Voices of Scottish Librarians

The evolution of a profession and its response to changing times

Ian MacDougall

Edited with notes by
Alan Reid and David Fletcher

The Scottish Working People's History Trust
Scottish Charity No SC020357

In association with

John Donald

First published in Great Britain in 2017 by
John Donald, an imprint of Birlinn Ltd

West Newington House
10 Newington Road
Edinburgh
EH9 1QS

www.birlinn.co.uk

ISBN: 978 1 910900 09 3

The publishers gratefully acknowledge the support of
The Scottish Working People's History Trust
towards the publication of this book

British Library Cataloguing-in-Publication Data
A catalogue record for this book is available on
request from the British Library

Typeset by 3btype.com

Printed and bound in Britain by T J International, Padstow, Cornwall

Contents

List of Illustrations

1. Andrew Carnegie, in the library of his home in New York, c1913

2. The 'Torch of Knowledge'

3. The reading room, Newtongrange Miners' Institute

4. Scotland's first mobile library, introduced by Perth & Kinross County Library Service during the early 1920s

5. Andrew Fraser and Midlothian County Library Service colleagues, c1938

6. M W (Bill) Paton

7. Peter Grant

8. W B Paton

9. Joe Fisher

10. Gavin Drummond

11. Alan White

12. John Hunter

13. Blackhall Library 1966. Inset – Blackhall Library 1948

Foreword by Peter Reid

Professor of Librarianship and Head of Department of Information Management, Robert Gordon University, Aberdeen

Let us see the pride and glory of a public library . . . in the magnitude of book circulation among the people, in the number of new readers enrolled, in the speed with which enquiry for any book is satisfied, in the quality of books lent for home reading and in the number of children led to good reading and the use of the library.

Marcus Milne, for more than 30 years City Librarian of Aberdeen, quoted these words of Lenin in his *Aberdeen Public Library Annual Report* for 1941–42. They capture the essence of what public libraries are for, what they do and what they can achieve. Many of the images conjured up in that quote are potent but, perhaps, the key message which Milne was trying to convey can be best seen in the phrase 'the magnitude of book circulation among the people'. This is at the very heart of what public libraries are about; they provide universal access to books and reading material, of every type and to every citizen. These principles have always been constants in the public library landscape and continue to be relevant today.

The notion of libraries being for the benefit of society can be seen clearly with the establishment of one of Scotland's earliest public libraries. Innerpeffray Library, established by Lord Madertie around 1680, was for the benefit of all. It was originally founded as part of a school but Lord Madertie was clear about what he wanted with his will recording: 'I have erected a Library . . . which I appoint and ordain to be preserved entire for the benefit and encouragement of young students.' Scotland's oldest extant public library is to be found in Kirkwall and it is traditionally assumed that it was founded in 1683 when William Baikie bequeathed over 150 books to the 'Publeck Liberarie of Kirkwall'. It was originally housed in St Magnus Cathedral before moving to the Tollbooth. In 1684 the library of Bishop Leighton was given a home near Dunblane Cathedral and so became the first purpose-built library in Scotland.

Throughout the 18th and early 19th centuries, libraries of various descriptions came and went. Many were subscription libraries such as those at Leadhills (founded in 1741) and at neighbouring Wanlockhead (founded in 1756) which were clearly important and valued institutions for the mining communities of those villages. Circulating libraries of various models also thrived in Scotland and elsewhere across the British Isles and were an engrained part of 18th century life in many towns; Sir Anthony Absolute, in Richard Brinsley Sheridan's *The Rivals*, has cause to say, 'Madam, a circulating library in a town is an evergreen tree of diabolical knowledge.' Although these libraries were underpinned by the belief that they facilitated self-improvement and education, as well as entertainment, they were not truly public institutions and were far from being universally accessible.

As the 19th century progressed and the movement for social and political reform gathered momentum, a strong movement in favour of the provision of free public libraries emerged. The fundamental principle which this movement held to was universal access to books and to reading materials, not just for those wealthy enough to afford to have their own collections. William Ewart, the MP for Dumfries Burghs, was instrumental in bringing the Public Libraries Act of 1850 to the Statute Books. Ironically, however, it did not apply to Scotland, despite Ewart sitting for a Scottish constituency. Three years later, the Public Libraries (Scotland) Act was passed which allowed burghs to raise the rate by one penny and to spend the revenue generated on library and museum buildings as well as collections for them. The Scottish Act enabled the rates increase to be approved by a two-thirds majority at a public meeting of those who owned or occupied a house valued at £10 per annum or more.

Over the succeeding years many towns would adopt the Public Libraries Act but often the building of libraries was assisted by benefactors. However, many towns and cities went through protracted debate about the Act. In 1864, the citizens of Edinburgh rejected a proposal to adopt the Act by 1,106 votes to 71 on the grounds of the extra taxation it incurred. It took a further 20 years for the nation's capital to adopt the Public Libraries (Scotland) Act.

From the 1880s onwards, the public library landscape changed radically because of the intervention of one benefactor, Andrew Carnegie (1835–1919). His family had emigrated from Scotland to the United States in 1848 and his first job was in a bobbin factory; later he became a telegraph messenger and steadily rose through the ranks of that company. Eventually, he went into the steel industry and ultimately created, after a series of mergers and takeovers, US Steel, one of the biggest and most successful companies the world has ever known. His wealth at its peak has been estimated at around $300 billion in contemporary values.

His first public library was the Carnegie Library in his home town of Dunfermline which was opened in August 1883. Four years previously, he had given £5,000 to his birthplace. It was the success of this library in Dunfermline which proved the catalyst for his decision to fund library building throughout the English-speaking world. By the time of his death in 1919, there were more than 2,500 Carnegie Libraries, many of them in his home country. Edinburgh, as has been noted, was decidedly reluctant to adopt the Public Libraries Act and, indeed, it was the last city in Scotland to do so. Carnegie initially offered £25,000 to Edinburgh which he then doubled, helping to overcome lingering opposition in the capital to a public library service. Carnegie laid the foundation stone for the library, on George IV Bridge, in 1887. At the opening, three years later, a message from Carnegie was read out. It said, 'We must trust that this library is to grow in usefulness year after year and prove one of the most potent agencies for the good of the people for all time to come.'

This attitude was central to Carnegie's approach. He had fixed views about wealth and philanthropy and famously declared in his book *The Gospel of Wealth* that a man who dies rich dies disgraced. As a consequence, he was determined to use his enormous wealth for the greater good of society. He had a strong attachment to learning, self-improvement and education, and all of these formed the cornerstones of his philanthropy. Libraries played a part because of his affection for, and gratitude to, the libraries which he himself had been able to use during his formative years. His underlying philosophy to life helps explain much about his philanthropy. He said that a man should spend the first third of his life getting all the education one can, spend the next third making all the money one can and spend the last third giving it all away to worthwhile causes.

Thanks to Andrew Carnegie the period from the mid-1880s through to the First World War became a felicitous time for public libraries. Carnegie was, however, stringent in his requirements of councils through what came to be called the 'Carnegie Formula'. This required that councils demonstrate clearly that there was a need for a public library, that they provide the site and contribute 10 per cent of the cost of construction and support its running costs (for which Carnegie rarely gave money). Most importantly, as far as Carnegie was concerned, it had to provide a free and universal service. It was Carnegie's staunch belief that the recipient towns had to show an ongoing commitment to maintain and enhance the library. Without that, he would walk away and, indeed, on some occasions, he did just that. The ethos of building *and* maintaining libraries had also been enshrined in the Public Libraries Consolidation (Scotland) Act 1887, which granted all local authorities the power to purchase, rent or construct libraries and to maintain and furnish them.

Carnegie's philanthropy had indirect consequences too. With the establishment of so many new libraries, it became increasingly imperative to ensure that they were staffed adequately and professionally. In 1908, the Scottish Library Association (SLA) was established, bringing together all of those involved in the profession. This marked an important turning point for libraries and for those who worked in them. The SLA became the key professional forum for the sector, interested in the development and enhancement of libraries as well as the skills, knowledge and expertise of those who worked in them. In time, as with the Library Association south of the border, this would lead to the introduction of professional examinations for library staff and ultimately this would evolve into degree courses in higher education institutions.

The First World War and its aftermath led to many significant changes in society and libraries and librarians were not immune from this. In the difficult inter-war years, the public library network throughout Scotland had to adapt to tough fiscal times but also remain true to the ideals of education, entertainment and self-improvement. In many respects, it can be argued that these inter-war years of hardship fostered a coherent and, indeed, enduring narrative for Scotland's public libraries. Carnegie had used the torch, a beacon of light, as a decorative device in many of his libraries. Libraries became important sources of diversion and improvement for many people dispossessed by social or economic circumstances during the 1920s and '30s. It is not an exaggeration to say that they were beacons of light during these dark years but they were also, for many, beacons of hope. Libraries were open to all, accessible to everyone, offered endless possibilities for socially inclusive life-long learning (decades before those terms became fashionable).

It has often been said in the Scottish library community that some of the most remarkable innovations emerge during times of adversity or hardship. During those inter-war years, a number of innovations did indeed emerge. In 1921, Perthshire became the first library service anywhere in the United Kingdom to introduce a mobile service, from a converted Ford van, kitted out with wooden shelving and containing between eight and nine hundred books to provide library access to more remote communities without a branch. In 1924, the same idea was taken up in Kent and gradually Perthshire's innovation was adopted across the British Isles and far beyond.

Another innovation was the deliberate and conscious decision of public library services to collect all types of materials about their local areas, both historical and contemporary. The advent of the Edinburgh Room in the Central Library of the capital in the early 1930s was the first step to a network of Local Studies collections throughout the country. Admittedly, the Glasgow Collection had been integral to the Mitchell Library since its inception; however, it did not have the traditional public library remit alongside it at that time. Unique and important local collections have, over the intervening decades, been developed right across Scotland with some being exceptionally fine such as those in Orkney, Moray and Perth to name but a few.

Another important innovation during the 1930s was the move to the professionalising of staff. There remained a significant number of librarians without professional qualifications and, as Andrew Fraser recalls in his interview, 'They were good librarians, by Jove. They knew their job but they had no qualifications.' New entrants to the profession like Fraser, who joined Midlothian Libraries in the 1930s, were however strongly encouraged to pursue the syllabus provided by the Library Association and to study for the professional examinations required to be an Associate of the Library Association (ALA) and the higher qualification of Fellow of the Library Association (FLA). In 1931, articles of understanding affiliating the Scottish Library Association and the Library Association opened up the examination curriculum of the latter to members of the former. Fraser studied at home, three nights a week, using books from the staff library, attaining his ALA shortly before the beginning of the Second World War.

The Second World War placed many pressures on library services including depleted budgets, staff being called up or moving to other war-related jobs, difficulties in obtaining stock and many authorities having to cope with transitory populations of service personnel. Some libraries, such as the Central Library in Aberdeen, served as fire-watching points during air raids. Despite these upheavals, service continued to innovate. Marcus Milne, City Librarian of Aberdeen, saw a time of crisis as a chance to try new things. In October 1941, conscious of the need for the library to do its bit to try to raise morale by providing distraction to the conflict, he introduced a current awareness bulletin, *Books you can borrow*. It continued successfully for a number of years.

In the years after the Second World War, further important developments took place. Prominent among these was the establishment of the School of Librarianship at the College of Commerce in Pitt Street, Glasgow. Gavin Drummond, in his interview, recalls going there to study the one-year course and having to pay for it himself. He points out that the city authorities were often more generous to their staff, paying for them to undertake the qualification, but many of the rural authorities (such as Perthshire where Drummond worked) did not. Drummond notes that 'like most courses – interesting while it lasted but . . . not the kind of thing that really helps you run a library service'. The Scottish School of Librarianship was later to become part of the University of Strathclyde and, in 1967, a second school was established – after not inconsiderable debate – at Robert Gordon's Institute of Technology in Aberdeen.

In the 1970s, the public library landscape changed significantly in Scotland with local government reorganisation. Not only did the administrative entities change but the library service clearly became part of the responsibility of the district councils rather than the regions. In many areas, this had little obvious impact where boundaries did not change but in other parts of the country the redrawing of administrative boundaries had a significant impact. In other respects, legislative changes had a major consequence on the provision of services. The Local Government (Scotland) Act 1973 places local authorities under a duty to 'secure the provision of adequate library facilities for all persons resident in their area'. In the years since the Act was passed the definition of the word 'adequate' has been a source of much debate and often political tension in some local authorities.

That said, Scotland's public libraries continue to play an important part in communities right across the country. They are accessible, neutral public spaces which enhance and enrich the lives of much of Scotland's population. They have undergone enormous change since the 1990s with the advent of the Internet and the delivery of so much digitally. However, they have adapted and changed as they always have. Joe Fisher in his interview speculated on whether the printed book will be made redundant by technological advances. Probably not. Books for pleasure and learning, developing literacy and encouraging life-long learning will always be core functions of our public libraries but these will sit alongside digital products and services.

The voices to be heard in this volume chart the evolution of a profession over much of the 20th century but, more than that, they tell us the story of our libraries and how they have served society for generations. They tell of a profession committed to high moral principles of public good and belief in society, echoing Carnegie's belief that public libraries are one of the most potent agencies for good. There is much of interest in the stories these men and women tell and all of them exhibit their pride and glory in Scotland's public libraries.

Acknowledgements

The author and editors would like to acknowledge the help of a number of people and organisations who have kindly and generously provided information and assistance in the preparation of this book.

Our special thanks go to Mike Jackson who read the edited interviews, commented and made valuable suggestions and improvements. The Local Studies service of Midlothian Council Library Service has been an important source of information and illustrations. In particular, the helpful and efficient support of Dr Ken Bogle, Midlothian's Local Studies Officer, is gratefully acknowledged.

The public library service in Scotland is a much-cherished resource and the help of the following librarians in providing information about former members of staff in their authorities has been invaluable: Colin Duncan, Inverclyde Libraries, Graeme Fraser, Stirling Council Library Service, Douglas Garden, Shetland Library, Patricia Grant, Glasgow Life, Judith Legg, Aberdeenshire Libraries, Jill Lewis, Fife Archives, Margaret McGinty, North Lanarkshire Heritage Centre, Lyn Mee and Sharon Murray, East Ayrshire Libraries, Kirsty Miller, West Lothian Libraries, Laura Neil, Clackmannanshire Libraries, Graham Roberts, Dumfries and Galloway Libraries, Information and Archives, and Allan Wright, Falkirk Library Service.

Thanks must be expressed to Catherine Kearney, Director, Chartered Institute of Library and Information Professionals in Scotland (CILIPS), and Sean McNamara, Policy and Digital Officer, CILIPS, who helped in a number of ways with research and illustrations. Rhona Arthur, Robert Craig, Karen Cunningham, Don Martin and Joyce Wallace all provided contact information for the purpose of preparing notes and sourcing photographs and we thank them.

We are most grateful to individuals and organisations who have provided photographs and given permission for their use. They are individually acknowledged in the captions to the illustrations. Michael Graham, The Studio, Penicuik, expertly photographed an original 'County Library' enamel sign from Midlothian's Local Studies collections for use in this book and supplied high-quality prints for the illustrations.

Introduction

Among the objects of the Scottish Working People's History Trust, formed in 1991, has always been a commitment to recording the recollections of working people about their lives and their housing, educational, recreational, cultural and other experiences, then transcribing them verbatim and editing and publishing them.

Until the mid-1990s, however, the Trust was obliged to concern itself chiefly with three activities. First, gathering funds to enable it to carry out all its objects. Second, publicising as widely as possible its existence and its aims, and building support among a wide range of organisations, institutions and persons. Third, resuming the work of the academic Scottish Labour History Society, formed in 1961 and in which the origins of the Trust lay, in searching for and encouraging and arranging the deposit in public repositories throughout Scotland of surviving records of working people's movements and organisations, such as trade unions, political parties, Co-operative and Friendly societies, as well as of individual activists in those movements and organisations.

Early in 1996 the Trust, having raised £17,000 by appeals to working people's organisations such as those mentioned above, and also to local authorities, grant-giving institutions and a wide range of individuals, decided to appoint a paid part-time research worker to carry out its archival work and who now at last also would be able to begin interviewing and recording the spoken recollections of working people in Scotland. The present writer, elected at the Trust's formation as honorary secretary (which office included fund-raising and archival work), was thus further honoured by becoming its research worker too.

Interviewing and tape-recording the recollections of working men and women began in April 1996. Each interview usually took about three hours, a few took two or three days. Verbatim transcription of recordings took much longer. Editing was inevitably a time-consuming task as it included the provision of end-notes explaining, correcting or enlarging on references in the texts, arranging relevant maps, photographs or other illustrations and compiling a full index.

A consistent attempt has been made by the Trust to record men and women veterans in specific occupations, especially those occupations which had already more or less disappeared or were in process of changing.

It was between August 1996 and March 2002 that 14 former library staff (ten men and four women) kindly agreed to be interviewed and have their spoken recollections recorded by the Trust. Included were librarians – those who had obtained professional qualifications recognised by the Library Association (LA) – and others who worked in libraries in different capacities. Now at last in the following pages are those recollections duly published.

Most of these contributors worked in public libraries but one worked in Edinburgh University Library and another in the National Library of Scotland. Their careers cover, roughly, the period from the early 1930s to the late 1990s. Therefore some of them had experienced the limitations and restrictions of the inter-war period and the austerity of the years of the Second World War and the post-war era.

Once economic conditions improved, however, it was the generation of librarians represented here which recognised the opportunities for their service and had the ambition to introduce change and create a modernised, well-resourced service. They were the builders, the ones who used the foundations created by their professional predecessors to expand services, to introduce new facilities and new delivery models. They were the ones who planned the opening of branch libraries to serve new areas of housing in the cities and larger towns and to replace the inadequacies of county library collections in schools, miners' institutes and public halls in the smaller towns. They were the ones who extended mobile library services, who introduced local studies services and services to housebound readers, who expanded services for children and who increased borrowing entitlements.

Much of the confidence among librarians during this period was associated with the development of professional training. Previously, the route to professional qualification – Associateship of the Library Association – was through the LA examination system which necessitated independent study or supported, work-based study. Things began to change with the establishment in 1946 of the Scottish School of Librarianship where students prepared for the LA exams on the basis of full-time study. When the Scottish School of Librarianship became the Department of Librarianship of the University of Strathclyde in 1964 the courses related to the LA exam syllabus were replaced by new degree and postgraduate courses. Indeed, demand for places to study librarianship at Strathclyde University was such that a second School of Librarianship was opened in 1967 in Aberdeen at Robert Gordon's Institute of Technology, now Robert Gordon University.

During the period when those interviewed were engaged in their profession, libraries still relied to a very large extent upon printed resources – books, newspapers, journals and so on. Most of them had been readers themselves from an early age: their recollections of books and authors are a feature of these accounts; they have fond memories of favourite comics such as *Eagle* (1950–69, and relaunched 1982–94), classic D C Thomson titles such as *The Beano* (1938–present), *The Dandy* (1937–2012), *The Hotspur* (1933–59), *The Wizard* (1922–63, and relaunched 1970–78) and others. From the 1960s and '70s onwards libraries had expanded the range of formats and materials they offered their users. Several of those interviewed for this book, however, sensed that a greater change was under way and that libraries, while still providing access to 'traditional' resources, would have to face and embrace the challenge of a digital future.

Most libraries today are modern, well-designed, welcoming places offering a wide range of resources, materials and services; they contribute significantly to community life and to individual development. They are staffed by well-trained, knowledgeable professionals who deliver services which support literacies, learning and access to knowledge and information. Much credit for this is due to the generation of librarians and library staff whose voices are heard in this book.

It is worth stating also that although these recollections obviously deal with the devoted public service provided to readers and with the work experiences of those who were interviewed, they also provide information about and personal insights into a wide range of other aspects of the recent past.

This book is the outcome of a distinctly collaborative effort. Though I was responsible for finding, interviewing and recording these librarians and other library staff, it has been Alan Reid, retired Chief Librarian of Midlothian Council and a former President of the Chartered Institute of Library and Information Professionals in Scotland (CILIPS), who has voluntarily borne all the hard work of editing the recollections and generally preparing them for publication. Susan Reid, Alan's wife, most competently undertook the transcription of all 30 audio-cassette tapes, the number of words recorded on which was 396,284. David Fletcher, a member of the Scottish Working People's History Trust, who has had a lifetime of experience in printing and publishing, provided invaluable assistance with the editing process and generously helped push the work onward toward publication. The Trust has been fortunate, too, in having Professor Peter Reid of Robert Gordon University, Aberdeen, agree to write the Foreword for this book. Neville Moir, Publishing Director of Birlinn Ltd, and Mairi Sutherland, Academic Managing Editor (John Donald), have also made major contributions. The Scottish Working People's History Trust is most grateful to the Scottish Inheritance Fund for its generous financial support which has made possible the publication of this book. Above all, thanks are due to the 14 librarians who kindly provided their recollections. It is sad indeed that because oral history in this form tends to present the recollections of older men and women, and that the process, particularly of transcription and editing, does necessarily involve a great deal of work and time, many, even most, of these 14 voices will not be heard again.

Ian MacDougall
Edinburgh

Dorothy Milne

My name is Dorothy Christina Milne. I was born in Aberdeen on 7th June 1911.

My father was born and brought up in Aberdeen. He was a Post Office worker. He started as a telegraph messenger and then became a telegraphist and after that he was a branch postmaster.

In the '14–'18 War he started off in the Gordons.[1] He was in the Territorial Army[2] before the War and so was called up immediately the War broke out. He was wounded in the leg so he was transferred to the Signals.[3]

I can remember a bit about the War. That naval battle that they thought they had lost and then discovered they'd won – Jutland.[4] I can remember the atmosphere in Aberdeen. I was just a toddler at the time but I can remember that. I can remember changing from light-colour blinds to dark ones. We had green blackout blinds. Then we moved out into the country. I had twin brothers who were born in 1914 and we needed a bigger house. We stayed out in the country until my father came back from the War and then we'd to move into town because he couldn't travel.

My oldest sister is Mona Isabel. She is four years older than me; then Alastair Ker – he's three years older than me; then comes me; then the twins in 1914 – John McGregor and Magnus Ramsay; and then my young sister, Ruth Agnes, 1918.

My father's father started off as a cooper and then became a boilermaker. He was born in Peterhead but he worked in Aberdeen. He was dead before I was born. My father always said, 'Don't think of the past, think of the future.' But I remember my paternal grandfather left Peterhead because he quarrelled with his father. I think his father had a quarry in Peterhead. My father's mother was a glover before she was married. She would give up her job when she got married. She came from near Stonehaven[5] and I think her parents were English. They were Episcopal Church anyway. I don't remember her.

My mother was a telegraphist as well. She went to a business college and took the exam, and then she was in London for a bit and then came back to Aberdeen. I have a vague memory of my mother's father. He was a granite merchant in Aberdeen, engaged in the buying and selling of granite. He was a monumental sculptor as well. He was a partner with Taggart[6] before he retired. It was quite a good-going business but it wasn't a big one. I think Taggart expanded after that. Mother's mother was a farmer's daughter. They came from, I think it was Turriff.

I can just remember before we went to the country. As I said, I remember the blinds and I can remember the milk carts, the horses, horse-drawn vehicles. I can't remember the first house I stayed in in Aberdeen, but I can remember I think it would be the third one. It was in Forest Avenue, Aberdeen – before we went to the country. I can just remember playing with neighbours. I couldn't tell you anything about the house. But I remember the one in the country, in Tullahill[7] – you go over the River Dee and up the hill.

We rented the whole house. It was a cottage and we had a pump at the sink. I really don't remember how many rooms there were, whether it was four or five. At that stage the twins were babies and I had an older brother and sister.

I didn't start school at Tullahill. My older brother did. My sister had been at school before we went there. We were at Tullahill just under two years. I was back in Aberdeen before I went to school in 1916.

The house in Irvine Place, Aberdeen, was a flat with its own entrance, a two-storey house – people upstairs and we were downstairs at that time. It had four rooms but it had an attic which we lined and made into another room. So it was five rooms and a scullery.[8] We didn't have a living room, it was a kitchen and scullery then, not living room and kitchen. Gas lighting. There was a tank in the kitchen range[9] that you could heat water in, a fire with an oven at one side and a tank at the other. My mother browned her oatcakes at the fire. She didn't cook on the fire, she had a gas cooker. There was a bathroom with a flush toilet. The girls slept in one room and the boys . . . there was a bed-recess in the kitchen and then we had the place upstairs later on.

As a girl I was a keen reader. The Milne family motto is 'I read to learn'.

If I see print I read it. As a child I always read. As a wee girl when I got my reading book I read it right through and I lost interest in it. I got comics: *Comic Cuts*, and I can remember when *The Dandy* came out. I used to read fairyland tales – that was my reading rather than comics.

As a girl I always did a lot of walking. It was mostly just walking but I did some hill walking as well, just went with friends. I went up Lochnagar[10] by the Black Spout once. That's the most ambitious thing I ever did.

I attended Sunday School fairly regularly, although my parents weren't members of the church. I think they had too much when they were young. They belonged to different churches. My father was Congregational,[11] my mother was Parish[12] and we went to the UF[13] Sunday School. I joined the church when I came to West Lothian. I've always been attached to the church in one way, the Church of Scotland.

When I was little I went on holiday with my parents; we've got photographs. But when I joined the Guides,[14] my holidays were the Guide camps. I joined the Girl Guides when I was 11 and, after more than 75 years I'm still in them: I'm West Lothian County President. Camps always took place in Aberdeenshire, and when other girls left the Guides I stayed on and became a Sea Ranger,[15] the next group above. We used to meet down by the River Dee and take out boats and we went sea fishing once or twice and when I think of it, we just didn't take the proper precautions, but nothing happened. I was Captain of the Sea Rangers before I left Aberdeen, and when I came to West Lothian, among the members of the Education Committee interviewing me was the District Commissioner of the Girl Guides. When I got the job, she said, 'We're needing a Tawny Owl[16] at Blackburn. Will you do it?' So there was no break: from Sea Ranger Captain down to Tawny Owl.

I attended Broomhill School, an Aberdeen Corporation primary school. I quite enjoyed the school. I just took my lessons for granted. Classes were large – 40, 44, and if everybody attended all week you got away early on Fridays. It wasn't the sort of area with deprived pupils. I know that some of them were poorer than us, but there was only one sub-normal child and he stayed in the class for two or three years and then went to a special school. Everyone just treated him as if he was normal. They make an awful difference nowadays.

There weren't any subjects I had difficulty with, not until the secondary school. After primary school I went for six months to an intermediate school and then I sat an exam for Aberdeen Central School, which is now Aberdeen Academy. You had to get a standard in the exam to get in there. Aberdeen Central School was a Corporation school; you paid 10/- per annum and you got it back if you stayed three years. It was to encourage people to stay on. The move to secondary school didn't bother me at all although I had difficulty with foreign languages. I think it was more or less memory – to remember the vocabulary. You got French and Domestic Science the first year, and French and Latin the second year. The Latin teacher I didn't like. I remember a girl came from another school and she'd had Greek at her school and they gave her special lessons to keep it up. My English was all right, Maths and Science I was better at.

I didn't have any particular ambitions. I just fell into the Library. I left school in the third year when I was nearly 16. I tried several different things, exams – the Post Office was one of them. I got a scholarship for the business college. It was De Bear Schools Ltd Business College but it became Gregg's Schools later on, and I was a shorthand typist. It was Gregg's shorthand. It was a one-year course and I studied English, French, shorthand and typing, bookkeeping, business knowledge, Mathematics. I didn't pass the French but I got the Royal Society of Arts shorthand, typing, business knowledge and English. By the time I left, I could do 120 words per minute in shorthand. I think that was more or less average. I could do 140 for short times. For typing I think I could do 40 words a minute, something like that.

When I left the business college I worked in different temporary jobs in offices as a shorthand typist because it was hard getting jobs in those days, the end of the '20s, not like it is now. Then I applied for a job as a shorthand typist in Aberdeenshire County Library and got in – it would be 1929 – and worked my way up from there. The headquarters was in the City of Aberdeen. We were doing library work. It wasn't a shorthand typist's job. They just called it that for some reason, but we really were library assistants. It didn't bother me. I just seemed to take things for granted. I liked the job. I started, I think, with 10/- a week and your insurance stamp came off that; it was just a few pence.

In Library Headquarters there was five of us: K B Milne,[17] no relation, the Chief Librarian, and there was a young man who drove the van that went round the County, and then there was Miss Miller, the Deputy, and another girl and myself. I kept in touch with Miss Miller for a long time. The other two married each other. Before he went to Library Headquarters, the young man was some sort of technician, making microphones and things like that, so when the War came he was called back to his old job.

K B Milne was quite a good boss. It was a happy building. In the County Library Headquarters it was nine o'clock in the morning till five at night. We must've worked Saturday mornings, nine till 12, I think. But if you went out with the van, which we did occasionally, you might come back later – no overtime pay. We used to work for the Education Offices as well. We did their ordering of supplies, the school orders, and we used to have to work overtime on that to get it done in time, unpaid. We didn't work overtime all the time. It was just one time of year, and we would work for maybe a fortnight; we would work an hour or two a night. It wasn't every night, but it might be two or three evenings. It depended how the orders came in from the schools. We got an hour for lunch and we all went home for lunch. I could walk home and back in good time. We stopped for a cup of tea in the morning; it wasn't official but we did. Well, the boss knew about it. He got his coffee as well. We didn't have a stop in the afternoon. We got a tea-break if we were working overtime. I was a member of NALGO,[18] I joined in Aberdeen. Someone came to tell us all about it and we all joined NALGO. I'm a life member although I might as well not be – they never send me anything.

The Library Service in Aberdeenshire when I first started was mostly in schools. It was run by the Education Authority. We supplied books to the schools as well as the continuous readers. These were for use in the classroom and the library books were for taking home. But we supplied books for the adults. The fisher folk, Aberdeen, Fraserburgh, Peterhead, were very keen readers.

There was one local library – Aboyne was it? Someone had donated money to keep it. The trouble was, the way that the money was left they couldn't combine with the Education Authority.

Books were sent out from Headquarters in the van to schools. The van went out every day, and when it went out Strathdon way it was away two days. There were two of them always on it. Mr Milne, the County Librarian himself, went out. He didn't have close contact with the actual readers but it was the schools he was dealing with and the schoolmaster that ran the local branch library in the school. It was the head teacher who was normally responsible for receiving the books and making sure they were available to the public who went to the school to borrow their books. That would be after school hours. The school staff would be working unpaid overtime. The head teacher wouldn't dare refuse. The Director of Education would've known about it and he wouldn't have got promotion at all, I should think. I never heard of a teacher who'd refused.

Generally the libraries were open to the public just a couple of hours a week, after school, but not every evening. It was just expected of the teachers, issuing the books and filling in the statistics. They didn't seem to mind at all and some of them came into Headquarters. We issued books from Headquarters as well, but the people that came into the library there were mostly the teachers. We had a teachers' library as well as the other ones. The teachers paid a small subscription and these books were available for them and they came in and chose them, educational books, to do with their school work.

I was there until 1936 and I went to night school and took university prelims while doing the job. I took Higher Physics, English and History and Lower Mathematics.[19] I needed a private tutor for a bit. He did the Physics, the Maths and the English, and I did a correspondence course for the History. I sat all the subjects in the one year and passed them at first attempt. I tried French as well but didn't get it.

I went before I knew there were such things as library exams.[20] There were no library degrees or anything in those days. The idea was to try the Library Association exams, and you could take correspondence courses or you could go to London University. I was quite content to study at home, but I discovered that in Scotland, you had to go to Glasgow from Aberdeen for the exam, so I didn't sit it then. It was what they called, I think, the First Professional. It wasn't so much library subjects; it was English and a certain amount of Maths as well, sizing things for setting up a library, that sort of thing.

When I was still with Aberdeen County Library I didn't consider taking up some other line of work. I just sailed through life not worrying. Took things as they came. There's enough variety in library work to keep you interested.

Then I tried for the Deputy Librarian job in West Lothian, and got it. I didn't sit a librarianship exam until I came down to Bathgate, but I had seven years of library experience and I think the Director of Education in Aberdeen spoke to the Director of Education here. I was 26 and had always lived and worked in Aberdeen and had a certain amount of regret. When I came to Bathgate, where the office was, there was only the two of us. Miss Paton was the Chief Librarian.[21] Shortly after I came here, there was a junior appointed and then there was three of us. We did the typing as well.

West Lothian at that time was much smaller than Aberdeenshire and a much smaller area, with Bathgate in the middle. It was a different sort of area to Aberdeenshire – shale and coal mining. When I came for my interview I remember thinking, 'What funny hills they have here!' – the red hills coming from Edinburgh. It was the bings![22] I'd never seen anything like it before. But I just take things for granted. I didn't feel homesick – we were just brought up to be independent. Bathgate's a nice little town to live in, and it was very well run in those days with the Town Council rather than part of the County. We say about Bathgate, it was very easy to get out of it! Roads in all directions; the north of Bathgate is quite nice for walking. It would be '37 when I joined the Youth Hostels.[23] And I was back into Guides and made a lot of friends straight away. The Brown Owl[24] was in the Education Offices and we were working in the same building, so I had a friend straight away. And I still have her.

When I came to West Lothian in 1936, to start with I digged with a member of the Education staff. Couldn't afford anything else really. I started at £2 a week. At that time librarians were among the less well paid of public servants, and the staff was mostly voluntary workers. Here there were more libraries in the miners' institutes[25] with a local person doing it, and I think they got paid five shillings a week.

In West Lothian they used boxes for the books, and the books were changed once a term, so we were always doing different areas every week or so. The Council had a lorry to take the coal to the schools – they cleaned it up and took the library boxes! In Aberdeen we supplied any books the teachers requested but they could also choose books from the van. Whereas here the library staff chose the books and checked that they hadn't had them in the last three years. That took a lot of checking, but we all did it. No one stuck to one job. Everyone stuck in and did their bit.

It wasn't unusual that there were two women in charge of the County Library. There were a lot of women working in libraries, chief librarians. I knew ever so many lady librarians: Dunfermline, Renfrew, Rutherglen, a couple down at the Borders, Stirling – well, not when I was appointed but later on a friend of mine was made Stirling County Librarian – and that's just round about here. It was one of the areas where women had made a breakthrough. They got in on the ground floor, so to speak, because the County Library movement is not all that old. From 1918, when the Education Act[26] was passed, four successive West Lothian County Librarians were women. When I came Miss Paton had just newly become the County Librarian. The first one married a local man and became Mrs Wolf. The second one was Miss Adams and she just worked about a couple of years and then she went to a job in England. Miss Paton had been her Deputy. Miss Paton was a local lady. The other two had come in with experience from other places.

Miss Paton died in office before she was due to retire; she was very young – I think it would be 1941. I was appointed 'Acting' and didn't get the full salary of the County Librarian because it was during the War, and it wasn't confirmed until after the end of the War. I don't know what Miss Paton was being paid, of course, but I was on a scale and it went up every year and it wasn't until some time after I was appointed Acting County Librarian that I was put off the general scale on to the other.

In West Lothian, we didn't know who the readers were. To begin with, I wasn't dealing with the public at all. It wasn't until after Miss Paton died and I was in charge that I started to meet the public. Shortly after I came, in the infant school across from Library Headquarters two rooms were put into one and made into a branch library, which was open two evenings a week and a Saturday morning, and the teachers did voluntary work and the library staff did unpaid overtime. The teachers were beginning to object by then to working unpaid.

We were sending the books out all over the County. When I first came to West Lothian every village had an outlet for books and some of the places two – Linlithgow, two schools. Where there was a school there were library books. Bo'ness was a burgh and they opened and ran a library under the Public Library Act and we just sent them books every so often to augment their stock because they were paying rates as well.

Working conditions in the Library Headquarters in Wellpark, a mansion house, were cramped. The Education Officers were in it as well and we were a very minor part of it – we had what had been the kitchen and the scullery and a stockroom built on. Then they built new County Offices in Linlithgow and the Library just – wheech! – took over a whole lot more of the ground floor with another big room.

There were a lot of other things came in: the fire service and the water service, the youth organiser and, during the War, the man that checked the milk and the fuel officer that checked the coal. I was actually lent to the fuel office for a while when I started. They thought that I wouldn't be called up if I was in the fuel office. Then they discovered that responsible librarians were reserved.[27] I was back in the Library! I was never asked whether I would like to do that or not. I was just told.

The Second War had quite an impact on the Library Service in West Lothian. People read twice as much. Well, there weren't so many things they could do. I think it was men being away at the War. Dancing, for instance – there used to be dancing practically weekly; I don't think there was so much during the War. If there were soldiers or sailors or airmen for that matter, then the dances went on because there were partners. In Bathgate they'd have dancing in the school halls and church halls if the minister didn't object to dancing, and in Union Road – that was a dancing place.

I don't think it affected the type of reading at all. There wasn't a great surge for non-fiction books. There were soldiers round about the Forth Bridge and we sent them books. I can remember they started cutting the hard covers off the books to put inside their hats to make them sit properly! We objected to that strongly!

The Library Service wasn't engaged in any activity to promote literacy during the War although we helped register people for war service; everyone had to register, and it amazed me the women that didn't think they could sign their name. They'd no reason to write until the War so they couldn't write. If you wrote out their name for them, they would copy it out rather than put a thumb print on.

We had some bombs but they didn't hit us, the Library. There were three bombs, but they never hit anything. There was one outside Broxburn where a farmhouse was hit and the farmer and his grandson were killed although the grandmother and granddaughter were all right. They were in different rooms. One half of the house was damaged. I think there was a light showing and they dropped a bomb. But we were lucky – they went over towards Glasgow.

Not having any proper branch libraries at that time, the blackout didn't make much difference. But as local government employees nearly everyone was doing some sort of war service and when the siren went, you stopped what you were doing and went to the first aid post or the Civil Defence headquarters, or something like that. I spent an overnight at the Civil Defence headquarters. I was on the staff there. Nothing to do with the job – I volunteered.

The end of the War in itself didn't mark any particularly dramatic changes in the Library Service. As County Librarian I went to the Library Committee meetings, and I've seen me going to other meetings as well and being the only woman there, although there were women councillors. As far as relations with the Committee were concerned, I remember one councillor saying, 'Oh, well, it's just like keeping a shop.' It was sheer ignorance. Most of them weren't really terribly interested and didn't think much of the Library Service until I got one Chairman, Jimmy Boyle, a miner that was invalided out, I think. He ran the trade union in the Labour office. After the War he was election agent, I think, to the Labour MP. He was really interested in the Library. He had left school at 12 because he'd lost his parents and he'd educated himself. So he knew the value of the Library. I'd been trying to get branches and when he became Chairman, he said, 'This is the way to do it', and in the years after the War he got one. Of course, as soon as one town got one, all the other councillors wanted one for their area.

When we got the branches it made a big difference – the readership increased. When a library opened you got a huge influx of people and it calmed down a bit later. And we got a rise in our book funds every year. In Aberdeen I wasn't in a position to know about the book fund.[28] In West Lothian we managed. It wasn't too much, but it wasn't really all that little.

There was a book selection sub-committee and they liked to go to Glasgow with me to choose books once a year. We dealt with W & R Holmes mostly for that. And they liked going to library conferences. Of course we bought books at other times as well. W & R Holmes was the principal supplier but we bought from other firms as well and travellers came with book lists. It was my particular responsibility as County Librarian to choose the books – roughly 2,000 or 3,000 books a year.

As a County Librarian you had to buy the books, you had to oversee the staff, you had to do the bookkeeping. I always did the special requests

– people wanted special books – and I did that as well as other odd jobs. The staff were very good. You just let them get on with it – a very good team. I can remember coming back from one of those buys in Glasgow with Mr Boyle and it was after five o'clock. I stayed in the mews house at the back of the Library and he took me home and he said, 'Is that the library staff still in there?' Ten past five and I wasn't there even! By the time I resigned I had about six of a staff at Headquarters and paid staff in all the branch libraries. I didn't have a deputy. I had a senior assistant. They wouldn't pay for a deputy. But as soon as I retired and the other man came, the first thing he did was get a deputy.

I remained County Librarian for over 30 years, but I don't think there was a difference in reading habits during that time. Television came in in the mid-'50s. It was the Queen's coronation. Everyone wanted a television then. I wasn't aware of it affecting the reading. There weren't that many people had television sets then. By the time I retired in 1974 borrowing was increasing but not all that much. Some of the miners' welfares had books, but I think it was a failing thing, it wasn't kept up. There may have been individuals among the miners who were keen readers. The Chairman, Mr Boyle, who'd been a miner read Westerns! That was his light reading. He also taught himself German.

I think there was more interest in local history after the War. Not genealogy so much – I think they would go into Edinburgh for that, to Register House, the Scottish Record Office, for parish registers[29] and things like that.

Before the War schools had what the County Library sent them. After the War, they got school libraries with their own books, and when they started I got the job of seeing how much money they should get. Until I retired in May '74 the Library Service was still part of the Education Authority. School librarians, however, were separate; they were part of the school staff although there was co-operation between ourselves and the school librarians.

Before the War it wasn't common for children of working class parents, shale miners or coal miners in West Lothian, to go to university. By 1974, far more youngsters remained on at school and far more were going to colleges and universities. We were able to give students – people doing their Highers or at university – a better service. They were able to go to the branch libraries, find suitable reading that supported them or ask for books through the Scottish Central Library,[30] and, within reason, you could get any book. We borrowed books from abroad as well, through the Scottish Central Library.

I wasn't aware that industrial developments after the War – there was the decline of shale – affected the libraries in any way. The villages would know the difference because that was when the motor factory started, the BMC at Bathgate.[31] But it didn't make any impact on the Library. It meant that the shale miners got jobs, and then of course they had to close it down.

In West Lothian there's a large Roman Catholic element, much of it of Irish descent, but our staff was mixed. And there still is a fairly strong Orange element in West Lothian. I'd never even heard of them up in Aberdeen. I didn't really know about the Orange Order[32] even until fairly recently when I saw a parade and was quite shocked. A private army! But that didn't present any difficulties as far as the Library was concerned.

We had contacts with other libraries, could all borrow from each other through the Central Library in Edinburgh, and I had friends in other libraries. We met at conferences – the Scottish Library Association and the British Library Association[33] had their conferences. I was a member of the Library Association and I went to both of these every year. Sometimes I was accompanied by a councillor and sometimes I was on my own. We also had library seminar things, not schools exactly, and I would go and maybe take one of my staff with me. We had local meetings as well. The men had a club and the women librarians had a club that met maybe once a month; nothing to do with the Library Association, just personal friends. We would discuss our difficulties and things like that.

But I didn't go to international conferences in Europe or elsewhere. Only the very ambitious librarians went to those or those from the big authorities. West Lothian was one of the smallest local government areas. People who went to foreign conferences and things were wanting to get on in the Library Association as much as for their work.

I worked in libraries for 45 years and I've never had any regrets at having become a librarian. I liked my work. I did consider applying for a job as County Librarian or Chief Librarian outside West Lothian. When Miss Paton was still alive I applied for a job down in the Borders, but I didn't get it. It was County Library, Roxburgh, based in Newtown St Boswells. But I didn't apply elsewhere once I became the County Librarian. I was quite content then.

There have been changes I've witnessed – libraries became much more important. With all the branches round the County, it was a much bigger job. Including part-time staff, I must've had about 40 people on the staff. If I had been joining library staff now, I would never reach County Librarian because you've got to go to university and take a degree if you want to get on. Before, if you could do the job, that was the thing. Now, you can get a job but you stay a junior, a general staff. You could do more important work than just stamping books but you wouldn't get the pay for it.

I didn't have any regrets about having left Aberdeenshire. We all left Aberdeen – and nearly all my friends as well. All the Aberdonians have gone! I've no regrets. When I retired I thought, 'Oh, I'll miss the Library terribly.' But I went to a Soroptimist[34] Conference in Australia and I was away just about a fortnight. I came back and I didn't miss it at all.

Interviewed 10 May 1999

Isabella McKinlay

I was born towards the end of the First World War in Glencraig,[1] in my grandparents' house. My father was in France at the time, fighting in the trenches. He and my mother were married just before my father joined up. They didn't have a house because he was going off and my mother just continued to live in the grandparents' house. I had one sister, born in 1920.

My father's father was a member of the territorial unit[2] attached to the Black Watch.[3] At the beginning of the First World War, he was called up and sent to a place near Norwich to train the recruits. He told my father that conscription was coming and he didn't want a son of his to be conscripted so my father joined up with a lot of men from the Lochgelly area, and landed in Norwich beside his father. I presume that he was trained by his father before he was sent to France. It was the Black Watch he was in, but he never talked about his war experiences, they were so horrible.

My father's father was a miner. He was born in Pencaitland[4] and in the later 1800s, when he was young, he moved with his parents to Fife, to the coalfields. My father was born in Lochgelly in 1894. My grandfather manned telephones during the Second World War and died after the War. My mother was born in 1895 and her people all came from round Methil. They were called McAndrew. My mother's father was a contractor and had miners working for him. My great-grandfather, Chalmers his name was, came from Markinch, and one of the older relatives said that he was the village dominie.[5] Since he had five children he went to the mines, but in a non-manual job, because there was more money to be made.

My father, when he left school, was apprenticed to a licensed grocer. After his apprenticeship was finished, he got a job as a grocer with the

Lochgelly Co-operative Society. The customers were almost all miners and their families. My father used to say that it was their larder. Some people used to be in about half a dozen times a day. My father's uncle was the managing director. The first Co-operative shop in Lochgelly was built on the High Street on property that belonged to my great-grandfather. Eventually my father became a grocery manager with the Co-operative with his own shop and my mother was a clerkess. My father was never unemployed, he had good working conditions and holidays and we never were short of anything.

After my father came out of the Army, he got a privately rented house in Lochgelly, beside the school my sister and I went to. My mother used to just lift my sister over the school wall and deposit her on the other side. The house had a big garden which my grandfather used to dig. My father didn't do any gardening. He worked long hours and when he finished he was always bowling. Then we moved a few doors up the same street, Bank Street, the main street going through Lochgelly. We had our living room and a bedroom, and in the living room there were two box beds. My sister and I slept in the bedroom in one bed and my mother and father slept in the living room, and we had a kitchenette. For lighting we had a paraffin lamp but we had gas put in at our own expense. There was no hot and cold running water, no bath or shower, just a cold water tank. It had a flush toilet. We lived in that house for quite some years and then my parents got a council house in Lochgelly. It had two bedrooms up the stair, a living room, kitchenette and a bathroom; electric light; a little front garden and a garden at the back.

At the age of five I started at the school next door to us, Lochgelly Public School. I liked it. I liked all the subjects. There was one teacher, Mrs Taylor, who took a great interest in the brighter pupils in the class. At that time, one of the national newspapers was running a competition to find which school was a bit better than others. Once a week five of us used to go to this teacher's house and she gave us writing, composition and art work, some of which was passed to the newspaper. We didn't get a prize but it was interesting doing the work. There might've been about 30 pupils in the class. I did well at the school and because it was a higher grade school[6] I was there till I was 15 when I sat the day school certificate,[7] which I got with credit. That was in English, Mathematics – Algebra, Geometry and Arithmetic – Geography and Science.

I liked the subjects where I had good teachers. Discipline was strict, although there were one or two teachers who weren't so strict, but we didn't respect the ones who were lax. Although I was good at Mathematics and knew that he liked me, I was frightened of the Maths teacher. He was very strict and he had a temper he didn't always control. If he went out of the room and came back and found that we had been talking, making a noise, everybody got the strap. Not just the person responsible, everybody. The children used to throw stones at his window at his home because they hated him so much. I was absolutely scared of him but I was sorry for him. He'd been in the First World War and had had a bad time of it. When my sister followed in my footsteps, I said to her, 'Don't be frightened of Mr Lyle because he's very nice', and he was always nice to my sister. We had a good English teacher. We did a lot of Shakespeare's plays and the teacher expected every member of the class to learn a passage and then he would go to anybody and ask them to stand up and recite what they had learned.

My teachers wanted me to go on to secondary school, but at that time my mother wasn't well. When I left school at about 15, I was looking after the family while my mother was recovering. Some of the children in Lochgelly were awful poor and poorly dressed. They always had something on their feet when they came to school, but out of school they went with bare feet. Shoes would be kept for school so they wouldn't go to school without shoes and be shamed. Some of the boys became miners when they left school, one or two of them got apprenticeships, a painter and joiners.

I would have liked to become a doctor or a librarian. I was very fond of reading. I was friendly with one or two families who had young children and lived near us, and we all changed books. As a family we were all readers. My father had a bookcase full of books and some of his school prizes were there, like *The Pilgrim's Progress*[8] and *Annals of the Parish*.[9] I went through all the books, although he had some cowboy stories which I didn't read. To begin with my father would choose something for me but then I got to the stage where I got the books myself. There was one book he had called *The Woman Thou Gavest Me* by Hall Caine.[10] I was reading this and my father said, 'What are you reading?' I let him see and he said to my mother, 'Who gave her that?' He didn't think it was right for me and it was taken from me. We've had the book in the libraries I've been in and I've never been able to read it. When I had nothing to read I would read the Bible. When I was at school we had boxes of books sent from the County Library and exchanged every three months. Whenever the new box of books came, one girl who was older than me was always first to get her choice. She was big and strong and used her elbows probably. There was a *Complete Shakespeare* which she took, and every week I asked her if she was bringing it back and she never brought it back until it was time for the books to go back to Kirkcaldy, to the County Library Headquarters. So I never got that *Complete Shakespeare*.

I went to Lochgelly Library for books with my father. I don't know whether it was a subscription library which predated the opening of the branch library by the County Library. There was a grumpy old man in charge, but he would give me one or two books if I asked. Then the County Library opened up their branch library in the Miners' Welfare Institute.[11] It was a proper library room; the shelves and the desk were mahogany. It was a beautiful raised desk so the staff were standing on a dais. I used to get books there for my father. He would never talk about the War but he liked to read true books about the War. The branch librarian gave me a catalogue of the Fife County Library books – it was published about 1928 or '30 – and she said, 'There's a whole lot of books there so ask your father which ones he would like and I'll see if I can get them for him.' I suppose that started me, and when I was old enough I joined the Library. I think 14 was the joining age. They didn't have any books for children, only adult books. It was a well-stocked library, probably better stocked than some of the smaller branches are now. There was a plays and poetry section and I read all the plays, including all of Barrie's[12] plays, and some of the poetry before I left school, so I might have been using my father's ticket.

Although I was at home helping my mother for about two years after I left school, I did little odd jobs. My father's older sister worked for the local printer. Alec Westwater owned the *Lochgelly Times*, the *Cowdenbeath Advertiser* and the *Kinross Advertiser* and had a printing department in his premises. Occasionally, my aunt used to say, 'Mr Westwater wants somebody to fold balance sheets', or things like that. So I used to do that and make some money. Then I was good at stitching and would get paid for putting up a hem on something. I would put it all in my bank book.

There was a furniture shop, newsagent and tobacconist run by three sisters, and while I was helping out there with the newspapers and things like that this job for an assistant in the branch library in Lochgelly came up. Because I was so fond of books I thought, 'Oh, this is just what I would love.' I applied and was interviewed by the County Librarian and her Chief Assistant. Although she had a degree from Edinburgh University and had been teaching in a private school, Miss Bonthrone[13] had been appointed County Librarian without any library qualifications whatsoever. When she was appointed, her father was on the Council. He was County Convener. From the moment I met Miss Bonthrone, I had the highest respect for her. I've never met anyone who matched up to her. On the day I started, I had to go to the County Library Headquarters in Kirkcaldy and she took me through everything herself. She didn't leave it to a member of her staff. She even showed me how to carry an armful of books. I thought, 'If ever I am a librarian, I'll do what Miss Bonthrone did.' She was a lady in every respect and expected her staff to behave like ladies as well. At Christmas time, Miss Bonthrone arranged for the staff to visit a show in Edinburgh, usually an Ivor Novello show. She paid for the trips out of her own pocket. She paid for the tickets and the train, and her mother, who accompanied Miss Bonthrone, paid for our afternoon tea.

When I started, my pay was 10/- a week and it went up the next year to 12/6. You got increments and when you got to your maximum you got no further unless you had further qualifications or there was something extraordinary that would give you a rise. I got promotion quickly because when the Second World War started Miss Bonthrone sent all the senior members of her staff to Cupar to learn how to do food rationing work and take charge of the various food offices. The ones who had been senior-juniors became branch librarians, and so I became a branch librarian then. I was never called up because Miss Bonthrone said that she had let all the senior members of her staff go to do war work and the ones who were left couldn't be replaced. She said we were all doing war work of a kind, serving people at home.

I was just 21 when I became a branch librarian, but I'd been working in the Library for three or four years and knew exactly how it worked. I also knew the stock from beginning to end because I'd read quite a lot of it. I was always interested in art and was good at doing posters to publicise certain sections of the books. Every week or fortnight we had a different poster, trying to influence people, to get them interested in reading. We didn't do fiction. It was non-fiction work. I did a good one on golf because a lot of miners played golf. It wasn't a rich man's game in Lochgelly or anywhere in Scotland.

A lot of fine upstanding people used the Library. I noticed what people read; one man read a lot of books on sociology, and Lawrence Daly[14] is another who comes to mind. He was in his teens when he started to use the Library in Lochgelly during the War. We had Ministry of Information lectures once a month, held in a room at the back of the Library and Lawrence Daly came to some of those. At one of the lectures on social affairs he asked all the questions. He was very knowledgeable and could quote statistics. After the meeting the lecturer said to me, 'Who was that young man?' I told him, said he was a miner. He said, 'It's incredible. He knows such a lot.' He had been to Russia. He got a library book on Russian and after he came back said he was sorry but he'd left the book in Russia.

A lot of people used the Library. Some of them were in every day for books. Women used to come in for their Mills & Boon[15] love stories when they were shopping and they were always clamorous for new ones. One of the local doctors was a proper gentleman. He never went round the shelves but would just say, 'What have you got for me today?' He didn't read anything other than murder stories. We used to keep all the new ones for him because he'd read all those on the shelves. He would go off with his bundle of books and sometimes come back the next day – he'd read them and could give his comments on them all. There was one miner, an awfully nice man, he'd been injured in the pit and he used to come in every day. He used to come to the Miners' Welfare Institute to play billiards and to get his cowboy stories. When he put his books on the ledge, there would be two bars of Duncan's hazelnut chocolate,[16] one for me and one for the senior branch librarian.

We got a good proportion of new books and books from the County Library main stock. May Mitchell, the branch librarian, on the day that she was at Library Headquarters, would make up the new stock. Some stock of classics was always in the Library – Dickens and Scott, and things like that. There was a good selection of books about the First World War, due to my father maybe. There was a good stock of Westerns and murder stories, because the younger miners just wanted something light for reading, and we had a good stock of biographies.

From first starting in the Library I remember we had T E Lawrence's *Seven Pillars of Wisdom*[17] which was first published as a limited edition. It was fairly big and had beautiful red leather covers done with gold lettering and there was the poem at the beginning dedicated to S A, which I think was Saudi Arabia: 'I loved you, so I drew these tides of men into my hands.'[18] The book was done on hand-made paper with deckle edges and the illustrations were beautiful, done by Kennington.[19] It was a lovely book. Miss Bonthrone bought copies for Lochgelly, Kirkcaldy and Buckhaven and Methil libraries. She used to buy a certain amount of books for Kirkcaldy Library because it was double-rated – they paid a rate to the County as well as to the Burgh for a library service. That was a sore point with Miss Luke, the Kirkcaldy librarian.[20] She didn't see why Miss Bonthrone should buy her books for her. Buckhaven and Methil was double-rated as well. When I came to Buckhaven Library later, there was this beautiful copy of *The Seven Pillars of Wisdom* but by this time it was shabby and I kept it on the back shelves and had a modern one for the open shelves. After I left, I read that the original edition was selling for thousands of pounds.[21]

When I first began in the Library I had great holidays. We got both the Christmas and New Year holiday, two days at each, whereas shops and other places only got New Year. We got the local holidays in spring and autumn when the Library was closed, I had two weeks in the summer and we got the Easter holiday.

During the War, I was branch librarian at Lochgelly, and then I was transferred to Kelty and Lochore (I did the pair of them) and another librarian came to do Lochgelly. I did that for about two years, and then went back to Lochgelly Library again. When I worked there, I went to Library Headquarters one day a week and checked up Lochgelly Library requests, I got to know the reference books and the catalogue, and did cataloguing and classification because I had been learning those for my library exam. I was responsible for filing for the main Fife County Library HQ catalogue and used to take a bundle of slips away with me to Lochgelly, arrange them and bring them back next week.

I worked from ten o'clock in the morning until half past twelve, started again at five o'clock and finished at eight. In the afternoon, I was free to play golf. I was a keen golfer and played my first game in Carnoustie where we went every year for our holidays. We were always there when my father's uncle and family were there. They took their golf clubs, tennis rackets and bowls with them. I also worked on a Saturday morning, ten till half past twelve, or if I happened to be working at Kirkcaldy it was nine until one, but I had one Saturday off in a month. I didn't mind the hours because the second house of the pictures started at eight o'clock and I could go straight from work. There was an awful lot going on in the church too at that time. The church was the community centre. We had youth clubs, training classes for the Sunday School and I was a Church of Scotland Sunday School teacher.

In 1947 I went to Dorset. My sister wasn't very well and the doctor said that a warmer climate would suit her. So I had a look at *The Times Literary Supplement*,[22] where they advertised all the library jobs and there were library assistant jobs going in Devon, Cornwall and Dorset. I applied for them all and the first reply was from Dorset asking me to go for interview. It was February 1947, when everything was blocked with snow. Going south in the train I had a wee keek through the blind and there was a solid wall of ice and snow. I was petrified but when I got to Dorset there was not a bit of snow. The sun was shining, it was lovely and I thought, 'This is where I'll bring Nan.' I got the job as a library assistant at County Library Headquarters in Dorchester.

When I left home I said to my mother, 'I'll be up in the summertime.' I was home two and a half weeks later. I got so homesick; I didn't know a soul. I stayed in a hotel until I could get a place to live and I thought, 'If I don't get a place to stay I'll just pack up and go home.' Eventually though I boarded with a very nice couple and at work I got on well with everybody. The staff were very nice girls. It was a young staff, smaller than Fife County staff. I was doing different work in Dorchester, behind the scenes doing cataloguing and classification. At lunch times if they needed somebody on the counter I went and I met some very interesting people – the Earl of Huntingdon came in one time. A bit different from Lochgelly! Some of our clientele would tie their horses up outside the Library door. But everything was run like a tight ship, everything was to be perfectly done. We used fountain pens, and if there was a wee spot of ink on the floor the County Librarian would have an investigation. I was there for a year and five months but my sister decided she would rather be ill at home than ill in Dorset so there was no purpose in me staying. It was good experience though.

Before I went to Dorchester I had decided to take my library exams. Because I didn't have Highers[23] and the day school certificate wasn't recognised by the Library Association,[24] I did the university prelims at Edinburgh University in my own time at night. I passed four Highers – English, History, Geography and Maths – enough to sit the first library exam in which I passed in English literary history but came down in library administration. While I was in Dorchester, however, I continued to study for my Associateship,[25] and when I left it was with the intention to go to the Scottish Library College[26] in Glasgow. I thought there was no sense in trying to study at night and that I would do the thing properly. I wrote to the College and was admitted as a full-time student. It was awful difficult to get anywhere to live in Glasgow, so I lived in a hostel and went home every week-end. At the end of the first three months I sat the Library Association cataloguing and classification exams, much against the wishes of the head of the School who said, 'If you fail it looks bad for the School', but I got through and then completed the year at the College. I took my Associateship, didn't go back for a second year, thinking that if I wanted to do the Fellowship I could go back later, but I never did.

At the end of the course, Mr Paton,[27] head of the School said, 'Miss McKinlay, you're the only person who hasn't got a job to go back to. I think you should see Mr Robertson[28] of Stirling Public Library who is looking for a Chief Assistant and I'm sure he'll take you.' Mr Paton was an awfully good head of the School and I liked him a lot, but I said to Mr Robertson, 'I'm sorry, but I think I would like to go back to England. I don't think that I would like to go to a public library.[29] I would like to change to something different.' There was a job for me in Dorset if I wanted to go back. The County Librarian wrote and said that his committee had given him permission to buy a library van and he thought I might be interested in that. But I didn't want to go back to Dorset, I wanted to go on to something different.

I went for an interview for a job in charge of two branches in Northumberland. They offered me the job, but I said, 'I'm sorry, but I don't think I would be interested. In any case, I still haven't got my library administration, so I'm not fully qualified.' The Chairman said to me, 'With your confidence, madam, you'll get it at the next sitting!' Oh, that made me feel ashamed. There was another job I'd applied for in Norfolk County Library, but when the Deputy County Librarian took us round I wasn't enamoured. I thought, 'I haven't got a job but I can have my pick because there's lots of jobs going every week, every month.' And I didn't have to worry about money because my father was always there. However, the Deputy Librarian mentioned that there was a job coming up for an exhibition van librarian. When I went in for interview, before the interviewing committee said anything I said, 'I'm very sorry that I'm not interested in the job that I made application for, but I am interested in the one that's going to be advertised soon, the van librarian's job.' The Chairman says to me, 'Can you drive?' I said, 'No, but I would learn.' So they asked me some questions and I got the job which hadn't even been advertised.

I lived two miles outside Norwich, in Thorpe. The Norfolk people I liked; they had a chuckle in their voices. I liked it there very much. The County Librarian was a Welsh woman, Miss Protheroe. She and another woman had driven a truck or an ambulance together in the First World War, and when the War finished they started the Norfolk County Library Service with a van of books. When I started there were three vans, and I was told that I wouldn't be driving the van – there was always a qualified driver with me. There were two male drivers and a female driver. If anything happened to the driver, however, they expected that I would bring the van back. I was rather an oddity, therefore, being a van librarian and not being able to drive, so I took driving instructions and passed at the first attempt.

We did the whole County and took collections of books to the branch libraries and changed them about every three months. We went to all the village schools, to manor houses, vicarages and wherever there was a centre for book distribution. The van was shelved and we carried fiction and non-fiction for adults as well as books for children. We didn't issue books from the van. When we went to a centre, the people in charge chose their books, I would put the tickets in the books that were being returned and the driver would do the carrying backwards and forwards. In the country the people spoke a different language from people of the town. When we went into the first school on my first outing, I didn't know a word the headmistress said to me! Monday to Friday I went out and would maybe do four centres in a day. We got paid an allowance for lunch, and if we were later we got a tea allowance as well. Twice a month we did a King's Lynn run, which meant we stayed away overnight. The driver that I had to begin with was the youngest sergeant-major in the British Army, and another one was the youngest petty officer in the Navy. Och, everybody was nice and I got on well with them. Nevertheless, every long week-end I had I went home, and it was so nice going home.

I was in Norfolk for about four and a half years. I was beginning to feel I had been going around the countryside long enough and it was time to move. I was offered a job at the American Consulate in Edinburgh where a new library was being started to introduce people to American books and what was happening in America. I saw Miss Protheroe and said I'd been offered this job and would hand in my resignation. Well, the weeks went on and I never heard a thing so I rang up the American Embassy to ask what was wrong. Then I got a letter to say that they didn't have the money to start the library. So I went to the County Librarian to say, 'There's no job at all', but she hadn't told the committee I was leaving and said, 'Your job's still here.'

A few months afterwards, the job as editor of the Scottish Union Catalogue[30] came up. The Central Library for Students was an inter-lending system for students who wanted books for study purposes. You couldn't go in to the Central Library for Students, but your own library could make application to it. The Scottish Central Library was set up as an extension to the Central Library for Students and part of its work was the creation of the Scottish Union Catalogue. This had started in Glasgow Public Library and its purpose was to make a catalogue of all non-fiction works in Scottish libraries which could be used by the inter-lending service.

In April 1954 I took over from Miss Carbis, the first editor. Mr Pottinger,[31] Librarian of the Scottish Central Library, said he was to engage four typists while I did the preparation for them, and later I got a senior assistant who was like a deputy. I got on fine with Mr Pottinger. Sometimes he came in to see how I was getting on, but he never interfered and left everything to me. There were still a lot of library catalogues to be copied and, because a library couldn't do without its catalogue, it was a case of getting parts of them at a time. For instance, Dundee hadn't been done. I went to Dundee and saw Mr Small,[32] the Librarian, and he said he would give me so many drawers at a time of his card catalogue.[33] So I went backwards and forwards to Dundee and fortunately I had my car to do that. I didn't always have to fetch a library's catalogue. Sometimes the librarian would send the catalogues to me. When I took the cards to Edinburgh, they were checked with our existing catalogue that had been prepared from the Glasgow and

Edinburgh ones. There was a grid system with participating libraries assigned a number. If the entry from Dundee was already in the Union Catalogue, it was a case of putting a wee asterisk in the Dundee number to show that it was in Dundee stock. If there was a peculiarity, something that was different, we would note that. For things that were not in our Union Catalogue, I had to check with other catalogues to make sure the details were absolutely correct. I did most of my checking in the National Library of Scotland. Sometimes I went to the Public Library[34] to check books from the Reference Library.

Although not many libraries had catalogues that had to be checked for correctness, a badly-done catalogue would be sent back to the library concerned, and sometimes we were having to rewrite catalogue entries for new additions. The university libraries had printed catalogues that we held in the Scottish Central Library, and if I was busy their additions to stock would be filed until I had time to check them. I always had quite a backlog of stuff to check. The typists checked things against other catalogues and would lay aside entries they couldn't find, and these were the ones that I worked on and had to prepare for typing. The Union Catalogue was in a binder form, and if the typists caught up with me I got them to put the slips in but not clip them in because I checked that they were right; if an entry had been wrongly filed it was lost. We had a lot of binders covering the Bible, and a lot of binders covering the works of Robert Burns and Shakespeare. The Union Catalogue was kept in my office, but I was also doing a duplicate copy for the general office. A third copy was sent to the British Library.[35] There were seven editors in England and there were two regions in Wales, somebody doing the service in Northern Ireland and Miss Kehoe was responsible for Eire.[36] The editors had a meeting once a year at the Library Association conference and during the year we had a private meeting in one of the regions.

I travelled every day from home in Lochgelly to Edinburgh. I was going to get a flat in Edinburgh but after I started I was glad to get home at night, away from the crowds. I lived about a mile from the station and walked there in the morning. It was then an hour's journey, because the train stopped at all the stations picking up workers. I was in Edinburgh at ten to nine and that gave me time to get up to the Scottish Central Library. Nine till five were the hours. I would get the train at ten past five and get off at Cowdenbeath Station, two miles from Lochgelly, get the bus along and be home about six o'clock. When I got my car I drove to Inverkeithing Station, left it there and got the train.

The staff at the Central Library was small: Mr Pottinger, Miss Swinton, Mr Wright, and three other girls – less than a dozen including the Union Catalogue staff. The janitor made the tea in the morning and brought us a pot and biscuits on a tray, and then in the afternoon he brought up another tray for us. Mr Wright had started to do a catalogue of the bibliographies in the Scottish Central Library, and Mr Pottinger asked me if I would finish it as well as doing my editor's job. It was published under Peter Wright's name and my name, so I've got a wee entry in the National Library of Scotland catalogue.

I really did enjoy the work. I felt that I was doing a worthwhile job. This was a catalogue that was going to be used for finding books for people all over Scotland. When libraries couldn't supply books through their own stock they applied to the Scottish Central Library. It was a job that could never be finished because books are being published all the time and I was getting in additions every day from the public, county, special and university libraries participating in the project. I liked the contact I had with librarians, and with working in England I knew quite a lot of librarians there and met them at meetings. Then when I became editor of the Scottish Union Catalogue, going to the regional centres I got to know more English librarians. I felt I was right in the middle of librarianship.

Although I was very happy it was not the sort of job you could do for a long time. It was too wearing and was beginning to tell on my eyesight. However, Bill Paton,[37] who had been at library college with me and who I met at meetings and conferences, said he was going to Aberdeenshire as County Librarian and that I might be interested in applying for his job as Librarian in Buckhaven and Methil. At conferences, the Library Committee Convener usually accompanied the Librarian so I'd met one or two of his conveners and they always struck me as being nice. I was in two minds, however, as the area's pretty small and I understood that it was a man they wanted. But Bill took me to see the Library and I thought it was a nice little library. I made application and was called for interview with one or two others. The whole Library Committee were there, six householder members and six delegated Council members. I got the job. That was 1960.

The Library Convener was always a Council member because that person could go to Council meetings and fight for the Library's place in whatever was going on. The householder members were ones who used the Library and could see things needing done. We'd Dr MacDonald, one of the local GPs and very outgoing. We had a woman director of a local firm in Leven; she was good, she was interested and a reader. And the headmaster of Buckhaven High School was on the Committee. The Committee could change every year. The annual general meeting was advertised in the local paper and new householder members were asked to come forward. Although we had a few changes, usually it was the same individuals. The Committee was always a good one and wholehearted in support of anything that was proposed for the good of the Library.

I was sorry to be leaving the Scottish Central Library but glad to be starting something new, looking forward to some other aspect of the job. For the first few months I was travelling every day by car from Lochgelly. It was only about 15 miles. At the interview, however, they said that they liked all their officials to stay in the Burgh and they would give me a council house. I was to tell the housing officer what kind of house I wanted. My father had retired a short while before then and said that he and my mother would move to stay with me. And my sister said that she would come as well. I said to my mother, 'What would you want?' She said, 'It must be a house that's on the flat and it must be near a bus stop, and near one or two shops and it must have a garage at the door.' So these were the sort of things I told the housing officer I was hoping I would get.

There was a branch library at Buckhaven, a small room in Buckhaven Miners' Welfare Institute, with a part-time worker who worked seven hours a week. It was supplied with collections of books from the main stock at Methil. I thought it was time something was done about Buckhaven as it was not suitable as a branch. It was too small and the Miners' Welfare Committee had their meetings in the room and sometimes there were cigarette ends lying on the floor. Once or twice I had to speak to the cleaners to tidy the place up a bit. We moved from the Miners' Welfare Institute into a small shop-front opposite the Town House which we rented from Deas, the baker, for about two years. Next to the Council offices there was a shop with a house upstairs. It had been bought by the Burgh, and one of the Library Committee members suggested that it become a branch for Buckhaven.

I was delighted and thought, 'We'll have a library downstairs and upstairs we'll have a lecture room and museum room with artefacts belonging to Buckhaven.' There was a stair made between the Town House and this building so that when the Library was closed we could have our library lectures in the lecture hall.

Our first speaker was Jimmy Shand.[38] The year before, he had given a lecture in the main Library in Methil on his musical reminiscences. He came down once or twice before he gave the talk and went over everything with me. He said, 'Do you think I could do it?' I said, 'Of course you can if you can stand in front of the television camera and play. You're speaking to your own people, not to people that don't understand you.' He came just after we started the gramophone record library and we had quite a number of his records. He'd brought his box[39] so he played excerpts from them. He was shy, but he spoke well and carefully and with a sense of humour. He said he always looked for the best couple on the floor and played to them. You would never have associated Jimmy Shand the speaker with the Jimmy Shand you saw on your television playing the box without a smile. He was meticulous in everything he said. Oh, he was good.

The lecture room was a picture gallery as well. I had been given one or two paintings, and the Library had one or two paintings and this was a chance to show them off. Buckhaven High School loaned us two paintings done by Houston,[40] and one or two library members gave us some paintings that relatives had done. A shopkeeper in Lower Methil got a local artist to do three paintings of the area, and a Buckhaven man who was quite a good local artist gave us a lot of paintings of old Buckhaven and some of Wemyss and Dysart. This same man gave us a model of two sailing ships including one of the old Buckhaven ships, a Zulu.[41] I got two display cases from the Buckhaven Co-operative Drapery and we had things that were quaint and of interest in there.

The main library in Methil is all on one floor. It was extended by a third about four years after I started and we used the children's library for a lecture room until we had the lecture room in Buckhaven. Before I came, Bill Paton had six winter meetings and I continued them. Some of the speakers were paid by Fife Education Committee and I tried to get other speakers who would speak just for their expenses but that was difficult.

There was five of a staff when I started, all of whom had two late nights and worked till half past six, and when I left it was nine staff not including the part-timer at Buckhaven. I had a good senior assistant who was partly qualified and then gained her qualification through correspondence courses. After she qualified she couldn't get the salary she should have been getting so she went to Clackmannan as the chief assistant there. It was a completely female staff as it was in Fife County too. I just felt that men in libraries were out of place, unless they were in college or university libraries.

It was mixed clientele. Although some were miners quite a number of men in the area worked at the National Steel Foundry,[42] and for Balfour's[43] and the Central Farmers.[44] Then the power station[45] was built and we had men from there. Although there was a library in Leven, a large proportion of our members came from there because we had a better stock and a better library. We had members who came from Kirkcaldy, Glenrothes, Windygates, Kennoway. There was one shopkeeper who came from Edinburgh every day and he was a member of our Library. He said it was better than the Edinburgh Public Library. A man called Charles Brister used to come in. He was a lieutenant-commander in the Navy and had put into Methil docks during the War, liked what he saw and came back and settled. He became a miner and wrote a book entitled *This is my Kingdom*.[46] Ron Thompson,[47] who writes in *The Courier*,[48] came to the Library quite a lot. He edited the book.

Among the readers there were a couple of old women always looking for Mills & Boon stories. One day, my chief assistant said, 'They bring back books but they don't put them all on the counter. They put some of the books on the shelves and take other books but don't get them stamped.' I said, 'Next time they come in, ask them if they would like extra books because they come up from Lower Methil.' Nevertheless, in spite of getting extra books they still continued to take out books unstamped. But they always brought them back and we never said anything – they would've been so ashamed.

There was one old man, a retired miner, who, although he read Westerns and other things, was also fond of Mills & Boon, particularly ones about nurses and doctors. I think he had a daughter who was a nurse and knew a lot about nursing because he told us that there was something not right in the book he'd been reading. He'd written to the publishers to tell the author and got a nice letter back saying that the author was pleased he had drawn her attention to this. He was a nice old man and came in every day. He said he had written to one of the local papers to say that Buckhaven and Methil had the bonniest 'book belles' in any library. One of the journalists asked if they could do a feature on the staff, the young ones. They photographed the girls and were going to put their vital statistics in and I said, 'Oh, keep it decent. They're not Miss Worlds, just nice decent girls.' My staff changed every other year, they were always getting married they were so bonny. Whenever I got a new member of staff, I took her myself through all the different things she would have to do, and one of the things was to be courteous to readers and treat them with respect. You teach by example, so I never gave the girls a row.

After we got the new extension we had plenty of space although the stock didn't vary much because we were adding and discarding all the time and were limited by the money we had to spend on new books. In May 1973 the stock total was 52,626 volumes, roughly half-and-half fiction and non-fiction. The interests of readers spread over quite a range of subjects. A lot of miners were interested in the social sciences and politics. We took an assortment of newspapers including the *Morning Star* and *The Daily Worker*.[49] We were given a Chinese newspaper. One of our readers was an ex-miner who got his back broken in the pit and was in a wheelchair. He had been to China and got Chinese books and newspapers and brought them to the Library. I put them on display because a librarian is supposed to be unbiased. One time somebody wrote to the Town Council and said that the Library was biased towards Communism and I said, 'We display everything, every political shade.' Mr Watters, before his back was broken, was one of the first to come in the morning I started in Methil Library, and he said to me, 'Hello, hen, I've come to see the new Librarian.' Wasn't that a nice welcome?

We had one or two that used to come in to the reading room for the newspapers and start their conversations and we would have to 'shush' them because the Library was open plan. One time, my senior assistant went to a group of women who were talking and said they would have to be quiet because they were making such a noise. One of them says, 'Away ye go, Beth, we're not doing any harm.' Some of the men from Balfour's used to come on Saturday morning and play chess in the reading room. I was pleased to have anybody come to the Library.

My job title was Burgh Librarian. I was involved in everything and was always included on special Burgh activities and visits. I had to turn out at the Armistice Day[50] service and at the Kirking of the Council[51] after elections. The first Citizens Advice Bureau[52] in the area was started in the Library when I was there, and I was the adviser. We started up the housebound library service at the same time as we started Meals-on-Wheels. One of our Council members was on the Age Concern[53] committee. I went along and was put on the committee. Then I took on the secretaryship and a year later I became the treasurer, a post I held for about 20 years. We started up the Meals-on-Wheels service on a rota basis with so many women going out every day, Monday to Friday, and we charged sixpence for the meals which came from the Fife Council food kitchen. The Burgh then gave us the use of a van which could also be used for the housebound service. However, I did that round myself and used my car because it was much more convenient and I'd special baskets made by the Blind Society[54] to carry the books.

I was always keenly interested in local affairs and local history and through that the Library received a deposit of papers from the widow of a militant miner, David Proudfoot,[55] depicting the struggles of the miners between the two world wars. His widow sent me his letters, papers and booklets, and later his books were deposited with the Library.

I was in Buckhaven and Methil for 15 or 16 years till local government reorganisation in 1975 when I went to Kirkcaldy. The Library in Kirkcaldy was so old-fashioned and I had left a modern library. I was there for a year and a half then I retired. I could've gone on for another five years but I was glad to retire. When I left Methil Library to go to Kirkcaldy I invited all the girls up to my house. They all brought me something and I said to them, 'You've all brought me something and I've got nothing for you', and one wee girl said, 'You gave us yourself, Miss McKinlay.'

I have no regrets about becoming a public librarian. I always loved books and before I became a librarian, I was a library user. I used to love browsing around the shelves. I could spend hours in the library. Nothing can replace the feel of a properly produced book. I'm glad so many people are going back to reading again and that J K Rowling[56] has aroused so much desire for reading in children. I've read the Harry Potter books myself.

Interviewed 22 November 2001

Andrew Fraser

My name is Andrew Fraser and I was born on 21st November 1917, in Bonnyrigg I assume. I'm not very sure. That's where we lived anyway and it was quite common these days to be born at home.

My father was a lithographic artist. He should've been an artist, he had that skill but there wasnae the money to put him through school for it. He belonged to Edinburgh. He worked first with a firm in York Place, Bannerman & Steel, designers and lithographic artists' draughtsmen. When the last partner died or gave up, he took over the business and kept it under Bannerman & Steel, right up until he gave up. The Second War killed it. It would be '40 that he left. He wasnae retirement age because he got a job as clerk in the Roads Department at Bonnyrigg, Midlothian. We were in Bonnyrigg till '48, I think, before we moved into Edinburgh.

His father worked in the distillery. I don't remember my grandfather Fraser. By the time I was growing up he was dead and unfortunately my elder brother died when he was very young and my elder sister died nearly ten year ago now.

Before she married, my mother worked in the lace department at Patrick Thomson's.[1] In fact, she was head of the department latterly, but I've no recollection of my maternal grandparents. I think they were dead by the time I was growing up. My mother was an Edinburgh woman, she was a Bone. I think her father was Alexander.

The house in Bonnyrigg where we lived was 103 High Street, close on the railway station. The house is still there, Devon Cottage it was called. It had four rooms down the stair and three up the stair. There was a poky little thing, which I believe was originally for the maid. As far as I know it was only rented by us at first – a private landlord, a woman in Edinburgh. My Dad bought it from her, but as far as I know, it had been connected with the carpet factory.[2]

At that time it was oil lamps, paraffin and candles. We used quite a bit of candles. We got gas installed first and then later on we got it replaced with electricity. It might've had gas in it when I was born or maybe soon after. I just can't remember. Although they would have candles because you put the gas off and your candlelight let you get into your bed and what not. I was still at the school when we got the electric. It must've gone in late '20s or early '30s. I was thinking on the wireless set that my Dad built, but it was off batteries and we had to take the batteries down to the garage to get them charged. We used a paraffin stove for cooking. We had one of these Primus things although to begin with it was the open range[3] – an oven at one side and all these darn flues that you had to clean! There was hot and cold running water in the kitchen. There was no bathroom, no bath. The toilet was three-quarters of the way down the stair on a bend so if you didnae watch what you were doing, you were doon the stairs when you came oot! It had a flush which froze up in the wintertime. It was a good house for those days though. I had a room to myself – I started off in the maid's room and then graduated into one of the bigger bedrooms.

I was the youngest of three children. My brother's name was William, I think. He died while I was still an infant-in-arms. I don't remember but my mother spoke about it . . . the doctor warning her that if she didnae watch what she was doing she would lose me as well. She was so broken-hearted that he had to rap her over the fingers and tell her tae pull herself together. My sister was five years older than me and he was older, so he must've been another two or three I would think.

I went to Lasswade School. When I went it was an all-through school because the primary didnae go up till about the early '30s, but I was never in it. I was all my schooldays at Lasswade. I sat the Qualifying Exam[4] when I was about 11 or 12. I passed it and went into the secondary department. If you didn't pass you would've been kept back another year and had to sit it again. Occasionally you got a brilliant one who was moved up because it was too elementary for them. I don't know whether there was anybody who failed. They might have transferred them to Bonnyrigg School, which wasn't senior secondary and where pupils left at age 13, 14. They either left to work or they came on to Lasswade at that stage.

I liked English but I was a peculiar lad. I read a lot as long as I wasnae asked to. I'm very ignorant on the classics that we got as set textbooks, although I've read most of the other ones. Now what was the Dickens that we got? I struggled through it, and yet I had got *A Tale of Two Cities* from the Qualifying teacher, and I thoroughly enjoyed it. I think it was being *told* to read it. I preferred to do my own selection, because I read quite a few. I havenae read them all, but I've been through most of the classical writers, and thoroughly enjoyed them. I didnae do any borrowing from the old Carnegie Library in Bonnyrigg – I had never been in. We'd get books from the school library. The County put in a collection and I think it must've been the only place that I got them. I'm not aware of my mother or father being readers. I got *Adventure* comic and we swopped. We all had different ones.

I quite liked Maths. I could always get a high score in Maths and I still like to do the odd puzzle. I wasnae very good at languages – French I could scrape through on, but Latin, phew, I never got a pass in that after the first term. I could read it, I could say what the things were but make no sense of it. It's damned annoying because I could use it now. There's so much in the Record Office that's in Latin. I'm still doing research and anything I don't understand I copy down in the Latin and then come home and look up the dictionary.

I was never very good at Geography. I did manage to pass my Highers[5] eventually. I passed in English, which included History and Geography. I passed in Maths. I think in those days you had to pass a group of subjects to get the Higher. I took my Highers before I should've because I got the wrong date in for my birthday, so I was actually a year ahead when I sat the exam.

I wanted to maybe become a road-roller driver which horrified my parents! Oh, it was just a passing thing. I was quite interested in railways but I had no idea when I left the school really what I was goin' tae be. I would probably have been a chemist or a pharmacist, except the place in Morningside – he would have taken me – meant I had to go in and get the suburban train and the chap said, 'No, I'm terribly sorry but I wouldn't like to have you travelling, having to come in and change buses or change into the train, and have to hang around. It makes it too long a day.'

Then I was in for insurance and I was turned down – I suspect because I sat down when the chap said to me, 'Oh, just have a seat', and he hadnae sat down. You were supposed to wait, and I should've said to him, 'After you, sir', and then he would have said probably, 'No, no, it's a' right, just sit down.' I never thought.

I was at a college, Skerry's in Hill Place.[6] I took a course there for entry to the Post Office but I came seventh in Britain and they only wanted three candidates that year. I thought I had done quite well when I came seventh. I can't remember any other interviews that I had, but the next one was Midlothian Library. Copeland, the headmaster at Lasswade, was friends with my Dad and he said to my father, 'Here, why do you no' get Andrew to go in, they're looking for an apprentice librarian.'

I was interviewed by the Chief Librarian, Angus Mackay.[7] Apprentice librarian at a salary of £40 a year. It wasnae as well paid as a lot of things, but it wasnae too bad. I think it started £40, £50, £60, and then it jumped to £80 or something. As an apprentice librarian it was 9 till 5, Monday to Friday, 9 till 12 on a Saturday.

'Apprentice' was the term used because we were expected to study for the professional librarians' exams. I didn't go to evening classes or get time off. The Library Association (LA)[8] had a syllabus that you could follow on your own. I just studied at home, because we had the books to study in the library. We'd a good staff library. It was about three evenings a week I devoted to the course because there was quite a lot involved. I got my ALA (Associateship of the Library Association)[9] just before the War. When I joined the library, probably half the librarians in Scotland were unqualified. They were good librarians, by Jove. They knew their job but they had no qualifications.

It was the Education Offices we were in – Drumsheugh.[10] There were two adjoining houses and the library was down in the basement, plus an extension outside. We would be sent out to change books at miners' institutes[11] or some of the schools. The County Library provided a service through the miners' institutes and the like o' the Cowan Institute in Penicuik, a paper mill workers' institute. We had branches in Dalkeith, Bonnyrigg and Musselburgh, with the old indicator system.[12] Well, it wasnae in vogue when I joined but the remnants were still there.

With the indicator system there was a catalogue you referred to and it had a number opposite the title. So you looked up and said, 'Oh, I'd like to read that.' You didnae get to see the books. You didnae handle the books. You just looked it up and then you said to the librarian, 'I'd like to have number 263', and there was a board – blue was oot and red was in or somethin' like that. So he could look and say, 'Oh, aye, it's there', and he took down 263 and changed the indicator. Most libraries in Scotland ran this indicator system. All early libraries did as far as I know. In fact, during the War, I was stationed for a bit in Dumbarton. I found the Burgh Library, and they were still on the same system at that time.

The branch librarians came in on a Saturday morning to solve any problems they had and for requests to get books. West Calder was an odd one, because we stocked it but we never saw the librarian unless we were out there. She never came in.

The institutes were done by the caretaker in each case. There was no librarian and they were only open whatever convenient time suited them; they varied – but Arniston was open one morning and maybe an afternoon and an evening, or something like that.

All the books that these institutes and schools issued came from the County Library which got the books out in strong wooden boxes which held 50, depending on how thick they were. There was two wee slots that you could slip a shelf into. The idea being you sent the books just packed, and then when you got there they upended it, opened the lid up, put the shelf in and then you could have a little bookcase. But I don't think anybody ever did. I think they just left them in the boxes and let folk rummage! The Headquarters got the books out by local carriers. We had a certain number: Robertson for the Calders, there was somebody up in Penicuik, and somebody doon here in Musselburgh, and us mugs had to help them to humph a' the books up the stairs to the lorry.

My tasks as an apprentice librarian were very simple. You spent most of your time stampin' and labellin' books. I had a sort of boss, an older librarian, Bob Strathdee,[13] and when the collections came back we had to unpack them, they were put on the shelves and then he would check them over. Latterly, as I got a bit experience, I was allowed to help, but to begin with he did it all. He checked each book to see if it needed repair – if there were any pages torn, if the date label was needing replaced or the pocket for the book card had got torn, that sort of thing – or binding.

The boxes of books were sent out probably just twice a year. It wouldn't be more than three times. They were only partial changes of course. Schools were complete. We always went on the Gala Water run – Stow, Heriot, Temple, Carrington. The boss went sometimes. It was a link with the schools really, particularly down there. The headmasters of the nearer schools were into Education and could come down, but the teachers of the little ones werenae much in.

It took you a' day. It didnae need to but it did! You went with the contractor's lorry, just a flat lorry. There was a cover to put over if it was raining, but other than that it was just open. You sat in the cab, and there was only the two of you. The first time I was on, I just let him get on with it because he knew where he was going and where he would stop for lunch – we carried a sandwich – I think it was between Heriot and Fountainhall that we stopped on the back road.

The schools and the institutes didn't have a very sizeable stock of books. Fountainhall School, for instance, would probably have three boxes – 150 books. It might've been more because we did not only the school. The school there was really the branch library and there was a sign with the torch on it.[14] The adults went in the evening but it was a fairly restricted choice of books. In the schools the teacher, the headmaster probably, did it himself.

When I started, six people were employed in the Headquarters of the County Library. There was Mackay, Chief, Jimmy Hearn, Chief Assistant, Bob Strathdee, Assistant, and myself and we had two typists. I think they started off part-time. They werenae really employed by the library. They were part o' the pool but allocated to the library permanently.

I joined NALGO[15] once I started. The boss was keen on it. I think he was president of the local branch for a while and he encouraged you to take it up. Everybody in Drumsheugh was in the thing, the whole buildin'.

We'd a lending section as well for anybody who cared to come in, but it was mainly councillors or teachers. There were some big nobs. You got the like o' Sir John Clerk as a committee member, but some of the councillors werenae a' that bright. The books at the lending section in Headquarters were issued by anybody who was knocking around. Normally it would be one of the girls, but if there was any query or somebody wantin' help or advice, we were whistled through.

You always got somebody who wasnae satisfied, but people had to accept that you had a limited budget. I think Mackay himself was only on about three and a half hundred a year so you can imagine what the budget was like! Librarians weren't well paid, but you had job safety.

There were no paperbacks to begin with. The Penguins[16] came in round about the '30s. At that time you could replace virtually any book that you had, now you just have to take other stuff in. We used to have a tray with all the books, and Mackay used to go through it and decide that he would want this, this and this. He went along with the list to the bookseller and behold, they turned up. They kept them in stock. They don't now. There werenae as many books churned out and so they could afford to keep them. They were thick, it was thick paper. That was a normal novel at 2/6, 3/6, 4/6, depending.

Probably the stock was a third non-fiction and two-thirds fiction. In these days, you did get students asking – normally at the libraries, but sometimes at the institutes. Somebody would be at an engineerin' college or something, and they would ask for particular titles. We had quite a good minin' section and paper-making because there was a terrific amount of mining in Midlothian at that time.

Some o' the councillors or the teachers, head teachers borrowed quite extensively. In these days, maybe no' the councillors, but the teachers and the headmasters were in every week. You were allowed two books at one time – one non-fiction and one fiction. It was gradually relaxed. The non-fiction tickets were written in red, the fiction in blue. It sometimes caused a wee bit o' a stushie because somebody maybe wanted two non-fiction or somethin', but I don't think our stocks were that big that we could have stood it at that time.

We must have had 50,000 or 60,000, I would think. We were still on ledgers that you wrote in all the details: author, title, publisher, bookseller, price and then there was a space for discards, replacement and this sort of thing. With the population of Midlothian somewhere around 200,000[17] it wasn't an enormous stock. I don't think the demand was there. Not everybody read. It was a limited readership at that time.

Before the War provision for children or young people was done through the schools or the branch libraries or the institutes. I'm not aware that the library had particular policies to encourage children and young people to read.

We started in the late '30s doin' short book lists, sometimes on a particular topic and sometimes just general, and we put out bookmarks, but of course they would only go to readers. These were publicising the library because somebody would take it home and then their friends would be aware that there was a library service – because it wasnae always terribly obvious.

The County was a relatively young service in those days. They only started in '21. A lot of the librarians felt that they were pioneers. The counties tended to stretch out more than the burghs did, lookin' for a wider area and less capable readers. You had all the work in keepin' tabs on where everythin' was because if somebody asked for a book you had to be able to tell them whether it was at Headquarters or, if it wasnae, where it was and when it had gone. The schools got a typed list, we kept one copy and then you just checked against that when it came back and rung up and said, 'Where's so-and-so and so-and-so?'

In Midlothian, none of the burghs had its own library.[18] There were a lot of burgh libraries right up until reorganisation in the '70s but not in Midlothian. There were private circulating libraries but the County Library didn't regard those as rivals.[19] Boots and some of the other ones would have non-fiction, but an awful lot of the stuff was just light fiction and possibly some light non-fiction. We could buy more serious stuff.

At that time, the County Library didn't issue anything other than books. There was an abortive attempt after the War at a record library. It was a cock-eyed scheme: they brought in all the school stock because they felt that there were records lyin' in the school and if they werenae always using them, somebody else would borrow what they needed and bring it back. The poor schools who had built up their libraries, although they werenae very big, were losin' out because some other geezer had taken the thing and was hanging on to it like grim death! The thing really fell through until we took it up ourselves a lot later.

I was really enjoying the work and I think it was helped by the fact that I've always been interested in local history and although not a vast collection, they had enough to whet my appetite. And I suppose just gettin' around – you went oot to the institutes to change the books and you were always meetin' somebody else.

There was a County Library Circle which met probably four times a year in different localities. It was largely confined to qualified staff or staff who were trying to qualify, and they had occasional week-end conferences which I went to. Then there was a library course run every summer at Newbattle Abbey.[20] I attended a couple of these, maybe three, at that time. You got time off for that, it was part of the work. I can remember we sometimes supplied some of the books. One time I was on a bike and Bonnyrigg to Newbattle isnae any distance so I just popped back and forward.

Before the War, I went to the Scout Jamboree in Holland in 1937.

Although I was never in the Cubs I joined the Scouts[21] when I was probably 11–12. I think it was because one of my pals at school was goin' tae join. It was pure chance because we had a BB[22] company too. I enjoyed the Scouts and by 1937 I was an officer in the pack so I reduced rank to a patrol leader and went to the Jamboree. I think there was only maybe three or four patrols from Scotland. There was an officer went from our thing, Clark Fisher, and probably just two boys. We had a parents' committee which ran functions, raised funds and so on. Of course you had to be able to afford it. The committee did a lot of hard work raisin' money but you still had to put into the thing.

I certainly hadnae been abroad before and the furthest my parents travelled was down to London. So that was a great adventure to go across to Holland. It started on Friday, July 30th and it finished on Friday, August 13th. We toured around quite a bit. We were in Amsterdam, we were at Schiphol, we were in some of the fishing places, and you were meeting folk from all over, including one Red Indian. There were none from Germany nor Italy.

I was called up in November 1939. Didnae know one end o' a rifle from the other. You were called into the recruitin' office in Edinburgh, were given a medical, you registered and then in due course a letter arrived. It was the KOSB[23] that I was posted to, doon in Berwick. I was there for about three month. It was primitive – have you ever stood oot in pitch blackness wi' candles flickerin' while you tried to wash and shave in an open basin? It was cold water, if they managed to get it. They had put up this camp, wooden huts, and it was just up. Half the roads werenae completed. There was nothing really except the huts and what looked like a pig-trough wi' a pipe running along and taps off it and you washed and shaved there.

We did our basic training there, and then they shipped us oot to France in March 1940 – Rouen. We had been pushed out as a patrol. There was an officer, sergeant, three corporals, and they each had their patrol. I don't know what we were supposed to be doin' – stoppin' the German advance, I think. We were between them and Rouen and we just walked into them. There was nowhere for us to hide and there werenae enough o' us to do anythin'. They had tanks, artillery and machine guns, and we had three Brens[24] and three o' these damned anti-tank rifles. They sent a tank round the side, and they were lyin' behind hedges blatterin' us wi' everythin'. A couple o' our lads were wounded. I was carryin' the

Bren and I opened up. It was a token gesture, but I emptied what I had. I think I only had four magazines. We were a' scattered aroond in this open field, nowhere you could retreat to so we were made prisoner. That wasnae long before Dunkirk.[25]

We were marched into Belgium, got a train, landed up in Holland and were put on barges. There was nothin' to tell me where I was and I don't know how far we went. We got back on to a train and finished up on the other side o' Germany. We were always short of food because they had so many prisoners they werenae geared for that. I've often said to folk that the best meal I ever had was a raw turnip oot a field! We stopped for a break, and there was a field o' turnips. It's a wonder we werenae shot! We were taken to a prisoner of war camp, Stalag VIII, in Poland. We were sent out to Zychlin and were in the old schoolhouse. We were ditchin' at that time. The Germans were sortin' up the Polish roadside ditches because they were overgrown. They had their engineers, surveyin' and decidin' how far down to go and we were the ones that did the shovellin'. We did other things – we were on tattie-howkin'[26] one time.

It wasnae too bad because the Poles had no time for the Germans, and the farms round about were responsible for our meal in the middle o' the day, and we got the best. We got schnapps in our coffee, we got bread; we never got butter but sometimes a light bread – almost a cake – and lashin's o' beautiful coffee, creamy – farm, you see, they would have the milk – and sweet, but then they had sugar beet. But their coffee . . . I can't remember now what it was made out o' – hickory or somethin', and they roasted barley or something for it.

At that time Germany had half of Poland and Russia had the other. We were only six mile off the dividin' line and we saw all this stuff rollin' up, trainloads. We knew there was somethin' on. Then we were shot back to the main camp again, out the way, back to Stalag VIII, herded into cattle trucks and shipped back. You were just stuffed in. Very often you couldnae lie down, could hardly sit down, never mind anythin' else.

We werenae long back in Stalag VIII and we were sent to a coal mine. We objected, but you cannae argue wi' a rifle! This was in Bobrek – that's how it sounded. We were shovelling coal. The only Germans were what they ca'ed the *Overhäuers*, the overseers, and the boss himself was a German, but a lot o' the workers were either Silesian or Polish and

we got on. I had a very good man to work under, he was Silesian –
Hanisch, I never got his second name – we got on well together.
Shovelled coal until we had to be pulled away when the Russians came
back – three and a half years probably. We had a camp locally and were
marched down in the morning or whatever shift you were on. There
were three shifts. I was never on anything but either day shift or back
shift. Probably about 100 prisoners worked in that coal mine. They
were all strangers. I was the only KOSB person there.

You just coped, nothin' else for it. You did get better rations than
you did in the camp. The pit supplied it, and the Red Cross were on the
ball and we regularly got parcels through and then you did a bit of
tradin'. You got cigarettes and various things. I didn't smoke then. I did
take it up when things got a bit tight towards the end and I was gettin'
a bit hungry and that took the pangs o' hunger off. But even when you
smoked, you still had spare. You would probably get 50 in a packet,
you'd have plenty to spare and you were allowed to smoke doon the pit.

It was a massive coal seam. We reckoned it was probably 22 feet
high but you were workin' it in two sections. We were working the bottom
section, aboot 10 feet, 11 feet high. The pit was linked to another one
and in the first one we were shovellin' into the hutches to be hauled to
the pit shaft. It could be a bit tricky sometimes because you would have
a slope doon and a' you had was a length o' wood maybe three inches
square at the most, to brake and if that broke you were in dead trouble!
Or sometimes the tunnels were a bit low or narrow. Maybe four, six of
the prisoners were killed in the three and a half years that I worked
there, and we had quite a few injuries. I was walloped once or twice.
I'll still be carryin' some of the marks because once coal dust got in . . .

In one pit, they had what they ca'ed the shaker pans. You tipped it
on and it took it out on to a belt and the belt took it to the pit. They had
a different method o' measurin'. Wi' the hutches, it was how many
hutches you filled. Wi' this one it was how far you went in. Somebody
came round just before the end of the shift wi' a measurin' rod and
measured how far, and there was a great deal o' argument.

News of the War filtered through. They would maybe have a
newspaper doon the pit and you swiped it when they werenae lookin'.
The Germans issued a newssheet. It came out regularly, and gave the
German angle on things. But then we had a wireless. Illicit but we knew
better than the Germans what was happenin'. It was probably in the

commander's hut, the sergeant-major who was in charge. If there was the least suspicion that somebody might be comin', it was taken out, put into this oven, almost up the chimney, a very small fire was lit and the Germans were so thick that they never tumbled to the fact!

The word was passed on, what was happenin', or what the British said was happenin', and you compared the two then, but you always knew that the Germans would play it down unless they were winnin'. At the school there were maps, and I copied the local one on sheets o' toilet paper but I was able to copy a map for France and part o' Germany, and I made little flags. Once the British landed in France we used to stick them in accordin' to where they were comin'.

We had lads that broke out from the pit camp but they were aye caught. At that time the Germans had half o' the hut and our lads were in the next one, and they used to carry on a sort o' conversation – they had a certain amount of German. They shifted the stove and then started diggin' a tunnel, and I can remember one o' the lads sayin' afterwards that he had been chattin' to the Germans while they'd been diggin'. The Germans had been sayin', 'Well, what are you up to the night?' and he says, 'Oh, we're digging a tunnel', and the Germans had just laughed. Unfortunately they didnae go down deep enough and they went through the garden plot and one of the Germans went to dig somethin' up and fell into the hole! That was the end o' that. They could've been quite successful because about 100 yards off you came to a steep bank down to a railway, a mineral railway probably for the coal. They could've got out but they had no civvies so they would never have got anywhere. Nobody got away successfully. There were one or two managed, I don't know now how they did it, but they were very quickly caught and just brought back.

When the Russian advance got closer we were moved away from the pit. Everybody was being evacuated on foot. The Germans had a horse and cairt – I dinnae think the German Army had very much more. It's the only time that I've known Nestlés cream to freeze, the condensed milk. It was like ice cream! Tasted lovely. Sometimes we just slept at the side of the road but mainly they got us into farms or covered accommodation. Heaven help them if they kept us more than a couple o' days, because somebody would find oot where the tatties were stored or their grain and then everybody helped themselves. You could cook out in the open and there was always wood that you could acquire.

The worst experience was when they were movin' some o' the labour camp. I've never seen anything like it. Walkin' skeletons, and if they dropped, they either dropped dead or if they dropped frae exhaustion they were shot, and the rest of the inmates just stripped them o' anythin' they could get because they were in rags. We were startin' to protest and say, 'Here, here, here, what's goin' on?' Right away up came the rifles, and then we were quickly lined up and marched away oot the road.

We were hungry. It depended where we were. You went through Hungary and everythin' was hunky-dory because they didnae like the Germans. You went through Austria and they were a' for the Germans, so you copped it short. We were a good few weeks on the march, and the Red Cross werenae gettin' through then. Then they made the mistake of marchin' us by night and stopped in a village. Yours truly, along wi' a few more, found a very convenient barn and it was dark, they didnae see us and they didnae take time to count or check. They just 'Heraus, heraus!' into the column and away they marched. We were left there. No food, of course, no nothin', just what we stood up in. We then split up into two twos and went our own ways. I was with Benny and we travelled at night. We'd no idea where we were. We had no idea what direction to go in but we took off. When it was just daylight we looked for a house or a farm and knocked on the door and cadged some grub. It usually worked because I dinnae think they realised we were prisoners. There were so many odd-bods by that time kickin' around.

Then you found a nice wood, disappeared in there and towards dusk moved oot the other side and found somewhere to get some grub. We did that for quite a bit until we arrived at this particular village, and on the outskirts moved into a barn. In the morning I went down to cadge some grub. We had made two mistakes. One, the wife had lost her husband in the War and hated the British, and two, the German Army had just moved into the village the same night as us! She gave us somethin' to eat, but she reported us and we were nabbed.

This was in Germany. We were taken to the headquarters of a training battalion – youngsters to be thrown in as soon as they had enough experience. They thought, 'What are we goin' to do wi' them?' because they couldnae just let us go and there was nowhere that they could lock us up. So they came up with the brilliant idea that we could work in the cookhouse, in the lap of luxury because you were well fed. We werenae very popular wi' the blokes that had been in the cookhouse because they were put oot on to manoeuvres! We must've been a week wi' them, and kept on the move.

The night I got stomach-ache we stopped in a field and I was in agony and said to Benny, 'I cannae go any further, mate.' So we got down into the ditch and the German Army walked on and left us. By this time we were near the fighting. You could hear the guns, so each day you took off towards that. Eventually we were lookin' for grub at a farm and there were Serbs working on it, and the boss said somethin' to the farmer and he took us back to their billet. Billet? – feather mattresses! We were maybe a week there. Then we were on the march – us, this boss bloke and three Germans came along and they were scared oot their wits! Would we look after them, would we protect them? They handed ower their weapons and everythin'.

The Americans were about a mile away so we salamandered across and the first convoy was comin'. We flagged it down and were whipped to some camp and fed like fightin' turkey-cocks. My God, they lived! They even had doughnuts mid-mornin'. Then it was a question o' them gettin' us to a transit camp, and they were flyin' you out from there to the French coast. We landed in Britain, were deloused and given clothin' and a ration book, train ticket, and a leave pass.

That was before V-E Day.[27] In fact V-E Day landed while we were on leave because they told everybody on leave to stay another week. I'd been home and then had to report to the West Riding, to this camp. You got a certain amount of trainin', but they were just really holdin' on to you until they could demob you. Then we moved up to just ootside Dumbarton. Then they moved us down into Devon to clear the beaches, get rid o' the barbed wire but you had to watch in case there was anythin' lethal left. Then I think from there we were just demobbed.

I can remember we came up the west coast, had to change at Carlisle and come over to Edinburgh. We had a wee bit to wait for the train, so went into the buffet to get somethin' to eat, and I took the money oot ma pocket and it meant nothin' to me. The lassie wanted 1/11½ or somethin' like that, and I'm lookin' at this and I said to her, 'Oh, here, take what you're needin'.' You, see, Marks and Pfennigs[28] – I'd been so long accustomed.

When I went back to the library things were a bit different. The libraries werenae doin' a great deal because print wasnae available really.

I went down to London for a year on a course for my FLA (Fellowship of the Library Association).[29] This was the Army arrangin' the thing – resettlement. There was no difficulty from the County Library. They were only too keen to have you qualify if you could. I stuck in at the thing and I enjoyed it but my brain wasnae holdin' it. There'd been too long a gap. I'd lost the facility of studying. As a prisoner I had a little pocket Bible which I read twice frae cover to cover. Then through the Red Cross they were offerin' courses to people, and I opted for English literature, so I got one or two books. They were textbooks, purely teaching material; we didnae get novels or anythin' like that.

I never got my FLA. I was just short o', I think, two papers. I had lost the urge by that time because I could've re-sat them, but I'd been too long away and I couldnae concentrate properly. I would've had to have done it at home and I thought, 'Och, phooey. I've done enough. We'll just leave it at that.'

But, och, London had one vast advantage – I managed to buy an awful lot o' local history books when I was down there. I hadnae a lot of money to spend but you got two or three here and there, and I got maps and prints and things that you never saw up here. I had quite a decent library at that time.

I came back to the County Library after the year's course in London. The apprenticeship was completed by then. Mr Mackay was still the Chief Librarian. The two girls were still there and I think they had extra girls in to replace us. Jimmy Hearn was dead. Bob Strathdee came back about a year after me and became Chief Assistant and I moved up to Assistant. But no other apprentices were taken on. The organisation remained much as before the War although the Headquarters had moved from Drumsheugh out to the old Fisherrow School.[30]

I was on the first mobile library in 1950. I was driver-librarian. I learned to drive just before I got on to the mobile. One of the Assistant Directors of Education took me sometimes at night and gave me some lessons and I got lessons on one of the County Council lorries because it was a heavy vehicle I was goin' on to.

We did Currie, Balerno, Ratho, Ratho Station. It was later extended and then I did Newtongrange, Danderhall, Newton, Woodburn, Birkenside, Carrington, Temple, Heriot, Fountainhall, Stow. Monday, I was there in the morning, I was off in the afternoon and then we did Currie, Balerno at night and I always had an assistant for that because you were busy. Tuesday was what we called the Gala Water run. We finished up at Stow at half past four. Wednesday was Birkenside maybe into Gorebridge itself and I had my tea. I had an assistant there. I dropped them off and I carried on at night to do Newton and Danderhall. Thursday I had the mornin' off and then I went over to Newbridge and picked up an assistant there and we did Newbridge, Ratho and Ratho Station. Friday was Danderhall, Woodburn, I came back into Edinburgh, picked somebody up and went out to Pathhead in the afternoon.

We later extended, got other mobiles and the routes were all changed but for the first five or six years I was the sole librarian-driver. After that time we were really lookin' for smaller places as we were at the stage of building more branch libraries. Mayfield was built somewhere about '62 or '63. The first one we built we sneaked through because there were building restrictions. Penicuik got the first one – we built it in the grounds of the school so it got through as a school library but it served the whole community.

I enjoyed the mobile library. You made a lot of friends. They came for books and then they would maybe discuss things. I was certainly an unpaid carrier because, particularly on the Gala Water run, somebody would come in at Carrington and say, 'Oh, here, do you mind taking this to . . .' It was usually just a small parcel. There was one wifie from Heriot and I did quite a bit for her to somebody in Stow. She would come wi' parcels o' eggs or somethin' but she would sometimes give me somethin', and certainly at Christmas I used to get a' sorts o' things – packets o' cigarettes and handkerchiefs and all sorts o' things. You got to know people and they would ask you for advice on what books we would recommend. I used to keep my eye open when I was in Headquarters and I would say, 'Oh, Mrs So-and-so would like that.' It was a very friendly service.

I'd never driven in snow. I was still learnin' to drive this thing. So snow was just a nuisance to me. I took it up to Temple, a narrow street and nae openin's onywhere. So I had to go up the road to a farm and back in, and I did this wi' aboot three feet o' snow and how I got oot it, I dinnae ken. I got to Middleton Moor and I managed to complete the run. There was one wife in Stow said to me, 'My, I wasnae expectin' you. You're the only thing that's got through here the day!' It was my proud boast that only once I didn't manage to do my whole round – and that was mechanical failure.

The mobile library service was supplementary to the delivery of books to the schools and institutes. The sort of books asked for were really much the same as before the War but by that time we were givin' out three. I think we were still restrictin' to one non-fiction and two fiction but we didnae have the stock to be able to support anythin' else.

The War gave me an ulcer. Well, I stuck it on the mobile as long as I could, but it was far too heavy and far too cold sometimes. My doctor eventually said to me, 'You've got to come off.' I wasnae very popular but they made a slot for me and I came off it, and then of course some time later I had the op. I got the job o' comin' down to Fisherrow and receiving the books and allocatin' them. The boss had it all worked out, what was goin' tae go where and they coded the boxes. There was more space at Fisherrow than at Drumsheugh.

We married in '52 and moved down to Musselburgh and I just walked to work. I was there until I was 65. I wasnae working when I retired because I'd had a massive heart attack a year before and it took a long time to get over it.

Mr Mackay was down at Fisherrow for a number of years but he died suddenly before he reached retirement age. He was followed by Mr Strathdee, and I was stepped up as Deputy. That was an automatic step then. Mr Strathdee was there until reorganisation and before he retired I was interviewed and given the job so we were workin' as a team, the two of us. Well, we always did, but some o' the stuff he dealt wi' he had to pass over to me because it was District.

Staff numbers were increasing during the '60s and '70s. Headquarters must've been roughly 12, must've doubled frae what we were but then we had an awful lot more libraries by that time particularly in the County. East Calder was in the school there. Then in '60 we built Penicuik, and that was followed by Newtongrange, I think, and very shortly after by Loanhead and Mayfield because the two o' them are almost identically built. Gorebridge, Danderhall – I cannae remember just the order they were in. Bonnyrigg, of course, moved oot o' the old cramped place and into the new one. All the principal places in Midlothian came to have libraries before reorganisation. Towards the end we got Currie in the school and Balerno was in the school. West Calder of course had its own.

Livingston got a new one because it was a New Town. It was the oddest set-up. The planners decided that the school population would be primary school and they would work up to secondary, so they had planned it that we were up against Almondbank and the boiler was to be installed in Almondbank to do the school and us. But they discovered that they had an awful lot of secondary pupils and so they built a secondary school up the hill. They put the boiler in there and I don't know if you've ever tried putting hot water doon a hill! It was hopeless. The school was higher than our buildin'. They eventually got Almondbank Primary built but I don't know whether they ever shifted the boiler down or no'.

At reorganisation in '74–'75, I became the first Midlothian District Librarian. I'd gone from apprentice to Chief Librarian. I never moved. I was in for East Lothian as Chief Librarian but I didnae play golf. Enough said! I was in Musselburgh, and Haddington doesnae get on very weel with Musselburgh, so it all went against me there. I didnae get it. However I wasnae bothered. I was approached by Edinburgh at one point but I turned it down. Well, what's now the Royal Bank were openin' a library down in London and it was in the offing, and so I turned Edinburgh doon. The bank job fell through but I wasnae bothered. I never regretted it. I was quite happy in Midlothian.

With the setting-up of the District we lost all the west – Currie, Balerno, right out to the Calders. We lost Musselburgh and Inveresk, Heriot and Stow; we also lost the schools. The Education Service went to the Region,[31] but Libraries were Recreation and Leisure, which was District. The funny thing was that we only lost one member of staff at the changeover.

We also had Library Headquarters in Musselburgh, which was in the area of another authority, East Lothian. Not only that, but we were in a Regional Council buildin', because it was a school. My Director, John Gilfillan, and Chairman, Councillor Sam Campbell, did support us but we were so far away, we were off the beaten track. People had no idea of what you were doin'.

The chief frustrations in the District Library Service were the same frustrations as in the County: the problems wi' committees and gettin' things through and tryin' to screw some money out and you had to try and calculate how much you would need. You would be puttin' something forward and it would go in front o' the Library Committee and would be passed. It would then go to the Finance, and half of the Finance were the same folk that had voted for it and they voted against in the Finance.

I enjoyed my years as District Librarian until I retired in '82. I had my own ideas and I would argue wi' anybody – Chief Exec and councillors, the lot, if I didnae agree. I don't think it did me any harm, you know. I always got on well wi' them.

I've had no regrets about having chosen librarianship as my career. I would do it again, although things have changed. I noticed when we came down here, whether it was the bigger staff, we lost a lot of the fun and the co-operation that we had up in Drumsheugh.

Interviewed 23 May 1997

M W (Bill) Paton

My name is Matthew William Paton. I have that full, posh name but I'm known as Bill and that started right at the beginning because my mother didn't like me being called Motha, the Kilsyth rendering of Matthew. I was born in Kilsyth on 24th September 1922. I was an only child.

My father fought in the First World War. He was in the KOSBies, the King's Own Scottish Borderers.[1] He won the Military Medal[2] for bravery and finished up a second lieutenant. He fought in Flanders, and I think he was at the Somme. By occupation he was a coal miner, a face man and a fireman[3] and worked most of his life in Manor Powis Colliery near Stirling, Causewayhead, an anthracite pit. My Dad worked with his father who was a contractor. The mine owner used to break down areas and put them to people who would operate them for themselves and for the mine owners of course. I've been told that my grandpa Paton was a pretty hard man to work for.

Miners always want out of the pits but once they get out, they find they don't like it above ground, and all my father's brothers and sisters emigrated to America or South Africa before the Second World War. Sometime after he was married my Dad had gone to the States. He went to Detroit and got a job driving a tramcar, but my mother didn't want to go abroad so he had no choice but to come back. I think I was a baby when he was there and my mother was left on her own here and that was partly what brought him back. My Dad had a very serious accident about the middle years of the Second World War when a runaway rake of hutches[4] caught him. That allowed him to get out of the pits shortly before he was due to retire because they found that he had something akin to silicosis. He had a poor chest in the War years, the accident exacerbated this weakness and he could hardly drag himself up the little brae close to home. Despite that, he lived to 95 and was still looking after himself at that age. I don't remember my grandpa, Matthew Paton, or my grandma, Isabella Jarvie. My great-grandpa was James Paton from Ireland; he was an engine-keeper.[5]

My mother was born in Sauchie and worked in Patons & Baldwins Mill,[6] the woollen mill in Alloa, where 75 per cent of women worked between leaving school and getting married. She also worked in the Sauchie mill at one stage. After the First World War, my Dad was working in the shipyards in Alloa, and that's when he met my mother. Then once she got married she stopped working; that was the usual. When my granddad on my mother's side was doing anything, he was also a miner but he wasn't given too much to working. My grandmother had a difficult time and there were five in the family. I don't know anything of my great-grandparents on my mother's side.

Our first house was a tenement in Alloa, Tullibody Road – the main street from Alloa to Tullibody. There were four families sharing a two-storey block, two up and two down, a common doorway, a passageway, and sharing the inside flush toilet. We had two rooms: a living room and a bedroom. It was gas lighting and my mother had a range[7] with an oven and a hot water tank at the other side. I remember washing my face at the sink. The other families weren't miners' families. We were always conscious that my Dad was a miner and that put him a step or two below the neighbours, especially before the baths were opened at the pit. Prior to that, people didn't want to sit beside them because they were dirty. It wasn't nice to find that people avoided you. I can remember my Dad washing every day when he came from the pit in a metal bath with a handle at both sides. I remember his pit clothes in the living room, drying off. There was a washhouse outside which was shared with the other three households. It contained a tub with a fire underneath that had to be kindled every day. My mother had a mangle and the wee scrubbers. We were in that house till I was ten and then we moved to a council house in Alloa. It was an exchange. We had one bedroom, one living room, a kitchen, a separate scullery[8] and a bathroom. Electric lighting. We had a garden front and back. My father liked gardening. He was a great vegetable man. I can remember what moving to the council house did to the spirits in the house, what excitement there was at this and how my Mum was bucked up by the idea.

I started at a wee primary school in Alloa – two classes, maybe an infant school. It was some distance from home and we had quite a way to walk, but I enjoyed the school at that stage. I had two years in the first school, and then when I was seven I went to Sunnyside Primary School, and worked all the way up to Control, the Qualifying class.[9] I didn't like it but I didn't dislike it any more than anybody else. If we got the teacher we wanted we were lucky, and that made a difference. I was good at sums. I was good at Mental Arithmetic. I was quite good at school. I was more the teacher's pet than in with the crowd. I wanted to do well. I wanted to please the teacher. At that time we had two or three women teachers coming home to have lunch in our house. My mother provided them with lunch and charged, of course. We all sat at the table and had our dinner,[10] then went back to school.

I passed the Qualifying, and went to Alloa Academy. We didn't really know the difference between senior secondary and junior secondary. If you did well, you went to the Academy and learned all the useless subjects like languages and Algebra and stuff like this. Otherwise you went to the Grange School, the junior secondary, and learned to be a mechanic or a joiner and that sort of thing. However, there was a realisation that if you didn't go to the Academy, you maybe wouldn't get too good a job. I found the change daunting. Up to the top primary class, I felt I hadn't learned an awful lot and then all of a sudden you had to learn Latin.

I got Latin and French for the first two years and Algebra, Geometry, Arithmetic. I was scoring reasonable marks and it kept me out of trouble with the teachers. And I wasn't in trouble with my classmates because I wasn't top of the class – I would be maybe second, third, something like that. I didn't enjoy Alloa Academy though as much as primary school. On the social side, I wasn't popular either with the pupils or with the teachers because I was a wee fellow, poorly, my health wasn't good. I was a delicate lad and had various childhood illnesses all about my tummy. Rugby was the game that was played. Well, I was never built for rugby, and I wasn't interested in other sports. Funny, I was OK at gym, I enjoyed the gym. It was the games, and I was always the last person to be picked for a team. But I felt that towards the end of my time at secondary school, I was getting in with the other lads a bit more, holding my own.

I left school at the end of third year. I didn't really want to remain on at school. I felt I wasn't getting anywhere fast and there was an influence from home that I should be thinking about bringing some money in. I was good at Art; I was first equal in the exam but Art didn't bring in a weekly wage packet. Although the rector[11] urged me to stay on, I remember thinking, 'I'm wasting my time here. I should be doing something else.'

As a boy, I enjoyed reading adventure stories, and I liked Richmal Crompton,[12] Percy F Westerman,[13] Biggles,[14] R M Ballantyne.[15] I got comics – *The Wizard, Adventure, The Hotspur, The Rover* – not all of them but I changed with my pals. I got pocket money from my parents, but very little. I had some pals who belonged another level socially and when the shows[16] came to Alloa they got money galore, and that was the worst time. I joined the public library when I was still at primary school. It was in Alloa Town Hall. Reading was my principal interest as a laddie although I got on quite well with the boys round about. I had my place and used to go out playing – hide and seek, kick the can, levoy.[17] I joined the Cubs[18] and went right through but never became a Scout.

After I left school, my first job was as an 'apprentice' accountant. An uncle of mine had a newsagent's business and this accountant, James Frame, kept his books and I got the job with him. It was a one-man firm and I was the one man! It was largely a matter of doing audits for small-time local businessmen, shopkeepers mainly, like my uncle. The first month was frightening because I hadn't taken book-keeping at school. He would tell me how to do it, but there was no training as such. I got into awful trouble with one of Jimmy Frame's main clients because I hadn't 'posted to the ledger'. All the money that had come in I'd put in the cash book but I hadn't taken it back to the ledger. When it came time to send out the accounts, Jimmy said, 'Did you post to the ledger?' Of course I said, 'Yes', so out they all went and were charged for last month's work, which they had paid for. There was a right old stramash about that, but I didn't know about book-keeping. The work was interesting, I was paid ten bob[19] a week and it was a good enough job so far as prospects went. I was in the office all day myself while he was out doing audits, and I was doing bits of audits back at base. Then he used to come in at half past five when I should've been going away and he used to hold me there till eight o'clock or whenever. I had no life beyond that and so after six months I left.

My second job was a splendid job with Hibbert's Bottling Company which was associated with a brewery. I was supposed to be an assistant despatch clerk, but it was mainly making up presents, gifts, to consumers of the beer abroad. My wages didn't go up – they were still ten bob. The hours were all right; they were regular hours and I was free in the evenings although I worked on a Saturday. I enjoyed it and went home on the bike for dinner. I was there only another six months because there was no future in it at all. I was still in touch with Jimmy Frame, we got to talking about me going back, but I conveyed to him that I needed to get finished at the finishing time at night, and he promised, 'Oh, that's no problem. We'll certainly do that.' I moved back, but the hours kept extending and it was just a rerun. So I left after another six months.

This time I went to the Library. The job was advertised in the press. I didn't want to go there because it was the spring of 1940, the War had started and it was a temporary job to take the place of an assistant who had been called up, so I couldn't see a clear path forward. I don't remember in detail the interview, but Clackmannanshire was a small education authority, we tended to know each other and the Director of Education seemed to know about me. There were two of us interviewed because there were two jobs. One was a permanent job, one a temporary job, and I was applying for the temporary one. I wasn't eligible for the permanent job because I didn't have my Highers.[20] I really went in the expectation I'd be able to move on quite quickly to something else; library work didn't attract me at that stage. Although I was a keen reader I could see that there was more to the Library than reading Billy Bunter.[21] They had a big board saying what was there – Philosophy, Religion, Sociology, Philology – and I thought, 'What am I doing here?' There's a popular idea that to work in a library you've got to read all the books, and I was worried about that. I was conscious that I didn't have my Highers and there were words I didn't understand: what on earth was Philology, and things like this?

Anyway, I was appointed. We worked shifts – two late nights a week until eight (later it was brought back to seven) but with some hours off in the morning, and alternate all-day Saturdays. I don't remember what my wage was but it would be more than the ten shillings a week I'd been receiving. I was working alongside another library assistant, George Malley, who had been in the same class as me at school, and that helped. It was stamping the library books out, taking them in, checking them off, putting them back on the shelves. Gradually we got into other things like cataloguing, which was not much more than typing out the author, title, date and that kind of thing. There were branches throughout Clackmannanshire: Sauchie, Tillicoultry, Alva, Dollar, Clackmannan, and so we exchanged the books there. We didn't select books; we labelled and repaired books with a brush and glue – Gloy.[22] I enjoyed it, you met a lot of people and we got on well with them. The staff consisted of the boss, the two ladies who had run Alloa Public Library, George Malley and myself.

The boss was the County Librarian, Jack Egarr,[23] and a terror! He was a character, a Yorkshireman and a hard worker. He was a good librarian, a good man to have as a boss, but Heaven help you if you weren't pleasing him. He would sort you out in front of the Library packed full. It was a bit daunting, but we all realised that Alloa Public Library was a dead loss, and when he took over he transformed it into Clackmannan County Library system. I found that I was being given preference above George by Mr Egarr. I was the one who was first chosen when we had to staff one of the branches, and that was really something. If there was an advance[24] I got it first, and that was confidence-building. I also found that borrowers looking for a particular thing would come to me, they wouldn't go to others, even for quite difficult things like student loans where you had to borrow from another library.

I remained there until I was called up in 1942. My call-up was postponed because my Dad had had this awful accident and was near unto death, and I was given compassionate postponement that went on for longer than just the few months that it should've. I was quite glad to get away because my contemporaries, my pals, were away and I was still at home, forgotten by the War Office. So I wrote to them and was called up. My preference was for the Navy, but my mother lay awake at night thinking of me being sunk and landing in the cold sea, and proposed that I shouldn't join the Navy. It was the RAF I joined as a ground wireless operator, and then I volunteered and passed the medical for aircrew. I also passed an intelligence test for pilot, navigator, bomb-aimer, but I wasnae big enough to be a pilot. They sat you with your backside against the wall and you stretched out your legs and if they came to a mark on the floor, you were in. If they didnae, your legs were too short for the controls. There was a waiting list for training in navigators, and already I was late, so I opted for wireless op/air-gunner. I went for training in England for the wireless op, and for the air-gunner in Evanton.[25] Then in September '43 I was posted to Egypt to get crewed-up, to get into a crew, and they emphasised that you had to get on well with your crew. Then the pilot failed his course, I was without a crew and so I was put into another crew whose pilot was Sergeant Harry Cohen. It transpired that when he was training on Wellingtons[26] he had crashed this kite and killed some of his crew. He just couldn't face being responsible for another crew. He was a gentle man, a lovely man.

Thereafter we went to a holding camp in Palestine to get us off the aerodrome and let others come in. Then there was the question of where we were going, and we had a choice, believe it or not. We could choose to go on a certain aeroplane flying in the Far East, or another flying in Italy. I fancied Italy and was accepted. I was based near Naples but again that was just the holding camp. We then went to an operational station from which we did bombing raids, and that was a place called Cesenatico[27] on the Adriatic, in the Rimini, Ravenna area. For a start I was flying daylight close-support work, and then the whole station went onto night armed reconnaissance which was more interesting because you were on your own and had to find a target. If you didn't find a target, they would give you a target and you bombed it on their aiming instructions from back at base. Harry Cohen was still having problems with his flying; his take-offs went wrong, the plane didn't have flying speed and he would have to pull it up. We were subject to far more danger from Harry's piloting than from the enemy. Eventually he was seen by the high heid yins and was stood down,

The flying was OK. You had a wee thought for what you were doing because sometimes it was bombing towns. The worst instance of this was close to the end when the Germans were retreating along the south of the Alps and we were to make sure they didn't get the heavy armour across. So if there was a bridge, bomb the bridge, and we found a bridge in the middle of a wee town. To cut a long story short, we missed the bridge and the bombs fell on this sleeping Italian town just about a fortnight before the War finished. Even prior to that, before we took off Harry Cohen used to say, 'What are the people we're going to kill tonight thinking about?' I remained in Italy till the end of the War but then the whole squadron was posted to Kenya. The British Government and the Kenyan Government had agreed there should be an aerial photographic study of the whole country. We flew down in our own aircraft, and then the two governments fell out as to who was to pay for this, so in the end it was never done. We flew down to Nairobi, nothing happened and I was demobbed in 1946.

I was quite happy to go back to the Library. It was essentially the same job that I'd been doing. George Malley got to go on the full-time library course[28] a year before I did, so I had to kick my heels at the Library until George had done his first year. There had been Library Association (LA) examinations, but no organised course of study, or if there was I didn't know about it. At the end of the War, however, the LA syllabus was extended and so a course was put together at the Glasgow and West of Scotland Commercial College in Pitt Street, which later became Strathclyde University. I was given leave of absence and went there on the full-time course about 1947–48 to study classification, cataloguing, English literature, bibliography, things of that sort. For a time I stayed in Glasgow in digs and then I started to travel back and forward from Alloa where I was still living at home. Money didn't really figure. My folks, one way or another, were going to see me through. The tutor was W B Paton[29] – no relation. He was a marvellous man, because he had to take this new syllabus, learn about it and lecture on it – the only lecturer on the course, except for English which was a small part of the course. He was Mr Libraries, Scotland. When he left the College he became County Librarian of Lanarkshire.

I quite enjoyed studying. It was a two-year course. The first year was full-time and I passed that to become a chartered librarian, an Associate of the Library Association. The next year I did in my own time, studying at home and working at Clackmannan County Library, but I didn't pass all the subjects and had to pick them up by part-time study later on. When word came through that Mr Egarr had been killed in the War, W R Aitken,[30] an academic, decent, gentle, kindly man, was appointed as County Librarian. I worked with W R Aitken for a period before he got the County Librarian's job in Perth. I followed him there. He wanted me to go and I would never have got the job otherwise. I worked in Perth with him for three years. I liked him, we got on extremely well. It was my first senior job. My designation was Chief Assistant Librarian – second person in charge.

Perth County Library operated on very traditional methods and there was scope for development and better organisation. For example, there were lots of branches and little service stations throughout Perth and Kinross counties but there was no regular programme of book exchanges.

W R Aitken was quite content to just keep it going as it was. To be fair to him, however, it wasn't an easy job getting Perth going. The Council wanted to keep the rates down, and he was maybe better working at a national level, being a member of committees and that kind of thing. Nevertheless, we got a timetable for exchanges going, but that was really the only improvement we achieved. It was an easy job, I got on well with the staff but we were doing nothing.

I was living in digs in Perth and I used to go home to Alloa to my wee lassie and my Dad, because my mother had died by this time. After three years I was pleased to move on to become Burgh Librarian in Buckhaven and Methil Burgh. It was very small – I had three assistants, the Library was in Methil and one wee branch in Buckhaven. I got on well with the local people. There was still the vestige of a fishing community, but it was mainly mining. You could tell the miners apart somehow. I'd nod and catch their eye and get a nod back. No smile. I used to walk to work, back at lunchtime, walk to work again and walk home. There was an old fisherman standing, and four times a day I would pass and nod to him. Then one day, he sauntered over, and it was obvious he was going to say something, so I stopped, and he said, 'Wha are ye?' On one occasion, I was going up the steps of the Library with the caretaker, a big, physically impressive chap, and there were a couple of lads, one of whom said to him, 'Hey, mister, whas library is that? Is that your library?' And the caretaker replied, 'Yes, that's right. It's your library.' And the other wee boy piped up, 'Oh, no, it isnae. It's that wee man there's library!'

The readers were not dissimilar from those in Clackmannan. They were keen readers, but didn't have a very high level of taste: Westerns, mysteries and love stories, there was an awful lot of that, but more than that too. Working in Buckhaven and Methil wasn't a totally happy experience. I don't think I did much for the Library Service, to be honest. It was a decent enough job although I don't think I did it terribly well. My book selection wasn't too good and didn't suit the clientele. I was trying to raise their taste a wee bit. I was there for four years, and lived in Buckhaven. I got married in 1958 while I was there – an Alloa girl.

Then in 1960 I left. I was needing to get on and Aberdeenshire seemed an attractive prospect. There was a short leet[31] of four, and the first interviews were held in front of a staffing committee established to make this appointment. Two were knocked out and the other two, myself and Neil McCorkindale,[32] were to come back the next day and speak to the whole Education Committee, but we were told, 'Now briefly, because we've bigger things to do than appoint a County Librarian.' The one question we were asked was, 'How can the County Library Service help the School Library Service?' A big question. I started and was speaking away, doing my best and then every person I looked at dropped his eyes. I said, 'Am I speaking at too great length?' And the Director said, 'Well, maybe', so I cut it short which saved me. Neil and I were good friends but I got it on one casting vote, the whole of my future. I was appointed County Librarian.

We lived in Aberdeen itself, and Aberdeenshire County Library was based in the city. Library Headquarters was in Crown Terrace and we had a branch in every school. Until local government reorganisation in 1974–75[33] when libraries went to the district councils, the county library system was based on a few words in an Education Act[34] which authorised county libraries to provide books to persons residing in their area. These county libraries were run by the school teachers with boxes of books delivered periodically. The teachers didn't complain. They seemed to feel that went with the job. That's what I inherited when I went to Aberdeenshire, but we changed all of that. Aberdeenshire was my glory days. We were responsible for the public library service and the school library service, and shortly after I was appointed the Education Department called for a report on school libraries. Why are we doing this? What are they for? How should we operate them? What staffing do we need? What stock should be purchased? All that sort of thing.

It was a glorious opportunity and I worked on the report all week-end and put it to the Assistant Director of Education on the Tuesday, and he was thrilled, and it went to the Director and he was duly impressed, and it went to Committee and was accepted. That was the school library service sorted out but we still had this old-fashioned system on the adult side. We'd done one or two wee things here and there. In Peterculter we took over a shop, set up a library and that was my first branch. The use of the service there increased greatly. But Aberdeenshire was a big, spread-out county. So I put together a report on the public library side, referred to every branch and what we felt we should do: some should be improved; some required an extension of opening hours; others just needed redecorated; I called for mobile libraries. The Director and the Committee accepted it and we gradually made progress based on it. Also there had been a start towards gramophone records and framed art reproductions – which didn't take at all. I always had good relations with my staff. I started with ten members of staff and finished with 15, 16, something like that and we had a splendid library service and this was recognised by my colleagues. When I left a reporter came from the P&J[35] and the headline was, 'Not so much a library, more a way of life.'

As far as political control was concerned, when I was in Clackmannan it would be a Labour Council, and in Perth a Conservative Council, in Buckhaven and Methil, a very strong Labour Council and in Aberdeenshire certainly some Liberals and Independents. I didn't have any difficulty in working with any of these very different councils although it was only in Aberdeenshire that I met with the Committee.

In the late '60s, I went from Aberdeenshire to become County Librarian in Renfrewshire. It was a case of the grass on the other side always being greener and we thought, 'Let's go someplace else.' It was nearer to Alloa where our relatives and friends were, it was a bigger job and it had a well-developed library system. However, I got off to a wrong start and got a degree of opposition from the staff. We had catalogues in all our junior sections in the branches but nobody ever wanted to look up a catalogue. I argued that there was no need for the catalogues, that providing them was a waste of staffing. Also, our headquarters school staff selected pretty powerful, intellectual stock and not all Renfrewshire schools could cope with that. They were buying encyclopaedias at £200 or whatever, and not two children out of ten could have made anything of them. I became labelled – I had come from a small place, I didn't realise that it was important to select quality stock. There was a strong schools' and children's librarian and she had a lot of staff following her, and I didn't have their confidence.

Then there was the cataloguing system. The cataloguing we did was straight from the manual but that level of cataloguing was never needed so I proposed that we cut back on that and transfer some staff from there to other activity where they'd be serving some purpose. Of course the people in the cataloguing department didn't like that. This sort of thing constantly came along. I got some things done: got exchanges going, got staff into the schools, but there was so much that we had done in Aberdeenshire that I simply wasn't able to do in Renfrew, in part because the staff were so set in their ways. To some extent, this may have reflected the different approaches of the two schools of librarianship. The Aberdeen school was liberal in outlook; the Glasgow one was more traditional, textbook-based and detached from service delivery.[36] Not everybody was against me by any manner of means, and one colleague said of me, 'He's Scotland's best librarian!' Still, I simply couldn't get the service going.

In maybe my third year at Renfrew, I felt I made an important contribution at national level by way of my involvement with the Stimpson Working Party.[37] Questions had been asked among teachers, their representatives and teaching organisations about professional recognition, and so the Scottish Education Department appointed a working party under the chairmanship of D E Stimpson to look at the function of librarians and other professional groups in schools. The library profession was to be represented on the Working Party, and in recognition of my interest and involvement in school librarianship, the Scottish Library Association[38] appointed me. In addition, there was one social worker and one educational psychologist. All the rest were teachers or educationalists and trade union people. The trade union folk were reluctant to recognise that other professionals contribute to the life of the school and I wasn't getting much attention at the meetings. Ultimately, however, it was a most positive report although when it was published there was a scarcity of funds and cutbacks for years. Nevertheless, it was a point of reference for future developments.

When we were in Renfrewshire we lived in Paisley. Irene, my wife, was very unhappy by this time. She had left her couthy[39] Aberdeen friends, the accent was different, attitudes were different, she was on her own. Norman, our son, would get tormented about certain things, about his accent for example, and he wasn't happy. Education wasn't as successful in Renfrew as it was in Aberdeenshire, and although the teachers in Renfrew were great, there were social problems they had to deal with. By this time, my number-one objective was to get out of Paisley. I was six years in Renfrewshire – 1969 to 1975. It was local government reorganisation which let me away from Renfrew, where I had a full-time equivalent staff of 100, and I came back to Aberdeen as Grampian Region Schools' Librarian[40] where I had a staff of four. The Education staff that I'd left years earlier knew that I was very unhappy but when I applied for that job, they said, 'We've been keeping it for you.' We moved back to Aberdeen and got a house diagonally across from where we had previously lived. It was a satisfying job. There was quite a bit we could still do in the schools, and we worked on it and had the Schools Library Service going great again. I continued in that post for 12 years until I retired at age 65. My pension was based on my Renfrewshire County Librarian salary level, the highest salary I'd ever been paid.

I worked in librarianship for almost half a century, from 1940 to 1987. Libraries have changed for the better: there is more money, a far better selection of stock and the type of materials has extended, local studies services have improved, more professional staff. And although people still come down to the library and choose their books, it's quickly going to change with technology. The government is giving libraries quite a part to play in educating people, making them computer literate.[41] Now that's a great opportunity. I wish I was still there; it would have been great. I have no regrets about giving up the accountancy with Mr Frame or packing in the bottling plant in Alloa.

Interviewed 4 December 2001

Tom Gray

My name is Thomas Murray Gray. I was born in Greenock on the 27th of March 1924.

My father worked as a plater[1] in the shipyards in Greenock. Most of the time he worked at Kingston, which was Lithgows'[2] yard. He was in the artillery during the First World War although the only place he was willing to talk about was Mesopotamia.[3] I think he joined up in 1914. He was unemployed during the '30s until 1938 when rearmament took place and the shipyards started. By then, my Dad would be back at work, working long hours. In the first years of the Second World War, he would be away for days on end because they were refitting the lease-lend ships.[4] Then the ships had to go on trials in the Clyde. Greenock was a busy place during the War. A lot of American troops landed there. A lot of convoys came in and sailed from there.

As was the norm, my mother had given up work as soon as she got married but, from necessity, during that time she went back to work as an operator in the Merino Mills,[5] where they did weaving and spinning. My mother's family were all dead before they got married when he came back from the First War. My paternal grandfather was dead by the time I became aware of the world. The only one still alive was my paternal grandmother. She was an interesting character, the traditional matriarchal figure. There was a big family of them, most still living. My father's brother lived in Glasgow; another one went to live in New Jersey, but the rest of the family – my father, another brother and three sisters – wouldn't take any move without discussing it with Granny Gray, and if they did, there was hell to pay!

We lived in Regent Street, a traditional tenement block in the centre of Greenock, on the third floor and it was just a room and kitchen; gas lighting. There was always a row about the stair lights getting knocked out. Just cold water, no bath; a toilet on the landing shared with one other family. No garden. The whole thing's now demolished. I was the oldest of three children. My sister Flora, who was two or three years younger than me, was born there. Then we got a new council house; that was the east end. It was there my brother William, who was quite a bit younger, was born. Again a street that's been demolished, Fullarton Street. It was a dead-end street: two blocks with three closes in each block, two houses on each flat and we had a downstairs flat. We had two bedrooms, a living room and kitchen and a bathroom. Electric light, running hot and cold water and a bath, the water heated from a coal fire. A wee bit garden at the front, but at the back it was a common green.

I remember being dragged up the hill from Regent Street to Holmscroft School when I was five year old. I was only there a matter of months and when we went to Fullarton Street, I went to Ladyburn School which was predominantly a primary school but it had secondary classes accommodating people up to the age of 14. In present-day terms, it would be first year, second year and third. We got Science, Mathematics, English, Art, PT,[6] Woodwork and I got on well with French. I thoroughly enjoyed the school.

By the time I was in second year, we had moved again to a much bigger house, up the hill in a big new slum-clearance place. It was an upstairs flat in Burnhead Street. We had a good garden; we were on the end of the block and had the ground to the side of the house, and there was a common green for the two houses and then over the fence for the two houses next door. Then there was a strip of ground running along the back of the houses but below the green, and it was all railed off with iron railings, and each of these plots was split in the middle, half to the bottom flat and half to the upper flat. When we moved there, I continued to attend Ladyburn. It was a good 20, 30 minutes' walk. I used to take a flask and sandwiches and was allowed to go into the cookery room and sit and have my lunch there.

If your parents were posh and could afford the fees, you went to the Academy, but I transferred to fourth year in Greenock High School which was even further away to walk. There was no bus services in those days. I enjoyed the High School. The subjects were much the same: Science, Physics, Biology, Chemistry, Mathematics, Geography, History, English, but I didn't get Art, Woodwork, Metalwork or Technical Drawing. I liked

Geography – that might have been because of the teacher – and English. Mathematics was a puzzle to start with. I didn't have a uniform to wear to the High School.

My interests outside school were mainly Boys' Brigade.[7] I wasn't in the Life Boys but went straight into the Boys' Brigade when I was about 12. I had older cousins and there was a Brigade company associated with the church and we all had to go to church, Church of Scotland – the Martyrs' North which has been demolished. There was these two cousins in particular: one was a sergeant and the other one was a drummer in the pipe band. So I got joined up and thoroughly enjoyed it. We went to summer camps. More often than not we went to Bute, Kilchattan Bay, where we occupied the village school and slept on palliasses[8] which we had to go to the farm and fill with straw. The more straw you put into your bag the more comfortable your bed was. I put too much into my palliasse and kept rolling off!

I don't know whether this was the start of the library influence, but there was a fine gentleman who was the Librarian at the McLean Museum[9] in Greenock. He had been running a choir drawn exclusively from the boys in the 4th Company of the Boys' Brigade. That was the Company I was in and there was over 100. You're lucky if you get ten now. Mr Henderson played the piano and conducted. We used to go round various institutions, lead the singing in the church choir, go to old folks' homes dressed in our BB uniforms and we entered into song competitions at the Greenock annual festival. Herbert Henderson was in charge of the Library. There was a separate subscription library, an ancient institution, and the Museum. The two were separate although in the same building, and the Librarian's living quarters were in the McLean Museum building. He used to invite small groups of us to the house for practice. He lived with his sister and at the end of the practice we got a slap-up tea! We're still in the depression years and Herbert Henderson was giving us tea and sandwiches, scones and cakes – things we would not normally have had at home.

Our diet at home was all right. Breakfast was porridge and toast, milk; rolls were a treat. On special days, we got walked or sent down the road to a butcher who specialised in making black puddings the size of horse-collars. That was a delicacy. At the High School I still took sandwiches and a flask. Sometimes if there was money we were given enough for school dinners. Otherwise, my main meal was in the evening when I got home – potatoes, vegetables and mince or sausages or something like that, stew every now and again. While we were living in Fullarton Street, we used to go down to the quay where the boats were landing during the Loch Fyne season.[10] There were no plastic bags in those days. You took a bucket and every now and again the crane-man loading the lorries would give the basket a nudge and then swing away and we got a chance to go in underneath the lorry and pick up the herring. Then the next two or three nights we would spend gutting and filleting them as best we could and making them into rollmops: herring in vinegar, baked in the oven. There was no fridges or freezers but there was a ventilated cupboard where food was kept and they would be packed away in trays and plates. That would keep us going for a couple of weeks. Occasionally we had fruit.

When we were in Burnhead Street I started learning how to dig. This scheme of houses was built by Greenock Corporation as a slum clearance. A big central area of dilapidated tenements in the town centre was cleared and somehow the Quakers[11] made it available as an allotment to help the unemployed. They had an allotment committee with a secretary and a chairman, and they had a scheme whereby they would supply a spade, a fork, a rake and a hoe for a shilling. Now, a shilling was a lot of money in those days, but it didn't come anywhere near the price of a spade. I think I still have that spade. Then it was a question of getting plants. We had blackcurrant bushes, and we had to go to the Library and get books or buy magazines. I was sowing seeds, weeding, thinning and taking an interest in how things were growing. So we had fruit and vegetables in season. Occasionally it was tight while my father was still on the Labour Exchange but I didn't go without meals because my parents couldn't afford it.

I was a keen reader and my father was. While we were in Fullarton Street they opened a branch library nearby. There always had been a poky wee branch library, a wee room with books in it but they opened this big, new, posh branch library in Sinclair Street which I eventually worked in. Sometimes I'd go with my father but sometimes I'd be sent by meself to get my father's books and I had me own ticket. Children weren't allowed in the reading room but I remember getting a special privilege from the library staff to sit in the reading room and read the *National Geographic*[12] magazine. I had to behave meself. There was plenty books although I didn't do any selecting. Jimmy Hamilton,[13] the librarian-in-charge who became the Chief Librarian in Greenock years later, would select some stuff. Usually out of the four books that we were allowed, there would be a couple of interest to my father. It was easier to get books for my mother to read. She was a good reader as well. So I'd be up and down the street, a regular reader at the Library, a regular borrower.

As a child, you only had one ticket so you were only allowed one book at a time. I read practically anything: some of the detective series, Biggles[14] – there was always a squabble to get the new Biggles. I went to the shop and got a comic regularly and swopping went on. Things like *The Rover*, *The Hotspur*, *The Wizard*.

As a boy, I don't think I had any particular direction. It was the question of when I got my Highers[15] what would be next and, of course, by that time the War had started. Was I goin' tae look for a job, what kind of job, or was I going to stay on in sixth year and do another couple of Highers? There had been a suggestion that I might go to Glasgow University but the War was on and there was uncertainty whether you would be allowed to work your way all the way through a degree. The matter was fortuitously sorted when W B Paton,[16] the Chief Librarian from the Library in Greenock, came to the school to interview young men specifically for two vacancies he had on the Library staff. W B Paton was a distinguished figure in the library profession and, as I learned in retrospect, he had determined to build up the male component in the profession. He had appointed two the year before and he appointed two the year after. I was interviewed and was offered the job from when I left school. As a matter of fact, I left before the end of the school year because I'd passed five Highers.

It was the early stages where W B Paton started to influence the whole of librarianship in Scotland. Oh, he was a great guy. He'd tremendous influence on a lot of people and right there was this nucleus of six young men, all librarianship-career oriented. There wasn't anywhere else in the whole of Scotland like that. The two that came after me were Peter Grant[17] and Jimmy Neill[18] who has now retired from the library school in Newcastle.[19] The fellow that joined along with me was killed during the War in an air accident, training in Canada. Another guy finished up as Chief of the Kenyan Police Force. Another one was Richie McCallum from Gourock. As war service he joined the Merchant Navy and became a purser on one of the big transport lines and eventually stayed there. The last time I heard of him he was somewhere out in Australia. There was another fellow, called Neil McCorkindale.[20] Even Bill Paton became a captain in the Royal Artillery. We all went our different ways and left the womenfolk to run the Library.

But for a time we were all there. We used to go to the Morton[21] matches on a Saturday afternoon in a bunch. We arranged it that the lassies did the Saturday afternoon shift and we did the Saturday night shift. The lassies wanted to be off in the evening. There was never any aggro, aggravation or anything like that. It wasn't every Saturday, it was just the home games and the occasional international, but that was usually on Wednesdays and Wednesdays were the half-day.

I began in Greenock Library in 1940; I was only 16. I left the school on the Friday and started in the Library on the Monday. The Library was open from ten o'clock in the morning, though the staff was in at 9am, and it closed at eight o'clock at night. There was a separate reference library up the stair which had to be manned. There was a shift system, including the split shift system, whereby you worked in the forenoon, you had the afternoon off and then started work again at five till eight. We had it down to a fine art, so it was just a matter of shunting the last few borrowers out, getting our coats and hats on, put the lights out, and there was a janitor so we had none of the locking-up. You did three days of split shifts, and the other three was either the half-day or you worked nine till five. You had an hour's break for lunch and a tea break. I gave my pay packet to my mother who was pleased I had become a wage-earner, although by this time my father was working overtime so the financial situation in the family had eased considerably.

Library tasks included tidying up the shelves, doing a bit of cataloguing, seeing to binding collections, sitting in the reference library upstairs – it was just a sort of caretaker, watching; you didn't do anything. Well, you tried if somebody asked you. One of the jobs was to make yourself familiar with the books there. There was an awful lot of old crusty, dusty books, of which 95 per cent were totally irrelevant. But that's where the serious periodicals were. I remember an old guy used to come in regularly to read *The Tablet*[22] and he was usually there in the morning of it being put up. W B Paton's desk was in the general workroom, same as everybody else. He didn't have an office to himself, and he was quite approachable. Everybody respected him. It was a great encouragement, a great experience; I enjoyed it and there was a lot to learn. I used to go to evening classes in Pitt Street[23] twice a week: cataloguing, classification, administration and things like that towards an Associateship. It was just one year I did that until I went off to do my war service.

Greenock took a terrific battering in the air raids in 1941. I was working in the Library at the time and although the service shut down the library staff still went in and were in charge of record-keeping. I carried on in Greenock Library until I joined the Forces, although in the early years of the War I gave up the Boys' Brigade and joined the Air Training Corps[24] as soon as it was formed in Greenock. So when I joined in March 1943, aged 19, I was automatically put in the Air Force. I reported to the initial-training unit for air crew at St John's Wood in London where we got kitted out for square-bashing. We lived in a requisitioned block of flats. Then we got bundled into trains to Aberystwyth where we had arms drill. I remember spending bleak days on guard duty round an installation that turned out to be a very early radar station. Doing the two-till-four, the four-till-six shift was dreadful: the cocoa was always cold. In the evening, if you'd no guard duties or anything like that, it was a very pleasant place to be. Holidays with my parents were days away down the coast, a day trip on the bus. Getting to Aberystwyth and St John's Wood was the first time I'd been away from the west of Scotland.

Then we were sent on embarkation leave. And then we got on a boat, and eventually landed at Durban and had the lady of the docks[25] standing there in all her glory, singing out loud. She was a lady of quite ample build and a beautiful soprano voice. She always made an effort to be on the dockside when a shipload of troops were coming in, and she sang 'Welcome to South Africa' and things like that. We were in a holding camp in Port Elizabeth for a short while and as I hadn't been selected to be a pilot I ended up at navigator school in Queenstown, which was quite a pleasant place to be and where we spent about nine months. That's where we got our flying and navigation training. When we got our passing-out parade and our 'wings,' we came back to the UK, to Tempsford in Bedfordshire. By this time, 1944, the need for air crew was beginning to fall and we were retrained. At Tempsford there was a small group of Lysander[26] aeroplanes, and their job was to take the spies out. They also had Lancaster[27] bombers with bomb bays adapted to take the canisters of weapons and food which was parachuted to the Resistance in France.

From there I was sent to Singapore in late 1944 and finished up on an island called Labuan[28] where we had an airfield that was a staging post between Australia and the islands all the way up as far as Siam[29] and places like that. At Labuan we had Japanese prisoners working the laundry machine and doing menial tasks. That's where I ended the War. I spent a period back in Singapore at Seletar,[30] a service station for flying boats going up to Hong Kong. On one occasion we saw Lady Mountbatten[31] with her purple hair come ashore and into a limousine and wheecht away off. Part of my job was air traffic control but they just had the odd flight in. Eventually we were put on a boat and came home to Liverpool in the winter of '46–'47.

I'd been away for nearly four years. It was something over which an individual had no control. You were names on lists and people decided this and arranged transport for you and you did this course and that course. You just did what you were told. Then you got a fortnight's home leave, and by the end of the leave your discharge took effect, you got your demob suit and other bits and pieces, you went home and, as far as I was concerned, got back to work as soon as possible. That's when you started picking up the pieces, connecting up with people. I remember trying to find some of the people who'd been in the Brigade, in the choir, and while most of them were still around there was a significant number that werenae coming back at all.

I went back to the Library as if nothing had happened. The Library hadn't changed in any way during the War. W B Paton came back, although he left soon after to start the Scottish Library School in Pitt Street. All there had been before were evening classes, part-time lectures. In '48–'49, I went to that in second year, for a year, travelling every day. Jimmy Hamilton came back from the Navy, and was now Deputy in Greenock. He and Neil McCorkindale went off to the first year. After one year doing the full-time course I qualified Associate Librarianship. The course was demanding, studying cataloguing, classification, reference, bibliographies, administration, printing, publishing. The principal tutor was Bill Paton who was an excellent teacher and who did the librarianship side with supplementary tutors for bibliography and English language and literature. There were 25 or so students, men and women. It was essential and you had to do this. It was quite obvious by then that unless you were a qualified librarian you were going to get nowhere; even in your own local establishment you weren't going to get in.

At that time libraries were beginning to expand. There was more branch libraries, more specialisation, a wider range of services being proposed. There was a tremendous amount of reading, of course, during the War and that contributed to the development of libraries after the War. It was professional librarians themselves who widened the development however. You had to convince the committees that this is what a library should be doing.

After that year of study I returned to Greenock Library, although much of the time I spent running the east branch. The original east branch library was bombed out and a temporary place was established and it was my job to run that. Of course, I was an east-ender and knew a lot of the people there. Most library users were perfectly normal and if they came in regularly you got to know them. Some were a bit more demanding than others. There was one guy who was in practically every day. He'd a big family and through his benefits he could afford not to work. Then one day he came in, dumped his books on the counter and says, 'You're not going to see me as often as you used to.' He explained that he was going back to work: 'Ma oldest daughter has left school.' That upset the balance of his benefits, so he was goin' tae go back to work.

In 1951 I moved from Greenock to Morpeth in Northumberland; it was just a promotion. There was no way I was going to get a better-paid job in Greenock because the people who had joined before me all had the designated jobs. At that time there was plenty of jobs all over the place. I travelled quite a distance in those days looking for jobs. I was offered the job of Assistant Librarian for Northumberland. That job title didn't really mean much. It was just to designate you as a professional. When I got there, I discovered what they wanted me to do. We had this van stocked with books and the driver and I went to various library centres every day. Sometimes it was a two-day trip to the far west and we'd stay the night somewhere. If we went up north, we stayed the night in Berwick occasionally. It was an adventure, staying away at night and getting paid for it. We went to schools, village halls, miners' institutes[32] and places like that, and off-loaded a collection of books and collected the books that they'd already had, picked up the statistics, had a chat to the local librarian and then moved on from centre to centre. I would assist the local librarian to pick a new collection, get that into crates, we'd do the paper work and these books would be taken in. The driver did the donkey-work of collecting the existing books, sorting them out and putting them back on the shelves. Four days a week on average it would take, with the rest of the time at headquarters.

It was a complete contrast with Greenock where you were stuck in one place. I hadn't been to Northumberland before and enjoyed exploring. It was the rural areas I worked in, the people were generally friendly and there was no difference in readers or readers' interests compared with Greenock. They all wanted the same. If they had a subject they wanted chasing up, then they asked, or if it was just something nice to read then they got plenty of that. If they wanted information then they asked for it and we found it and sent it to them in various ways.

It was a three-month cycle but we didn't cover the whole of Northumberland. The bottom south-east quadrant is mining country, from Ashington down skirting Morpeth, round to Gosforth and back to the coast, round Bedlington and Cramlington and places like that. They all had their miners' institutes or, in Bedlington's case and Ashington's case, they had a branch library with paid staff. We didn't touch them; that was a different servicing arrangement. The collection at a miners' welfare had 1,000 books, and we would change 250 of them every three months. That collection of 250 books would be made up at headquarters and put into trays, like old-fashioned bakery trays, and the van was fitted out with rails that these trays fitted in. I didn't have anything to do with the mining areas. The driver went on his own to a miners' institute and the local person would be there with 250 books chosen. The new books would be off-loaded and the old books would be put back in the trays and taken back. Then back at headquarters, the paperwork and the shifting of record cards would be done. The record cards for the books that had been delivered would be added to the file, and the record cards for the incoming books would be extracted from the file and went on to the next stage.

Some of the miners' welfare institutes still had remnants of their own original collections and they were all political and very self-improving. But in my experience, the dust on them was about half-an-inch thick, which indicated they were no longer used.

I enjoyed my time in Northumberland and that's where I met my future wife. After two years I began looking around for another job, something with greater responsibility. In 1953 I applied for Coatbridge, for Deputy, and I got it. I was quite happy, I went up there, started work, settled down, got married in 1954 and started raising a family. We bought a little house and then got a big council house and I had an allotment there. As Deputy I was doing practically everything. There were about a dozen or so staff; just one library and one small part-time branch in Whifflet. I got on well there. It was great fun and rewarding and I started studying at Pitt Street for the Fellowship. Then I signed on for a two-year course at Glasgow University and got a Diploma in Public Administration. I tried me hand at applying for purely administrative jobs but they didn't come up. I kept studying for the Fellowship because you could do it in parts.

I remained in Coatbridge for ten years. By this time Bill Paton had given up his Library School and it was transferred to Strathclyde University. He was a leading, even dominant, figure in Scottish libraries; charismatic, highly professional, much respected and admired and he was a good organist, too. He was a church organist. He went back to run Lanarkshire and did the same there as he had done in Greenock: he set about recruiting, only this time, instead of raw school-leavers, he recruited a bunch of chartered librarians, men and women. Bill Paton introduced what you would call team management. He made his senior staff individually and collectively responsible for the service, how the service was provided and where it was going.

In Lanarkshire there was a greater sense of co-operation, although they all wanted to be in charge. They formed a kind of study group in which library principles and practices, in general and with particular reference to Lanarkshire, were hammered out. There was this brain-storming session in Hamilton we used to have once a month. That's where this group worked out systems, practices and proposals and then took them to Bill Paton and he mulled over them, polished them a bit from his greater experience, and then put them into operation. I knew most of the ones that were there and that's how I got to know what was going on. It was highly professional because we were all at least chartered librarians and some of us were half-qualified Fellows. We had some of our own ideas at Coatbridge. We pioneered photo-charging,[33] for instance. They thought about it in Lanark but they never got round to doing anything about it.

One of the things we used to argue was that the Library School course in Scotland should be a full degree course authenticated in an established university. Eventually that's what happened. It started with the degree course at Strathclyde, then a Library School was started in

Aberdeen.[34] You can go in straight from school and do a three-year course specialising in librarianship. Alternatively, you can do a degree in another subject and then go to the Library School and do a diploma course in librarianship. Then after, I think, a couple of years in an approved post, you can apply to the Library Association[35] for recognition as an Associate. These Lanarkshire discussions were what I missed more than anything when I moved up here.

There were no differences between readers in Coatbridge, Northumberland and Greenock. They all wanted lots of new books. Coatbridge was the one place I've been where the book fund[36] was not a problem. It was the impetus of Alex Dow, the Chief Librarian.[37] At that time, the Library Committee was a separate committee of the Council, not responsible to anybody. It was a completely separate budget, whereas in Northumberland the Library was part of the Education, and it's the same in Ross and Cromarty.

After ten years as Deputy in Coatbridge I wanted to be the boss. There weren't all that many chiefs' jobs going, so it was a case of applying for each and every one. I applied for Aberdeenshire. Neil McCorkindale got that. I applied for Inverness and Dick Milne[38] got that. Then Ross and Cromarty came up and I was appointed Chief Librarian there in 1961. The headquarters was in Dingwall. They'd never had a chartered librarian in charge before. The guy who had been in charge since the War was a retired Army captain, a local worthy. There was no professionalism about the place at all.

Ross and Cromarty as a county was beginning to pick itself up. The Council was not as dominated as Inverness-shire by the lairds, the landowners, and the main object in running the Council wasn't to keep the rates as low as possible. Eventually they were very generous. There was a Library Committee, subservient to the Education Committee, and it was lucky that the Chairman of the Library Committee was Mrs Linklater, wife of Eric Linklater.[39] Another one was Rev MacIntyre from Strathpeffer, and he and I got on well and he would say, 'Where can we go from here?' I would take every opportunity to brief him, so when matters got to Committee it wasnae me that was doing the talking it was the Chairman – particularly important when it got to the Education Committee where he was reporting on Library Committee business because that's where the money was. There was a great surge of improvement with him and with Marjorie Linklater.

There were service points that had their own accommodation and there were other service points that had shared accommodation in schools and village halls. There was one or two places, like Cromarty, where they still called themselves a Library Committee but to all intents and purposes it was run by the County. Stornoway was independent, but they had a mobile library there and the librarian in Stornoway was, to some extent, responsible for supervision of the County Mobile Library. There was a library in Tain, run by the Town Council. There was a library in Invergordon, which was supposed to be run by the Town Council. In the rest of the area there was nothing that you would call a branch library. There couldn't have been more than a dozen full-time staff. At the so-called branch libraries, they were all part-time people, and there was no other professional staff, just meself.

One of the things I started doing was to get some professional recruits, and also to look at the branch libraries and tidy up the legal position. We had to get the Town Council of Cromarty formally to give up their library powers, and the same at Tain where we had a helluva battle. Invergordon Town Council were astonished to be told that they were responsible for the library. Strictly speaking, Dingwall was the Library Authority, and that had to be sorted out. Eventually we did the same in Stornoway and that resulted in one helluva party after the Council were agreed. The hospitality from Stornoway Town Council was out of this world!

It was a question of persuading the Committee of the idea of spending money, extra money. When I came, the only mobile library was the one which served Lewis. There was none on the mainland, just the delivery van. I got them to get, first of all, one mobile library, and then two. That must've been '65, '66. It was a bit of a struggle getting the idea accepted, and then getting the money and getting the thing designed and built. The mobile library on the mainland didn't cover the whole of the County because the east coast was considered to be covered by places like Tain, Invergordon, Dingwall, Cromarty, so it covered centre and west, the less populous areas.

The delivery van was staffed only by a driver because it was just delivering and picking up. When the mobile library went on, we didn't have a qualified librarian, just the driver but paid as a library assistant. There was a couple of weeks when the mobile library was away from Dingwall for four days – three nights. On those occasions we had an assistant with him, usually the relief driver. There was plenty of bed and breakfast places. The mobile library stopped in centres of population, and gradually it came to be a centre for the exchange of local information. People came and had a blether. Even although they lived within a couple of hundred yards of one another, they might not have spoken for a while. There were some cases where we had severely disabled people and, if we had time in the schedule, the mobile library would stop and the driver-assistant would go into the house and do an exchange that way. There was a social welfare element there.

When it became Highland Region[40] I discovered that in the schedules for the mobile library working out of Brora there seemed to be an awful lot of time not very well used. We discovered that the guy was not only taking medicines out but was also running an insurance book! With the Region it was difficult keeping in touch with staff who were out on the road and left to work at their own initiative.

Winter weather could bring difficulties for the mobile library. There was one occasion it slid off the road. Nobody was injured, but we had to wait for the snowplough. Nevertheless, it's not unknown for the mobile library to be the first vehicle into a community after a snowstorm. In a rural county the mobile library is the local government service with which most people have contact, and that contact is voluntary. People come to the library of their own volition, for their own purposes and in their own time. At the time I'm talking about, they didn't have dustbin lorries, they didn't have nurses and welfare offices just down the street. If they wanted them they had to go and get them to come. Whereas the mobile library was toddling up every month, every four weeks, regular as clockwork.

We had good relations with the Council Roads Department. An awful lot of the success was relationships, and that is what has gone wrong with local government today. In the old Highland Region days, relationships were built up. I knew people in the Council offices in Wick, Thurso and Golspie. At the time of the reorganisation of local government in 1974–75, the Library Service in Ross and Cromarty became part of the regional Library Service and I became Regional Librarian. Under the rules of reorganisation, the post was closed to anyone from outside so it was entirely competition within the professional staff of the Highland Region. The five Chief Librarians from Inverness burgh, Inverness-shire, Ross and Cromarty, Sutherland and Caithness, all put in for the job. And I got it.

Prior to reorganisation I had been asked to organise meetings of these Head Librarians, and we drafted a report on the future provision of library services in the projected new Region. The strongest recommendation was that the Library Service should be part of the Education Department for administrative purposes. Mainly for political purposes, however, the shadow Council decided that libraries were going to be part of Leisure and Recreation. To smooth things out it was eventually called Libraries, Leisure and Recreation, so we finished up under the control of a Director of Leisure and Recreation instead of being part of Education. As a result, the School Library Service was developed along separate lines, and I think it was a serious inhibitor of the Public Library Service because we were forced to compete against parks, museums, leisure centres and all kinds of sport. At that time, grants started to become available for those activities. For example, if a grant was available to fund 50 per cent of a park ranger then the Council was prepared to produce the other 50 per cent. Now that had to come from somewhere in the total departmental budget and it tended to be from the Library Service which had brought something like 80 or 90 per cent of the departmental budget in the transfer in 1974–75. At the same time there were no grants to buy books or engage more staff or buy more mobile libraries.

As far as I understand, the School Library Service has only recently come together with the Public Library Service as a result of an enormous rationalisation. Libraries, leisure and recreation and culture have now been subsumed under Education, which is what we recommended in 1975.

At least we had a job, and in the Region it was very similar to the job I'd had in Ross and Cromarty – sorting out and pulling together a diverse group of service points: getting the librarian in Wick to realise that he was no longer an independent agent, and the same with the chap who'd been in Caithness, in Sutherland; pulling the disparate bits together, but over a much bigger area with a bigger staff, a lot more service points and four mobile libraries.

Financially, things became much tighter. In 1974 I'd been working on the County Council to build a new library in Dingwall. I got plans drawn up, I got costs, I'd a site and it was in front of Committee for approval. The Chairman of the Committee suggested I was missing a chance in not having proper stone facing on the building and would prefer that the extra money be spent. The Committee agreed to approve the plans subject to estimates being ready for the next meeting. In those days the Council met every six weeks and between one meeting and the next central government clamped down on all capital spending.

There was plenty of good points with regionalisation, however. We got a warehouse in the Longman Industrial Estate in Inverness and money to tidy it up and furnish it, and it meant I could move out of the County Buildings and make space for somebody else. I was detached from the Department, however, and it was very handy to be in the Department and keep an ear to the ground. On the other hand, a lot of business done in various places was brought together into one place. We started getting some advantages of economies of scale. More things got done with the same staff and the staff were happier to have proper accommodation to work in. Nevertheless, the money wasnae there for additional staff or for upgrading posts. Most of the staff were local people, quite happy working in their own local library. It was back to the task of moulding the original disparate bits together. By this time, we'd lost Stornoway and Lewis which went to Western Isles Council and that eased problems of communication. At the same time it removed a uniqueness in Ross and Cromarty, in that there can't have been many County Librarians who had to use British Airways scheduled services to visit the service point!

I retired in '84; I was only 60. I found I was stagnating. I was running like blazes to finish up half a mile back from where I started. There was a lot of budget cutting, plans that had been approved were disallowed and we didn't seem to be getting anywhere. Complaints were beginning to come in that there weren't enough new books, and there was demands for mobile libraries here and bigger branch libraries there. I built a big library in Alness, in Ross and Cromarty days, modified a branch in Invergordon, tidied up Wick and Thurso libraries and, in the first few years of regional libraries, built a big new library in Culloden. After that, nothing much was happening and, with the Library budget the biggest single element in the department budget, when cuts were required, it tended to come from the Library Service. If I'd stayed on I might have had the benefit of the publication of Scottish Library Standards.[41] I gather that when the Council considered the Standards in terms of qualified staff, premises, equipment and various other things, the Library budget was improved to a tremendous extent.

Interviewed 6 December 2001

Joe Fisher

My full name is Joseph Alexander Fisher, and I was born on the 26th November 1925, in Shettleston, Glasgow.

My father was a clerk in Beardmore's[1] at Parkhead, and then in the Depression he was sacked, and eventually got a job with Glasgow Corporation, the City Improvements, 20 Trongate, and was employed there as a clerk. He was born in 1890 and died in 1960. It was said that he got allowed off to look after his mother so he didn't serve in the First World War. What my grandfather did I don't know. The only time I traced my ancestry, I looked up the Mormon fiches[2] and there was Fisher, Joseph, currier[3] in Glasgow, and it was obviously my great-grandfather.

There were blacksmiths too somewhere on my mother's side. My mother was a housewife, wife, mother, grandmother.

As a boy I lived in a tenement in, I think, Fairbairn Street, a little street off Wellshot Road in Shettleston. It was Begg's Building. Presumably Begg was the person who built it. It was a very average tenement house – red sandstone though, which elevated it above the more jerry-built ones.

Before I was at school, my mother's mother died and our family moved in with my grandfather to look after him. It was a divided household. It didn't affect the children, but it was unhappy because my father never had a house of his own. It was further acerbated by the fact that my mother's sister wouldn't have anything to do with it, and ma mother was left to carry the load alone. My grandfather's house was in Wellshot Road. It had five rooms, rented though, a private landlord. In fact, we lived next the factor. He had taken a house beside us. This was a row of semi-detached, dormer windows in the roof. He was still using gas lighting. Fairly common when the houses were built, but not by the 1930s. We had an indoor flush toilet, a bathroom with a bath, running hot and cold water. My grandfather was a buyer in Arthur's, the Warehouse.[4]

I had a younger brother, Robert – Robbie. We shared a bedroom. Typical of most people of my generation, I doubt if I ever slept in a bed by myself. When you were a child or a youth, you slept with your brother or if you're a girl, with your sister, and then when you got married you were in another bed.

I went to Wellshot Road Primary School at the age of five. I was not unhappy. I liked drawing. I had joined the public library as soon as I could, which was about five. It was just down the road. I didn't need anybody to take me. When I was walking home from school, if I was chased by big boys, I always ran into Shettleston Tollcross Library for shelter. I became a librarian's pet. I was allowed to take whatever books I wanted and go in behind the counter. In my final primary year, the teacher said, 'Anybody in this class read Warwick Deeping?'[5] And I held my hand, and he says, 'Now, Joe, I knew you were going to hold your hand up.' I didn't come from a bookish background. There was very few books in the house. There was my grandfather's glass-fronted bookcase, which was mainly religious and Harmsworth's *Encyclopaedia* and stuff like this.

We read comics all the time, the *Rover* and the *Adventure* and so on, with the wee print. My father was convinced it was bad for the eyes, so he wouldn't allow us to buy them or read them, but we read them and he didn't know. If you had several you exchanged them like mad. Funny enough, my grandfather paid for a copy of *The Children's Newspaper* for my brother and I. It was a dreadful paper! That was Arthur Mee's[6] publication.

I just read and read and read. I read a lot of Percy Westerman.[7] He wrote exciting adventure stories and 'W' came at the end of the fiction works, and immediately after that was the start of the classified sequence. When my parents said what was I reading, I said philosophy and religion because that was the sign above, and they were very puzzled by this. What was on the library shelves was what I read. And non-fiction.

I sat the Qualifying Exam.[8] I must've done quite well. Eastbank Academy was nearer but I went into Whitehill Senior Secondary School, my parents' choice, until I left school at 18 or whatever. We didn't have a sixth year, it was fifth year. I'd no problems, no great things happened. No discoveries were made. I just carried on with my education. I don't know whether it was me or a type, but we took things as they came. The school was there so you went to it. You didn't wonder why or if you could get out of it. It was more or less an unspoken thing that you educated yourself.

The only ambition I had was not to be like my father. I wasn't going to be a clerk because it didn't seem an interesting job. I always thought something to do with science or technology, not the literature aspect. I was good at Science at the school not at Maths but at Science. English as well – essays, writing. I was interested in history, too. Quite a spread of interests. The only thing that I had problems with was foreign languages. We took French and we had Latin at one time but I had no aptitude whatsoever for that; I was no good at French.

I'm not a sporting type at all. There was a period when the boys played football. There was a group who were so abjectly miserable at doing this that they were kept out and I was in that group. We pretended to play rugby. We just took a ball and ran up and down with it. No interest. My father was a runner. He was in Shettleston Harriers,[9] and he was always trying to get me involved and I wouldn't have anything to do with it. I cycled a lot. I acquired a bike when I was 13 or 14. It was purely amongst my friends. We once cycled out to Lenzie, little knowing I would later live here. And we went to Loch Lomond and south into Lanarkshire and so on. Thirty miles there and 30 miles back.

I remember the outbreak of the War. We were evacuated, my brother and I. We went to Wellshot Road School where the evacuation was arranged, right at the outset of the War, the first wave, Friday, 1st September 1939. It was extraordinary how quickly they got us away – as if the whole of the city was going to be destroyed. This was a common belief. They said the bombers will always get through. We were the only ones amongst my pals who went. The boys that we played with weren't evacuated. We didn't know where we were going. We were told that it was about 70 miles so I remember using a compass and sticking it on the map with a 70 mile radius and drawing a circle and wondering which of the many places it went through we were going to.

We went to stay with this elderly couple who lived on the outskirts of Lockerbie. They were well off. The maid was the one who looked after us. Eventually though the folk in the house decided to get rid of us, for reasons I don't know, and we went into a house in the centre of Lockerbie at the other end of the social spectrum. My grandfather and my mother came down from time to time to visit us. We weren't miserable or ill-treated, it was just a different lifestyle. To us it was a great adventure. We got friendly with boys from some of the local farms and we went to play in the stack-yard and so on. We made bows and arrows, I remember. My brother and I went out and shot sheep until the farmer saw us. No great harm done. Typical city boys!

The teachers came with us and ran our own school in a church hall. They tried to teach us Latin then for some unknown reason. We were there for three or four months and eventually ma folks came down and took us back home in the winter of '39–'40. By then it was realised that the cities weren't going to be bombed to pieces. What surprised us when we went back was the blackout, big, long streets entirely dark and tramcars with no lights zooming about.

Thinking about a job after leaving school might have been something as simple as being a draughtsman or a surveyor. A boy of that age has no idea. You don't know enough to choose. I left school about the middle of the War, went to what became the Royal College of Technology – BSc, electrical engineering – where my inability to do mathematics caught up with me. Eventually I left. It was the mass radiography and I had a shadow, and was in hospital, Robroyston, for a while. When I came out there was an understanding that the Royal College course wasn't for me, that I was having to struggle so hard that it was most unlikely that I would finish it.

One of the problems about going to tertiary education in the place where you were born is it's just really an extension of school. You leave house in the morning to go, you come back home in the afternoon. You almost feel you should have a playtime or something when you're there. I don't think it releases what gets released if you go right away from home.

I wasn't called up because I was a student and then because of the illness. I was unemployed for a while after I came out the sanatorium. One of my friends, Daniel Hood, says, 'Why don't you try the Libraries?' He was a school friend from Whitehill and he was in the Libraries. A lot of the boys didn't come back after the War. I think there were four killed and others survived but decided to change to something else. There was quite a number of vacancies – a window opening and I happened to step through it.

I wrote in asking if there was anything, and was asked to come in and have an interview. There was no personnel officers then. It was the City Librarian, Mr Paterson,[10] that interviewed me. I don't know whether that was his common practice to be interviewing somebody who wanted to start at the bottom. However, he said, 'Come back and start work,' and I did. That was 1947. Ending up in the Libraries was good for me. I can remember my first pay packet was £4 a week. I started in the Mitchell.

The Mitchell Library was entirely due to a bequest from Stephen Mitchell,[11] one of the later tobacco barons. I don't know if the firm still exists as such. Their most famous tobacco was Mitchell's Prize Crop. He was a bachelor. He retired to Moffat, died there in 1874, and left a very large sum of money – £66,998.10.6d. The conditions of his bequest were that it had to stay until it reached £70,000, and then they were to use it to build a free municipal reference library.

Glasgow didn't have a free public library at that stage. The Glasgow Libraries were set up under a Tramway Act. In these days, when you were putting a Parliamentary Bill through you tacked everything you could into it so that it was cheaper, and that's how they got the main Library Act passed. But the Mitchell was quite distinct, and it opened in 1877. One of the most remarkable things about it was he said that no book was to be denied entrance merely because it contradicted current opinion either political, religious, or anything else, and we're quite proud of that and tended to stick with it. He was a Unitarian – whether that had anything to do with it.

It had moved from place to place. Nineteen eleven was when the present building in North Street opened. There was a great furore at the time because they were moving out of the centre of Glasgow. In fact, you could say that Glasgow's followed the Mitchell Library, because that's where all the office buildings and so on are going up.

It's a pity that nobody – possibly me – has taken note of all the folk who've put in their memoirs or their autobiography that they came to the Mitchell. I don't think there's been a single person educated to a professional level in Glasgow who hasn't used it. You could say that it's a student's library, but what else would it be? A lot of ordinary people, I've found from taking them round the Mitchell, are in awe of it. They think it's not for the likes of them. It's very difficult to get rid of this notion. It is unique in Scotland. The other cities, like Edinburgh, have no general reference approaching the Mitchell, nor Aberdeen nor Dundee.

Because of our unique nature the Mitchell was regarded to some extent as a training place for reference librarians before the Second War, and a lot of them went down to England and got posts there. On the other hand, we had to go to Birmingham to get our first Mitchell librarian, Mr Barrett,[12] who was 81 when he retired. Came up from Birmingham. He was a Glasgow figure. Whether that was because of the times, but no social function didn't have the minister of the Cathedral and the Librarian of the Mitchell at it and other dignitaries. He got a doctorate from the university. They couldn't get rid of Mr Barrett. He wouldn't go. There was no retiral age, and he went on and on and on. And even when he went, he got permission to come back and have some oversight.

And we went to England for Mr Black.[13] He came up, not as City Librarian, but as Superintendent of Branches, and then he moved up to Depute Librarian and from Depute up to City Librarian. They say he got the Superintendent's post because support for the two Scots candidates was so evenly divided that they had to agree on a third person. Also it was said Harold Laski[14] recommended him.

In 1947 I would think there were about 30 members of staff in the Mitchell as well as probably two janitors. There was a fairly rigid gender discrimination. They wouldn't take girls in the Mitchell and they seldom took boys in the branches. The work was supposed to be so heavy in the Mitchell, carrying heavy newspaper files and books. They'd to allow women in as readers, and make provision for their needs and one of them was a ladies' loo. It opened off a room called the Ladies Room and they had to have somebody in the Ladies Room to staff it and it had to be a woman. It was a period when it would have been considered not right for women to sit indiscriminately amongst men. So there were two or three women on the staff. Also, during the War because of boys being called up, they asked for girls to come in from the branches. Boys didn't work in the branches, period. They weren't employed direct into the branches. Oh, you did go out at a senior level when you got promotion. That was later.

The other thing about the Mitchell was – I don't know if incestuous is the right word but nobody came in from the outside. We never recruited from elsewhere. I only found out later how strongly this was felt by folk like Don Martin.[15] People working in the library profession in the surroundings had no chance of getting into one of the biggest municipal reference libraries around.

They would recruit but it would be to start. They probably came in through the Corporation Exam. This was a well-established thing. You sat the Corporation Exam and you got marks and then you got offers from various departments. This would be white-collar workers. It was considered a step up for a lot of folk to get into the Corporation, mainly because of the superannuation.

I've a feeling that you only sat the Corporation Exam when you were at school. I don't think people of 23 sat it. I think it was purely recruiting from school and they moved up as people retired. The ultimate goal was to go out as a district librarian into a branch into semi-retirement in many cases. You stayed in that branch until you left, and it might be 10, 15, 20 years.

The problem is we had no standards of comparison. Nobody was coming in bringing fresh ideas. Two people came in as sub-librarians – Fred Guthrie, and I forget who the other one was – and they hadn't a very happy time of it because they couldn't suit them to the *mores* of the Mitchell. The problem was they were enthusiastic, and enthusiasm wasn't a Mitchell characteristic.

Roman Catholics were excluded. I should imagine they would look at the name of your school and if you came from St Philomena's or St Augustine's you kicked wi' the left foot. This is a characteristic of Glasgow, commonly accepted as a hurdle for anybody looking for employment. It was the Catholic vote to a large extent that put Labour in, yet it was widely believed in the whole of Glasgow that Catholics were discriminated against! Do you know how many Catholics were in the Mitchell? Three. How it could possibly have been done I do not know. You would find no instruction not to employ Catholics, but it seemed strange that no Catholics were employed.

The most obvious example was Tony Hepburn, Anthony G Hepburn,[16] an excellent man, a marvellous bibliophile, everything you could have looked for in a superior librarian. Yet he never got a good post. He was a very good Catholic. He was very much involved in *Catholic Truth*[17] and so on. He was a man of great abilities, and there he was, Mitchell Librarian (which is a post we don't have in these terms now) but it didn't amount to a hill of beans. Tony, although he had that post, was always overseen by the City Librarian and would be called up to explain things or told to do things.

The Mitchell was there before the branches so the City Librarian started off as the Mitchell Librarian, and always had a keener interest in running the Mitchell than running the branches. There was a superintendent of branches who looked after that and although they had responsibility for the whole system, the City Librarian and the Depute Librarian were located in the Mitchell. This is why they have always exercised more oversight of the Mitchell than maybe they should have, and if anything happened of a serious nature, they're on the spot and would be called in.

Though the Library was open six days, we weren't working six days, we were working five days. There was shifts. I've never had a car and at one time to fulfil split-day duties[18] I was on 12 buses. Most of the staff were on in the morning and the evening, which was absurd when most of the readers were coming in in the afternoon. Yet when the City Librarian decided to change that, there was a lot of opposition from the staff, and two or three of the traditionalists were allowed to continue the old style of working. The Mitchell suffered from holding on to old ideas when any reason for them had passed. The shift working was badly arranged but it was the law of the Medes and the Persians.[19]

The Mitchell used to open on a Sunday in the winter from two to five so they wouldn't interfere with people going to church. That remained the case until the Council decided what was the point in paying wages and heating a building when it was used almost entirely by people from outside Glasgow. Almost nobody but students came on a Sunday. If you didn't want to do your Sunday duties you gave them to somebody else. A number of branch librarians volunteered for Sunday duty for a bit of extra money but also to get into the Mitchell. Mr Hepburn, on religious grounds, wouldn't work. He was the only one who was allowed out of it.

Each day a worksheet was made out of the duties for the following day, and you had your two shifts. Under ordinary circumstances one of these shifts you would be on duty at the front desk, and the other shift you would be on duty on one of the stack floors. Being on the floors at night was a favourite because you had bugger all to do.

When I began in the Mitchell in the late '40s, there was the Main Reading Hall and there were separate rooms including the Magazine Room. There wasn't a Glasgow Room at that time. The Main Reading Hall was the nerve centre of the Library because that was where all the work of the Library was carried out as far as readers were concerned. As a reader you approached the front counter and handed over your application form for particular books or documents. And we would say we'd serve it. It may have been a book to hand but if it was a book in one of the stacks, then the slip was sent up. There was two vertical shafts and there was an endless rope – a pulley at the top and a pulley at the bottom – and attached to that was a large leather bag. On the front of it was a series of small leather pockets, one for each of the floors. You took the slip from the reader, rolled it up and stuck it in the appropriate pocket, or pockets if the books were coming from several floors, then pressed a button that buzzed on all the floors. Whoever was responsible would pull the rope, take out the slip, get the book and put it in the bag.

There was a ledge at each floor where the bag halted and the person on the stack who'd found the book and put it in the bag knew when to stop the bag by looking down and watching it. You could look down, and you saw when it came into the light. Now there was two schools of thought. One was you let it go, and the other one was you lowered it gently and, by God, if it was maybe *Lloyd's Register of Shipping* it could have taken somebody's head off. There was a notice saying not to put your head in the book hoist.

The book hoist worked, but if you had ten books in it you could take the skin off your hand if you let it go down too fast and for the person at the counter there was no way o' catching it. If it ran away you just put your head back out and waited for the crash as it went down into the basement.

We had no internal phone system in the Mitchell, and communication was by shouting up and down the book hoist. Aye, this super-efficient organisation. If you wanted to get in touch or there was a visitor for somebody, you would buzz First or Inter and ask them to tell Mr Campbell that somebody was wanting him down the front. You just shouted up the hoist. There was one old lad, Bernard Deagan, who had never got anywhere and was restricted to the first floor stack. They never put him at the front or anywhere else. He had very slack false teeth. Anyway, when he leant over to shout down his teeth would fall out and every now and then you'd be told, 'Go down to the basement and take Bernard's teeth back up to him.' There was a book hoist on either side but only one was used. The other one had been turned into a wee telephone booth – we still had the old candlestick phones in these days. Every now and then the leather would wear out, and the electrician who was the odd job man would take the bag away to stitch it up and he would sometimes put a new one in place. This is the point: it ran. As soon as we got the electric book hoist there was a hell of a trouble, trudgin' up and down the spiral because the electricity thing had failed.

One thing we could do in the old days, when almost the entire issue was done by slips across the counter, we could check on where the readers came from. We did that once or twice and found almost a third would be from outside the city. We played our part in tracking down the people who stole the Stone of Destiny.[20] The most important job that Bernard Deagan had to do was to take the slips from the previous day's issue and count them up. They were stored until the storage space got too full and we'd throw some out. Somebody had the brilliant idea of going back over these and finding out who had been taking out guide books to Westminster Abbey. And they found them. I don't know whether to be proud of that or not. It was too high up for me to be involved in it but this is the story that came down to us.

Of the 30 staff, at any time some would not be on duty because of the shift system. If you take the afternoon, half o' them would be off. At the front desk there would be from seven to ten serving the public and on the floors there would be maybe four, each one to a floor, but generally speaking there was seldom staff on Third, because there was very little work up there and Intermediate there was often nobody on there, apart from my wife, 'cause that was where the telephone exchange was and it was run by the librarians. So it was mainly First and Second.

The ones who took charge of the front desk were sub-librarians. There was six sub-librarians on the front desk rota who took turns at being in charge. In a sense, that person was the Mitchell Library. He had responsibility. The day-to-day working of the Library was in his hands. He allocated the duties. He answered the enquiries when the assistant couldn't deal with them. So it was an interesting and a hard-working person who was in that job. It was the senior librarians in the staff that we had most contact with, and we'd ask them about problems we had and so on. The Mitchell Librarian was on a level with the people in the staff at the same age as him. You would as likely go to him as you would to anybody else. There was no side there. How much of that was due of course to the person who filled the role, I don't know.

The serving staff were interchangeable. The serving staff did the book processing – the stamping, labelling and collating new books. Every book had to be collated – God knows why. You'd to go through them and ensure all the pages were there. You went through page by page to check the pages were there. The bulk of them would obviously be new books. We didn't collate donations. The theory was that if there was a fault in the book it might not be found until it was no longer replaceable.

So from '47 to '52 I was more or less just going on like that. It never bothered me, because to be in the middle of almost a million books was sheer heaven. And if you were on duty on one of the quiet floors in an evening or a Saturday, you'd a fair amount of spare time. No doubt you should have been doing something to further the Library, but I would look along the shelves, find things and make myself acquainted with the stock. So it wasn't a soul-destroying task as far as I was concerned.

The cataloguers were separate. They were sub-librarians: it was a promoted post, and some of them did it full time, others combined it with being in charge at the front. Some of them would be in charge at the front desk half the time they were on duty. There was about six, I think, more or less one for each day, who took a turn at looking after the front. There was one for the morning shift, one for the afternoon shift and one for the evening shift. So in a week you would maybe be in charge three times. Some of the others were totally cataloguers. Some of them combined cataloguing with maybe binding or periodicals or PSBs.[21] There was a cataloguing room, where about six or seven cataloguers worked.

I enjoyed my work in the Mitchell very much. There was an *esprit de corps*. The Mitchell staff all knew their work and were good at it, and took a pride in it which is almost totally lacking now. When you became a sub-librarian it freed you from the wheel. You were no longer designated to be here or there. You did whatever your work was. I don't think there was a recognised minimum period of years for qualification to become a sub-librarian. It was dead men's shoes. Merit didn't play a part; it was purely seniority. Your place on the staff was how you moved up. Somebody could stay behind because they didn't get the exams, the Library Association exams – ALA.[22]

There were occasions on which it proved impossible to find what a reader was looking for. Sometimes it happened because what the person was asking had never been answered anywhere. Other times it was because we didn't have or couldn't find a book that would answer it. Sometimes an item was marked as NOS – Not on Shelf – which meant that it wasn't where it was supposed to be: it had been misplaced, or possibly stolen. It happened from time to time.

It was a sub-librarian's job every morning to walk round every single shelf in the Library and look for slips of the previous day's colour.

There was three colours: red, yellow and white. It changed each day and his job was to go round and see if any of the previous day's books hadn't been returned to their place. Shelf-checker. It was a helluva job. An important job but it was very easy to dodge it because nobody checked on you. You'd to walk round from the basement to the top floor. Not done now, because the books are issued from the shelves in the open access.

As well as an accession number[23] each book was given its shelf location and that was where the book stayed for ever. The shelf number was generally four digits – we had no shelves beyond 9,999. So you'd to take the accession number, look it up in the location book and find out its shelf. When I started these location books were recording accession numbers round about the 600,000, 700,000. That's not the actual stock but it must've been proportional to that because they're now well over a million. And the Library had its own classification system.[24] A letter of the alphabet and a broad classification. A, I think, was theology; H was fiction. By my time it was used for practically nothing.

The Mitchell wasn't such a big library as, say, the National Library of Scotland or Glasgow University Library. There was some problem of establishing its exact identity because it was unique and difficult to put in a category. It wasn't an ordinary reference library; it wasn't a research library; it was something in between. That has always been a bit of a problem as to what its stock should consist of, what level. I think our endeavour was not to specialise but when the Mitchell was being set up, one of the ways that the stock was acquired was by buying up several big libraries. I think we bought the library of the historian Cosmo Innes.[25] We bought quite a number like that and they were very strong on Scottish history and all the standard works. We were well represented in that because nobody was keeping big libraries in science or technology in private hands.

This was one of the great things about working in the Mitchell: you'd pick up this old book, look at the bibliography and it would say some obscure book and we had it. Whether you could say that about the books published in the last 20, 30 years, I don't know, but then there's a great many more books being published. A lot of people think we're like the copyright libraries – we're not. Every book has to be bought.

There were discussions among the staff, about these principles, although in the staff room, the main talk would probably be about whether to stick or twist.[26] There was a tea towel conveniently kept on the table so that if a senior member of staff came in you dropped it over the money. We also played ping-pong, though the staff room was only roughly 25ft by eight or so. When I started, the cooking equipment for the male staff was a Baby Belling electric cooker and that was what you made your coffee with. It was someone's job to fill a very large cast-iron kettle and put it on this electric hot-plate and if you didn't put that kettle on your name was mud! One single refectory table ran the full length of that and everybody sat round it except the City Librarian and the Depute Librarian. You sat next to people with 20, 30 years' experience, and after the sort of hurly-burly of whatever game they were playing was over, you could have a wee chat and learn an awful lot from them. It was marvellous.

The female staff room was about the size of a scullery,[27] but it had to accommodate what was called the clerical staff, the office girls. There was a number of them. I was never in it. You weren't allowed in it anyway.

I undertook more or less from the beginning to study for my ALA. There was no point going into the Libraries unless you were going to do that. Every year a number of staff – three, four maybe – were given leave of absence without pay to attend the Scottish College of Commerce library school, whatever it was called, in Pitt Street.[28] They went through the course and they came back to the Library, and depending on the results they got an increase in salary and were then capable of going further up.

There was an evening course you could do, but by my time few people did that, because you got leave of absence, although Molly [Mrs Fisher] would have wanted to do that but her parents couldn't allow her because of their need for her wages. Mine's did, and I went to the College, Monday to Friday, full day, during the College terms. You weren't being paid while you were there so that meant that your parents were supporting you. I was living with my folks, and they managed. The Corporation must have paid your stamps or something like this – there was no interruption.

I joined the Library Association.[29] It was the Association that set the exams, so you had to join it to sit the exams. But when somebody got promoted to the districts, they came out of the Association. I did. Then Mr Black insisted that there would be no more promotion for anybody who wasn't a member of the professional body so there was a big rush back. I'm still in it as a retired member. There's the Library Association and there's the Scottish Library Association. As it so happens, we've dissociated ourself from the Library Association. We now have a lot of functions that used to be carried out by the Library Association. It shouldn't be the Library Association, it should be the English Library Association. They're entirely oriented towards circumstances in England. What was the exams we sat? Cataloguing and classification, bibliography, administration and English literature. That would never be contemplated now. That shows the ethos of the Association in these days. It hadn't caught up with science and technology.

I gained my ALA in 1952 and became a sub-librarian which meant a slight increase in salary. You were no longer serving staff then. You became the middle group and you would be given a specific duty or range of duties to carry out, and I was put in charge of periodicals, so I did my work up in the Periodical Room. I didn't particularly enjoy that. Och, you had to spend a lot of time writing for overdues[30] and watching out for subscriptions, so it was sort of clerical work. I also worked as a classifier and cataloguer. The main thing was that you were no longer being told where and how and when to work. There was an element of freedom. You could move about the Library which was great because I moved about the whole of the Library from top to bottom.

I continued that way until there was a vacancy at my level in one of the district libraries and I went out there – in charge of Hutchesontown. Now this was the anomaly: all the boys had been trained in the Mitchell as reference librarians, worked their way up, eventually got to the promotional stage, and where did they send them? District libraries. Not only to work there but to be in charge over women who'd been there since they were girls and had been nowhere else. Very odd. But that was the way it worked.

I knew nothing! We knew nothing of the branches apart from administration. We were expected to pick it up. For a week I went to Shettleston Library where the District Librarian was supposed to show me round things. There was anything from six to eight in a branch, and when I went to Hutchesontown, there was a librarian, a sub-librarian and then there was a first senior and so on. This first senior there was scatty, she was hare-brained! And I got all my ideas about branches from her.

There was a big difference in librarianship in a branch and librarianship in the Mitchell. In the Mitchell we were dealing with undergraduates,

graduates, post-graduates, researchers, assistant lecturers, and you had to know what they were talking about. If they talked about the transhumance of sheep in Spain in Philip II's time you had to find out. Whereas in the branches, you needed a right hand to stamp the date in the books and to put the books back on the shelves. It wasn't boring though because I was interested in the children's library and the children.

Hutchesontown wasn't a good library at all. I was there for a year or two then I went to Riddrie Library, which is next Barlinnie Prison, in a typical Glasgow scheme. It was marvellous having children coming in. Adults wanted the latest book on this, that or the other. The children didnae; they never looked at the date of the book. It was a book that they wanted to read, and to introduce them to all the great children's literature was marvellous. I enjoyed that. I enjoyed talking to the readers, too. We used to get the governor from the prison coming down and the chaplain and warders. We had local notables coming in. You can build up a rapport which is satisfying. But I was a reference librarian above all. A very different clientele, a different approach. One wasn't better than the other but they were different.

I settled down and to some extent, that was goin' tae be me. I was in Riddrie until I came back into the Mitchell. I might have been five years in the branches, so I'd be back in the Mitchell by about 1964. Once again it was literally dead men's shoes. In 1959 the Glasgow Room was opened. There hadn't been one before that, an open access department, and the fellow who got it up and running died in tragic circumstances and I got a phone call one Friday to say, 'You've to report at the Mitchell on Monday.'

It was Tony Hepburn who had asked if I could take over as Librarian in Charge of Special Collections, which included the Glasgow Room, the Poets' Corner, and the Strong Room – all the stuff that nobody knew what to do with. It was the best job in the world! The Glasgow Room: the whole city was yours. The Scottish Poetry: then I became an expert on Burns; I did the Burns Catalogue and I'm still giving talks on Burns. The archives, the Strong Room, was all the manuscripts: that was terrific! For instance, the Dunlops of Garnkirk, an important 17th, early 18th century account of a laird close to Glasgow and three or four genera-tions, and finally they set up the Clyde Iron Works.[31] It was interesting to see the transition from being country lairds to becoming industrialists. There was the family down in Largs – Brisbane, we'd the Brisbane

Papers.[32] Marvellous rental books, contracts, everything. Oh, a lot of miscellaneous things.

This was a new world to me, handling manuscripts. No training or anything. 'Where ignorance is bliss, 'tis folly to be wise.'[33] I went ahead and did things in my own way. I prepared a catalogue of the Dunlop Papers[34] and it's a marvellous catalogue, but arranged on entirely the wrong principles from an archival point of view. That was my first catalogue. I came across the Dunlop Papers in a strong box, which there was no key for – I broke it open.

Another chest, one which was even more important, had the correspondence of the Glasgow Chamber of Commerce[35] from before it was founded up until about 1870. All the letters between the Chamber and their agent in Parliament about Bills passing and what to do. I think the Chamber was started in 1783. There's some preliminary stuff in the 1770s, leading up to the founding of the Chamber, and there's a whole mass of papers from a lawyer, Bell,[36] who's famous for having written the first textbook on civil law in Scotland, I think. And Campbell of Succoth,[37] whose picture is still on some of the pound notes, about a bankruptcy Bill that was going through Parliament.

Another chest had the papers of the Glasgow East India Association. At that time, the 1830s, the East India Company[38] had a monopoly with trade, and all the out-ports – Bristol, Liverpool, Glasgow – started lobbying to get this done away with. These were the Glasgow papers to do with that lobbying. A companion volume was the Glasgow West Indian Papers, 1807,[39] to do with trying to stem the emancipation of slaves in the West Indies.

They were busy years, new responsibilities. When I came back there wasn't a Glasgow Room staff. What I got were people from the front desk. You'd no continuity at all. There was no training. You'd different persons the whole day long. I was a boss without a staff. So I just concentrated on learning as much as I could about the stock and left the day-to-day running to the staff coming in. That changed eventually and we had a staff to train. At the beginning there was four of us altogether, including me. I don't know how we managed. This was the period when Glasgow history was becoming topical. A lot of queries. The main thing was the letter enquiries from all over the world. Where else could they write if they wanted information on Glasgow? Science and technology, if you'd a query in that field, you could write to Liverpool Library or

Birmingham or Edinburgh and you would get as good an answer. But if you wanted a Glasgow enquiry answered, there was only one place – that was us.

We used to keep an eight-by-five catalogue card for each letter and for each reply and an unwritten rule was, if you couldn't get it on to that card you were saying too much. You had to reduce it. There was a survey made of all the metropolitan libraries, like Liverpool and Manchester and Birmingham and Edinburgh and Glasgow. One of the questions was the average time given to a query. At most of these other libraries, the length of time was five minutes, ten minutes. Ours was something like 20 or 30 minutes.

We hadn't a standard that we took from the library profession as a whole as to how long you should spend. We worked on it till we had an answer. These were non-Glasgow ratepayers. I always pointed out that we were not only acting as a library department, we were a tourist department, we were a media department, we were raising the name of Glasgow all over the world by giving full, clear answers to queries about the city. So I didn't grudge the time.

The main thing with readers is to establish what they're after. It's not what they say they're after. They don't know enough about their own subject to know what to ask.

Reader: 'Have you got a book on Glasgow, mister?'

Librarian: 'Aye, 4,000!'

Reader: 'Well, it's the north of the city.'

Librarian 'Oh, aye, here, there's this, there's that.'

Reader: 'It's round about Maryhill.'

Librarian: 'Well, there's a wee history of it.'

Reader: 'No, I want tae know if ma sister-in-law's still in Shamrock Street.'

Librarian: 'If you'd said that first, I would have looked it up in the valuation roll or the voters' roll.'

They want tae spare you. Give them the book and they'll do the hard work.

There was a fellow came in – he had an ancestor in Anderston, but he didnae know their address. He was looking through the entire census returns for Anderston for 1851, '61, '71. Two and a half years he spent doing that, found it and he wasn't the slightest bit better for it. He had filled in a name. Family historians are a waste of time. Generally speaking, people with hobbies o' that kind, they're not worth the effort spared on them.

What I liked were the two ends: the children and the professors. The professors were always approachable, able to think of your problems, able to help you to find what they wanted, able to accept you on their level. The children were the same. But the ones in between – they wanted something: 'Get it.' 'I want this, I want that.' It was mainly people new as lecturers or schoolteachers. They treated you like a member of their class. Readers get the service they deserve. There's no end of trouble you'd go to for a reader who was polite and sympathetic and explained things. You would go to extreme lengths for them. These other kind, they've no idea what they've missed through rudeness. I don't know how these folk get on in the world.

The higher echelons in the library system supported what we were doing, they left you to get on with it. We had no contact with the councillors at all. It always struck me as odd when I would go down to the William Patrick[40] or talk to others, to find out how intimate the relations was with the Council because the councillors came in, borrowed books, their voters came and spoke to them about the library.

All the time we were building up the stock of Glasgow books and literature. We were always scanning second-hand booksellers' catalogues. There was very few Glasgow books of any importance we didn't have though. All we were watching was for new stuff coming out. It's different now. About ten or 20 years ago if there was one Glasgow book every two years you were lucky. Now they're coming out the wall. Local history societies are flourishing too.

Once the Mitchell was departmentalised each department had a budget, except the Glasgow Room. There was so little new Glasgow books being published there was no point, and anyway we would suddenly have to spend maybe £100 on a rare item coming up and for the next three months we would spend nothing. There was a fund for general purposes that we drew on and I never found any problems there.

I was usually called Librarian of the Glasgow Room, but strictly speaking it was Special Collections. Later the Archives was set up as a department on its own, and the Scottish Poetry, once there was the Department of Language and Literature, went there. So I was then in charge of the Glasgow Room alone. I retired as Librarian in Charge of the Glasgow Room.

In 1962 the St Andrew's Halls went on fire.[41] There was no damage to the Library. There was a gap between the back of the Mitchell and the back of the St Andrew's Halls and that's what saved us. The glass in the window was cracked and the asphalt on the roof melted but that was about all the damage. The firemen used it as a basis for their hoses up there. If the usual prevailing wind in Glasgow had been blowing, which is a south-west wind, the Mitchell would've gone up. It was a north-east wind. There's an aerial picture of it and you can see the smoke and flames are all being blown away from the Library.

Then the notion developed that the old St Andrew's Halls or the site thereof, should be incorporated into this marvellous new complex with a theatre, conference hall and so on. The fact that the new library had a café which hadn't existed before has helped. People could spend all day there without leaving the building. The staff used the café but I never used it.

The Main Reading Hall, the front desk, were things of history and subject departmentalisation took over. It had occurred before the opening of the new Mitchell in a very tentative way. The first open access subject department was the Music Room in 1930, and the next one was the Glasgow Room in 1959. The problem was lack of room. The Music Room opened in what used to be the Committee Room – at one time the Library Committee met there. It was shut during the War and opened up afterwards. There was a Students' Room, which now is where they issue the newspapers and which used to be the Glasgow Room. This offered some peace and quiet, but it was just one single, open room. That was closed during the War and was used by the cataloguing staff who had nowhere else to go.

The new Mitchell Library, the whole present complex, opened in 1980. We had room to spread, we had room to have displays and so on. It didn't bring anything radically new in train, but it meant that we could do what we were doing better. The staff increased. By the time I retired there were eight or nine staff members in the Glasgow Room. As for the people who used the Glasgow Room, there was more genealogists. I think we had more students and younger people. The Library became a meeting point for a lot of young Glaswegians who were in tertiary education, many to run into members of the opposite sex, particularly amongst the Asian community. They were a damn nuisance! They weren't there to study. They went there to winch or whatever you would call it.

Glasgow Corporation had a closed shop policy so you joined the union, NALGO.[42] *Faute de mieux*. I wasn't an active member. There were no active members in the Library. The representative, the NALGO man, paid very little attention to anything to do with the union. There was no discussion with management as far as I knew. There was never anything coming up. Then things began to change. We had young folk coming in as representatives, and there was changes taking place in employment and there was a much more abrasive interface, let's put it that way. It started when Mr Black, City Librarian, went. Mr Black couldn't have stood that. He was an autocrat. Never had a day's illness in his life. Couldn't understand other people were ever ill: they were malingering. He was unpopular but the strange thing is, once he went he was spoken of very highly because we realised that you never went to Mr Black and didn't get an answer. It didn't matter whether you liked the answer or not, he would say yes or he would say no and that was it settled.

Other Librarians would dodge the issue. 'Well, we'll see about that, Joe. I'll think about it a wee bit. You come back to me and I'll see.' Mr Black was concerned with everything in the Libraries. Nothing could happen but he was there. At one of the meetings of the District Librarians with Mr Black – not, you'll notice, with the superintendent of branches – he had me explain why I had spent five shillings on a tin of heat-resistant black paint to paint round the boiler! There was another poor soul who had electricians working in the library and what it was doing to the electricity bill was nobody's business! And Mr Black tore this poor librarian to strips. Penny-pinching.

Mr Black wasn't a bibliophile. He depended on Mr Hepburn, the Mitchell Librarian, who was. Whenever they went to a professional meeting, Mr Black would, 'Eh, Mr Hepburn, this gentleman here is asking me about the Audubon.[43] Could you tell him?' Mr Black was followed by Mr Alison,[44] a gentleman with every connotation for good and bad. He was also a Christian. It was said he opened the management meetings with prayer.

There was a peculiar break by the War. There seemed to be very few who knew the old Mitchell before the War. Mr Dunlop was the one with the old memories. He was another gentleman. To a lot of people, he was 'Mr Mitchell'. He had a presence. He went up to be a librarian at Baillie's[45] after he retired from the Mitchell.

Baillie's was a failure from the time it opened. It was no fault of the staff. It was run on a shoestring and it kept moving. It couldn't purchase books, it couldn't employ staff. Generally the librarian was a retired person. The university took it over. I think they sold a lot of the stock off. It's now with us – we're running it on behalf of Baillie's Trust. We get some extra money, and we've got the stock and there was material in it which we didn't have. The university professors went off with most of the good stuff!

There's two good aerial maps of Glasgow, one about the 1850s, part of a series that appeared in *The Illustrated London News*[46] for all the big British cities. There was another much earlier one, a lithograph done by a Glasgow artist, a beautiful work of art apart from anything else. We only knew of one single copy, the one we had, but ours had a fold down the middle. There turned out to be one in Baillie's, a complete map in excellent condition. Disappeared off the walls! I went up to get it and it was away.

I retired in 1990. My career was in two halves. The latter half was the Glasgow Room and the first half was just a general librarian. It was the Glasgow Room that I most enjoyed. When I retired they published *Essays in Honour of Joe Fisher*.[47] It was mainly done by Biff Carmichael,[48] but Hamish, a friend of mine, and Kevin McCarra, who wasn't a librarian, are the editors. I want to read what Cliff Hanley[49] said:

> We shouldn't inflate him too much because you can't applaud a gink who just does what he enjoys. Selfish beast. He should've spent his life doing something terribly important and painful. He backed away from that serious duty and devoted himself to selfish fun.

And somewhere he said that if they'd only known, Joe Fisher would've paid them to employ him. I never thought of undertaking any other job. I applied once for a job in the UK atomic establishment! It was when I was in the branches and about the time my first-born was on the way – Kenneth. I went down for an interview and the chief thing I can remember is getting into a terrible argument about Nennius.[50] One of the interviewers and I just argued the point and I think that was what lost me the job because it was obviously no interest for somebody going into a library in an atomic establishment. Anyway that was the only time I tried elsewhere. I don't think my heart was in it. I think it was the money.

Looking back libraries, librarians and librarianship have changed because the whole system of conveying information is changing: the Internet and satellites and so on. Nobody knows what the future's goin' tae be. There was a fellow on television saying there'll be no more printed books soon. There's a great many scientific and other types of journals which are only published in computer form. We're also being changed because of financial pressures. Both in universities and in local government from Mrs Thatcher[51] on, a measure has become profit, saving money. Libraries are having to cut back on book funds[52] and on staff and on everything else. They're more professional. You'll see a lot of senior figures in the library world with an MBA.[53] In some places you don't have a director or a librarian, you have a manager of libraries, sometimes with no library qualifications. I regard that with some despair.

This business of new means of information – librarians aren't properly trained in it and I don't see how they can be because they say every six months there's a new filing system comes out, there's a new computer programme comes out. We in the Mitchell are now quite well off that way. There's a great many CD programmes and they're terribly useful but they're not easy to use. They're not user friendly. The technology of computers is outpacing relationship with humans. But then look at what they call OPAC.[54] All additions from about 1970 onward are on that, and what a boon it is! I was looking for something which would give me facsimiles of inventories in the 17th-18th century and I didn't know how to approach it. I knew that notary publics in their protocol books were involved with these things. So I keyed in as a keyword 'protocol' and it brought up all the books that have been published since 1970 about notary publics and their protocol books, and I got one which had exactly what I wanted. I could never have found it any other way. I used to find these things by serendipity. Now you find them through the OPAC. Modern technology has revolutionised searching for information.

I don't know whether the printed book will be made redundant by technological advances. At one time I would've said no. But this man was even talking about fiction, reading *Our Mutual Friend*[55] or something. You read it, it goes into your imagination and becomes part of your memory. If that was linked up with Dickens's life, with Victorian literature, with the history of the law in the 19th century, so that when a solicitor's name comes up, you could key in and get details of what the legal set-up was, it's hard to avoid the conclusion that that would be helpful, in which case the printed book will go because people will get more this way.

Librarians act as a gateway so that the readers can make their way through to information. What if the readers don't need the gateway? What if the readers can ask the computer? My wife and I were in Paris last year and we visited this lovely old hospital, Hôtel-Dieu de Paris. My son was showing me his Internet access and I asked him, 'See if you can find something about the Hôtel-Dieu de Paris.' He did and gave me a printout of about 16 pages. I could never have done that in any other way. I could never have found it. I could never have got a copy of it. I could never have afforded a copy. When my grandson goes to university and on into the world, he's goin' tae be part of a population that expect to get it on a computer. That's when we'll see the big changes. I won't live to see it but it's coming.

Finally, the overriding thing is how damned lucky I've been in working there and being allowed to a great extent to go my own way. At one time we had three graduates, four graduates, and it was great because there's one thing about graduates – they can at least write and spell fairly well and are capable of putting their thoughts down on paper.

Interviewed 19 May 1997

Peter Grant

My name is Peter Grant and I was born in Greenock on the 26th of August 1926. I was the oldest of the family. I had a sister who was born in 1930 but she died when she was 20 years old.

My father was born in Alves parish in Morayshire where he was a farm servant. He wasn't an educated man. I think he went to school in Alves but had left when he was 13. Even when he was in school he was doing farm work and driving cattle from the Forres side to the Elgin market and back. There's that oak wood when you come out of Elgin and he would be driving cattle back on a winter's day, and instead o' walking behind them and driving them on, he walked in the middle o' them because he was so feart of ghosties coming out! He was a first horseman, and had the first pair of horse on the farm. He moved around; he fee'd [was hired for a fee][1] to various places. I can drive through Morayshire and say, 'My father worked there – Barmuckity and Waterside and Calcots and all over there' – farms this side o' Elgin and west to Forres and Alves.

He had various stories about the bothies[2] where he'd stayed from about 14. The first farm he worked in was Waterside where he stayed in a loft above the calves, and once he was up in the loft the farmer took the ladder away because he was frightened the calves would injure themselves bumpin' against it. If he came home he had to cross the River Findhorn. There was a ferry, a rowing boat wi' a rope, and you paid the ferryman a penny to get across, but his mother was so afraid he could get drooned crossin' the Findhorn that she never told him about the ferry and so he had this long walk. He didn't get eating with the farmer, and this was a small farm, he had to eat separately. Then the farmer took ill and his brother, who was on the tramways in Glasgow, came back and he had different ideas and says, 'No, no, if the loon's good enough to work wi' me a' day, he can eat wi' me at night.' It was a rare thing for them to get beef or even bread. Baker's bread was a thing they got at the week-ends. It was oatcakes all the time and porridge and soups. My father's sister, who was in service in Elgin, had mutton ribs to make soup and the girls in the kitchen had a plate of soup and then ate the meat off the ribs. The wifie, the woman o' the house, came looking for the mutton, and they said they'd eaten it. They got a helluva row for this!

My father left Moray probably 1910 when he was about 22 or so. There's a bothy ballad – I was quite familiar with bothy ballads at a young age:

> I often thocht I'd like tae be a bobby in the Force,
> Or maybe join the tramways and drive a pair o' horse.

So my father became a bobby in the Force and was a police constable in Greenock from 1910 till the Second World War ended. He had extended service because of the War. The north was a fruitful recruiting area. There was a lot of my father's friends in the police from Aberdeenshire and Morayshire, from Islay, Skye and the Western Isles. I think it was economic reasons. My father had thoughts of emigrating and he was quite advanced about going to Australia but something had happened about clearance and he hadn't gone.

My father wasn't away in the First World War although some of his friends volunteered to go. He was in a reserved occupation, and the oldest of a family of 11 and there was brothers that were away. After the First World War police salaries were being reduced. He was the spokesman for protesting against this, and after that he knew he wasnae goin' tae make anything. Captain Christie, the Chief Constable, never took him on after that and he remained a police constable.

My father's father was a farm worker too. He came from Tomintoul where there's two graveyards, one the Roman Catholic graveyard and the other, but both of them are full of Peter Grants. It seems to have been a common name. My grandfather was still alive when I was growing up. He was retired and my grandmother and grandfather Grant stayed in Rothes. During the '30s, when some people didnae get out to the next town, we had holidays up to my grandmother's and to my mother's side in Jura. It was a big family and we had relations and friends all over

Morayshire. In the '30s, my father got an old Morris Oxford car and we spent our time on holiday going round these farms and old friends and relations. His oldest sister had married Andrew Munro, a grieve[3] on a big farm called Stynie between Fochabers and Mosstodloch. He had been a pal of my father's. They'd both been on farms and we spent quite a lot of time there. They had eight pair o' horse on that farm, a cattle court in the middle and a thrashing mill.

That gave me an interest in farms and the language, and I later became interested in Scottish literature, poems and the Renaissance[4] – MacDiarmid and others. I understand Burns, too, of course, and find Burns easy to read. My grandmother spoke broadly and my father never lost his Morayshire accent, although his was diluted wi' being in Greenock.

My mother was born and brought up in Greenock but both her parents had come from Jura and there were still relations in Jura. My mother's father was a tugboat captain and I have an old Bible which says 'Alan Rankin, Captain, *Flying Dutchman*'. The firm was Steel & Bennie's,[5] one of the tugboat companies, whose boats were all *Flying* things – *Flying Falcon*, *Flying Eagle*. I think Rankin was an Ayrshire name originally, although there were Rankins in Islay and Jura. There was a movement at one time of putting Ayrshire people with experience of agricultural work to these islands.

I don't know what my mother's mother did before she got married. MacPhail was her name, and there was a big family of MacPhails. On the maternal side further back was McColls who were shepherds and worked on the land. That McPhail family were Free Presbyterians[6] and when we used to go up in the '30s and '40s and stay with my grandmother's unmarried sister Peggy we had family worship in the morning, the afternoon and the evening, every day, and Sunday you did bugger all. I liked Jura as a place but it certainly put me off religion. Peggy was a kindly soul but she read a lot, big books of sermons in Gaelic, and when we had family worship she prayed in Gaelic. My mother spoke Gaelic conversationally but she couldn't write it. That family were clever people, my great-uncles, and Neil MacPhail, one of my grandmother's brothers, used to write Gaelic verse which was published in *The Oban Times*.[7] They were in Lealt in the north end of Jura, near where George Orwell[8] stayed, and then the whole family, the MacPhails, moved to Glasgow, including the grandparents, for economic reasons. They had a shop in Raeberry Street in Glasgow, a general ironmongery.

My mother was a Greenockian, and left school at 14 although she was a bright woman and could've gone on. There were four in that family, two boys and two girls. My mother was the oldest and she was in a higher grade school[9] but she was put to domestic service. Her first job was a maid o' a minister's house, and then she was a long time with a family called McCurdy who were connected wi' shipbuilding, and Kerrs and she was there during the First War. She used to speak about twin nephews of Miss McCurdy she worked for, and they were in the Argylls[10] and were both killed at the Dardanelles.[11] Then she was in the munitions in Greenock, at Rankin & Blackmore,[12] but she hated it. Her experience had been Free Presbyterian and sheltered in these big hooses and gentry, and the rough language really repelled her. I don't know if she lasted the whole War there, but she was then in shops, working in women's coats, hats and clothing. Miss Bowie's was one of the places. Then she was in an umbrella shop to which she went back during the Second World War when they were short-staffed. It was when she was in the shops that she met my father and they were married in 1925. Somebody had drawn a comic postcard of my father leaning on this wall in his uniform and cape and there was snow all over him and the umbrella shop sign.

I've always been interested in ships and shipping and many of the MacPhail-Rankin side of the family were in ships, yachts, shipbuilding, engineering; my mother's brother worked in Hastie's Steering Gears[13] in Greenock and my uncle was in MacBrayne's[14] office, and cousins of my mother were in Clarks' yachts, the thread makers.[15] They had a fleet of yachts which all began with V: the *Vedura*, the *Volga* and so on. My mother's unmarried sister was a French polisher in the yards. I had jobs between school and getting a proper job and during summer holidays, and it was great to be a purser or a ticket collector on a river steamer. I had a long summer on the *King George V* – that was MacBrayne's – Greenock to Ardrishaig: Dunoon, Innellan, Rothesay, Colintraive, Tighnabruaich, Tarbert and Ardrishaig.

We stayed in a good tenement in Captain Street in Greenock. It's no longer there. There was a big kitchen and front room – a sitting room only used on special occasions – a bedroom and a bathroom. My parents used the kitchen box bed. I was four when my sister was born; my father and I slept in the bedroom and my mother and sister slept in the kitchen. It was gas lighting first but then they got electricity in the '30s.

We had hot and cold running water. There was no kitchenette. Everything was done in the kitchen. There was the sink, a dresser and a black grate, a range.[16] My mother had gas – two rings on the top and gas in the oven and she baked and cooked there, not on the fire which kept things hot – soups once they were ready. Latterly she got the grate taken out.

At the age of five I started Grosvenor School, an annexe to Mearns Street School in Greenock. You went there for the first two or three years, and then you went into the main building. Holmscroft Street School was nearer but all my mother's family had gone to Mearns Street and she was keen on sending us to it. It wasnae that it had a great reputation. It had coal fires in each classroom and the jannie [janitor] came round and put coal on. I don't have very strong memories of primary school but I got on quite well. I wasnae overjoyed with it but I didnae dislike. I liked readin' and writin'.

At 11 or 12 I passed the Qualifying Exam[17] and went to Greenock High School. There was two schools that you went from primary school. There was a higher grade school, Mount School, but the ones with better scholastic marks went to Greenock High School, or you could – not that any went from Mearns Street – go to Greenock Academy which was a fee-paying school. Greenock High was non-fee-paying. I finished primary at Christmas and New Year, and Greenock High School started after the summer holidays, so they had an arrangement called preparatory and you went for six months to the High School. I think they were looking for subjects that would be useful before you started the proper first year. You got a lot o' local history. It certainly gave me an interest in Greenock, the sugar trade and sugar refining in the town, the relationship with the West Indies and the street names: Antigua Street, Madeira Street, Jamaica Street. It gave me an interest in graveyards too because I would go to the library to read up things. I realised you could get a lot of social history in a graveyard and I still go to graveyards when I'm on holiday.

When I was 13, 14 I took rheumatic fever and was off school for a whole year. It was the end of second year, so when I went back I went into third year. But personally, socially and scholastically it had quite an effect to be away for a whole year. My mother looked after me. I was in severe pain and the bedclothes had to be tented over my legs. After the first weeks I wasn't in such great pain but the doctor kept me in bed for a long period and gradually brought me to my feet, and so I didn't have any heart disease or long-term effects. At secondary school I was interested in History, English and Geography and I was quite good at Art. They wanted me to take Higher Art but that year off unsettled me and I didnae work very hard. I only got three Highers:[18] Physics and Chemistry, which was just Science, English and History. I left school at 18 at the end of the fifth year.

I was interested in football. My school years were almost exactly the War years. The regular school team goalie was a young chap and quite small and we used to play a lot o' service teams – soldiers and sailors – and I used to get games as a goalkeeper but I wasnae very good. I was all right wi' high balls but I was a bit slower in getting down to the right-hand corner.

I went to Sunday School and Bible Class because I was sent and we went to church. My father just went along, but my mother was keen on the church. She'd been brought up a Free Presbyterian and had back-slid into the Free Kirk which was a bit more liberal, and it was the Free Church we went to. It was the same dreich stuff – no organs, nae kists o' whistles.[19] There was a precentor[20] blew his wee trumpet to get the note and then led the singing, which was pretty execrable. I kept going to please my mother but since my teens I never attended church. I don't attend church now, although I was married in a church.

I didn't get a lot of children's books. My mother was suspicious o' books as a corrupting influence. We did get a few books but none that are reckoned to be classics for children. There was a very good library in Greenock High School. There was a friendly relationship between the then Burgh Librarian, William B Paton,[21] and the English teacher and the History teacher who ran the library. It was in a separate room and was catalogued and classified with the Dewey classification scheme.[22] They had a lot of novels, and P G Wodehouse[23] and John Buchan[24] were the ones I ate till I was told to stop reading P G Wodehouse because it was influencing my essays. I joined the public library when I was in secondary school. I read a lot o' Buchan. It didnae do me any harm but I don't think Buchan's a great author. The *Just William*[25] books was another thing I read. I wasnae reading classics. I've never read *Treasure Island*, for example.

We got comics but very controlled. *The Wizard* and *Hotspur*, *Skipper*, *Rover*, *The Champion* and I exchanged them. An aunt gave me a subscription to a scientific sort of thing, *Modern World*, and I sometimes got *The Children's Newspaper* but I wasnae very keen on that. My father bought the *Children's Encyclopaedia*,[26] ten volumes of it.

As a boy, I wanted to go to sea, to be a deck officer in the Merchant Navy. The rheumatic fever knocked that on the head. When I was working in Greenock Library there was an ex-assistant who was a purser on the big boats, and I thought maybe being a purser would be a compromise, but it never came to anything. I had one school summer holiday on the river steamers and then I was a cook-deckhand on a naval boat, *The Gay Queen*, RN 375.

I tried to get into the university and got the length of going for an interview to Gilmorehill.[27] The Highers I had might have been sufficient in a normal year but there was this great flood of ex-servicemen comin' in to the universities at the end of the War and they, quite rightly, were gettin' preference. For a time I was knockin' aboot doing damn-all. I hadnae a job and I didnae know what I wanted to do and there was all that pressure on you, social disapproval. My father had retired by this time and I was a sort of layabout for two or three months.

When I was lookin' at books in the central library in Greenock in Wallace Square, which hadnae been designed as that – it was the old General Post Office – this English teacher, Miss Irvine, came in and asked, 'You wouldn't like to work in here? I'll give you Mr Paton's address and you write to him and see if there's any jobs.' It was Miss Irvine that had got Richard Wilson[28] started in the theatre. She had a school drama club and got scripts from the Citizens Theatre,[29] Robert McLellan's[30] things. So that's really how I started – sort of drifted into it. I wrote to Paton, who had been the Burgh Librarian. He had left Greenock by that time. He'd been a captain in the Army during the Second War, came back for a wee while and then they opened the Scottish School of Librarianship in Pitt Street in Glasgow and he was the first head of it.

There was a stand-in, Miss Bryson, who ran it during the War when he was away and continued when he left to be head of the Library School. It was Miss Bryson I saw during the summer of 1945 and she employed me as a library assistant in Greenock. Then I went to Library School.[31] It was a year's course at that time. It's now a three-year degree course, but then it was just startin'. After that year I went back to Greenock. You worked shifts of course. The lendin' library was open till eight o'clock and the reference library was open till nine o'clock, on Saturday too, and you had to take a turn at that although not too often and usually Saturday nights were quiet and you could sit readin' the magazines and you got a day off in compensation. It was a weekly pay but then they went on to monthly pay and I was never out of debt for a long time. My father subbed me; I paid him back. Then it went on to a fortnightly pay but I can't remember how much it was. Nevertheless, it was a good while before I settled in libraries. There was a man appointed to succeed Paton as Burgh Librarian. He was quite a decent chap but an unimaginative Chief.

However, there was vacancies coming up in Lanark County where W B Paton was the Librarian by this time, having left the Library School, and I got a job there in December 1950. Lanark County had been a good service before the War and was expandin' rapidly. The headquarters in Auchingramont Road, Hamilton, had been a house, then a bank but then they built a big extension at the back as a library headquarters, an administrative and distribution centre. Before the War they had opened branches at Bellshill, Larkhall, Cambuslang, and Blantyre was the next one which opened in 1955.

We were buildin' stock for branch nine, or branch nine had opened, when I went there – that was Strathaven. When I left nearly 20 years later in 1968, they were buildin' stock for branch 48 or 49. I worked in all the departments in Library HQ. At the beginning, there was no mobile libraries, and it was all centres in schools and miners' welfares,[32] and so you built up collections and exchanged them every three months or so. Then the books came back and they had to be checked off, physically examined and distributed again or sent for rebindin'. Some of the bookmarks they came back with – like fishbones! One famous occasion there was a condom used as a bookmark – unused fortunately. It was embarrassin' because these two girls didnae know what this was. 'Oh, look, what's this?' 'It's a balloon,' says Jack Watson. Och, anyway, it was a lot of physical work, unloadin' vans, puttin' the books out, checkin' them off and examinin' them.

I'd been round the different departments in headquarters, and then was on the request department, which was more interestin' biblio-graphically, dealing with requests for subjects, books and so on. Then Blantyre came up. I was the first branch librarian at the new library there, in charge of settin' it up, gettin' stock together. They'd a good system in Lanarkshire with book selection meetings every week. You were buyin' books for existin' libraries, but you were also buying for branches being built so that when the branch opened they had a basic stock all ready and it was just a matter of toppin' it up. It was in '55 I went to Blantyre which had a reputation of bein' a pretty tough place, and we said, 'Oh, they'll be carvin' their names on the shelves', but nothing like that happened; it was a nice place. I enjoyed and was very proud of Blantyre. The main library was very attractive. It was all wood. It had a red cedar floor, display places, troughs for plants, a staff-room wi' a cooker and a good reference library which was far too big and advanced for the use. Another mistake was that the children's library was far too small. That's where the pre-war design failed. It was more like a miners' welfare design than a library. The branch librarian had an office to himself, which he could hardly use because there was somethin' wrong with the heatin' system. It was freezin' in the wintertime. We worked shifts and you were on to eight o'clock. Many of the readers were miners and miners' families, but I had been in Hamilton for a good while so it wasn't really strange to me. I had ten years' service, I was in charge of a new branch library and my salary in Blantyre was less than £600 a year.

Vaguely, I thought I would be a Chief Librarian some day. I was increasingly interested in Scottish literature and art, a sort of cultural nationalist, although I was never in the SNP.[33] When I was in Lanarkshire I stayed wi' an aunt and uncle in Glasgow and used to go on my mornin's off to Kelvingrove and went round the Barras and bought art books and first editions o' poetry. During that period I'd read Masaryk,[34] the first president of Czechoslovakia, and he had said something about the greatest patriotism was to go out and see things in your chosen occupation, get experience, then come back and give it to your own country. That was in my mind, but I had been winchin' wi' Betty for two or three years and we were talkin' about getting married. This opportunity came up and she very kindly agreed that I go to America, take the opportunity and even paid my National Insurance while I was there. That's how I went to Brooklyn, and Brooklyn's a tremendous difference from Lanarkshire or even Glasgow.

Brooklyn is one of the burghs of New York City with a population of three million. They used to say it was divided between Jews and Roman Catholics, Presbyterians and Arabs. I was in the YMCA at first, but was invited to share a good flat with two other fellows, a Canadian and an American from the Midwest. So I got good accommodation at a reasonable cost, and had quite a lot to spare. My salary was $4,000 a year, which was quite good – at that time it would be maybe £1,500, roughly.

I was sent first to a branch at Sheepshead Bay, a double shop that had been adapted. It was very busy and it took a wee while to settle in. I remember the difference from what you expect of American children, and this boy came up to me and said, 'Excuse me, sir, I don't want to seem bold but what country are you from?' They werenae all like that. When I was in another branch at Midwood, the centre of a prosperous Jewish area, this youth about 15, 16 says, 'Say, mister, were you imported?' Midwood was a very busy and demanding place. There was Brooklyn College, which is of university standing, Midwood High School and primary schools. At that time, the children had to find out for themselves and write up things, so you got requests for information and books thrown at you from university level, high school level, primary school level, and a lot of it was strange to me, the language was strange. Bein' a professional librarian, you were on the desk and all the queries came to you. Things like puttin' books away and issuin' books was done by what they called clerks, not qualified librarians. You came off an hour or an hour and a half at that desk and your brain was tired. Then I was on the mobile libraries and went all over the city from Coney Island up towards the Bronx, into these concrete jungles, and it was mobbed with kids. You would go into cafés for your cup of tea and the guy in the shop would say, 'Are you from Glasgow? Oh, great place, Glasgow.' They were servicemen and had tried to arrange their duties so they'd get to Glasgow for the dancin'.

Then I was in the central library, Grand Army Plaza, Brooklyn, and it was reference work there and quite hard work. I'd done reference work in Greenock but it was small scale, and yet in the evenin's you were often the only person in that department. There was a main desk in the foyer area and people were supposed to go there first if they didnae know their way around. Then they were directed to the appropriate department. Mine was history and biography, so I got to know a bit about American history.

The hours were long and they were open on Sunday too, afternoon and evening. So you could build up spare time and have a week-end. I went to Washington for a week-end, another time to Virginia, and another time my friend and I went up to his home in Ontario. Then I got a month's holiday. This other chap, the Canadian, had a station wagon and we went right across America to Montana and then up to Calgary, the Rockies, down the Pacific coast to Monterey, Cannery Row and Carmel, where Clint Eastwood was the mayor, and then back across through Salt Lake City. It took a while to settle down after I came back.

I was in Manhattan a lot, the art galleries, Museum o' Modern Art, tickets for the Metropolitan Opera and concerts. When I came back I was in Bellshill and it was quite a difference, and you went trundlin' in the bus through Bothwell, through the schemes, and even the grass seemed worn oot. Folk at Blantyre were keener; it was new to them and anythin' would please them. Bellshill was an older-established place. The Library was a '30s place above a clinic, and the design of the clinic dominated the Library. There was pillars came up from the bowels o' the doonstairs; not an easy place to work. A lot o' folk were steel workers and a lot of Lithuanians. There was a big collection of Lithuanian language books in Bellshill. I think the Library had bought them. The impression I got was that they had been used at one time, but by the late '50s, they weren't used. I shifted them all out. They were in the main Library takin' up a helluva lot of space. By this time I'd got married in 1958, and we stayed in Motherwell in furnished rooms.

I became a member of NALGO[35] when I was in Greenock, and I was, of course, in the professional association, the Library Association (LA).[36] There was a Scottish Library Association which was separate in a way but which had amalgamated with the LA to which you paid your money and they set the exams. In Lanarkshire we were encouraged to get involved in the professional association.

In my time W B Paton was the outstanding public librarian in Scotland and became President of the LA. He was a Glasgow man, brought up in Glasgow, but he got out quickly and was only in his 20s when he was the Burgh Librarian o' Airdrie and then in Greenock. He was a big man. He wasnae big physically, but he was a major figure because of his intellectual ability, enthusiasm and energy. A lot of people get to the top because they've got physical energy. Mr Paton became the Lanark County Librarian in 1950, the service built up after that and its strength was as a lending service. We had reference and local history, but primarily it was a lending service, exceptionally strong on the methods of book selection, ordering and distribution. The turn-round from shop to shelf was far ahead o' its time. Book selection was delegated to the branch librarians who knew their readers. It was co-ordinated centrally to ensure a balanced selection and avoid simply chasing issues.[37] Paton wasnae a literary man, but he was an organiser.

Although there were a lot o' local people on the staff, Paton was hauling in people from all over: young people keen to go to Lanarkshire because a lot of them were his ex-students. There were people from different parts of Scotland. It wasnae like Glasgow and Edinburgh that tended to be local lads. Paton was a big shot in IFLA[38] through which he was meeting people, and we got West Indians, West Africans, East Africans, Ceylonese and Indians comin' to work for extended periods with us for experience. That gave an uplift to the staff. We thought, 'We must be quite good that a' these folk choose to come.' Most of them fitted in very well. East Africans were a bit more difficult but the West Africans, the Nigerians, were good fun. The West Indians, of course, were a great laugh. There was a Madrasi, from Madras. He was a great Communist. He'd come to the university, got a degree but he wanted to be a librarian. So there was a great mixture of folk.

Paton was a decent man: he looked after his staff and built up staff structures and went to NALGO meetin's and shouted the odds about conditions, standing up for his staff against other departments. I think his ambition was to be City Librarian of Glasgow but he didnae get that job. I think he had applied at one time before he got Lanark County. Whether he thought Lanark County would be a good springboard . . . But he built up Lanark County. It was world-known. Paton spent a lot of time in London. He was sometimes criticised for being absent so often, but by that time his staff had built up and he could leave them conscientiously.

He was keen on music, a church organist all his life and ran choirs, and he was secretary and pusher of the Scottish Junior Singers in their heyday in the '50s. We used to go as ushers, ticket collectors and programme sellers to St Andrew's Halls[39] at their annual concert, three nights in succession. A great choir! I was quite interested in choirs too. I had been a member of the Greenock Gaelic Choir and had two uncles in it. I'm no' a Gaelic speaker but I was quite a good singer. I used to sing solo, Scots songs.

Paton was a church man, a Congregationalist,[40] and he used to give sermons but he was never a goodie-goodie sort o' guy. Sectarianism is considerably stronger in the west of Scotland than in the east as I found when I came to Aberdeen. There's not so many Catholics in Aberdeen. In the west of Scotland, the big influx of Catholics from Ireland was deemed a threat, an economic threat as well as a religious threat. There was sectarianism in Greenock. There was Orange Lodges[41] and flute bands and even the primary school always wanted to beat St Mary's, the best football team in the primary league. You were conscious o' it and there was plenty folk that would say, 'He's a Fenian.'[42] Sectarianism certainly existed, but it wasn't overt in our area of work and there was Catholics on the staff in Greenock and you could joke about it. I was never conscious that being Catholic affected your promotion. Paton didnae say, 'Which school did you go to? We don't let Catholics in.' There was quite a number o' Catholics in Lanark County Libraries and we all got on very well. There was never any sectarianism among the staff. In fact, my wife was in headquarters and two or three of her closest pals were Catholics, and mine, too.

Paton was humorous and would laugh heartily at ridiculous situations and things people said, but sometimes he seemed to lack a sense o' humour. There was one ribald incident at a new branch where the librarian was Sam Brunton and I was the overseer settin' it up. We'd been openin' so many branches and I set up quite a lot of them. In his office Paton had this paintin' of a cockerel, an impressionistic thing with magnificent colours. He was very fond of this paintin' and so I don't know what persuaded him to shift it to this new branch near Baillieston. Nothin' was finished; a day to spare, and Paton looks around and says to Sam Brunton, 'Well, Sam, you can always say you've got my cock looking down on you.' I don't know if it ever dawned on him.

He retired in the early '70s, after I'd gone to Aberdeen. He had kept everything from his career: all his speeches and talks, a' his notes, his jokes. He had this bound into three volumes, one of which he gave to the Scottish Library Association. I knew him all my working life and when I was asked to do his obituary in the Scottish Library Association magazine[43] it was quite easy because I was able to use his own collection.

I was with Lanark County for 18 years, but it was never the same job because the authority was big enough to shift you around. I don't know if I would've left but during the '60s there were reports within the profession and local government about reorganisation. With counties to be done away with, I realised that after all these years and at my age – I was about 40 or so – I would be better in a city rather than a county.

As it turned out, this fine library that had been built with such enthusiasm was just broken up. The books were used but the organisation disappeared. Anyway, I came to Aberdeen in '68 as Depute. I had to be persuaded to come. In Aberdeen, the Chief was Marcus Milne,[44] and Bill Critchley,[45] the Depute in Motherwell, an Aberdonian who had previously worked in Aberdeen, got the Depute's job. Some years after that Milne retired as City Librarian, and Bill was made Chief. I knew him; I was a part-time lecturer at the School of Librarianship and so was Bill. He was keen that I apply for the job as Depute which I did and I got the job. Then in '72 he took a heart attack and died, and I was promoted. I got in without interviews or anything, I was just promoted.

So, suddenly, I was couped[46] into this new job and local government reorganisation, and there was lobbyin' and meetin's, and then in '73 my wife announced that she was goin' tae have a baby! We had been married for 16 years and hadn't had any family up to that point, but we had a boy in November '73. So that was another upheaval, domestically. It was a very busy time. The Library came out of the reorganisation very well, but it was a lot of hard work. I was always going to meetin's in the Town House, proposin' things, workin' to accepted standards, and Aberdeen was a hellish system – backward, out of date and under-financed. In the league table of expenditure per head of population on libraries and book funds,[47] the only worse places at that time were Helensburgh and Maybole. Marcus Milne had claimed, 'Oh, it's the best library service in Scotland', and it palpably wasn't.

Because of its location, comparisons were difficult. In Lanarkshire there were favourable comparisons with neighbouring authorities: wi' Motherwell, which was a good service, and wi' Glasgow. There was nothing similar here. But Aberdeen County started to improve and they had branches close in, like Cults, Culter, Bridge of Don and Dyce, and folk were beginnin' to make derogatory remarks about the city service. It took a while to identify the folk that had influence and made decisions. One of your problems was that councillors tend not to be readers. But we had a committee room in the Central Library and the committee meetings were held there, and as we gradually got more books we had a display of new books and you could find out what they were interested in. There was a tendency, still is, for officials to look down on the cooncillors, but I never did. Although it was older than a lot of other departments, Libraries were too small politically within the Council.

You had to look for allies and identify officials that could help you. However, my predecessor didnae get on with the finance officer, the chamberlain as they called him, which was a mistake – he was too influential. Anyway I liked Dargie, without any deviousness about it, and found out that he was a great birdwatcher, sea-birds in particular. I was interested in that too and he used to tell me places to go like Crawton and Newburgh, and if there was any bird books, I made sure that Dargie saw them.

I wasnae crawlin' but you've to build up support and credence that you're honest and worthwhile, and I did that wi' the councillors. Then I was very lucky. The Chairman of the Libraries Committee, Harry Rae, and I got on very well. There was a sort of *simpatico* relationship and we went to conferences together. I worked hard at conferences wi' whoever was with me. A lot of folk say, 'Oh, Christ, I've got to go to conference with that old so-and-so.' You had an influential man for a whole week to yourself. You could pump in ideas o' your own. That was important. So we gradually built up the thing but it was hard work and it took a lot out of me. Just before reorganisation, I had a notoriously low book fund of £58,000, and that was after a lot of increases. I had worked out that with the new branches that were bein' developed the book fund should be £128,000. Goin' to the meetin', I was thinkin', 'Should I reduce it?' I was drivin' round Queen's Cross and I says, 'Oh, bugger it. It's up to them to reduce it. That's what it should be as can be shown statistically.' So I put it to them, but before I went into the meetin' at the Town House I walked roond the buildin' twice, takin' deep breaths. But we got that and a good staff structure out o' it.

The next obvious campaign was to get the Central Library extended and refurbished. They agreed to do that but it was hard work, lobbyin' and reports before they decided to do it. The extension was at the back and so the building was divided into two. The reserve stock and some of the reference stocks was taken out, kept in order and put in unused wooden fish boxes, of which there are plenty in Aberdeen, and then the mobile shelving[48] was taken off its rails, the rails were relaid in this big hangar sort o' place, and the stock was reshelved. This went on for years, but the reserve stock was always accessible. It was never packed away in cartons where you couldnae get anythin'. It was a major job, the whole place was gutted and it took about six years before the whole thing was done. There was bulldozers in the basement! They had to strengthen the walls. The extension in floor area isnae very much but it's multiplied seven times because it's like a tower of seven floors slapped against the old building between the church and the Library at the back. The high Victorian ceilin's allowed them to put two mezzanine floors in. Lookin' at the front o' the building, it's no' changed much really, but there was about 60 per cent more floor area. And there was lifts – didnae have any lifts before – and there's a loadin' bay, there was a new heatin' system, new electricity, lightin', the whole lot carpeted. And we never closed durin' that time.

We advertised the Library on Grampian TV – three seconds or something. There was a photograph of the Central Library from the front and we advertised what we did, what you could get. We were twice on next to *The Sweeney*.[49] And we advertised on local radio and on the inside of buses. After all these efforts we increased the usage of the Library, no question about it, because we had the resources and pushed them. We also had a commercial department, a business and technical department, and we put a lot of effort into that. We made contact with business firms and provided books, magazines and information and computer services. This was all goin' on through the Thatcher[50] period. North Sea oil had arrived and we provided technical and commercial information services to support industries. The annual bibliography of our holdings in oil and gas was in demand from all over the world with similar situations as ourselves: Newfoundland and parts of America with offshore operations. We were in touch with the Chamber of Commerce to get these guys to say, 'Oh, it's a great Library. I phone up and they can tell me where to get this and that and financial information and all the rest of it.' We never had any complaints about spendin' too much on that Library.

I had been goin' at the leader of the Labour Group about our budget, and when he became Lord Provost I could hear my own voice as he told a full Council meetin', 'We increased the book fund. The book fund is the lifeblood of a library' – one of my own phrases. It was tryin' to get this balance for the branches, for reference and for local history and to keep the family history folk in check because they would run away with everythin'. It was a very good period and very hard work.

I retired when I was 62. There was an internal reorganisation of departments; it was '88. I probably would've stayed on, but when the offers came . . . I don't mean by that a big golden handshake but I did get an enhanced lump sum. So I've really no regrets. The only regret, and I fought this more than my retiral, was that I was a chief official, which wasn't commonplace. Being the City Librarian gave you access to a lot of people; you went to chief officers' meetin's; there was a separate Libraries Committee. Elsewhere you were under Leisure and Recreation and in some places it was Education. It's the kiss of death for public libraries to be under Education and I always fought against it. There had been arguments in '73 about where Libraries should be. I had to jive myself up to speak at one big meetin' and told them all, and the Director of Education was there. He was wantin' Libraries under him and I said, 'It's one-way traffic. Education takes everythin' from Libraries and gives nothin' back.' That got a laugh! You had to fight Education all the time. We shared buildin's in some places – branch library and community centre – and if they had trouble with the heatin' or the water, they just shut the place and we were left. We had to buy gas heaters to keep the library open and get water into the toilets. They're quite ruthless and don't bother.

I was lucky to get the opportunity to do so much in Aberdeen. Betty eventually got a job in the County Library, quite a responsible job in their headquarters. In Lanarkshire we spent a lot of money on books, servin' 300,000 of a population. Aberdeen, being a city, is more compact, an easy city to administer, a city of character with a university, a whole lot of colleges and higher education, an airport and medical facilities. It was always a prosperous city wi' the fishin', a big market town and then the oil came over and above that. I used to go down to the harbour at lunch time and you would see these funny-looking boats comin' in. I didn't know what they were doin' but they were all connected wi' the oil industry, supply boats.

Looking back over all the years, libraries now are much freer and more inviting, furnishings are better, libraries are carpeted throughout. There's also the professional organisation in Scotland which has a sort of devolution and a full-time director, Robert Craig.[51] He's a good bloke. I'm friendly with Bob. He's a nice fellow and very competent. If he's in Aberdeen he stays wi' us and gives us the gen. That helps a lot to have a man like that.

The only connection I have now is that I read a lot, and so does my wife. Every fortnight we go to the Library and a woman I worked with all the time in Aberdeen lays aside books she thinks we'll be interested in – that's the only perk I've got. Apart from that I don't run aboot to aged and infirm librarians' meetin's and that sort of thing. I don't believe in it. I saw a lot of folk that did that, and they just get in everybody's road. You soon realise that the way people looked at you was because you were the City Librarian. When you're Peter Grant, what Peter Grant says is worth bugger all. I deplore the fact that libraries are goin' through such a tough time. My wife was speakin' to this woman that's retirin' soon and she was tellin' her they've been told to stop orderin'. After all this struggle. To get up to that level and then it's just gone doon the stank and it'll take years, if ever, to build back up again because the will's no' there. I think there's goin' tae be closures and in Aberdeen there's goin' tae be curtailment of hours. Looking back, the Thatcher period was halcyon days. You may have gathered, I'm no' a Tory and have been strongly supportive of the left wing all my life, but I cannae see the pattern in the present attitude to local government at all.

Interviewed 21 January 1998

Philip D Hancock

My name is Philip David Hancock, born 23rd September 1928 in Edinburgh, 20 Marchmont Crescent, I think it was. I was an only child.

My father was a Guernsey man. He was in the Army Educational Corps,[1] a regular. He was a sergeant-instructor when I was born, stationed at Perth, attached to the Black Watch.[2] My mother wanted to come to her sister in Edinburgh so I was born in Edinburgh, then we went back. I was in a pram parked by the side of the parade ground, the Queen's Barracks,[3] in the first year of my life. My father's father was in the Army too. I'm not quite sure in what corps or regiment. On my father's side I do recollect that my great-grandmother came from Athlone in Ireland.

Mum was Edinburgh. Her father was a self-employed tailor in Ardmillan Terrace. After leaving school, she was determined to get to India somehow. She was nurse to the children of various Army colonels out in India where she met my father. She had this fascination for India and thought of being a missionary at one time. She had proper training as a children's nurse and was with one or two families in Edinburgh first. The first family she went out to India with in the early 1920s was Colonel Turnbull's; he eventually became a councillor or something in Edinburgh.

After spending my first year in Perth, my Dad managed to wangle a posting back to Guernsey, and then we moved to Reading and then to Bulford Camp[4] near Salisbury. There's a big Army training area all over the Bulford Downs. I can remember going to the Army garrison school in Bulford. We were housed in married quarters, one of the tin huts, prefabricated corrugated iron buildings in long rows, built as temporary accommodation during the Boer War. There was a sitting room and a bedroom at the front, a kitchen affair at the back, in which I had my cot or bed, and the scullery[5] at the side. Outside flush toilet for the exclusive use of the family. Then they were trying to get back to India again but ended up in Malta in 1936.

We were in Malta four years. We weren't able to go out straight away when my father went because of the Italian-Abyssinian crisis.[6] Malta, of course, was right south of Sicily, and could've been in the middle of things if anything had happened. There was a state of alert then on Malta. When we got there we found that one of the rooms in the house had been given wooden partitions outside the doors and a curtain that could be rolled down to convert into a gas-proof room, in case of gas attacks. All the time we were there we were subjected to pictures of Mussolini on his balcony ranting and raving. And the Maltese were very patriotic.

We would've lost the nice married quarter which my father had out there if Mum hadn't paid her own fare to go out privately. It was in Tigné Barracks, an offshoot of Sliema,[7] one of the main suburbs on the other side of the grand harbour from Valletta. It was a house which some previous Army schoolmaster had managed to get built for himself. It was far more opulent than a warrant officer, which my father had become by then, should've had, which was why everyone else was after it. So Dad said, 'Come out or we'll lose it.' There was a veranda, then a big entrance hall with a marble staircase going up to the top floor, kitchen, scullery, dining room and a main room on the lower floor, three bedrooms on the top and a toilet, a box-room, a bathroom and a garden at the back, and quite a big courtyard as well. Possibly the most opulent house we've lived in.

My father was a WO2[8] at first and then a WO1 but he had become the headmaster of the Army garrison school then – the school I went to in Malta. The thing I recollect about it is that there wasn't any homework. I enjoyed the school. I was always keen on English and Art. Not so much History, but History became my subject when I went to the Darlington Grammar School.

My interests as a boy were the good old toys – Hornby Railways,[9] Meccano,[10] toy soldiers. Toy soldiers especially, of course, with being in the Army. I was a keen reader. I gather I could read before I went to school. I think I started off on *Chicks' Own*. Mum used to read books to me. In Malta, I read anything from *The Magnet* and *The Modern Boy*,

The Wizard and *The Hotspur*, through H G Wells,[11] Kipling[12] and everything. I was always reading. We used to take the comics to school in our suitcases or bags and swop around.

·It was actually a five-year posting to Malta but Mum and I were evacuated in May 1940, just before Italy came into the War. We came back by ship, the *Oronsay*. My father had to stay and he got all the initial bombing but he got home in late 1941. He was transferred during the War from the Educational Corps first to the Intelligence Corps[13] and then to the Royal Corps of Signals,[14] because he was working with ciphers. Posted in London for most of the time, in the end he managed to get a posting to Scottish Command. He ended up as a captain but got out after the end of the War. He got his Long Service and Good Conduct Medal. He could've carried on but he didn't want to so he got a teaching post at Currie Junior Secondary School until he retired.

When we came back we stayed with an aunt at Darlington for a year. There was good discipline and there must've been quite good elementary education in the garrison schools because my aunt said, 'Oh, you're going to a proper school now, the Darlington Grammar School', and I discovered I was well up in everything. I'd passed the age at which they'd have sat the 11-plus, so I had a general knowledge test, an oral test and a written test and I passed and was in. Anyone who passed was in, no matter from what background they came; there were no fees, school books were provided and they had a homework programme. I was most impressed by the Grammar School, and the History master, Mr Hemingway, really brought History to life and encouraged me.

Then Mum came back to Edinburgh at the end of 1941 and I went to George Watson's.[15] I was still only 12, 13 years old but Mum had this vague idea that if you went into the Civil Service, that was good. One of my cousins was a draughtsman, so that was another possibility. I'd never thought of librarianship

There was an entrance exam much like the one in Darlington. Mum had thought of getting me to Heriot's[16] where one of my cousins had gone but Heriot's were full. But a lot of the pupils at Watson's had been evacuated to Canada, so there were vacancies. Dad was just a second lieutenant at that time and it must've been quite a thought to pay the fees. I think the fee was something like £15 a term, much more reasonable than they are now. At one stage the headmaster told Mum that I could apply for a Merchant Company[17] bursary. I got pushed back a year and started in first year at Watson's which was just as well because they'd started Latin in the junior school in Watson's so I was way behind in that. And I was no mathematician, so having had elementary Algebra in Malta, then again in Darlington and again in Watson's, I think that was what finally managed to get me through Higher Maths.

I went right up until the sixth at Watson's. I quite enjoyed it but the pressure was on. You got into what they called the U-stream – university or upper – and then you were really expected to work. Some evenings we got piles of homework. We'd protest to one master, 'We've already got Maths and History', and he'd say, 'That's none of my concern.' There was no co-ordination between departments. But there was a friendly atmosphere between the pupils and the masters. One of the things that shocked me at the beginning was that it was all Christian names at Watson's, instead of being 'You, Hancock.' It must've been a deliberate policy. There were a couple of masters who were feared, but most of them were approachable. All the masters at Watson's, of course, had the sanction of the belt. In the Darlington Grammar School, it was only the headmaster. One master at Watson's, the French master, Mr Dawson, would give what he called a quarter measure: one of the thongs, just a slight tap, for just getting a question wrong or anything. I got a couple of those, but no real hammering for misdemeanours.

In English they encouraged you to read widely. You used to hand in reading lists to one of the masters who liked to discover what you were reading apart from the set book. When I first went to Watson's there was an Art mistress who seemed to understand my sort of art. It was more the representational draughtsmanship type, which was old-fashioned at that time. The master who returned from the War and took over after her was more modern and he and I didn't really gel. A pity, but if I had gone in for Art it's a very precarious existence, and most artists find they have to take up teaching.

In the later years, there was the Highers[18] looming and you were supposed to be going in for the bursary competition for the university. I was in two minds. I both entered for the bursary competition and applied for a scholarship to the Art College. I sat the Highers and passed everything – English, Science, Maths, French, Lower History and Art. By the time I left Watson's I still hadn't made up my mind apart from knowing I was going to take History if I went to university. I didn't know what I'd do after that. I won a bursary in the bursary competition and the art scholarship didn't come up so I went to Edinburgh University. I didn't even think of going anywhere else. I was living in Edinburgh and Edinburgh University seemed the thing. In fact, all the business about moving around to other universities seems to have developed since the War. That was in 1947. They didn't want me for National Service[19] because I was medically exempt – eyesight and various other things.

In the first year you took a variety of subjects, including Economics and English. I could've taken joint honours in English and History, but I decided to concentrate on History. There was a course in British History and European History, and eventually you specialised and I took Scottish History as my special subject in the last two years. I enjoyed the course and graduated with honours, first class, in 1951.

I never thought of teaching because I had the remnants of a very bad stammer. It started when we went to Malta, and my mother always blamed a shock that we had when arriving on the boat and Dad was on a raft thing. Something came along and nearly knocked him into the water, and apparently I started stammering after that. At Watson's it was very bad, and the headmaster suggested I should go to a speech therapist and I was still gradually getting back to normal speech when I started the University. So teaching was out despite my father having been a teacher.

Nevertheless, I had thought of maybe teaching History at the University. It was Professor Croft Dickinson,[20] who taught Scottish History at the University, who first put the idea of librarianship into my mind. Professor Dickinson mentioned that he had started off in a library and then moved on, and he said that would be a good way for me, with the eventual prospect of becoming a university teacher. But first of all he got me on to compiling a bibliography of works relating to Scotland, which was a supplement to Mitchell and Cash.[21] I got a Carnegie Scholarship to do this, and I thought that this was the equivalent of doing a PhD. It was only after I'd been doing it for about a year and a half that I learned that it was just something Professor Dickinson had wanted someone to do.

Professor Dickinson had misled me but I don't know if it was intentional. He was a very nice man. It was quite a shock though and I was a wee bit aggrieved for a while. And I wasn't given particularly good instructions as to how to go about it. After I had become a librarian, I discovered all the things I should've been doing so it wasn't nearly as good a work as I would've liked to have done. That certainly did put me off academic research. For my first few years at the Library I pondered the possibility of working on some sort of thesis for a PhD but I decided I'd had enough of that by that time.

So anyway that's what introduced me to the University Library because I did quite a lot of the work on the bibliography in one of the little alcoves in the upper library hall, in the old Library.[22] I got to know members of the staff, so even before I'd finished I had an interview with Dr Sharp, the Librarian.[23] All very informal, not like the thing you'd go through now, and he said there was a vacancy if I'd like to start in the coming year. I think Professor Dickinson had mentioned me to Dr Sharp. I started in the Library in 1953 before my bibliography was finished, and I just carried that on in my spare time. The book was published in '59 – *A Bibliography of Works Relating to Scotland, 1916–1950.*[24] It didn't bring in nearly so much money as a book on model railways which I published later on.

The thought of working with books probably appealed to me, although I looked forward to joining the University staff with a certain degree of trepidation. I anticipated more variety than I actually ended up with. In fact, I had a great deal more variety at the beginning of my career than later on. I was taken on as an assistant librarian, a cataloguer, which was the routine procedure for anyone entering the staff of the Library who had good graduate qualifications. You had to be a graduate to become an assistant librarian, the idea being that you could, at a pinch, deputise for the Librarian, although it didn't actually work out that way. The idea was that I should just have a year there and then move on to the National Library but after a year I felt quite at home. I knew someone at the National Library and had a chat with him, looked around, and it didn't seem quite so friendly there – much more formal.

The cataloguers were expected to do cataloguing and other things as well, as required. I worked on inter-library loans,[25] assisted in the reading rooms, had a certain amount of time in the book-order department but all this was extra to cataloguing which was supposed to be the main thing.

We made the catalogue entry for each book, writing out a catalogue slip which was duplicated in various forms in various sheet catalogues. You had the author's heading or the society or whatever that published it, the title, other information about the number of pages and the rest. It then had to be classified according to subject. It was quite a slow process.

It was based on British Museum and Library Association (LA) cataloguing rules.[26] We had our own version of them which the Deputy Librarian, Dr Corson,[27] a keen cataloguer, was evolving throughout his career, trying to make it really logical. The logic behind it took quite a bit of grasping, but in the end you discovered it was a good system. It was almost like going back to school to learn a new subject. Dr Corson had this big sheaf of his rules but they weren't complete and when he retired in the late '60s he took them with him, so we had to then adopt more LA cataloguing rules. After that we felt that our cataloguing and our classification in particular wasn't so correct as it had been before but we had to accept it. In those days there were about half a dozen cataloguing staff. It gradually increased, then was cut back and now there are only a few trying to struggle with the new computerised catalogue.

The Library staff was small enough for you more or less to know everyone. It was generally a pleasant, friendly atmosphere. In the main building there might have been about 30 members of staff and also about 20 in the class libraries. Every subject tended to have its own class library. There might be an assistant librarian or merely a library assistant in some of the libraries. Some of them were smaller and more informal than others. It was only in the '60s that they tended to be grouped into things like Social Sciences or Science; at King's Buildings[28] the whole grouping came together. New College Library[29] was quite a big library on its own account, a Divinity Faculty library really, with a head librarian and quite a big staff under him. If you took History, for instance, there were only one or two members of the University Library staff in the Kirkpatrick Library. In the Law Faculty Library, another quite big one, there were two people there. And then each department probably had a room with books and maybe a permanent or part-time assistant for the students to consult when they were writing their essays. Even the Scottish History Department had such a room but there wasn't any official librarian there. It contained things like the Acts of Parliament.

As the Library expanded especially in the '60s, what had been the cataloguers' small part-time jobs were handed over to other library assistants. A librarian could end up with a department of, say, three or four people under him. Inter-library loans is an example of an area that expanded. When I started, I had one half of the inter-library loans, dealing with requests from other libraries for books. Then eventually that and our requests were all put under one librarian. When that became too much for him or her, other assistants were appointed and it ended up as an enormous thing. In fact, the people in charge of those services tended to become more highly elevated than the cataloguers who were left lower down, not so highly regarded as once upon a time.

Originally when I went there, cataloguing was the basic activity into which new entrants to the University Library staff were placed. Afterwards it didn't occur in that way. I was stuck with cataloguing, however, because, after a while, they began a new catalogue for the Library because the old one was a handwritten affair in what were called guard books.[30] Dr Corson evolved this new system of a typewritten catalogue with extra pages inserted for new editions, so it would be a sort of self-perpetuating catalogue. He never wanted to go on to a card catalogue. He always regarded a book catalogue as the easiest one to consult, which it certainly is, and he was always working out how you could evolve this in an ideal way. In fact, when we began considering the idea of a computerised catalogue, I acted as devil's advocate saying, 'Yes, we want computerisation, but we want it to be able to produce a book catalogue' – every couple of years, a print-out – and I still feel that would have been the ultimate answer. You could access it through VDU screens from other parts of the Library or elsewhere, but for actual consultation in the Library you needed a book catalogue. If you've got a long list of books to look up on computer it takes ages, because you've to type in every author's name, wait till it comes up on the screen, and half the time it says do this or do that, whereas previously you just flicked over the pages.

The idea that the book catalogue would be constantly replacing itself didn't quite work out because certain sections didn't replace as rapidly as others and the edges could get a bit tatty. Anyway, I and another cataloguer were put under Dr Corson and we worked on this new catalogue for, oh, it must've been ten years until it was finally completed sometime in the '70s. We were still working on it when the Library moved to George Square.[31] That was my major task in the Library.

I was also involved originally in inter-library loans which was growing all the time. We got either individual requests from members of staff for books which we didn't have and you sent off requests to other libraries, and also lists came in from the National Central Library[32] and the Scottish Central Library[33] of books which other people had requested. So you had to check whether we had those and if we had, you got the books off the shelf and posted them off. It was quite interesting because you could sometimes get involved with the people concerned and even get into correspondence with them. It became quite a sizeable job.

When we started there was still the idea that length of service would qualify you for advancement. It was quite a while before we realised it wasn't working that way and that to advance you had to apply for posts in other libraries and move around and prove yourself that way. At the beginning all you required was the graduate qualification but more and more the LA was insisting that people had their qualifications, the Associateship or the Fellowship.[34] I enquired about it at the beginning and Dr Sharp said, 'Oh, no. You don't require it.' I think it was the pressure from the LA made graduate librarians tie themselves up with the Association of University Teachers (AUT),[35] as being graduates rather than the same as public librarians. Now they require both graduate qualifications and LA qualifications. After I'd sat my final exam, I said to myself, 'I don't want to sit any more exams.' To some extent, I later regretted that I hadn't entered for an Associateship, although by that time I'd resigned myself to the fact I wasn't going to get a higher position in the Library, and possibly didn't even want it.

At some point after we'd moved into the new Library, when everything was getting bigger, it became clear there was no progression based on length of service. More people were being appointed to specific posts. People were brought in from outside to fill what were becoming the more important posts. It never really became a full-flown dissatisfaction. I can't be sure whether any representation was made to the AUT about it. Some of us did slip into higher posts. There was a period when they had an efficiency bar and that was where some of us really got annoyed, feeling we were held at the efficiency bar for a couple of years simply because we hadn't got the responsibility, say, of a department. Some of us pointed out that we were well-qualified for that. In fact, working on the new catalogue, Peter Berwick and I got some extra people to help us, but instructing them took more time than it was worth! Eventually it was accepted that we'd slipped past this efficiency bar.

Mr Fifoot,[36] who succeeded Dr Sharp, didn't have the appreciation of what was involved in cataloguing that Dr Sharp had. Dr Sharp was one of the last of the old style, scholarly, book librarians. He and I got on very well. When I was working in the book department, I'd say, 'These books on railway history are quite important', and he'd say,

'Right, well we'll take them.' Dr Sharp died in office. Dr Corson managed for a year but he didn't want the responsibility. I don't think he even applied to be Librarian. I don't think I got on so well with Mr Fifoot – he was a new broom sweeping clean. He came in the few years while we were preparing to move to the new building. In the case of cataloguing, he decided we didn't need to keep quite a few of the records and various supplementary catalogues that we had. Some were just swept away; others we kept surreptitiously because we knew we'd require them.

A later Keeper of the Printed Books was pleased we kept some of the old guard book catalogues. They were part of the history of the Library. So the strange thing is, we've got a complete set of the original guard book catalogues but the ones we'd been using before the new catalogue, we've only got half of them because half of them were thrown away. Dr Sharp was a Scot. Mr Fifoot, I think, came from Leeds University and possibly via a different course of things being done in the library to what we had done. He was a good librarian. He finally went to become the Librarian at the Bodleian.

He was followed by Miss Moon,[37] and Mr Freshwater[38] came as the Deputy. I got on quite well with them and, for example, got the task of producing a library newssheet, trying to make it more readable than it had been. It had been going for some time before that, but it was just an informal thing which could be done in odd moments. But a good way of getting information to the staff – tell them about new acquisitions and developments in the Library and also personal things like so-and-so's getting married.

I also got the opportunity to mount a few exhibitions. I enjoyed doing that. The first one was in Mr Fifoot's time actually. I was interested in coinage and suggested that we have an exhibition on decimal coinage because we'd quite a few interesting books on the subject. I'd even a coin collection in the Library which could be used. I hope they don't realise it's of some value otherwise they'll probably want to sell it! I don't know how it came to the Library but they had such things as gold nobles and Scottish unicorns – two Scottish unicorns, a very scarce and valuable coin – James I and II.[39]

The University Library almost started with donations from people: each student had to donate a book. Clement Litill[40] donated his large library of books to the University and the town – quite a sizeable collection

– and all sorts of professors and people since have donated collections. The Sarolea Collection[41] was a huge one. I put together a little collection from Professor Sarolea's H G Wells's books and pamphlets, some of which were quite scarce. For some reason they didn't want to take those and we'd to buy some of them later on at greatly increased prices. Half a dozen of us from the public library, the University Library and the National went down to his house to make a selection. The rest went to form the start of one of the red brick universities,[42] I forget which one. This sort of thing happened to me at the beginning – I was a sort of odd-job man – although it didn't happen all that often. With most donations, like those from a professor on his death, the librarian in charge of book donations would physically bring the books back to the Library and they'd be put on shelves. Originally that was part of the responsibility of the book-order department, but then that became something on its own.

Another of my first tasks was in book orders. There was a librarian and a library assistant, and recommendations for books were sent in by members of the teaching staff. Members of the Library staff could recommend books too. They also received a large number of book catalogues and would mark books that they thought would be of interest to the teaching staff or that the Library should have. Sometimes members of the teaching staff would be asked whether we should get particular books. The Keeper of Printed Books was really just one man with an assistant in a separate part of the Library.

When we first moved into the new building, we thought there's room here for ever but it's amazing how quickly it's filled up. Being a librarian has changed from being a member of a family to being a member of a large organisation. Student numbers have gone up enormously. When I went there as a student you almost felt the place was small enough to know a good many members of the teaching staff and that's expanded.

The Library move from the Old Quad into the new Library in George Square was a watershed: the much greater size of the new Library, the expansion of staff numbers – and they were becoming more scientific rather than academic – as well as the impact of technological advances. Many things were being kept on microfiche[43] or microfilm. We still had the large bound volumes of *The Scotsman*[44] and *The Times*[45] but the later volumes came on microfilm. When I first went to the Library, it had only just got a photographic department. Previously the Keeper of Manuscripts, Dr Finlayson,[46] had set up his own apparatus in a spare room and produced photocopies. There was a great deal of amateurism about our initial moves into the new world of technology which was rather fun.

I didn't come into contact with the students. There were all sorts of places where we were tucked away in the old Library. It's still a bit like that in the new Library. For example, Dr Liu, the Chinese librarian, more or less carries on cataloguing the Chinese books in his own way. I don't think anyone else quite knows what he's doing! It was the people working behind the service desk who would come into contact with the students. I only came into contact with them because I had a lunchtime period for some years in the Reading Room, issuing and receiving books. It made a nice change from the normal procedures. You felt you were in contact with the people who were benefiting from your work.

There were a number of characters on the Library staff when I first began. Mr Christie worked on the service desk, the counter as we called it in the old Library. He was the one whom the students really came into contact with and he'd been there since he was a boy, in the days when it was a much more informal set-up. I'm sure that for many of the students he was the Librarian. In fact the book issuers were junior staff really. They weren't necessarily graduates. He wasn't a graduate. When he eventually retired some of the students had a special dinner for him.

We had Harry Taylor who used to assist in the serials department. He was an intelligent man and a keen member of the Edinburgh University Chess Club. Apparently he'd been told by some doctor or psychiatrist he had to assert his personality. So this was why he boomed. Harry was good at shelving books, and when he departed we discovered that you required three people to do the work that Harry had been doing.

In the Reading Room for a long time there was Miss Purves, who, like Mr Christie, became known to the students as the Librarian, very helpful to them all. Of course, the number of reading rooms increased too. Occasionally one had evening duties and I'd get landed in a reading room. I remember on one occasion getting landed in the medical reading room, which scared me stiff because I hadn't a clue. If people were asking for such-and-such a book, I didn't know. One was at the same stage as them, just had to go and consult the catalogue and search for it. I recount another story of how a girl in the Reading Room came up and asked if she could borrow overnight this particular book for last-minute revision before her exam. It was one of the books that weren't supposed to be lent because it was in constant demand. She swore she'd bring it back first thing next morning, and of course she didn't so I was in trouble.

When I started, I anticipated getting a greater variety of work throughout my career than I actually did. After these initial years working in cataloguing, inter-library loans, book orders and so on, it then became more and more cataloguing. When we started you could catalogue a book in any subject but eventually different people became responsible for, say, English or History. After I finished work on the new catalogue, I became responsible for some years for the books in the English Department and that got you in touch with the University staff there.

We had an annual book check and there'd always be books missing but thefts weren't common. There was no physical check of the students, no turnstile gate or anything. Anybody could go into the Library, everybody had completely open access to the shelves, except to the books in the special collections. It was only when we moved to the new Library that they installed a security system with each book given a metal tag. We had a few cases of discovering people who had been stealing books. Jean Guild became suspicious of one character and was brave enough to glance in his bag and discovered these books. It turned out he had piles of books from the University Library and the National Library in his house. He had, I think, 4,000 books stolen from libraries. He'd not merely taken the books, he'd taken plates out of the books. It wasn't that he stole them to resell. He just liked books to add to his own collection.

Mr Harley, another of the old members, was in charge of the fabric of the building, dealing with workmen and such, and he used to mention that there was one book which had been lent to a Russian library during the First World War. And it had been on a ship which was sunk, so it wasn't really a missing book because we knew where it was!

There was a period that I was keen on what was then called the audiovisual collection in the Library. That was a start to the move into things other than books. As a historian, I always knew the importance of films and other media. There were already some such materials in stock but I felt it should be encouraged, and there was a librarian eventually placed in charge of that. I was always keen as a small boy on ciné, and had one of these original Bing Pathéscope[47] things and you wound the handle round and round. I've got a collection of Super 8 films on that. There are audio-tapes there as well on all sorts of subjects – historical and recollections and even a small collection on gramophone record. And they've got quite a few reel-to-reel Grundig[48] tape recorders, but the tapes are unusable on anything else now.

I was employed full time in the University Library right through until I took early retirement in 1982. I was pleased I left when I did because cataloguing in particular is not quite the same. Now it's a case of working in front of a VDU screen. Also it was getting difficult looking after my mother. They were offering quite generous terms because they were cutting back, and just a few months after I'd retired my mother had a serious stroke. So I had three years of really quite hard labour looking after her.

Looking back over my 30 years plus a wee bit in the Library, I sometimes wonder what would've happened if I hadn't. Not having advanced as far as I might have there's a certain sense of disappointment. I'd have liked to have had more contact with the teaching staff and the pupils. But then it might have worried me. In my father's Army career at one stage someone commented in his report, 'Lacks drive.' I think I probably lacked drive as well. I was quite content to be a cog in the machine rather than one of the guiding lights. I always had my other interests as well. I was keen on the history of railways and railway modelling. I've always been a railway modeller. I published work on railways. I'm probably a railway modeller who was a librarian in order to earn the shekels to make the models! I've got a gentleman coming to see me tomorrow from America, who's apparently read my writings in the railway magazines for over 40 years. I have a certain notoriety in the model railway field. More so than in the library field. At one stage I was offered the editorship of the *Railway Modeller*[49] and I thought when a hobby ceases to be a hobby and becomes the bread and butter, it would probably lose its savour.

I was quite happy at the Library. I was never what you would call a dedicated librarian but I was quite pleased to be a librarian and enjoyed the work on the whole. I don't regret having been a librarian, I still keep in touch with the Library and I periodically go in and consult things.

Interviewed 14 July 1997

Margaret Deas

My name is Margaret Deas. I was born in Edinburgh in 1934.

My parents were 'Fifers', from Leslie. We went back there for holidays and all sorts of things. I'm 11 years younger than my sister Jean. She was born in Leslie. My mother was born in Leslie, but she spent some time as a child in Kirkcaldy where her father was working in a pub. Then he bought his own one in Leslie. He was too old to go, but he died during the First World War when he was 47, and my grandmother had to sell the public house because it wasn't right for her. I think it was my grandmother who had the money, such as it was in those days, and she had a dairy. My mother's grandfather was a baker and moved around a lot because my grandmother was born in Livingston and my grandmother's parents were married in South Leith.

My father was born in 1893 and he was in the First World War – I think he must have been a conscript. He drove ambulances, then when he came home they married. Father ended up with what's now called a market garden in a nursery. He used to also go round with milk until the Co-op started in the business. They came to Edinburgh about 1923 or '24, with my grandmother who also had a dairy in Lady Lawson Street in Lauriston, opposite the fire station. I seem to have spent my life behind a counter. One of my early memories is being behind the counter of the dairy, before five years old, with my grandmother but she sold it at the beginning of the Second World War. She died in 1951.

Both my father and my mother had to work very hard. He became an insurance agent; my mother became a theatrical landlady. I was born in Cornwall Street in a flat opposite the stage door of the Lyceum.[1] In the flat below lived the Patersons who became great friends. Then *Peter Pan* came and the Patersons didn't have enough room for boys[2] and said, 'You've got a spare room, why don't you take one in?' My mother did and it went on from there, and because she was opposite the Lyceum we're not talking about horrible digs, we're talking about the top end of the market here.

When I was two they moved to Lothian Road, diagonally opposite the Regal cinema.[3] They're 19th century houses, good solid stone. Because she had these theatrical boarders the house was full of people, and I was brought up to speak to other people and be polite. It tended to be actors from the King's[4] and the Lyceum, sometimes the Empire,[5] but the Empire and the Theatre Royal[6] were slightly downmarket. My mother always encouraged them into the kitchen and they were served a meal when they came back from the theatre which would be quite late. My sister talks about having to take food up to the stage door at the King's, possibly between a matinee and an evening performance. So from an early age I was used to dealing with all sorts of people, and I think this helped me deal with the public. At the beginning of the War she stopped taking in actors because they weren't coming up and then she took in students.

When war was declared my sister joined the Wrens.[7] She volunteered. My mother didn't want her to go and father encouraged her. Before that, we had a succession of servicemen through the house, including my cousins from Fife on their way back, arriving at midnight in the Waverley Station. The house was always full of people; she ran a sort of private canteen and it was great fun. She said it was her war work. My sister was invalided out: she fell and had a slipped disc. She met a soldier from East Lothian in our church at a Burns' Supper. His name was Burns. She married him in '47 and left to become an Army wife. Then things were really bad. We needed a roof job done and there was no money to do it, so when I was about 14, they sold the flat, bought another shop and we moved to Fountainbridge, Murdoch Terrace, where the shop was. We lived in one room, a small bedroom. There was a toilet, a coal cellar, a sink at the kitchen, and I was mortified! I'd always lived in a huge house, not much money like everyone else probably, and then here I was in what I considered a slum although it wasn't really. It was very much a working class tenement street, and it didn't make any difference to my friends. So I served behind that counter, even when I'd started at the Library, until we sold the shop. From the age of 13 until the age of 60 I had a counter in front of me.

Andrew Carnegie, in the library of his home in New York, c1913. Courtesy of the Andrew Carnegie Birthplace Museum, Dunfermline.

The 'Torch of Knowledge'. Reproduced from an original enamel sign in the collection of Midlothian Council Library Service.

The reading room, Newtongrange Miners' Institute. Courtesy of Midlothian Council Library Service.

Scotland's first mobile library, introduced by Perth & Kinross County Library Service during the early 1920s. Courtesy of Culture Perth and Kinross.

Left. Andrew Fraser and Midlothian County Library Service colleagues, c1938. Courtesy of Midlothian Council Library Service.

Above. M W (Bill) Paton. Reproduced from *SLA News* Jan–Feb 1976 (No 131).

Peter Grant. Reproduced from *SLA News* Jan–Feb 1978 (No 143).

W B Paton. Reproduced from *Of One Accord: Essays in Honour of W B Paton*, edited by Frank McAdams (Scottish Library Association, Glasgow, 1977).

Joe Fisher. Reproduced from *A Glasgow Collection: Essays in Honour of Joe Fisher*. ©CSG CIC Glasgow Museums and Libraries Collection The Mitchell Library, Special Collections.

Gavin Drummond. Reproduced from *SLA News* Jan–Feb 1985 (No 185).

Alan White. Reproduced from *SLA News* Jan–Feb 1980 (No 155).

John Hunter. Courtesy of John Hunter.

Blackhall Library 1966 (Inset – Blackhall Library 1948). Both reproduced from *Lum Hats in Paradise: Edinburgh City Libraries, 1890–1990*, edited by Norma Armstrong and Alan White (Edinburgh City Libraries, 1990).

One of my mother's students who was at Moray House[8] started on me when I was four years old so I could read and write before I went to school. We didn't go to school for the first two months or so of the War. I was shoved off to Leslie; not evacuated officially, just a private arrangement. I did go to the little school in Leslie two or three times but we came back. Then I went to Gillespie's,[9] a fee-paying school, for 12 years. Some of my friends were on a scholarship but I wasn't, same with Jean. My parents worked damned hard. They only took in once a year, and my birthday's in January so I started school at five and a half in September '39 when war was declared. I don't remember anything to do with the curriculum. There was two years when you were in the babies and then another two years in the junior and then another three. By this time we knew what was going on, and you were terrified with the guns. On the big map we followed the Army in North Africa and all the way through. We were taught French in our last year, our Qualifying year,[10] and I did quite well. I can still read it better than I speak it. I was not good at sums and if I got four out of ten for Mental Arithmetic I was doing well. I was always on the literary side. The headmistress then is well known – May Andrews. She knew every child, particularly if you'd started at five. It was an incredible education. In my Qualifying year, which was 1944 – I know it was because I came home for lunch and my mother told me that the invasion[11] had begun – there were 53 people in our class.

My memories of school are happy ones. I was in the junior choir. A new word – spastic – came into our vocabulary. They were opening a special home, the first in Edinburgh, out Corstorphine.[12] About 14 of us went out and sang 'Bless This House'.[13] It was opened by the Princess Royal. I remember going to the school concerts in the Usher Hall[14] when my sister was in the choir. They were all in white dresses and black stockings.

I was an avid reader and a member of the public library. When we were still in Lothian Road, I used to walk up Johnston Terrace and go to the Library in George IV Bridge. I did have a bad bout of whooping cough and was in my bed at the time we were learning joined-up writing. I was having a great time reading and my father who was a beautiful writer helped me to do joined-up writing. I was very good at grammar and interpretation, but although I was good at English it didn't carry over into an enjoyment of writing stories or essays. I expected to have the stories put in front of me in print. As a girl I read anything: girls' stories and grown-up books on all sorts of things. When I was a girl I got *The Dandy* and *The Beano* and I think we got them because my father liked them. And I read my mother's magazines, the *Woman* and the *Woman's Own*. I never got *Girls' Crystal* but I used to get a loan of it. By this time I was reading *The Sunday Post*,[15] I was into grown-up reading. I was reading serious stuff. I passed beyond the comic stage when I was relatively young.

My mother and father were both avid readers. My mother was very keen on historical novels, and that's what started my interest in history. I was reading quite a lot, and one of the times I was quite ill I read through the complete works of George Bernard Shaw[16] because there was nothing else. I read Buchan,[17] probably at the beginning of my secondary. I even read Frances Parkinson Keyes[18] and things like that. Dennis Wheatley[19] was later on: I'd be about 14; and *The Scarlet Pimpernel*;[20] I used to read Orczy quite a lot, to the detriment of my school studies, I may add. You know how children play games, and you'd have your grocer's shop and everything? I played lending libraries. I got all my books out and had a register.

But again, I was brought up in this most historic part of Edinburgh, and for the first 11 years of my life our back windows looked out on to Edinburgh Castle. I was taken up to the Castle before I went to Sunday School and by my grandmother. I knew where Bruce and Wallace[21] were; I even knew where Earl Haig[22] was and Ensign Ewart.[23] The West Port was really bad then. The wives were still going about with shawls, with their babies on their back. I was told where Burke and Hare[24] worked. We were marched out every Sunday afternoon when it was fine to walk the Braids,[25] Braidburn valley, the Hermitage, Joppa.[26] That was the background of my childhood, part of my education because of where I lived.

I was not a good scholar and I was serving in the shop. Then when Standard Life[27] were opening a branch in Drumsheugh Gardens my mother got the job as caretaker and so we moved to this gorgeous flat in the basement there in 1949. There was a huge garden at the back, French windows. I had to help my mother clean the offices. I was about 15 at that time. That was a blight on my schoolwork because I'd to get up in the morning, and my mother and I took it week about to clean the brasses and everything. I wasn't even able to play hockey, and I was good at hockey. I'd to go along to the shop where my father had opened up and make his breakfast. I did not have a deprived childhood. I never resented any of that. Poor man, he used to get scrambled eggs every Sunday and Saturday while my mother was obviously doing things at home. Then she came out about lunchtime and father and I went to Tynecastle.[28]

The first football match I was taken to was a reserve match at Tynecastle when I was 15, 16. I kept on falling in love with different Hearts players! One of my friends' father owned the Piershill Ballroom,[29] and it was the highlight of our social year if you were invited to Margaret Dargo's Christmas party because it was held in the Ballroom. One year for her birthday, her mother and father took us all to the Sevens at Murrayfield.[30] It wasn't my introduction to rugby, because my cousin had come home from New Zealand by then. Sport was quite important to me but the only competitive one I played was when they dragged me out to play for my house.[31] But I played badminton and I was very good at athletics.

I didn't have any particular ambitions. I used to think, 'What's going to happen to me?' Because I didn't do well at the school, I couldn't sit examinations. I was ill for the last two years of my school life and it was put down to that. It didn't stop me from playing. I went to Girl Guides, Brownies[32] as well.

My parents were Church of Scotland, Thomas Chalmers' old church[33] – a big bust of him in the hall – at the corner of Lady Lawson Street and the West Port. It's knocked down. The West Port was predominantly a Roman Catholic area and some of the Roman Catholic girls used to come to our Girl Guides. I don't think we were aware of religion in Edinburgh. I certainly wasn't. There wasn't this Glasgow business. There was one Jewish girl, but that was in the secondary.

At secondary school we had a great advantage because the primary school was in the same building as the secondary and we'd already been there five years. We knew the secondary teachers, we knew where you got your lunch and we must've been right little bitches to the new ones! What made matters worse was that the new ones came in with their brand new blazers and we were furious. In secondary, I was very keen on English, Latin and History and I liked Geography. I hated Maths. I could never master Trigonometry. It was my doctor who taught me Geometry, because he'd been in to see me and I said, 'I can't get this Geometry sum.' He sat down and said, 'It's quite easy, Margaret. It's this, this, this', and from then on I understood it. French I was OK with. I enjoyed school, but I did deteriorate and I think it was to do with the home life, and I think I just frittered my time away, and examinations were strenuous. I enjoyed Art. I used to go to the art club after school. From an early age I was also learning to play the piano. We'd an excellent music teacher who played us records of classical music, and those of us good enough were in the main school orchestra from the very first year, taking part in the big annual concert in the Usher Hall. We used to have a junior choir at church as well and I was in that and took the lead in three different things.

I sat my Highers.[34] I didn't get very many! Funnily enough, I failed English, and left in fifth year when I was 17½. We never even thought about going to university. People like us didn't go to university. Girls didn't think of that, and if you did you were only going to be a teacher. A month later I started in the Library which was still being built at that time. I got the job through the school. Henry William Meikle,[35] the Historiographer Royal, was a great pal of May Andrews and I knew about the National Library because he spoke to us about it one Founder's Day. You've no idea the number of Gillespie girls that were in the National Library. I was asked to go for an interview as a typist, the lowest of the low. I did typing and shorthand, which I hated, at school. I went for the interview in my school uniform, my wee box hat. It was Beattie[36] who interviewed me, Keeper of Printed Books at that time, and when I accepted I said I would like to have a holiday before I started. After I'd retired, Alan Marchbank[37] decided to have a big dinner for me and he read out the letters that I had written to Beattie. Oh, it was awful because the place was absolutely packed.

I started the third week in July because school finished at the end of June. The first day was awful; this great big place: silent, and a grandfather clock went tick-tock – Sir Walter Scott's, incidentally. There was three steps down into this great big room, and I went in and it was so quiet! But there was a young girl I recognised because she was three years above me at school. That was when the Library had the books in the Laigh Hall[38] – all these bookcases with wire on them, a great big coal fire and old Giles, the messenger. Then these men appeared with black gowns and a white wig who had their offices in the Library along that corridor. You couldn't distinguish the National Library from the Advocates[39] use of it. It was very 19th century.

There was a kettle, we made tea and there was Donald Brown and Bob Burnett just sitting there. Then we had to take the cups away and they said, 'We go down to the vaults, through the drill hall and then we go to L.' And I'm going, 'Vaults! Drill hall! Hell!' The wash-hand basins in the ladies' toilet was where we washed the cups. By half past eleven I'm sitting with my legs crossed; I'd just come from school, and you couldn't ask to go to the toilet in school, you had to wait. By the time I got out for lunch I was desperate. I ran along to the ladies' at the Infirmary![40]

I was just a typist on Grade I. I had to go to typing school and pass in speed of typing and accuracy, and do tabulation, which meant you had to measure and work out where to set the tabs as you're typing. We were only temporary at that time and then we sat an examination and became permanent civil servants. When I started in '51, there were about five typists, and Beattie had a secretary. Marryat Dobie[41] was the Librarian and Beattie was the Keeper of Printed Books. Willie Park was the Keeper of Manuscripts. James Ritchie[42] was an Assistant Keeper. Hamish Seaton[43] was an Assistant Keeper.

When I first went to work there, you started at nine o'clock in the morning and finished at twenty to five at night. The old Advocates Library opening times were 9.30am to 4.30pm, with an hour's lunch break and a morning tea break but not in the afternoon. There was evening opening once a week. We all did evening duty, down to the lowest typist took a turn. So from the very beginning I was again behind a counter, even as a typist. You got paid overtime for the evening or maybe a half-day off. We were also open on Saturday when everyone worked until one o'clock.

At that time there were 36 staff in the Library. Everyone knew everyone else. Everyone was very polite to everyone else and people were not looked down upon. No matter what job you were doing, you got your place. We typed the catalogue cards, a special job because it had to be accurate, but I had a great advantage in knowing Latin and French. The other thing we did was the shelf catalogue, a catalogue of books as they were placed on the shelf. The cataloguers catalogued by hand or if they could type. We were trusted to write the catalogue entries into these great big volumes. Two of us used to spend a morning or afternoon with one shouting out the titles while the other would type. Quite bright in those days, the typists.

One of the interesting jobs I got as a typist was working on the big

Newbattle Collection.[44] I and another girl who had been at Gillespie's – she was just clerical officer level – stuck the labels on this collection. We went right through this incredible collection; it was French, German, Latin – marvellous. Later they had to give it back, but as part of the agreement, they went down once a year to check that the books were all there. This didn't involve me by this time because I was in a different department, but the year I left, I said to Ann Matheson,[45] 'I have never been down to Monteviot and I would like to go because Evelyn Weinstock and I put all these labels on.' She said, 'Oh, there's no problem, of course you can go.' So I went down and it was great to see them on the shelf.

That was '51, '52, '53. By this time my mother was employing two ladies from Murdoch Terrace to come down and do the cleaning. In '54 we had to move from Drumsheugh Gardens and were back in the shop. In '55 I began to feel unwell, tired all the time, got thinner. I was diagnosed with tuberculosis in the October and spent the next nine months in the City Hospital. But I did everything I was told. Luckily I had what used to be called galloping consumption, the type that responded well to the modern drugs. Sunshine, open air, was the regime: a veranda at the City. It was the middle of winter and the snow used to come down. You looked right on to the Pentlands,[46] and the birds used to fly in and out. You could hear the mice in the lockers at night. I wasn't allowed out of my bed for the first six weeks and I'd double pneumonia. Then you were allowed up once a day which meant you could go to the toilet. Then you were given what they called full toilet, meaning you could get up in your dressing gown. And then you got your clothes on for half a day.

When I was in hospital I used to get parcels from the Civil Service Sanatorium Society. I was asked if I wanted to go to Benenden in Kent, all my fare paid and my mother could go down anytime. But I decided it was daft, I didn't know anybody down there and all my friends were coming to see me. Practically everyone in that ward smoked. I did even after my experience of TB. I still have a smoke now and again. I think I must've been about 19 when I started. For our generation it was just the thing to do.

Every experience you have can teach you something and it taught me that you're not immortal. I was 21. I remember going for the serious X-rays you only got once because they were dangerous. I remember praying all the way across. You laugh about it now, but frightening! It wasn't until you went out that you realised how weak you were and you got drugs to take as well. I was out in the summer of Suez,[47] and in time to see the Hearts come home with the Scottish Cup. That summer we all went to Europe in a car, staying in youth hostels – the first time I'd been abroad.

The building of the new National Library had been stopped by the War but it opened in '56. The Sheriff Court had been there and they knocked it down and moved the Sheriff Court. When I went back I was there for the opening of the new Library. At that time, there was a trustee called J Randall Philips, and his daughter had been taken on as a cataloguer. The list of people being asked to the opening came out and we weren't on it. Some of the staff were, but it was to a certain grade. Randall Philips's daughter went bananas! She'd only been there for two years and she was on it. She told us that she'd raved at her father, and I think I'm right in saying that the invitation list was then changed and it depended how long you'd been in the Library if you were to be invited to the opening. So we did go. That is an example of the Edwardian, Victorian values that still prevailed in the Library. I think it was that year, the Earl of Crawford,[48] the Chairman of the Board, invited members of staff to go to Colinsburgh to his house for a picnic. But we weren't invited to that.

Not long after the opening of the new Library they had a new job called the superintendent of typists. *Moi*! So that was me till about 1957, and then I was promoted to clerical officer (CO). I think I sat an exam for that at some point. And I was part-time in the public area.

By this time Beattie wanted to make the Library a seat of learning and have more qualified people. It was about then that the Library's status as regards copyright changed.[49] We've always been able to select the books, but now we had this big, lovely building we extended our claims under copyright, including claims to periodicals and newspapers. It was '53, I think, the Library began to stock newspapers in a way it had not done before. We always took the books, but we extended it to a certain type of book – this was the beginning of the paperbacks. So we had to employ a lot more people and after '56 there was great burgeoning of staff. People working in the wider Civil Service[50] got a transfer to us. They started to bring in graduates specifically. The manuscript department took on extra people as well. Hamish Seaton became the Secretary of the Library, and he bought foreign books, antiquarian, things like that. There was a lot of cataloguers, so obviously they were necessary, although not so many book fetchers.

John McKernan was a great Labour supporter, always fighting for the masses. He didn't actually do it with the union but he certainly was an activist. You weren't obliged to join a union and you're still not. I became a representative of the Civil Service Clerical Association.[51] I must've joined very early. It was the lower grades that were members until there was a national upsurge of feeling about working conditions. After the War, the men came back and there was a 'I'm not goin' tae put up wi' this' feeling. Of course we were slightly different. We weren't an ordinary Civil Service department; we were a cultural department and some members of staff had not much experience of trade unionism.

During the '50s, we used to have concerts in the board room, early stuff – the Baroque Ensemble. Madame Bozoni, the singer, was quite well known, and she would come in in the morning, you would hear her singing, and then she used to go and lie down in the sick room until it was time for the concert. Nobody dared be sick at that point.

I don't know when the next promotion came but during the later '50s I ceased to be a typist and became someone who dealt directly with the readers, the public. I loved it. A lot of it's to do with my background and upbringing. I always mixed with people no problem and I've to thank my parents that even though I didn't pass anything I still had this incredible education. When I was first promoted, I spent half a day downstairs and another half day upstairs. Downstairs was what used to be called the business room, and that was where you logged all the copyright material that came in, not from the London agent,[52] but direct from publishers. Writing down a big ledger of donations which included great parcels called the colonials – government papers from the colonies – and you used to smell it: you could smell cinnamon and things like that. We weren't busy with the public at that time, therefore I used to take them upstairs and do that work there. Then they decided to change it, and instead of going up dealing with the public certain days, we would be upstairs permanently. That's when it really became interesting – finding things out. I've always been curious, wanted to know facts and things about people and what goes on.

If someone outside the Library would say, 'Where do you work?' I would say, 'In the Library on George IV Bridge. Not the public library, it's the one on the other side.' 'Oh, you mean the one where all the clever folks go?' When someone says that, you know straight away you're going to have difficulty explaining what we actually did. It's not just clever people that come in.

People would wander into the Library by mistake and the men at the front would shepherd them away unless we got a difficult one. We had some weird ones, particularly on a public holiday when the public library was closed. One Monday holiday this man came in and you could see that he was ill at ease. He said, 'I want a book on dogs.' I said, 'What kind of book do you want? Illustrations? Do you want to know how to bring up puppies?' He leans forward and says, 'Ma dug's got fleas.' I took a step backwards and said, 'I don't think any of the books are going to help you. You need a vet.' He says, 'But they're all closed.' I said, 'No, they won't all be closed. Come on, let's have a look.' So we got the directory out and I managed to get an emergency vet. 'Thanks, hen,' he says, and away he goes down the steps.

There's many an argument when you had to tell someone they couldn't get in. 'I pay my taxes the same as everybody else' sort of thing. Then you had to explain that was why there was a public library, and the way you could get through to them was by saying, 'You can get that book over there. If we were to let all our books be read by anyone or everyone, they would not be there.'

Most readers were polite and grateful for any help. It was really the eccentrics. One of the occupational hazards was that you got people that the public library wouldn't tolerate. There was a museum curator at the Highland Folk Museum. She was never abusive, just difficult to deal with, an eccentric. She used to write as well. There was Willie Parker and he seemed to be almost like a member of staff. He was a journalist, an expert on Scott, Stevenson and things like that. He was in all our lives for years, always wanting books and things like that. Once he wasn't able to come in, he invited me out to his house in Murrayfield, and it was the first time I'd ever tasted Madeira and little biscuits. He was a nice old soul. After a certain time they become harmless!

We'd a tremendous amount of people from the Royal Edinburgh Hospital. It seemed to attract people who were looking for somewhere quiet. That sometimes could be difficult. One man used to lie down on the floor. There was once a guy holding a knife, but we did manage to get rid of him. There was another fellow, we thought he was a journalist or something like that, and he started shouting at the staff. He never came into the Library for three months after that. Not long before I left, someone said to me, 'There's a man crying in the reading room.' It turned out to be a patient from the Royal Edinburgh. I got in touch, explained what had happened, we put him on a bus and they said they'd meet him at the other end. We had a West African in and he began to behave very peculiarly, and started putting candles all round. We had to get in touch with the University and they had to get in touch with the Nigerian High Commission in London because this was the son of one of the paramount chiefs. He was shipped out.

But give the staff their due – I must have dinned it into them – you made no difference between one reader and another. George Pottinger[53] spent all that terrible time between being suspended and his trial in the National Library. He was writing a book. He was all right, no problem. I think he appreciated the fact we just let him get on with it.

There was always a challenge. I was downstairs in the stack floors, and there was a phone call to say, 'There's one of the readers telling us they've seen a man cutting pages out of a book.' He had left about a quarter of an hour previously. We had to find out which books he'd had out, who had spoken to him. Eventually the CID came and by then I'd discovered that he'd had out a volume of 19th century golf pamphlets all bound in and the rules of some of the oldest golf clubs. That was on the Tuesday and they were all at The Belfry for the Ryder Cup on the Thursday. I thought, 'He's down there, selling them.' Nothing happened. Then after I retired there was a phone call to the Library from someone in America who said, 'We've got something here that's got the Advocates Library stamp rubbed out.' It was one of these pamphlets and they were sent back.

I actually saw a guy use a razor blade on a book. I nabbed him. You've got to be fearless. Readers don't like to report things but you can't be standing over someone all the time. Most readers would be quite good, particularly the ones that started as undergraduates, graduates, and became authors, scholars. Ian Rankin,[54] for instance. He came as an undergraduate. We knew Ian Rankin. There used to be a member of staff seated at a desk in the middle of the reading room to keep an eye on readers. That was all right when there was only maybe 50 in the room, but when you had 156, you couldn't. Then they put the mezzanine floor in and you'd have to have somebody else up there. I'm not sure about security staff because it's such a soul-destroying job. They're wandering around probably thinking what they're going to have for tea or how their football team is doing. They might see something, it might not register.

One of the biggest problems we had, although not so much at the beginning when I was just a junior, was the admittance of university undergraduates. We did allow a few in but they had to have personal letters. They had to be honours students. Just after the War there was a tremendous influx of Americans. They'd all been in the Forces and were given scholarships and most of them were theological students. The girls got to know them quite well. Then there was an influx of Greeks and Egyptians through British Council scholarships. That was the beginning of the increasing numbers of our readers. Then we got the Indians and they read everything, but only if they were post-graduate did we allow the medical people in. Thereafter things became a little difficult because Willie Beattie's daughter became a student at Edinburgh University. Therefore admittance was extended, particularly to arts students, and we'd a dreadful time.

We were having trouble with History of Art students and the staff said, 'Some of these books are in bits', and we discovered English literature, and all sorts, were falling apart. And some of them were paperbacks that could be got in the public library. This was just through constant usage when there was too many people in there under false pretences. They were only supposed to read books they couldn't get. We used to get quite a lot of young lecturers from England, rather languid young men, and they couldn't understand why their students weren't allowed to see it because they needed it. It was difficult to deal with them. Some of them were just awful. So we summoned some of the senior lecturers, and, looking at this book dated 1936, I said, 'If we'd allowed anybody in there, your students would not be able to have what you call essential. Part of our remit as a copyright library is to keep and preserve.' That was the only way we got through to them. That's what people don't understand. They don't realise that we wouldn't get the copyright otherwise.

The expansion started during the early '60s. Things became more difficult when you got the bolshie students, particularly the first student Rector of Edinburgh University, Gordon Brown.[55] He didn't come in very much but he was in saying that they should be allowed in, that they were the same and why shouldn't they get . . . Robin Cook[56] was OK. Apparently he was sitting with his feet up on the table in the days when the men used to come round and hand out books, and John Allen had said to him, 'Please remove your feet from the table, Mr Cook.' He still used to come in during the recess and during elections before they went into office. Jonathan Miller[57] came when in Edinburgh with the Cambridge Footlights. I knew John P Mackintosh.[58] He came to the old building, when he was either in his last year or in his post-graduate year at Oxford. And he came in after he became an MP.

The years when Beattie was Librarian were exciting, things were happening. He never had time to write a great deal. He was interested in early Scottish books. Not long after I started, Dobie retired and they had the interviews. At that time the Lord President of the Court of Session, Lord Cooper,[59] who everybody trembled at, was Chairman of the Board. I was picked out of the typists to help Beattie's secretary serve the tea, and of course Beattie got the job. I'd known him from very early on. He either liked you or he didn't like you; you liked him or you didn't like him.

Beattie was followed as Librarian by Dr Denis Roberts.[60] He was Northern Irish and so was Irene, his wife. I knew him very well and I know his wife so well. He'd worked in the Library as Assistant Keeper in manuscripts, and then he went to Trinity College[61] as Librarian there. A different person altogether and these were entirely different times, and the Department of Education, that, I think, was in charge of us, were becoming difficult. That was the '70s and there was a squeeze on Library funding, and there was great changes in staff and in thinking. Professor Roberts wanted to allow access to senior school pupils, which I was very much against. However, they got stopped.

I cannot think that senior school pupils need to use the National Library any more than Open University students do. That is a big bone of contention. The public library in Edinburgh undertakes to have a copy of every book needed by the Open University. With school pupils, that was the time they were doing Sixth Year Studies and what they used to have to ask for, I could probably have answered all the questions without looking at a book! What one should do is not allow the pupils in but have a seminar for them and teach them from the books, let them look at the books. What were our books going to be like? One of our duties is conservation. These books could be made available somewhere else and we've got a damn good public library.

The inter-library lending service[62] has gone by the board now. It's too expensive both to readers and to libraries, and the public libraries are not buying any books because they've got no money. I come back to this conservation concept maybe because I'm a National Library and copyright library person through and through, but that is a function of the Library. We wouldn't be able to look at some of these books today that are 200, 150 years old and which are still needed if the Faculty of

Advocates hadn't looked after them. What's maybe a seminal book on a subject just now might in 50 years' time be necessary for somebody to write a PhD and it might not be available. We were thinking of future generations, not just the present. The present generation and those ruling over us don't seem to have any foresight or idea that what they're benefiting from now is what other people did years before.

Latterly, a much bigger part of our work was dealing with correspondence, letter enquiries, and I vetted every single one. The job got bigger and bigger and they cut down on the answers. Doing things for authors was very interesting, and they're always very generous. They weren't all academic questions. In fact, most of them came from ordinary people, including a tremendous amount from America. Family history was the bane of our lives and puts you against genealogy, but I'm more interested in it now and I'm going to do it for the sake of the younger ones. There was a letter of complaint written to Denis Roberts about me. A visitor asked about the MacGregors and I gave him all I knew about them and said, of course, they were like all the others: they were thieves, robbers. He wrote and complained and said, 'My ancestors were called thieves!' Hilarious. There was a time when you just did not ask Australians where they came from. Now every Australian wants to be descended from a convict.

One of the saddest things I'd to deal with was a probation officer who wrote to me from Northern Ireland and asked if I could find out something on behalf of one of his prisoners. It turned out that his father had murdered either his mother or somebody or other. The probation officer phoned me up and said, 'Thanks very much for doing that. The fellow's very grateful.' A couple of years before I left, this prisoner wrote to me himself. Wasn't that lovely? People don't realise that you are doing a lot of good work for others.

Many of the staff became friends and are still friends. There's seven of us meet every month and we were all contemporaries; apart from one, we were all in the Library at the same time when we were young. I've been interviewed on the radio about my work in the Library. My picture was even in *The Sunday Post*. My whole working life was in the Library and I've no regrets at all. I thoroughly enjoyed it all the time I was there. Had I married, it would've been different. I would've left. But I didn't marry and worked there for 42 years. We're into the computer age. I knew it wasn't going to involve me. I had to retire. I would've sat down and learnt it with everyone else. I certainly wouldn't mind being on the Internet but I've not got any room and I've not got any money. I've not got a computer, but there's a great danger that if I had it I would never be off it. As I've not, I read books all the time.

Interviewed 26 January 2001

Margaret Crawford

My name is Margaret Moffat Crawford. I was born in Edinburgh on the 1st August 1936. I'd one brother; just the two of us. He was a year and eight months younger than me. He died when he was 53. He'd a lot of illnesses. He had scarlet fever when he was about nine months old. He had a mastoid. When he was seven, and my Dad was away in the Army, he took diphtheria. I've often thought it must have been a dreadful time for my mother. He was very ill and was in hospital for a long time. He had to learn to walk again. I think that maybe did damage to the heart. He had his first heart attack when he was about 35 or 36.

My father was born in 1904. There was eight in the family and his father died quite young. He was a ladies' hairdresser. Work was very scarce at that time and I remember him saying the only openings were a chiropodist or a hairdresser and he didn't fancy working with people's feet. Both my parents lived in Glasgow originally, and he was trained at Tensfeldt's in Glasgow, which was quite a well-known hairdresser, but they'd to pay for their training. Then my Dad got a shop in Princes Street, Edinburgh, a rented shop. It wasn't a big place, a sort of office space. I can just vaguely remember the old dark wood cubicles. He had one assistant and a receptionist. He didn't have it all that long. When the War came he was called up, probably in 1940, so he'd to give up the shop. After the War he worked with Gilmour and Brown in Hanover Street, and then eventually got his own place again near Haymarket, in Maitland Street, and he'd two or three of a staff. He worked there till he retired. Not a well-paid job, even latterly when he got his own shop. His clients were all getting older, people didn't go all that often to hairdressers and he didn't like to put up his prices.

I didn't know either of my grandfathers; both died when they were about 50. My paternal grandfather was originally from Glasgow, but he was a bowling green keeper, and moved around and so my father was born in Carlisle, which he kept very quiet. He was the only one born over the border. Then they moved to Lockerbie and then came up to Glasgow. Two of my Dad's brothers were green keepers in Glasgow.

My father's mother was still alive when I was growing up. She was a Glaswegian, too. With six boys and two girls, she brought the family up with a rod of iron from all accounts. She would have very little, although the income from the older ones would help. In fact, my Aunt May, the youngest of the family, and Uncle Jimmy decided they wanted to get married, but my grandmother said no, they would need to wait a year. May's sister had got married, and my grandmother couldn't afford another wedding as quickly. So the two of them booked the Registry Office and got married. Well, they were separated – he was sent home, she was kept at my grandmother's; arrangements were made for a proper wedding and she'd to wear her sister's wedding dress.

My mother went to secretarial college after she left school and worked in an office, in exports. She could do shorthand and typing. When she got married she gave up work and then when my Dad got his business after the War she worked as his receptionist. By that time the family were away so she'd more time. My mother's father was a station-master in Glasgow but he died when my mother would be just in her teens. My Mum's mother lived till she was about 87. I knew her very well. Her parents had a fruit shop round about Hamilton. She used to talk about going to balls and things like that when she was young. She gave me a fan and it was like swansdown.

My earliest memory is growing up in a house in Carrick Knowe,[1] the four-in-a-block type – Mactaggart & Mickel.[2] We were downstairs. We were right across from the Union Park, plenty children around to play with. I went to Murrayburn Primary School at Sighthill and we got a bus. It didn't take long and we came home at lunchtime. It was a great school, quite a big school and there was always a double intake.[3] The classrooms were downstairs and upstairs, all to one side, and in a wing there were the hall, the sewing room and things like that. We had about 30 pupils in our class. The teachers were all very good. I liked reading but once got the belt: when I was in Primary 7 I was reading a book under the desk and he caught me. Of course I didn't say anything when I went home, but my Mum must've gone to the school and he said, 'Her face haunted me the whole weekend. She looked at me as much as to say, "I never thought you would do this to me."' He wasn't really the type of person that used the belt very much. I probably had been warned a few times. I definitely did not like drawing. I loved sums – Mental Arithmetic I thoroughly enjoyed.

I enjoyed the primary. I sat the Qualifying Exam.[4] I was at the top. If you got above a certain grade, you went to a senior secondary school. I went on to James Gillespie's.[5] You'd to sit an exam to get in. I was the only one in my class and there were two in the class below me. It was fee-paying but it wasn't as expensive as the likes of Heriot's or Watson's, although you had to buy your own books and your own sports equipment. There was a bursary and one girl went from our school on a bursary and didn't have to pay fees, but I didn't get a bursary. When I got to about third year, if your marks were high enough, the next year you didn't have to pay fees. So in the fourth and the fifth my parents didn't pay fees for those years.

I found the transition from Murrayburn to Gillespie's difficult at first. I would be just turned 12 when I went to secondary school. At Murrayburn you were top of the class, the playground organiser and then you went to this school. Some of them had come from the primary at Gillespie's so they all knew each other. A lot of us didn't know anybody else. The other two who had gone from Murrayburn had been in another class. I was in the top class of the first year, I worked hard at school and my parents always made sure I had my homework done. When it came to the first exam though, instead of being first or second as I had always been at the primary, I was about 20th. My parents didn't make any fuss about it. They said, 'You're in amongst an elite group.' Another difference from Murrayburn was that it was a purely girls' school. I liked that. In fact, after I left school and went into the Civil Service,[6] if you were under 18 you had to go for day release to the Regent Road Institute.[7] There were boys in the class and I remember saying, 'Thank goodness I went to a girls' school', because they were pests.

You had to wear a uniform with a wee nurse's hat and if you didn't wear it – boy! But I didn't find there was any snobbery, not in the school itself or in the teachers. When I was older and maybe going to dancing, we used to laugh – 'What school did you go to?' That is an Edinburgh thing. When I went into an insurance company at that time banks and insurance companies would not take you if you hadn't been at a fee-paying school.

At Gillespie's, I enjoyed languages. I loved Latin. I'd Latin and French from the beginning, and then in the third year I took on German. If you did all right in your two, you could take German as an extra subject. Two days a week we'd to stay on after school for a period to fit in the German class. Normally, we would finish at half past three, so that would be ten past four, and then people on the buses used to complain about school children: 'They shouldn't be on the bus at this time.' It was a long day, and then we'd a lot of homework. I enjoyed Maths as well although I wasn't so keen on Geometry. I dropped Science very gladly at the end of third year to concentrate on languages. Most of the teachers were women. There weren't many male teachers although our Science teacher was Mr Brash, there was a Music teacher, Mr Somerville, and there was a Maths teacher, a wee man. The teachers all wore gowns. When we went into the third year, we got Miss Marr, a Maths teacher, as a form teacher. A lot of the classrooms had double desks with fixed seats, but this classroom had separate tables and chairs, and she made us practise standing up and putting the chair back quietly. We were all terrified of her but she was a great Maths teacher. One of the PE[8] teachers, Miss Anderson, was a great country dancer. We did a lot of country dancing. She'd a lot to do with the Scottish Country Dance Association and made up dances as well. You did gym in your bare feet and your navy pants and blouse, and she inspected your nails. No rings or earrings, you weren't allowed anything like that.

I enjoyed Gillespie's and made friends quickly. I didn't go home for lunch. There was a school dinner hall but I was faddy about food at that age. I always loved soup. Well, we only got soup once a week and there was an awful lot of milk puddings and things which I didn't like. So sometimes I would take dinners and other times, when I got older, a crowd of us sat in the classroom and had sandwiches.

I remained at Gillespie's until I left in 1953 at the age of 17. I did five years. I sat my Highers.[9] I got A passes in English, French, Latin, Maths. When you got to fourth year, you took either History or Geography but didn't spend as much time, so they were done on a Lower[10] basis. And the German, because we'd taken it on late, was a Lower. It was four Highers I got and two Lowers and Arithmetic. Not all that long before I took my Highers if you failed in one subject you didn't get a certificate. The certificates came out at school; they weren't posted. You would sit in the music room and your name was called and you got your certificate and, 'Look, see how I got on.'

I left at the end of the fifth year because of the homework, especially in fourth and fifth year. You were sitting most week-ends with a lot of homework to do. At that age you've got other interests. I was always a reader. I joined the public library when I was about seven – Corstorphine Library. It was a great wee library. You tip-toed in and out and you'd sometimes get your hands examined. I did enjoy reading. I got lost in a book. I didn't know what was going on round about me when I read. I preferred books to comics but my brother and I got the *Radio Fun* delivered to the house. My Dad was a great reader of newspapers and got the *Express*[11] and the *Evening News*[12] and on Sundays he got the *Sunday Express*[13] and *The Sunday Post*.[14] I remember the cartoons, *Oor Wullie*[15] and *The Broons*[16] in *The Sunday Post*.

My parents were regular churchgoers, and I went about the church a lot because it was the centre of Carrick Knowe, so I still kept up with my friends there. I went to Sunday School most Sundays although often at school holidays we were through at Glasgow at relatives. I couldn't really sing but I was in the junior choir. I went to the Band of Hope[17] and got a copy of *Pilgrim's Progress*[18] for good attendance. I went to ballet for a long time. I'd been on the train to Glasgow and, because I'd a high instep, this lady said to my Mum, 'Oh, your daughter's got ballet feet. You'll need to send her to ballet.' So I went to ballet when I was seven. I loved it. I was in the Brownies and went from the Brownies to the Guides[19] and somebody came to the Guides and did country dancing. At that time we entered competitions and had country dances in the church hall.

As a girl I had a bicycle and went all over the place. We used to go to Gogarburn. You could cut through Broomfield and there was a path through and we went to the river for picnics. Often we went up Corstorphine Hill. It was perfectly safe. Other interests: I had a book with scraps in it and I had another book with film stars. You cut them out of magazines and swop. There was seasons for everything: skipping, your peerie and whip which you decorated. We played outside a lot. We played games on the road: tig and leevoi, umbrellas and banana-slides, peevers, statues, games where you'd to get from one pavement to the other.[20] With the park opposite, when they were cutting the grass you waited till they were away and then the grass used to get made into houses.

And you made up games. We played cricket at school. Corstorphine and Carrick Knowe both had cricket teams; Carrick Knowe had two teams, and the second one was for the younger ones. There were no girls in the teams but we followed the cricket team and did the scoring. I played tennis because there were tennis courts in Corstorphine but not an awful lot. At school we did running in the summer and hockey in winter. I went to badminton in the church when I was older.

The year the War started, we were at Burntisland[21] for summer holidays but we'd to leave the house because it had been requisitioned by the Admiralty. During the War nobody got away. After the War I remember being at Kirn[22] one year on holiday and then we went to Leven.[23] When I was about 11 or 12, we started going up to Stonehaven[24] and that lasted for a long time. We didn't go to hotels but had 'rooms with attendance', and then we got in with this old lady and went to her for a number of years. My Dad was a bowler, and there was two bowling greens in Stonehaven. We went the first fortnight in August and the same people would go year after year. I thoroughly enjoyed it. There were about 14 or 15 tennis courts and if you didn't get along early in the morning and get your name down, you'd had it! You went to the open-air swimming pool in the afternoon. When we were older, they had dances in the town hall. The harbour, Dunnottar Castle,[25] you could go walks along the cliffs. Oh, it was a great holiday place.

As a girl, I always fancied being a nurse. Then when my brother, Dougie, came out of hospital, he said, 'Sis, you don't want to be a nurse and have to empty these bed pans.' It didn't really put me off but my Mum was against it. In those days, you did what your parents advised. After I left school I joined the National Hospital Service Reserve[26] and went into the Red Cross.[27] When I was in the Civil Service I was allowed a week off a year to do training at the convalescent home beside the Zoo. It's a nursing home now.[28] You went to the Red Cross once a week and had classes. You sat exams: First Aid and home nursing.

Other than the nursing, when I was coming to the stage of leaving school I really didn't know what I wanted to do. At that time, getting into the Civil Service was a big thing so I sat the Civil Service exam while I was still at school. I got the position and more or less started when I left school. It was the Ministry of National Insurance, down in Leith, Commercial Street. There was about 30-odd of a staff. The No 1 bus went from Carrick Knowe to the foot of Easter Road but mostly I walked because your pay wasn't all that big, and I could cut down through the Links.[29] I started at 8.30am and worked till five and on Saturday morning as well till about 12 o'clock. I had an hour for lunch. There was a staff room and a cooker. You'd maybe get a tin of soup or there was Crawfords[30] on the Shore where we would go an odd time for a snack. If the weather was good, some of us used to go along to the Links, sit there and get some fresh air.

My appointment was Clerical Assistant. It was a great office, a friendly office. They had a wee social club, and we had Hallowe'en parties, we went out – not ten-pin bowling, it was skittles. I still keep in touch with some of them, although a lot of them now have passed on. There was nobody of my age group when I started. They were all into their 20s: 50/50 men and women. The work was very interesting. I was moved around all the different departments. The office handled sickness benefit, industrial injury benefits, there was a finance section, a pensions section which dealt with retirement pensions and a section which dealt with contributions queries. There were two offices of this type in Edinburgh: there was one in George Street and we covered Leith, Trinity and Ferry Road, Pilton, Granton. Then there was a public counter as well, the Labour Exchange,[31] which was separate. I loved going on the public counter; it was quite an eye-opener. Somebody once told me he was going to put my nose in a sling, but because I was younger they weren't too bad with me. By the time I left – that was three years I had been there – I had been round most of the sections.

When I first began my pay was about £12 a month, just over £3 a week, and was handed over to my Mum. She gave me back enough to cover bus fares, and if I was going somewhere, to a dance or something, I would just get the money. But £3 a week was not enough for me to have said, 'Right, I'm going on my own', and clothes were expensive. There was an annual increment on your birthday.

After three years I left the Civil Service. At that time, there was a big move on and a lot of the work was being transferred to Newcastle. There was no way I could have afforded to live away from home and I just didn't want to go. I thought about doing primary teaching, and I went to Moray House[32] to see about it but I would have had to study and go back to no pay. Then I thought about nursing again but I was goin' to have to move into a nurses' home and no kind of income.

I don't know how I heard about this, but I went to the Scottish Union

& National Insurance Company,[33] a big company. The head office was in St Andrew Square. You'd to go for an interview, have a medical and then I started. It was a big, very old-fashioned office, like something out of Dickens. There was the long line of wooden desks with stools. Spiral staircases that went up to where the files were. Initially, I went into the new proposals department, and then got a shift to the actuarial department, which suited me down to the ground because I'd always been interested in figures. It was a friendly office; they had dances every year, you went to the Insurance Ball in the Assembly Rooms[34] – that was all the companies – and you had your own dinner dance.

I travelled in by train from Corstorphine. My brother used to run me up the road and the guard was waiting with the door open, throwing me in! Then I met Betty Ramsay on the train. She was my Brown Owl[35] when I was in the Brownies. I'd gone through Guides and went into Rangers[36] for a short time. By that time, I was working at Leith and it was such a long day that I stopped going to the Rangers. So before I knew where I was, I was helping at the Brownies. Apart from maybe four or five years, I remained attached to the Brownies until three years ago. By that time I'd started the badminton as well, and I was at the Red Cross too. Then I went to the League of Health and Beauty[37] for a wee while. I still went to odd country dances but I didn't do it on a regular basis.

My hours at the Scottish Union & National were nine till five, and we had about an hour and a quarter, an hour and a half at lunchtime, because I went home.[38] In those days at lunchtime you had your lunch and it did have to be ready on the table. Apart from maybe once a month when you got your salary you really didn't eat out. It was a high tea you had at night. I worked on a Saturday at first but it went to every second Saturday. We got Christmas and when I went through to the west I was amazed how many places worked on Christmas Day. In 1964 I got married and at that time my husband worked on Christmas Day. Pay at the Scottish Union & National was done in grades. The insurance companies were quite good and I moved quite quickly up the grades, and by the time I left in December '63 it was about £800 a year; it was quite a good salary. When I was in the Civil Service and the Scottish Union & National I never joined a trade union and there was never any pressure.

I'd been working at the Scottish Union & National seven years and when I left it was to get married. My husband was from Hurlford.[39] He worked with his father and uncle who had a haulage firm and coal business and they had a garage there. I got married and moved to Hurlford. I didn't get a job at first. I wasn't rushing to get anything. I wanted to get settled in but after two or three months I went into the National Insurance Office in Kilmarnock on a temporary basis. Then I was expecting so I had to leave; Gordon was born in April and I didn't go back to work.

At that time, Duncan McClements, assistant minister at Carrick Knowe Church, was coming to Hurlford as minister. He got involved in the community and started up a lot of things, including a playgroup, a story time and he got me roped in to take his Brownie Pack although I was actually a member of the other Church of Scotland in the village. His wife and I did the story time in the Library and that was how I got started. The lady working in the Library was leaving to work in Kilmarnock College library, and she said, 'Why don't you apply for it?' I wasn't very happy about applying because I had two children. That was 1974, Gordon was nine and Gillian was about seven, and the school was very near the house. They were home at lunchtime every day.

The interview was in a huge room in the County Buildings at Ayr with three or four, including the Director of Education, sitting behind the table at the far end. You'd to walk up and sit and they were all firing questions. However, I was told there and then that I'd got the job. I don't think I slept for about three nights wondering if it was the right thing to do. But it was part-time with very suitable hours and it worked out. I only worked four days a week. On Monday I worked from two till seven-thirty, and the Library closed for an hour between five and six so I could go home; Tuesday was ten till one; Thursday was two till five; and Friday was two till seven-thirty. The hours suited the children because my husband was in. The business had been sold when the uncle and his father retired so he was there for the children coming home. It was 18 hours a week the Library was open, although you were paid for 21 hours, including three hours' background time for preparation behind the scenes, which was good, because it was busy at that time. At the end of the day you'd to count the issue,[40] record it in a book and deal with the money. By that time, I'd started the Brownies and they were a Wednesday afternoon so that worked in as well. It got me thinking that if Duncan McClements hadn't come to Hurlford, I might never have got involved in the Brownies, I might never have got into the Library.

It was a library assistant post; I've never gone through training to become a chartered librarian. Working at Hurlford was like being in limbo. I had two weeks' training with the lady who had been working there. After that I worked on my own and if I was on holiday, I'd to get somebody to come in. There was no phone, you had no contact with anybody. If I hadn't gone to my work nobody would've known. Every six months you boxed up so many books and sent them to Ayr, and you got another lot of books. Luckily, I'd only a year of that.

I had a stock of about 7,000 books although it was all just the same stock. You really weren't getting much new stock. The larger part of the stock was fiction and the Library was used by regular readers for light reading mainly. The lady before me had started this system to record on the date page who had read any particular book. For example, one gentleman who read Westerns was identified by the number 51, and I would write 51 in pencil on the page, so that when he came back, all he needed to do was open the book and if it didn't have 51 on the date page, he knew he hadn't had it before. The same system was done with ladies that read Mills & Boon[41] books. It was quite handy because when they got older and weren't able to come to the Library, if somebody else came to choose books for them I could pick something they hadn't had before. It was on the date page so you weren't defacing the book. There was a good selection of non-fiction but it wasn't used much. Some miners came in and railway workers looking for railway books. Some of the classics were still read in those days, probably more by women than men, and the older ones. You would get school pupils in with their reading lists. You did get a lot of the children in at that time, but then the secondary schools started their own libraries.

We came under Ayr County when I started, but that just lasted a year and then it was reorganisation.[42] When Kilmarnock and Loudoun[43] came in, the hours were extended because the Librarian believed that a library shouldn't be closed two days in the week. So the hours were changed and it was open every day, Monday to Saturday, 22 hours a week, and we'd no background time. Again it was mainly afternoons and evenings, so it still worked in, although it was every day, so you didn't get a day to yourself, and you were working till one o'clock on a Saturday as well. At that time my parents were still living and I couldn't get away till a Saturday afternoon instead of a Friday night although we had a car by that time. It wasn't a serious problem, however, as far as working in with the children, and it was a Wednesday morning I was open, so that fitted in with my Brownies in the afternoon. I was still working on my own, although if you were on holiday or off sick somebody was sent from the Dick Institute[44] to cover, and eventually they did put the phone in, which was a big benefit. There was much more contact with the headquarters in Kilmarnock and you felt you were part of a service then. Things improved and the stock improved as well. And it was much easier having a request system because prior to that there really wasn't one and there was nobody I could go to to get books for somebody unless it was serious non-fiction for which you might have gone through Ayr.

There was a good, well-used junior section and quite a number of children came in as readers. We eventually started up a story time which began with a teacher bringing her Primary 2s to change books every so often. Then they started up story-telling throughout the libraries, and so the infant departments came on a Wednesday morning before the Library opened and I told them stories or read stories. I loved it. When the children came, I told them about the Library and where the books were, so that encouraged them. Children's reading was very popular then but that has tailed off. Children are not reading and they're not reading the same type of book now. They're happy sitting in front of a television set, being entertained. It's quite tragic. The story time has carried on through the years, however, and you get a small nucleus who are readers, who will come back. There aren't all that many of them though, and once they go to secondary school they've certainly got a better library there now, but they don't remain as readers.

Somebody was doing a survey into problems with vandalism and behaviour in libraries. I have never had that problem because the children have come from the school, they know the Library, know me and I live in the village. They've always been very well behaved. Things got worse in some of the libraries – there was one closed altogether in a bad part of Kilmarnock because of vandalism. It had a flat roof and wee boys were standing on the roof piddling on people coming out, and sending dogs in and flinging fireworks in. Oh, they'd a dreadful time in that bit. One of the other libraries in a big housing scheme stopped opening at night because of the problems. Because of these problems we were asked to say we did not want to be on our own at night in the Library. Hurlford was all right but my husband said, 'That's selfish.

Just because you're all right', so I signed to say that we should have somebody else on with us in the evenings. So, the two nights a week the Library opened six till eight we have 'double-manners': there are two of you and you're not on your own at night.

It was quite a help because we started book rotations[45] which involved boxing the books, changing the despatch details on the boxes, shelving the books. That was a lot of extra work and, as usual, you were just left to get on with it. You'd no background time. And they brought paperbacks in, which a lot of staff didn't want but they lasted better than expected, and they were getting two and three books for the price of one. There was a lot more work put on to us. The book rotations were good: large print and the paperbacks, and at times we did the non-fiction and an odd time we did the fiction as well. You just had to fit it in.

Again, I didn't join a union, although they did try to talk me into it. There was a strike for something and I didn't go on strike. They couldn't make me go on strike because I wasn't a union member, and I'm saying, 'I can't go on strike. Imagine my Brownies passing the Library and the Library's closed because Mrs Crawford's on strike.'

Once we went into Kilmarnock and Loudoun, there were all sorts of courses to attend: health and safety and I don't know how many customer-care courses I was on. Crazy! I was never inclined to do library training although there were such schemes available. I still had my family, I had the Brownies, I was involved in the church and it wasn't going to make any difference to me at the end of the day. I had all the experience I needed for anybody wanting information, and I knew just about all the books and authors in Hurlford Library. You were part of the community and if somebody wasn't well, they would phone up and I would take books round. I used to take books to the sheltered housing unit. There used to be keen readers there at one time but not now. Whether it's television or maybe more people are staying in their own home, I don't know. The ones who are going into these places now are maybe past reading. I used to have quite a lot of people there, and they liked the big print books and it's human contact as well.

I retired last year. The Library was being computerised and I should have been computerised earlier but there was a break-in that postponed things for a wee while. I kept saying, 'I want to wait on and see it up and running, and get the experience of the computer myself.' Well, I had the year, and we got a bit of training, not an awful lot. I enjoyed working with the computer. Certainly for book reservations it is good. You could just bring up an author and a title and find out what library it was in, if it was on the shelf or on loan and you could borrow it from another library. Before, you'd to phone the Dick Institute and say, 'Right, who's got such-and-such a book?' Then you'd to phone maybe one or two libraries to see who had it on the shelf, because you didn't have that information. It was good for some things, for the information you can get from it, about the locations of books because there are far more people asking for specific books, for something they've seen on television or in magazines: far more requests now than you ever did have. I spent quite a bit of extra time writing postcards.[46]

But to me the old system worked a lot better. It's all right when the computer's working but not if the computer was down and the information on it isn't available. You can put books in and out on a disc, however.[47] We used to do all our own overdue postcards and letters[48] and if I knew somebody had had a death in the family or something like that, you wouldn't send it. With computers, you can't do that sort of thing. Or I could look and say, 'That can't be right, that person's in and out regularly. There's no way they've got a book that's late.' You could check, in case an item recorded as overdue had been returned. I felt as if I wasn't in control any more of what was going in and out the Library.

My experience and feeling is that things have changed but not always for the better as far as Hurlford Library is concerned. In earlier times, we had far more readers, more books, wider interests. Whereas now it's fewer readers, narrower interests and the issue was going down. At one time it was well over 3,000 books a month I would be putting out and it's down to about 1,600, although the last two or three years it's stabilised again. The Mills & Boon are not as popular with the younger ones. The older readers went for those, and some were reading maybe four and five books a week. They'd come in every week to change their books. But as they died off you weren't getting the younger ones in to replace them, and younger readers would only maybe take a couple of books and away for three weeks before they came back. Many of them are working and have families; they don't have the same time to read. That's a major change.

Latterly I still had a fair junior issue in comparison to a lot of the other branches, but nothing to when I started at first. When the school came out you would have a queue. There's no secondary school in

Hurlford. The majority go to the nearest one, Loudoun Academy in Galston, but Galston Library isn't particularly busier with the secondary school children, because I've worked there as well. The children are reading rubbish nowadays as well. They're not reading the classics or things that they used to read. They're nor reading real stories. It's all these *Ghostbuster* books[49] and science fiction. I suppose as long as they're reading, that's the main thing.

But they're doing new things. They have a reader development course[50] but it was goin' to be a full Wednesday that I'd to go to Lugar. Well, I'd my story time in the morning and my Brownies in the afternoon, and as it was to run for a three-year period there was no point for me because I wasn't going to be there for that duration. They did a Christmas promotion of adding a title picked at random to the books you'd selected. This was to encourage people to read something they wouldn't normally read and develop their taste in reading. That's quite a new thing but I don't know how it's going.

Libraries are trying to develop services. A computer was put in for the public to use and get on to the Internet – but used very little, and mainly by children coming from the school for a carry-on. One man used it to do family research, and there was somebody else, but that was the only two people to use the computer for what it was intended. They've got money from somewhere[51] and there are three computers. A whole corner of the Library has had to be changed, sectioned off, for these three computers and whoever's there will have to be able to show them. What had been a non-fiction section had to be changed and books moved around. It's taken away some of the shelving, cut back on the book side. They're certainly concentrating on IT.[52]

Eventually, they started to save money. One year they closed all the libraries for two weeks at the Kilmarnock Fair, but there was such an outcry that after that the Dick Institute stayed open. That meant that every year we had to take our holidays at the same time, the first fortnight in July. After years of moaning, it was decided to link the part-time branches with a full-time branch which stayed open during the holidays. So for a few years I worked at Galston Library for two weeks in the summer. I thoroughly enjoyed it and it was a busier library although you were still working on your own. Working on your own meant that there was nobody pressurising in any way, nobody standing over you. You could run the Library the way you wanted; you could run it to suit your customers.

I started a voluntary helpers scheme, and Primary 7 pupils helped after school. After they did 40 hours we had a wee award ceremony. It had all started with being involved with Brownies and Guides. The Guides did a Service Flash which involved service in the community, and some of them did that at the Library. It progressed from then and started in some of the other libraries after that. I'd a lot of contact with the school, I got to give the Primary 1s their prizes and when I left I got a presentation. You used to get them coming in from the secondary saying, 'I can remember when we used to sit on wee mats and you read us stories', and I thought, it's quite good being part of the community and you've given the children a pleasurable memory of the Library.

I was in the Library for 27 years and greatly enjoyed them, and yet it happened as an accident, purely as an accident really.

Interviewed 3 March 2002

Alan White

My name is Alan Grant Davidson White and I was born in the Elsie Inglis Maternity Pavilion[1] in Edinburgh on the 19th of September 1938. I was an only child.

My father ran a garage business in the town, buying and selling second-hand cars. He brought me up with the idea that I would take over the business. My early schooldays and latterly were spent working with cars, with the garage, with members of the public coming in. Although that didn't lead to the career I finally chose, it did me a tremendous amount of good because I worked with things, with my hands, and above all else with people. Librarianship is a very people-related profession, and if I could sell a ropy old second-hand car to somebody, I could certainly help them choose a book!

There's no history of librarianship in the family. My father's father, who died before I was born, had a cask-making business. He put the staves together, assembled the barrels and supplied them mostly to the whisky industry in Leith.

My mother was an Edinburgh woman and worked as a secretary at the time they married. My father and mother were divorced shortly after I was born so I didn't have very much to do with her in my early days. Her parents were Edinburgh likewise. I think her mother was dead at that time I was growing up. Her father was still alive, but I never met him. I knew nothing about them.

I stayed with my grandmother when I was a boy and we moved to Merchiston Grove, in the Ashley Terrace, a detached bit of Merchiston at Shandon. One ambition I had as a young boy was to drive a train, a conventional ambition, 'cause at the end of our Grove a lane led into Merchiston Station, and I used to spend hours watching the trains go by: the old LMS Coronation Scot[2] and various others going through the station during the War in khaki paint. At the other end of the street was the trams. No 4 trams used to run along Slateford Road to Slateford. That gave me a great interest in the transport of Edinburgh, which I'm still interested in and a hobby since I retired.

I used to play up and down Merchiston Grove on my tricycle. I was banned from going out on to the main road so, being an adventurous boy, I did. I wanted to see what it was like to drive on the tram track. So I drove my tricycle on the tram track and came to the cut at Maclachlan's brewery,[3] and my front wheel jammed in the car rail and I couldn't get it out. Meantime all the No 4 trams between Edinburgh and Slateford had to wait. All they did was ring their bells and say, 'You'll need to move your bike, son.' I ran home in floods of tears to get help.

I went to George Watson's Boys' College,[4] in Colinton Road in 1943 and spent all my schooling there. It was a family tradition, part of Edinburgh tradition. Both my aunts and my father had gone to Merchant Company schools.[5] I married someone who came from the same sort of background and our daughter went to Watson's Ladies' College. I remember my father signing my papers to go to Watson's the same way I signed for my daughter to go. I have mixed feelings now about the difference between Merchant Company education and the better end of secondary education. But at that time, there was no doubt that you were buying access to something which wasn't available elsewhere.

It was a splendid school. I look back on it warmly. A lot of people didn't enjoy their schooldays. By and large, I did and was lucky to meet schoolmasters who had been there before the War and had come back after serving. They were a different sort of teacher from the people who came in during the '50s and '60s. They had a different set of values, treated the boys quite differently and, if you responded to them, they would treat you as an individual. I think they led to my career in libraries.

I took Art and languages as my specialist subjects and we had a very good technical department, so I was able to try pottery, stained glass and things like that which you wouldn't have the opportunity to do at some other places. A lot of things people take at evening class, I learned when still at school. I had a very good Art master. My intention had been to take up commercial art, and he told me, 'You're quite good, but not good enough to make a living at it.' I hated him for that at the time, but he was quite right. It's a tough field and I've had many a reason to be grateful to him.

The other thing he gave me was an insight into architecture which remained a strong interest all the time I worked in libraries. I particularly valued Banister Fletcher's *History of Architecture*[6] which I'd been introduced to by this inspiring Art teacher, Ewan Walker. As a boy I'd had a copy which I'd lent to somebody and they hadn't given it back. When I retired, they asked me what I wanted and I had a copy given to me then.

I always enjoyed English, which you would expect of a librarian. I was lucky to have George More, head of the English Department, who's something of a legend – a man from Stornoway who taught in the Nicolson Institute.[7] He was an early post-war enthusiast for school libraries, at one time a secretary of the School Library Association in Scotland and well known in that field. During the War he'd served as a bomber pilot and could tell exciting stories of night raids over Germany. He and I got on well and I remember how I became involved in libraries in the first instance. I was at one end of the corridor, George More came out of his classroom and I realised he was waiting for me, and I thought I had done something wrong. When I got up to him, he said, 'I want you to run the school library.' Although I was a member of the public library and used Fountainbridge Library, I had had nothing to do with libraries. To this day, I don't know why George picked me.

A former pupil called Blair had left money to form the Blair Library in Watson's, and because the school didn't have a proper library it needed a planning team to decide how to spend the money – I think it was £20,000, a lot of money in those days – to fit out a room and buy the foundation stock. Of the 1,700 pupils, George More picked me to run that school library. I must have been 11, going on 12, had just moved into the secondary department and was tremendously chuffed. I got home, told my father and he said, 'Well, I don't know what all the fuss is about. Libraries are dull things. I don't know why anybody would want to have anything to do with that.' Needless to say, that only made it surer that I would do it.

That's what brought me into libraries. Until then I had used the local library at Dundee Street which I had joined, under my own steam, when I was about six or seven. Going past on the bus with my grandmother, I used to ask her what that new building was. It was designed and opened in 1939–40 with floodlighting and lots of glass. Because of the blackout regulations you weren't able to see in, and I was fascinated by it. So when the blackout came off after the War, I was one of the first people along to see what this fascinating place was. I used it and the tuppeny per night Shandon Library, which was on Bonaly Road, before Bonaly Road changed its name, just at the bottom of Ashley Terrace. He had one shop there and one in Comiston Road. He used to lend mostly fiction and children's books at tuppence per book per night. I read the Biggles[8] books, the Blyton[9] books and all the early things you were supposed to read in those days from that library before I moved on to the public library. Brownsmith, his name was, that ran those two lending libraries. He used to sell chocolate and sweeties, but predominantly they were lending libraries. The small shop libraries lasted into the '60s but have now gone entirely. Public libraries put them out of business. Why pay tuppence a night if you can get it for nothing? Boots[10] and Douglas & Foulis[11] outlasted the rest but they went quite quickly after that.

By the time I left school at the end of my fifth year, 1955, I'd made up my mind what I wanted to do. In those days you had to make a written application to the City Librarian saying why you would like to work in a public library, and give referees. I was able to give George More as one of my referees and George gave me a very good reference. If you particularly wanted to start in libraries as opposed to the Corporation in general, you had to wait until there was a vacancy and in those days there were very few vacancies – one of the reasons I waited from July until the following February to start at Stockbridge Library on 15th February 1956. The Corporation always started new people in the middle of the month – that's when the salary day was. It was a monthly salary.

Between leaving school in the July and the February, I worked in the Post Office, did a lot of driving jobs, did new car delivery up from Oxford, just enjoyed myself. I'd a driving licence, and I'd been brought up to drive since I was quite small. In my early days I was interested in motorbikes, and I've kept up that interest to this day. My father was very keen on motorbikes. He used to ride in scrambles and trials and so did I for a while. I did a bit of motorcycle racing on the sand at St Andrews and Leven.

My father didn't understand it. It wasn't that he didn't read books or wasn't sympathetic to books and reading. We had a lot of books in the house and my grandmother had books that had come down in the family. He just didn't understand that any son of his had found something to do with libraries. He expected me to join him in the business. I was the only son and it meant the end of the business. He didn't oppose it, he didn't stand in my way and, to give him his due, he paid for a good education which enabled me to do it. The beauty of it was that the library offered shift-work, and so I kept my contacts with the family business for about the first ten years when I was working – a nice balance between the practical thing and the librarianship. I always saw myself as a hands-on, practical librarian and I got it doing that in the early days. To some extent that kept my father quiet. He was pleased when I was able to go back and keep helping him and it allowed me to do what I wanted to do. I'd two sources of income and I don't think I had so much disposable income before that or again.

I was one of the very few people that took Highers[12] in my year who didn't go to university, and I think the school was disappointed. There were about five or six of us took up jobs that didn't require a degree. There was no tradition of any members of the family going to university until my own daughter, and nobody was around to tell me what university life was like. Nowadays, it's a degree-only-entry profession, but in those days it wasn't. If you wanted to work in university libraries and some college libraries you needed a degree, but not in the public library where I wanted to work. You didn't get a degree; you went to the Scottish College of Commerce in Glasgow, and studied librarianship for a year.[13] You came out with the same qualification as I got by doing it in evening classes. Taking the qualifications as a librarian at night classes meant you could work, you gained the experience which you had to have to get your qualification.

I enjoyed the variety that working with a wide cross-section of the public can bring. I reckoned I was quite good at it. To the day I retired, I retained that liking and I've never regretted my decision. As the junior assistant I learned my trade from the bottom up. There were quite a number of people in senior positions who had been there, not only from before the War but all of their careers. Edinburgh Libraries at that time hadn't moved forward since the War. It was still routine-bound, routines that I'd already learned in running the school library. I had to be careful not to say, 'I know all about that', and try to be a smart aleck. There was only five of us there and your tricks were found out very quickly.

One of the things that you had to learn was the Library of Congress classification scheme.[14] Edinburgh Public Libraries is probably the only public library in the whole of the UK that now uses that scheme. That was something I hadn't encountered before, so while I knew about the Dewey Decimal Classification scheme[15] for arranging books, I knew nothing about the Library of Congress classification scheme.

In the early days you were taught a number of slavish routines, and there were things you only did after you'd been there for about five years. Despite the fact that Stockbridge was a busy library, you weren't encouraged to do things you hadn't been fully trained on. I remember the excitement of getting to write, for the first time, a reader's ticket for somebody who'd joined the Library. You weren't allowed to use Biros; you had to use a dip pen and inkwell. About a fortnight after I was able to write out tickets, I got to underline the surname in red ink, equally with a dip pen, and that showed the thing had been properly checked. That was a senior member of staff's job.

The Branch Librarian was Sandy Barker[16] who came from Grangemouth. He was the first post-war import into Edinburgh Libraries from a library elsewhere in Scotland or anywhere else. That was ten years after the War. Because the other three members of staff were female and had been there a lot longer than either of us, it was him and me against the rest. Sandy was a shy, nice individual who lived in a boarding house along Stockbridge and cycled to work every day. Using Sandy's bicycle, one of my jobs was to recover long-overdue books in the tenements down by the Water of Leith – Saunders Street, Cheyne Street, Dean Street, places that have been pulled down. Stumbling along these dark corridors to recover books, my success rate was good till the day I came out and all the books I'd collected and Sandy's bike had been stolen. That was the last time I got to use the Branch Librarian's bike.

With 12 branch libraries in Edinburgh, there was a lot of to-ing and fro-ing on the old 29 tram. You were sent once a month, as the junior assistant, to the Central Library to collect everybody's pay, including the Branch Librarian's. You went on the tram because it only cost 1d. You were paid out in cash and carried it back in an attaché case. Years later, we're employing Securicor to do the same thing! I was getting the princely sum of £203 per annum at that time.

You were discouraged from using the telephone because the phone was an expensive thing. At least three branches weren't even on the telephone. You were discouraged from phoning somebody if a book came in that they'd reserved. Nowadays you would lift the phone and tell them, leading to a faster turnaround of books and more satisfied users. In those days you had to send out a postcard because it only cost 1d whereas a phone call cost 2d. A large number of people weren't on the phone in any case.

What I liked about Stockbridge was that it was a busy library. It drew people from the Colonies,[17] from the north side of the New Town and from Stockbridge itself. You had a tremendous cross-section of readership and that made it an interesting place to work. Attached to the Library was the Thomas Nelson Hall. Thomas Nelson, the publisher,[18] gave four halls to Edinburgh, at Stockbridge, St Leonard's, McDonald Road and Dundee Street, of which there are only two left. They were working men's halls for newspapers and games, a meeting place. They were administered by the Libraries Committee but they never had books so the link was tenuous. The building in Stockbridge is still there but the principle behind it has gone. When I started, one of my first jobs was to black out the racing results in the newspaper using a little roller and inkpad because it was thought to be bad for people to look at the racing results. The other thing was to go round maybe every three hours and spray disinfectant as widely as you could, preferably over the inhabitants of the room.

A lot of people lived in the various lodging houses round about. They came into the Library because it was warm, they had the papers and were able to play dominoes and draughts which we kept at the counter. When the game got very exciting, you used to shout over the top of the partition that they were making too much noise. That was days when everybody used to say Sshhh! in libraries. There were some interesting old guys – men who were retired, younger people some of whom would still be working if they had the chance. Most of them weren't too clean and the girls didn't like them at all. I remember a couple of Irishmen among them. They were nearly all Scots. A fair number came from north of here, from Aberdeen and that sort of area.

Although the Library closed at half past eight at night, the newsroom and the Nelson Hall used to close at nine o'clock. I was living in West Linton and because there wasn't a bus until twenty-five to ten I stayed on, let everybody else go and locked up the Nelson Hall after these guys. When the place was quiet in the evening, I used to have many an enjoyable game of dominoes with these characters. For years afterwards I would be walking along Princes Street trying to look respectable and out of a doorway would lurch a terrible, old, smelly, drunken tramp saying, 'Hello, Alan. Nice to see you!' These were all denizens of the newsroom where I played dominoes.

I was working 37½ hours a week. The Library opened at nine in the morning and remained open till half past eight, and a Saturday from nine until half past eight as well. I used to like the Saturday evening because you were always very busy and the time passed quickly. A lot of people didn't like working on a Saturday. Then it became eight o'clock, then it became five o'clock, then it became four o'clock, then it became one o'clock, where it is now.

Most of the Library Service, apart from a number of management posts, then and today, work shifts. In Edinburgh the shift system has been very good. You do a shift, you finish, go home and that's you finished for the day. Or you do a late shift. Generally speaking, the hours are configured on an alternating shift where you do a morning followed by an evening followed by a morning followed by an evening. You started about two o'clock and worked until half past eight or nine o'clock, and you started at nine o'clock in the morning and worked until four o'clock or half past four. I never minded working shifts. Latterly you were paid for working shifts. I was more interested in having time to pursue my other interests. Although the pattern of shifts was fixed you could get somebody to swop with you. I liked doing late shifts, working in the evening and other people liked to have the evening off. So I never had any trouble in switching shifts.

Television had a very positive effect on libraries. More people saw things on television that they wanted to read about than were put off using libraries by television. That's been a canard all my life in libraries, and I think we're about to see it again with everybody saying the Internet will see the end of libraries – I don't think it will. It's an unorganised source of information. It'll whet a lot of people's interest in a lot of things and they'll have to turn to books and to libraries.

I was launched into the Stockbridge branch and had no idea how I might go on from there. I was still learning the craft. Once I passed the stage of learning the alphabet to arrange books, I got on to the Dewey Decimal Classification scheme which was and is still used for the children's sections. I was familiar with that from the school library so

I was able to do a lot of work quickly in that area. Each day the children's fairy tales were in a terrible mess because children were always taking them. The idea of display in libraries was virtually unknown in these days. At home one night I copied an *Evening News*[19] heading they used for children's features that showed pixies, fairies and elves on to the back of an old chocolate box lid, and made a display. I think that was the first time anybody had ever done anything like that.

In those days a superintendent of branch libraries went round – he didn't actually run any of the libraries – to carry out spot checks and he saw this fairy tale sign and said, 'Oh, I didn't know we had an artist on the staff', and within six weeks I found myself in the Central Library with responsibility for dressing the showcases on the main staircase. That was done by the Reference Library in those days. Nowadays it's a full-time display officer. So I was able to use my art training and did about ten years' worth of exhibitions there. More interestingly for my career, I found myself working in the Reference Library by the end of '56 after only about six months at Stockbridge.

I spent part of the summer before going to the Reference Library working with the mobile library service, which I thoroughly enjoyed. It had been running a few years but was an infant service compared to nowadays. A number of counties had them but Edinburgh was the first municipal mobile library service in Scotland. It had two vans. The first took to the road in 1948, the second in 1955, both driven by the librarian, which is why I came to be on them because I could drive these things.

It went to the housing estates which at that time and for years afterwards didn't have branch libraries, and some of them still don't. I found myself going out to the suburbs, Moredun, Muirhouse, the Inch, Gilmerton, Pilton when the prefabs[20] were still occupied, providing a once or twice-weekly service to those new areas. It was seen very much as a stop-gap until a return to normal after the War and we were able to provide a full-time branch library service in these places.

There was a difference in the readers who used the mobile service compared with those coming into Stockbridge, governed by the kind of stock that we carried on the van. We didn't do children's books on the mobile libraries. That came much later. It was solely an adult service, largely fiction, popular books, do-it-yourself, gardening, very much a targeted service. Anybody who joined on the mobiles could also use a branch library. We found that people who wanted more serious books went to a branch library. People who just wanted two or three novels used the mobile service. We were part of the delivery-van culture that prevailed in these places because, particularly in Pilton and Muirhouse, a lot of houses were built very quickly but they had no infrastructure. The fact that the Library went there by van was really no different from anything else. In fact, a number of people when we came to replace the van with a built library said, 'Don't take the van off because we're used to working with vans.' At Pilton, I used to share a stand with a mobile chip-van who had a smoky, coke-fired range. He used to park on one side of the island and I used to park on the other. When this chap got his fire stoked up and the fish suppers were going well, the smoke used to drift across from his place, fill up the van and I had to move. The superintendent caught me one night about 50ft off-site to get out of this chap's prevailing smoke-screen and I got hell from him for having shifted the van from where it should be! My other problem with the chip man was that the people used to buy their fish supper, eat it at the van and insist on reading the books with their greasy fingers.

It was busy. We had our regulars who only used the mobile library. Long before we started making special provision for disabled people, people used the mobile library because it came to their street or stopped outside their house. The longest stop was about three and a half hours and the shortest was about half an hour. It went to about 20 sites in different parts of the town. Meeting different people from the community stood me in good stead later on; it gave me a chance to drive; and it gave me a lifelong interest in mobile libraries and time-tabling which I was able to use later to revamp the mobile service. Although I was out there for a short time that summer, they used to borrow me back during the summertime when they had nobody to drive the vehicle.

Then I got into the Reference Library to look after the exhibitions in the Central, and George Young, the museums officer, got his eye on me and asked Charles Minto,[21] the Librarian-Curator at that time, to have me transferred to the museum staff. I was quite interested, but Minto said, 'Under no circumstances! That man is staying with me. He's going to be a librarian.' Working in the Reference Library was a very much sought-after move. You didn't normally get there until you'd been in the service about 30 years. A lot of people were jealous of that. There was a pecking order; the Reference Librarian was the highest paid of any of the public departments in the Library Service at that time, and the staff that worked there were experienced and well qualified.

It brought you into contact with a different group of people. That was before the University Library on George Square was built. There was a great increase in the number of students and a great shortage in library places for students in Edinburgh at that time. The mornings were taken up with classes and you had to be up by two o'clock in the afternoon or you'd had it! You wouldn't get a seat, never mind the book you wanted, and we used to have people sitting on the floor. All the students wanted the same book and the same seat and that prevailed for years. I've never felt fitter than running up and down the staircase because at the back of the Central Library there is a stack 11 storeys high and four and a half miles long if laid end to end. The member of staff met the member of the public, went into the stack, found the book and brought it out.

It was a speedy service because all books in the stack are in classified order so people were able to ask, 'What books have you got on such-and-such a subject?' That's one thing you can't do in the National Library where they're in shelf order because they come in under copyright in an arbitrary fashion. We encourage people who know the literature of their subject to use the National Library. But you have to offset that against the improvement there's been in the college and the university libraries in the town.

There was a tremendous emphasis on the housekeeping side of librarianship. You had to check each afternoon that the books in that Reference Library room were in order. One junior assistant took one half, one junior assistant took the other, and you checked until you met in the middle. There were 12 bays of books – a lot of books to check – but you got to know your stock very well. One of the challenges that this chap who started at the same time and I set each other was to answer questions on 100 books from each of these bays – that was 1,200 of the most-used reference books on open shelves.

The Reference Library shut at nine o'clock on a Saturday night and I used to love working then. Most of the week was pretty busy with students and textbooks, but on Saturday night you got a lot of people from the Borders in for the day with their enquiries, or referred on from the local library there. They did their shopping and after the shops closed they came to the Library. There was a train on the old Borders line to Galashiels about half past nine and they all worked until nine o'clock and then got out to catch their train. We had a huge intake from the Borders and Fife.

We had people from the Tulliallan Police College[22] – you saw large feet appearing round the door and two large policemen. They never let on who they were. They'd obviously never set foot in a library before, but they'd been sent from Tulliallan and they'd come sidling up to the counter. We used to kill ourselves with mirth because we knew exactly who they were and what they were after. This huge guy, a big Glasgow bobby, would whisper to the assistant, 'I've got an essay to write for next Thursday and it's on love.' Some of the essay subjects they picked for them! We saw these policemen regularly and they were a hoot! Other groups – they were building the abbey at Nunraw and we used to have monks in for details of building techniques, wearing their clerical clothes. It was a real cross-section of people, particularly in the evening when all the students had gone to study or to the pub or whatever they did. It was an interesting place and I was there for seven years and thoroughly enjoyed every year of it.

During that time I took evening classes. That had been a condition of being taken on in the first place. It was made very clear that there was no future, particularly for a male, in libraries unless you had a qualification, Associate of the Library Association. You embarked on a one-year course and then a four-year course of four different subjects, taught under the auspices of James Gillespie's Evening College by members of the public library staff acting as evening school lecturers for two hours every Tuesday night in the staff library, a non-public area. It had been set up by a far-seeing librarian called Dr Savage,[23] the Librarian up to the start of the War, and he had built a fine collection of library textbooks from which the staff could borrow, get articles and so on. So you had your tea and went downstairs to evening school and then went home.

What you had to learn, apart from the entrance exam, was bibliography, reference books, assistance to readers, classification, cataloguing and literature of a subject, including English literature which I took. You did these under four separate tutelages, four separate papers, four separate years. If you were successful, you were awarded your Associateship. I got that at first sitting, fortunately. I was the second youngest person in Edinburgh Library Service ever to qualify by that route. One of my friends had just beaten me to it the year before. She was 20, I was 21. I stayed in the Reference Library for about six months after that.

The original intention had been to open the Edinburgh Room and the Scottish Library as a joint department with one person in charge of both, and day-to-day management of the collections in the hands of individual members of staff. However, Marie Balfour, the Librarian of the Edinburgh Room,[24] died and the chap who was to run the joint department got a job in Glasgow as superintendent of the branches. So it was decided to retain the separate management of the Edinburgh Room and the Scottish Library. Norma Armstrong became the Librarian of the Edinburgh Room and I became the Librarian of the Scottish Library. That was during the summer of '63.

The Scottish Library was the reference function together with a large lending collection. Unlike other major Scottish history collections up and down Scotland which are mainly for reference, we had a large collection of material that you couldn't get anywhere else for lending. The Art Room, the Music Room and the Edinburgh Room were opened in the early 1930s and they'd built up their indexes and expertise. From the day it opened, the Scottish Library was expected to behave like them, and of course we didn't have 30 years under our belt, so we had to run very quickly to be able to walk. I enjoyed that period very much because we were developing something which has stood the test of time. People asked us why we opened a Scottish Library when the Scottish National Library was across the road. We cater for a different clientele altogether. There was never any conflict between the two libraries, quite the reverse – nothing but co-operation.

I knew a superintendent of the Reading Room in the National Library, Bob Burnett. Bob used to break the rules and let us borrow books from the National Library and bring them across George IV Bridge for a trusted reader so we could put all the material together. We sent somebody over one day to pick up a book and she dropped it in the middle of the tram tracks, the oil, all the muck. The poor girl was in a terrible state, as was Bob Burnett because the book shouldn't have been out of the National Library in the first place! We had to have it cleaned professionally and then returned.

I was in the Scottish Library until 1966, by which time I had been in reference libraries for about ten years. I'd applied for a couple of jobs outside, and was offered one in Birmingham which would have meant promotion, but I decided not to take it. Looking back I'm glad I didn't. I'd made up my mind to stay where I was. I was very happy with the Scottish Library.

I'd married in '63, just at the time I was taking over the Scottish Library. Our daughter was born in '66, so I had a future pupil at George Watson's to pay for. I had to look into the future and about that time the new library in Blackhall was being built. It was designed as a very ambitious library by the same company that built Leith Town Hall and Library back in the '30s. I knew nothing about branch libraries, but if I was going to be a manager of libraries I needed experience in lending libraries as well as reference libraries. This library was running some nine months behind at that stage and was starting to embarrass everybody concerned. I was sent there to get it open and running within three months. My chief at the time, Charlie Minto, said to me, 'It doesn't matter who you fall out with, get the thing open.' But I enjoyed my time there, and was able to use my practical skills. One of the things our family did was build its own house, and as a boy the builders showed me how to do all kinds of things. I was acting as my own clerk of works for Blackhall Library. I said to the chief, 'The only way I can do this is to break a number of Edinburgh traditions and do it my way', and he said, 'I don't care. I trust you to get the bloody thing open.' So there I was with a new building, new stock, a new staff team, more or less carte blanche and a golden opportunity for the second time in my life to set up a library my way.

I was given a date, and got it open on time. It was opened by the Lord Provost on the 30th of September 1966, although it had opened to the public about May. We didn't have our troubles to seek from day one. In February '69 the place went on fire – an electrical fault. A spark went up and caught in the roof space and the whole thing was burnt up one side. Instead of opening the following morning at nine o'clock, we opened at ten past nine. We set up a caravan in the car park, one of my firm's caravans. I was able to get one at half-an-hour's notice because of my connections. We fed the staff coffee, tea and soup, they had a comfort break every half-hour, we kept going through the snowstorms with no heating and no lighting and we never closed.

It was a new library, a big library, it had a good stock and a staff that had a new approach. Blackhall Library was so busy that on Saturday afternoon they queued inside the building, outside the building, down the steps and into the car park and we had an attendant on duty to let the queue in in twos and threes. I did a survey on where the readership came from. The trend was that people would travel inwards towards the town to use a facility like a library. What we discovered was that if you gave them a library that they liked, car parking, a good stock and attentive service, they travelled outwards. We had people coming regularly, some of them by bus, all the way from the south side of town just to use Blackhall Library because they could get what they wanted.

There was a new building at Portobello in 1963, which was the first one after the War. It used to be in the old Portobello Town Hall, sharing it with the Police Station. It moved across the road to Rosefield Terrace in 1963 but was constrained by the site. Blackhall was the first and is the only library where we had a big enough site to match international standards. When you saw it with all the furnishing and books out, it was huge. It was the biggest branch library I'd ever seen. We also established a link with mobile library users in Muirhouse who walked up to use the library at Blackhall until Muirhouse Library opened in 1968 and the mobile library service there was withdrawn. Edinburgh has got what we call big branches, sort of area branches, and these smaller branches. We now have 23 libraries, whereas in those days there were 12, going on 14 with these two opening. The next one to open was Sighthill in 1968, which is marginally bigger than Muirhouse but nothing like the size of Blackhall. That taught me all I know about running branch libraries.

In 1972 there was a spate of retirements and a lot of senior posts became vacant. I found myself going back to take charge of the Reference Library at the end of that year. It was the next most senior public post, it paid more than Blackhall and it was a step in the right direction. It was something I knew, something I liked doing. I had ideas about what I wanted to do in charge of the Reference Library and I managed to do some of these. If I'd had a year there I might have been able to do more, but I'd only been back six months or so, when there was another round of retirals and I moved up to Chief Assistant Librarian, a third-tier management post, two down from the City Librarian. I was responsible for the whole of the Central Library and the staffing for the whole Library Service. So by that time, I had experience both of the Central Library and of what went on outside the Central Library.

What I missed was the shifts and direct contact with the public. Everybody who moves into a management position in a public library loses that if they're not careful. I liked getting out of the office, walking around the building and meeting people. One of the key things that gave rise to my retiral was that I could no longer get round that building in the way I liked. I felt very unhappy if I was cooped up in an office. I could do maybe two hours and then I had to prowl about a bit, see what was happening. It is in the nature of librarians. It's a very front-of-house profession. You can build up collections of books, but if you take away your readers, if you're not talking to the people who use them, it's very easy to get out of touch.

I became the Chief Assistant Librarian in 1973 for two years. Librarianship was still seen, wrongly, as a female profession. Not too many men go into it because it's not a high-earning occupation. You get your satisfaction in other ways, but if you had a family, a house, a mortgage you had to get a fairly senior position. Although I was working nine to five now as Chief Assistant, by that time my father had retired and I'd lost contact with the family car business. I still helped out now and again but it ceased to be a source of income about the time my daughter needed to go to school and various other things during the '70s.

During these years recruitment was difficult. One of the people I recruited was Irvine Welsh.[25] He worked for us for a short time as a library assistant and I recruited him to work on the mobile. However, Edinburgh was an atypical recruitment market. You were competing with the banks and insurance companies for female school-leavers, and they were offering better conditions. One of my jobs was to go round the schools' careers conventions and convince people that they would like to work as a librarian. I enjoyed doing it but it had limited success. Often people were having an interview, we were doing the paperwork and they were getting an offer of a five-day week with a bank. At one stage I was doing up to a dozen or more interviews a day for new assistants. A heavy turnover. That was one of the reasons that we stopped the Saturday afternoon opening and went back to one o'clock. That eased it a little.

Although I'd interviewed most of the staff at Blackhall, I now had to interview really for the first time, putting other people through the examination syllabus, advising them on careers, going out to libraries and all the administration that goes with keeping 100 staff going. We didn't have personnel officers, so I was a shoulder on whom they cried. You had to quickly learn about employment law, negotiating with the trade unions, hours of work and so on.

We had two unions. NALGO was the white-collar side of local government – it's now UNISON – and NUPE for blue-collar staff.[26] I never joined. I felt you couldn't run with both the hare and the hound. In management you couldn't be a genuine member of the union, not because I disapprove of the union or I didn't get on well with the unions. At the time I was looking after staffing things, I didn't always agree with the union but they were always somebody that I could talk to and they could always come and talk to me. Although I wasn't one of their members, I think they recognised honesty and I didn't make promises I couldn't deliver and didn't try and put anything over.

I was also responsible for the Central Library, the services there and the fabric of the building. That gave me an interest in the history of the place, and I decided to write a history of public libraries in Edinburgh as the thesis for my Fellowship of the Library Association (FLA).[27] Local government reorganisation was on the horizon, the old Corporation was winding up and it is now difficult to get the source material beyond 1971. People have asked me to update it but the stuff isn't there. I made sure we kept as much documentation as I could and we set up an archive but I was conscious of the people who'd been there their entire working lives, who retired and took another bit of the history with them. I was determined that when I went I would try and bring it all together. Everything to do with public libraries from the 12th century to 1971 is in that thesis, including the Advocates Library,[28] the Signet Library[29] and anything to which the public had access in Edinburgh.

You always think the things you set up or set in motion were the best things that ever happened. Looking back on the history of Edinburgh Libraries, there was a tremendous expansion at the turn of the century when Morningside, Stockbridge, McDonald Road, the first branch libraries, were opened. Then after the First War there was a dead period. I've got a marvellous quote that I used in the thesis by this chap Savage[30] who came north from Wallasey. On his first day he wrote, 'I found in Edinburgh a survival so perfect that it seemed an impiety to lay a finger upon it.' Dr Savage was a martinet. He used to sit in the room off the Reference Library, the Librarian's office at that time, and it had speaking tubes down to each of the departments, like a captain on the bridge. He used to send a memo down to the librarian in the lending library saying, 'On my way through this morning I noticed dust on the top of bookcase number so-and-so. Kindly assure me by midday that this has been dealt with.' He could turn up anywhere, anytime. He used to phone and find out, 'And how are you doing tonight?' 'Oh, very well, it's busy.' A couple of minutes later he would walk in because he'd just phoned from up the road, and you weren't busy at all. I never worked for him but I would've respected him and feared him at the same time. What he did between 1922 and 1942, when he retired, was quite remarkable by any standards. A friend of his had donated books to the school library and I met the pair of them in Savage's house, long after he'd retired. He died soon afterwards, but I was privileged and impressed to meet Savage. He wrote a lot of books about librarianship, and his biography, *Librarian Extraordinary*[31] by James Ollé, was published in 1977 by the Library Association (LA) as part of their centenary celebrations.

He was followed by Butchart,[32] who was the librarian in Midlothian. He was succeeded by Minto, his deputy. When Minto retired in 1971, he was replaced, on an interim basis, by Jimmy Cockburn,[33] his deputy, who stepped in for two or three years until he retired. I chose the departure of Minto as a closing point for the thesis. It was an end of an era because he trained under Savage as had most of the people around him. I was awarded the FLA in 1974.

The following year, at reorganisation, the Corporation was wound up, the District Council came into being, the Library Service was subsumed into the recreation function and Alan Howe,[34] the Librarian, became one of the Depute Directors of Recreation. Only Directors were allowed to have Deputes, so I became the Assistant City Librarian – Depute City Librarian in the old terminology although the job itself didn't change. I was the most senior person after the Depute Director of Recreation who acted as City Librarian. I was based in the Central Library throughout, the senior member of staff there and I did that job for the next 20 years until my retirement. Prior to reorganisation, when George Young retired, Museums were seen as important enough to stand alone, they passed from Library control and Herbert Coutts[35] was appointed City Curator in 1971.

The Library Services was adversely affected by the reorganisation because previously it had been a distinct department reporting to the Libraries and Museums Committee, and then we became simply part of Recreation and the Recreation Committee oversaw the Library. Those of us who'd been there for some time didn't like it. We had our history, our own administration, we'd had our own way of doing things independently and not unsuccessfully for years, and it served the Library perfectly well. Suddenly we were expected to be corporate. The department was divided into the intellectual bit and the jumping up and down bit – physical recreation and so-called cultural recreation. There were more votes in playing fields and children's playing parks than in libraries. It downgraded our political clout. In my professional life, I've always argued that it didn't matter if the Chief Librarian was the Chief Officer, as long as he or she had access to the committee controlling the Library Service. In 1975 and for a few years afterwards they didn't have that access, and I don't think that did us any good.

The first Director of Recreation was an ex-member of the Town Clerk's staff, a committee animal, to whom people with service expertise were made responsible. Aberdeen, Edinburgh, Dundee went down that road and it gave libraries a very poor image. Glasgow didn't, and to this day there's a separate Libraries Committee and a Director of Libraries in Glasgow who has direct access to his own chairman and committee, and it's a stronger service. Libraries never were sexy. In '75 all the big, sexy services went to the Region, so what was left in the District was housing or recreation. Since the whole Council couldn't serve on the housing committee, to find something interesting for the rest of the councillors they swept everything together and called it Recreation, and Libraries went into that.

In 1986, we changed administration. The Lord Provost, Jack Kane,[36] Librarian of the Dott Memorial Library, piloted the arrival of Newington Library, Craigmillar Library and Moredun Library. Prior to 1975, Jack Kane said the Libraries were to get some of the residue of the Corporation's Common Good Fund, and he carried the day although he wasn't of the prevailing party at that time. In 1986 the priority was for disadvantaged areas and communities. Up until that time we'd been doing practically nothing for them. If you think of Blackhall, it's a car-using, well-heeled area, middle class. Politically the ideal was to put a big library like Blackhall at a conveniently central point for all the bus routes so everybody could get to it.

From a professional librarian's point of view, because most of the radial roads go out like spokes, the ideal would be to put a reasonable-sized library at the convergence of each of these spokes all the way round the town, each big enough to sustain a decent stock. One of the most wasteful ways is a number of small libraries with a small stock which people read out very quickly and you've no method of changing it. That was one of the dangers of the mobile library: you had to keep refreshing the stock regularly.

We had to stop members of the administration from creating shop-unit libraries. Every time there was an empty shop, they wanted to put a few books in it and call it a library. Our strong advice was not to do that, but to wait until you could do it properly. It didn't do the Library Service much good. Imagine the euphoria in any political party that had suddenly got power and wanted to do things particularly for the people that had voted them in. But our job was to provide professional advice and sometimes that was contrary to what they wanted to hear. At that time we expanded the mobile library service from two vehicles to five, and that got round the problem of these shop libraries. We were able to increase mobile library sites from about 30 a week to nearly 100 per week, and the vehicles were bigger. They carried about 4,000 books as opposed to 2,000 books of the earlier one. I look back with some fondness because I designed and specified the trailers, the chassis, the bodywork and everything else. They are unique to Edinburgh. I knew enough from my motor trade days to argue with the body-builders and the chassis people. They're not attractive-looking things but they carry a lot of books, which is what they were designed to do to get round this problem of opening small collections.

The two smallest libraries we took over were at Granton which opened in 1936, and the one in the old primary school in Balerno which we inherited from Midlothian at reorganisation in 1975. These are smaller than anything we would have opened ourselves. They are expensive to run, to staff and to keep the stock up to scratch.

We established the ethnic collection, which I was closely associated with, based in McDonald Road Library. We were able to get an Indian chap who'd set up a similar service in Bradford many years ago. He came out of retirement and did the same thing for us. We were fortunate in getting a professionally-qualified Indian girl to take that over, and it's going very strongly indeed now.

Despite their caricature, librarians are not only interested in routine. They're not like that at all; outside the library they're the hardest drinking, hardest swearing, hardest living people that you could wish to meet; inside the library they're totally committed to what they do. A friend of mine died from drinking too much. He and I used to go drinking after late shifts. He was a bit of a philosopher, and I remember him saying that the one thing you learn about libraries is that they got along without you very well before you got there and they'll get along without you after you've gone and you can only do the best you can while you're there. You can't leave anything else behind you.

You had to be a member of the LA before you could take the professional examination, so I joined in 1956, and you paid your own way through the examinations, you paid your subscriptions and never thought anything of it. The Scottish Library Association (SLA) was founded in 1908 and affiliated to the LA when the LA started examining in 1931, because the qualifications were seen as being interchangeable nationally. It basically became the Scottish branch of the Library Association, although it retained the title Scottish Library Association, so if you join the LA you automatically become a member of the SLA. I first went to the Summer School at Newbattle Abbey[37] in 1957. I didn't want to go but Jimmy Cockburn said, 'It's a good thing to go to, you'll meet other people and it'll help with your exams.' Which it did – it was very much an exam-oriented syllabus at that time and I loved it and didn't miss a year for the next 21, 22 years. Everything seemed to be happening in the west of Scotland, particularly in Lanarkshire, where another of the giants of the profession, Bill Paton,[38] was the County Librarian. He had a number of people I got to know through Summer Schools and going to meetings and they had cornered all the professional activity. There wasn't very much happening in Edinburgh. The East of Scotland Branch of the SLA was fairly moribund but it did have a joint meeting with the West of Scotland part of the SLA once a year and we would visit a library or a bookbinder like Dunn & Wilson[39] in Falkirk, then have high tea. When you were sitting your exams these visits were part of your education and you gradually widened your circle of acquaintances. But that had virtually no part in the policy-making of the SLA, and the Association didn't have much to do with salaries, nothing that seemed to be moving the thing forward.

There was another national organisation, the Association of Assistant Librarians (AAL),[40] and a number of young firebrands set up a West of Scotland AAL Division to challenge the establishment, and the establishment said, 'Come back when you're an all-Scottish Division.' I became the hit guy to set up the East of Scotland Division of the AAL in the same meeting room in the Central Library where the SLA was set up in 1908. After that we recruited enough people from the north of Scotland, and we became a division of the AAL, which as a UK organisation wasn't answerable to the SLA. We could say what we wanted and we set out to have a seat on the AAL Council. We battled for that for a number of years. People were coming from all over Scotland, meeting on Sunday afternoons in each other's houses because we had to do it in our own time. We spent week-ends, days, evenings and nights scheming and were eventually successful – Scotland was given two places on the National Council of the AAL and I was one of these. After going to meetings in London for a few years, they asked me to be President in 1972 – the first ever Scottish President of the AAL.

That took me out of Edinburgh and down south quite a lot because there were 17 divisions throughout the UK and the President was expected to put in an appearance and speak at each of these. You had a Presidential address, you had four Council meetings a year and so I ran out of spare time. I started all this when I'd just opened Blackhall, and whether Charlie Minto thought he owed me one, but I traded in half my annual leave, he put in the other half and the Committee approved this arrangement. Otherwise it would have been impossible on the family, quite apart from anything else.

Out of that grew a tremendous number of contacts up and down the country, I represented the AAL on the LA National Council and met a lot of people there. I'd wrested one thing away from the west of Scotland, and thought I'd wrest another couple of things away from them. So in 1966 I started editing *SLA News*,[41] which hitherto had been largely a prerogative of successive people in Lanark County. In 1966 I also took over the organisation of the Summer School at Newbattle from Jimmy Cockburn. I was doing three things all at the same time, becoming more and more involved. I did the editing of the *News* for about six years, I ran the Summer School for 11 years. In 1980, whether in an attempt to get rid of me I don't know, but the SLA made me President.

As the President, you couldn't go on doing a number of things, so I passed on the Summer School and the magazine to other people. I've now been on the SLA Council continuously for 35 years – the longest-ever serving member. Then I'd a phone call from an old friend who thought I would be just the guy to take over from him as chair of the LA General Purposes Committee. I let my name go forward and was made Chairman of the Staff and House Committee which basically ran the LA: it hired and fired staff, it had relations with the union, it looked after the finances, publishing, the building, everything. We had about 100 staff. It's a big organisation with its own headquarters in London off Tottenham Court Road.

It was more or less a full-time job. Although there was a paid Secretary, the elected member was expected to play a major role. I did that for far too long until we revamped the committee structure, wound down the elected role and appointed as Chief Executive George Cunningham,[42] who had given up as an MP by that time, and a very successful Chief Executive he was. I worked closely with him in handing over the management to people paid to manage it. I think perhaps they were wanting to get rid of me again, and they made me President of the LA in 1990. I served my year as President, had two years on the LA Council after that – they made me Chairman of the Council – then it was time to move on. I was the only person ever to have been the President of the LA, the SLA and the AAL in 150 years of libraries in the UK. I look back with a lot of pleasure on it.

Then in 1993 I had a stroke. I was out of the game for about six months but I'd a number of things on the go in the Library so I wanted to get back and retire under my own terms. I went back and found what you expect after six months, that things are exactly as you left it. I finished what I set out to do and retired. I've got a photograph my wife took of me going to work smiling on my last day. To the day I retired I never stopped wondering what the day would bring. If anybody can spend 40 years in the one city, in the one organisation and still be keen to go to their work, that says something for it.

My motto has been, 'I'm here if they want me.' I spent the last year doing a feasibility study for a big extension to the Central Library, which went to an international architectural competition which we had 150 entries for, and I had to help with the judging. This was after I came out of hospital, and I enjoyed it thoroughly. At one time, the Corporation had brought back George Washington Pound,[43] the architect of the building, to recommend where to extend the Library when that became necessary. Pound was the chap who did the Old College Library and the Standard Life building on George Street among a whole lot of libraries in Hawick and Jedburgh and so on. His recommendation was that the only place would be out the back. The Committee decided that was to be reserved, and when I was in charge of the Central Library, we bought up bits of that land as they came on the market until we had that whole site immediately behind the Library. A number of times I've had to hold out against wishes to build houses or shops or car parks or anything on that site.

Edinburgh never spent a lot of money on its libraries. Of course, the extension wasn't built, and I doubt if I'll live to see it built. That was a big disappointment to everybody concerned because a tremendous amount of work went into it. We've got detailed plans which still hold good, will probably hold good for another ten years yet anyway. I think we could have financed the capital but not the cost of running it after we'd built it because it would more or less double what is there now.

I've no regrets at all at having chosen the profession of librarian. One of the things that I got which I was very touched with when I retired was a specially-bound volume of cuttings, a sort of 'This is Your Life' book. I was a terrible blether always. I used to say to people who wanted to see round the Central Library, 'Do you want the half-hour or do you want the four-hour?'

One of the things I insisted on in Blackhall was that you look up, you talk to the person using the Library. The nice things about serving in a library were that you knew their names, no money changed hands, apart from a fine sometimes, and they came voluntarily. They didn't come because they had to; they didn't have to buy something. You couldn't have a better across-the-counter relationship than that. Old Savage is quoted as saying, 'I will not have Post Office manners in my library!' I knew exactly what he meant, because in the old days of digging in tickets, it was all too easy to keep your head down. You just gave back the tickets and went on to the next one, particularly when you were busy. I used to smack knuckles, figuratively speaking, of people who didn't look up and talk to the people. The result is that, over the years, you meet and see a huge number of people and they say, 'Oh, it's you! Oh, I remember you when you used to work in the Reference Library.' It's a tiny village when you've been working in the public eye like that.

Interviewed 22 August 1996

Gavin Drummond, MBE

My name is Gavin Drummond, and I was born in Perth on the 4th January 1939. Created the War! I've been retired for two years.

My father had a chequered background. He was born in Glasgow. My grandfather had been a policeman in Glasgow, and during the time there were the Glasgow gangs around he was beaten up and eventually died as a result of his injuries. After my grandfather died my father and his mother moved around. He spent part of his childhood in Finavon, just outside Forfar. He also spent time in Dundee, London, Arran and so on. So he moved around.

My father was 63 when he died 27 years ago – 1975, so he would be born in 1913–14. He started off working as a chiropodist, trained as a chiropodist. He didn't enjoy chiropody at all. Then he worked in a shoe shop in Perth, and that's where he met my mother. She was the manageress of the shoe shop and he worked there for some years and then moved into the telephone exchange, a telephonist. In Perth.

My mother was born in Rattray and her father was a farm worker and they moved around farms in the Rattray, Alyth, Coupar Angus area in the days when the feeing[1] was going on. So her father was moving, not on a regular basis but an occasional basis. My great-grandfather was a farm worker, and my great-grandmother had been in domestic service. I think he probably was on the farm and great-grandmother was in the farmhouse.

I think the farm cottages they lived in were basic, but that was all they knew and they were comfortable with that. They knew the farmer had a more luxurious lifestyle but they didn't expect a luxurious lifestyle. They weren't entitled to it was the assumption. It was still a kind of feudal system where the class structure was very clearly defined, and they wouldn't expect to rise up the class structure too quickly. Expectations weren't great at all. I think my family were all traditional people who thought they knew their place in society. All these things have thankfully changed.

Then they moved into Perth, I think, in the late 1920s. My grandfather had given up farm work. I think that he was getting to the age where he was coming to retiral. So he worked as a gardener with A K Bell[2] of Bell's Whisky. Once my mother's father died they settled in Perth, and that was the base for the family after that.

My mother worked in the shoe shop from leaving school and became manageress in due course. My mother was one of these typical early '20s people. She was a very bright, intelligent person who had been very successful at Rattray School and at Blairgowrie High School. She could've achieved a great deal more in a different generation but I don't suppose they ever thought that. They were always happy with what they had. At school at that time there was an attempt to push some of the brighter pupils on to higher education. But the family couldn't afford it so she wasn't going to get that opportunity. Being a female, she had to go out and work and make some money for the family. She was the third of a family of seven.

She would've liked to have gone on to a university, and I think she would've liked to have taught because that was one of the desirable jobs at that stage – highly respected. So she would've liked to have done that but didn't get that opportunity.

My mother was about eight years older than my father so she was born about 1906. She died in 1958; I think she was 53 when she died. I've got a half-sister. When my mother died, a few years later my father married again, and I suddenly discovered I had a sister when I was 21, which was a bit of a change as I'd been an only child when my mother was alive.

We lived in a house in Rose Crescent in Perth and that was where I was conscious of life beginning, probably before I went to school, so about three, four, something like that. During the War my father was away in the Army; he was in the REME,[3] and was in India during his service. I think his view was he had a more reserved war than many others. My wife Muriel's Dad, for example, was in the front line in Europe and obviously had a very different war from the war my father had. What my father did talk about was that all the soldiers had servants.

They had 'boys'. I think a lot of them were West Africans who'd been taken out there to make their tea, iron their clothes, do their washing and so on. So in comparison to other parts, it was such a sheltered life that they had.

Alastair, our younger son, went off to do voluntary service in India, and the first impression he got at landing in Delhi was the abject poverty, beggars in the streets, kids looking for money, disfigured people all over the place, absolutely hellish sort of environment.

Rose Crescent, Perth, was a semi-detached villa. It actually belonged to A K Bell.[4] When my grandfather died, my grandmother had to move out of the tied house they had on the estate, and they were given this house, which eventually the family bought from Bell at a very reasonable rate. It was a three-bedroom house and a nice garden. All mod cons, electric light; it had all the facilities. We were extremely fortunate because in comparison to lots of my friends, the kind of accommodation we had was extremely good. While my father was getting a very small pittance of a salary there wasn't a lot of money elsewhere but the house was very comfortable.

At the age of five I went to Cherrybank Infant School in Perth, and then, age seven, I moved on to Craigie Primary School. School is something that's gone out of my mind pretty much. It didn't interest me a great deal. I think it was OK. I just got on with things. I don't consider myself to be an intellectual type in any way. I think to some extent, but I'm not an intellectual type. I think I've got through life really with good fortune, and I'm sure some of the things that I picked up in school and in life subsequently have helped me in that respect. But schooldays have been and gone.

I suppose it's more the arts, the literature cum arts subjects that I've been interested in. I don't think I'm particularly numerate. I can count but it's not at the forefront of my abilities, and I'm not a particularly scientific person. Always a reader. I got the traditional *Beano*, *Dandy*, *Eagle*, *Rover* kind of comics. We'd a newsagent who delivered and I also used to pick up a few from him and we used to swop them.

I think I began reading books from quite an early age and I read fairly widely. Biggles,[5] Enid Blyton,[6] I can't remember anybody else but I read them. Both mother and father encouraged me. Neither of them were particularly enthusiastic readers and I didn't see them sitting down reading a great deal but I did read a reasonable amount.

I think I must've been about seven or eight when I joined the public library and it has to be said it was a most off-putting experience. I don't know why I ever became a librarian because I think one of my earliest recollections is in the Sandeman Library in Perth which was the City Library. I went in one day just to have a wander round. That was when they had the turnstiles, and you could only get in if you could show you'd a ticket, a library card, and I didn't have mine with me. I couldn't even go in to look at the stock. I was furious! And maybe 20 years later I became the Deputy City Librarian and the person who refused me entry was still working there, because I remembered her.

When I worked in Dunfermline Public Libraries we were encouraged, forced to make sure that kids had clean hands. If they didn't have clean hands they were sent outside to wash them. And all they did, if there was puddles in the ground, on the pavement, they just stuck their hands in the puddles, rubbed their hands on their trousers or their skirt and came back in, and they were relatively clean. It embarrasses me greatly how we must have put kids off coming into the library by doing that. It doesn't happen now. It's a changed concept, changed attitude, which is wonderful.

As a result of sitting and passing the Qualifying Exam,[7] I went to Perth Academy, a six-year secondary school. There wasn't a junior secondary; you either went to the Academy or to the High School. Perth High School, was also a six-year senior secondary, but it did a different range of courses.

What I was saying to you about school – it was there, it happened and you went through it. I suppose at the end of the day there was obviously some benefit and you experienced the education and came out and made friends, and that was it. I took French. I didn't pass the Qualifying certificate to do two language courses. I did the one language course. French was OK but I wasn't motivated.

I did a Higher[8] in English and in History and did Lowers in French, Maths, Geography. I think that was it. I completed the course and I carried on till sixth year and left in 1956. I was 17, and went to work in Dunfermline Public Libraries.

My family were very much church-centred and at one stage in my life, while I was still at school, I was really quite interested in going into the ministry. At least one of my friends at school was moving in that direction so it was something that interested me. I know my folks would've been absolutely thrilled to bits had I moved in that direction. I didn't do it. I think I'm lazy by nature, and had I worked a bit harder

I'm sure I would've got the appropriate passes to get me there. I didn't. I didn't have the Higher passes to get me off to university. I think I'm quite glad, looking back on it now.

I was a regular attender at Sunday School and became a member of the church as a teenager. Mother's side in particular were very involved in the kirk, Church of Scotland. My father eventually grew into it. I'm not sure if he was just bulldozed into it or whether he really developed an interest. But he became involved as time went on and it was just natural for me to go along with them. There was a lot happened in the kirk at that stage. There was a whole group of us, we did a lot together – socially in particular. It was quite a social event and social gathering. There are still folk from that time that I meet with on an occasional basis. When we're in Perth there are still some of the girls or the guys who were around then, we meet and catch up with them. So it's still quite nice to have these contacts.

Scouts have been a lifelong interest and from being a Cub, I've done lots in the Scout Association since then.[9] And I've been involved in various sporting organisations, particularly golf and badminton that I still play, and played a few other things like football and rugby and cricket. I think rugby would be my favourite but I was a very flimsy little lad and got thrown around easily so I wasn't particularly efficient.

These were the main interests, and life was fairly full. Through the Cubs and Scouts and Youth Fellowship and suchlike, there were lots of things happening. Whether we were putting shows on or out doing things it was great fun.

I don't think I'll ever know what influenced me to become a librarian. It wasn't something that just suddenly came as a flash in the night or anything like that. I don't know what influenced me. If you ask about somebody who influenced me, yeah, Bill Aitken,[10] who was the County Librarian in Perth and who then moved to Ayrshire and finished up lecturing in Strathclyde. He spoke about libraries at a meeting I was at one night and I thought, hmm, interesting! I suppose that started me off. But I think I'd been a drifter and I saw an advert for a library assistant in Dunfermline Public Libraries just at the time I was about to be leaving school and I'd no idea what I wanted to do. I think I was typical of the generation. Lots of us had no idea.

It was in the days when there were trains between Perth and Dunfermline and I used to travel daily. I was only there for a year. I used to get a train in the morning, about an hour to Dunfermline and then the train home at night. I could be away at half past seven in the morning and back at half past eight, nine o'clock at night. It could be long days but it was OK, you could cope.

I was a library assistant. That meant you were behind the counter, issuing and stamping books, putting them back on the shelves, just doing the donkey work basically. I don't know if we learned any skills, but I think it was more you learned about people and learned how to relate to your customers, which I think was probably the most important lesson to learn at that stage. I think the pay was about £7 a fortnight – we got paid on a fortnightly basis.

We did a five-day week. Every second Saturday, we worked. That was from nine till five, and when you worked on a Saturday you got a day off during the week. Then two evenings a week we worked till eight o'clock. On the day you worked till eight o'clock, you would start at one o'clock. So it worked out about 40 hours a week.

Well, I worked that kind of shift for a good number of years and I used to quite enjoy a day off during the week because you could do things when places were quiet. Week-ends were OK. There was time to catch up with everybody at week-ends.

I was working in the central library in Abbot Street in Dunfermline. There was also a branch at Rosyth and I used to spend some time there, but most of the time was in Abbot Street. There was a librarian and a deputy librarian. There was a children's librarian. That's three. Maybe about 10 of us, 10 or 12 of us in total – very friendly, very pleasant people to work for or to work with. I enjoyed the year. It was an interesting introduction into working life – fairly gentle. I was just the junior in the library and got the dirty jobs to do. And because I was the only male on the staff, I was given some of the heavier jobs because it seemed appropriate for me to do them rather than the girls to do them at that stage. That was OK; I didn't have any problems. The only other males on the staff were the two janitors.

At the end of the year, a job came up in Perth County, and Bill Aitken, who was at that stage the County Librarian, encouraged me to apply for the job, which I got. Then when I got it he left. So I wasn't sure if it was cause and effect or not! But I went to Perth County and I was there for seven years, which was a most enjoyable place to be as well.

The county and the city were two separate services. At that stage the county did raise some of the rate, which was for libraries, so they paid the city a small amount of money back. It was the County Library I worked with for that period. I was a library assistant for most of the time. In between times I went off to Library School in Glasgow and did the course there.

At that stage Librarianship wasn't a graduate profession at all, and if you were going to qualify professionally you had to do a one-year full-time course at the School of Librarianship, College of Commerce, Pitt Street in Glasgow.[11] I just had to pay it. Some authorities did pay for their staff to go, but the rural authorities like Perth have never been known to be generous towards the staff. The cities, I think, were always much better, more supportive of their staff. It seemed to be that rural authorities like Angus and Perth and Kinross were ruled by the country gents, the Independent Tories. They wanted to keep the rates down as low as possible because if rates went up they'd have to pay their servants and their serfs a bit more. So it was a question of keeping them away down.

I was quite fortunate that we had relations in Glasgow, but we still had to pay them. It would've been more expensive if we'd gone somewhere else. It was the first time I'd been out of the sort of Perth environment and it was an amazing introduction to the big, wide world. You had the opportunity to meet fellow students from all round Scotland and beyond. It was a good experience and one I enjoyed. There were about maybe 20 students on the course with a pretty even balance between men and women, which was unusual because librarianship had a very strong female element.

The course comprised library-based subjects – things like cataloguing, classification, bibliography, historic bibliography. There must've been other things. I've forgotten them all. It's like most courses – interesting while they lasted but when you came back to work they were pretty irrelevant. Not the kind of thing that really helps you run a library service.

In these days, it was the technical skills that we were being trained in. I'm talking from vague, vague memories, but I suppose I discovered some theoretical procedures that I've used all my life. I think though it could've been a bit broader and could've been more about people/ interpersonal skills. These are things we talk about now. We didn't talk about them 35, 40 years ago. So I think that kind of skill would've been probably more useful than a lot of the theoretical, operational skills, because if librarianship's about anything, it's about dealing with people and matching people's requirements up with the information. Library education now has changed so much, and it's much more looking at some of these skills rather than the detailed operational skills.

I think it was about 1960 I went to Library School, and then when I came back a job for an assistant librarian came up which I got, and that was my first professional post when I was in Perth County.

The County Library HQ was in Rose Terrace, which was one of the old Perth Academy buildings, overlooking the North Inch and the River Tay. That building was used as the school probably in the '20s and then it moved to the present site at Newlands. There were branches in places like Blairgowrie, Aberfeldy, Comrie, Crieff, Kinross. That might be it. And then most of the schools around the county had small collections and the head teacher was the librarian. It was one of the jobs they had to take on in the rural schools. One of my jobs for a long time was to go round with the library van and we used to exchange the collections in schools all over Perthshire and places like Straloch and Kinloch Rannoch and Killin.

In these days, when the roads weren't as good as they are now, getting from Perth to Kinloch Rannoch and back in a day was not on. We used to spend nights in hotels in Kinloch Rannoch and Killin and Aberfoyle. So it was quite a pleasant life. The driver, John Balfour, and myself, we spent a lot of time together, got on very well with him. He was a fine guy. Another of these people who had huge potential, which he'd never developed. When he left school he went into the Army, National Service,[12] and then when he left the Army he moved into the County Library and he'd been a driver there all his days. He was about ten years older than me. I still see him occasionally when we're in Perth and keep in touch with him.

John and I used to go round all the schools in Perthshire, and it was an interesting life. We visited each school about three times a year, because there was only one van. That was in the days when there were lots of rural schools. The closures have changed that situation. It was a huge area to cover and such a contrasting area from Highland Perthshire down to Lochleven, round Lochleven-Kinross direction. So it was a fascinating balance.

It was a good job, and meeting the teachers and the pupils in the schools was good experience. We didn't take boxes. The van was filled with books and we just exchanged. If they had 500 books, we would just select 500 from our collection on the van. All we were doing really was moving stock round from school to school around the area. But different areas have different interests, so that was where you had to keep in touch with the staff, to find out what particular areas were of interest.

In one day we might do four or five schools. If we did that, say, four days in the week, well, about 20 schools in the week. I would imagine there must've been about 70 or 80 schools around Perthshire we were dealing with. They were asked beforehand if there were any particular things they wanted. A schedule was produced each year so they knew when we were coming, and they were asked if there were particular topics they wanted or particular titles to let us know and we'd try to take them with us. We couldn't always do that, but we always made an effort to do so. That was in the days of the Primary Memorandum Development when schools were moving into topic and patch work.[13] We were being asked for collections on particular areas of the curriculum. So that was changing the focus again because before, they just got a general collection and after that they were looking for much more specific material.

The problem was that ten schools would be doing the same thing, so you couldn't provide for that. I think it's one of the interesting things about librarianship, because the real purpose is to ensure that you find the material that's going to suit that particular community or that particular person. That's where the skill of the librarian comes in, because you've got to have the interpersonal skill of being able to talk to a customer.

You had a limited amount of material to choose from, so within that context you made up collections that you hoped were appropriate to the particular schools or branches.

John and I shared that work. We chose the collections and put them into the schools.

The library van could hold only about 3,000 books. On shelves. That's about standard for the County Mobile Library that operates. It was a mobile unit and it was on a solid chassis. So it's not a big collection, and when you think that collection was covering everything from popular fiction to non-fiction to children's collections, the operation was done within very limited confines.

I did that for seven years. I was with Perth County for seven years. It was time to think about moving away, because having lived in Perth all these years, I could've sat in Perth and probably finished up as

County Librarian, without being immodest, and I would've seen nothing apart from one local environment.

Then a job came up as Depute Librarian in Perth City which I applied for and got, and I was there for six months and decided this was not the place for me. Muriel and I got engaged about that time. She worked in the County Library. That's where we met. Then I moved away to the city, and I found that hard going. It had very little money. It had a lovely, charming guy who was the librarian. He was called Alex Tait – I think! He was a lovely guy, but professionally we didn't manage to hit it off. Personally we were fine. I really liked the guy but in professional terms I couldn't have worked there much longer. So I decided to go. His experience and mine were quite different – I suppose the arrogance of youth and impatience came into the whole thing – but I wanted to see things happening and do things and move things around. He wasn't interested in doing anything like that.

It was a good promotion and potentially a good job but it wasn't exactly a big library service. We were serving 40,000 population. Although I was only 26, professionally it would've been daft to have stayed there long. So that's when I decided to move and I moved to Bedfordshire, a super leap. I moved to a place called Houghton Regis, which was just outside Dunstable. When they were creating the London overspills, it was that kind of area. It had been a small village of about 1,200 population and it suddenly became a community of 12,000, and there were no facilities around. And they wondered why there was vandalism and all sorts of damage being done. Folk had come out from the comfortable, warm, scruffy and dirty areas of London into the country and they'd nowhere to do anything. Then a year later there was a new library built in Dunstable and I went to the new library as the librarian, which was great. Dunstable was a super place to be, a good-sized community, and the library was right in the centre of the town and it was really a lively, active place.

I was down in Bedford for six months and then we got married and Muriel moved down. I'd bought a house. It was in the centre of Bedfordshire, a place called Ampthill, which is a nice little Georgian village. It was a lovely place to be. We enjoyed it there and were down in Bedford for just under five years.

It was the time when there was a lot of development taking place in England. There'd been a new Libraries Act[14] and Bedfordshire had been a fairly sleepy service and suddenly money was becoming available, new buildings were being erected, new services developed. It was a fair revelation for me having come from somewhere like the Sandeman, which was pretty backward and not a lot of money to spend, the kind of old-fashioned concept of libraries being dull, studious, boring and dusty places. It was a sort of grace-and-favour thing to the customers – they were lucky to be allowed in and get this service as long as they had clean hands, and they didn't turn the corners of the pages down and such like, because that was another heinous crime!

Whereas down in Bedfordshire, there was a bit of a buzz about things, you were talking about new services, new buildings, trying to pull people in. It was much more promotional. You were out to sell the service and bring people in. It was a super experience.

That opened my eyes to lots of things about the profession and the role of the library in a community. It's been found to be the case in a number of surveys that a large percentage of the population use the local library service. Every child's got to use the school because that's a requirement, obviously. But in terms of optional services, libraries are pretty much at the top of the list. We did a survey on one occasion in Angus and something like between 55 per cent and 60 per cent of the population were using our service just for borrowing. Even more would be using it as a meeting place and just for information. So despite saying we've got a population that is thirled to television or to video games or something like that, people still are using libraries for information, for reading and all sorts of other activities.

Again, being a bit arrogant, I think if I'd stayed there, I'd probably have finished up as County Librarian of Bedfordshire and that would've been exciting as well. After the five years in Dunstable, I felt it was time to move on to a more senior post and I'd applied for a number of jobs. I had had an interview in Hartlepool, and Muriel and I went to see the place and decided there was no way we could live in this. The centre of the town was a coal bing[15] at that stage, and it was one of the depressed north-east communities. But it's all changed. I had an interview there and I was asked if I would like to come and live there and I said no. So I wasn't offered the job.

Then two jobs came up after that. One was the County Librarian of Selkirkshire, in Galashiels. The other one was Deputy County Librarian in Aberdeen. The fascinating thing was the County Librarian in Aberdeen had been the librarian in Galashiels. He'd moved up to Aberdeen succeeding Matthew Paton – Bill Paton as he was known.[16] My then boss in Bedfordshire discouraged me from going for Galashiels. He thought it was not a good idea, it was too small, and he was probably right. And I applied for Aberdeen County Library, became Depute County Librarian there in 1971.

I don't suppose we'd any desperate desire to return to Scotland. It was the job came up and the Aberdeenshire job seemed interesting. And it was. It was a very good job to have for that period. I found it absolutely fascinating. I'd moved when the Robertson Report[17] was talking about improved library services. Aberdeen County Library was part of the Education Department and the Director of Education, James A D Michie, was a great promoter of this service and really a good guy to have around because we got a lot of money for development. In every year I was in Aberdeen, we were either building a new branch and/or putting new mobiles on the road. I think when I went there, there were two mobiles and when I left I think we had about six.

It was a big county and we were developing mobile library services, branch library services, we'd built or renovated branch libraries all round the county at that stage. We were developing a school library service. At one stage it had been very much 'Just give a collection of books to the schools and they'll put them in a cupboard and if the kids are good on Friday afternoon, they'll get to read them.' Whereas it was really looking at a much more focused curriculum-supporting service. It was really a hive of activity. Money was coming in and services were developing. Neil McCorkindale,[18] who was the County Librarian at that stage, was a superb guy to work for. He's the guy who'd been librarian in Galashiels, and Neil was just one of my heroes, I suppose. He'd this great, very clear-sighted view of where the service was going, and I learned a lot from him.

We just lived outside the city, a suburb called Milltimber, on the way to Deeside. When we were in Aberdeen Graham was born.

I was there for about four years till reorganisation. The library authority before reorganisation had been Angus and Kincardine, and with reorganisation, Kincardine was going to join Aberdeenshire. So the last year or so of my life in Aberdeenshire was spent taking over the Kincardine service from Angus. Then the job in Angus came along in 1974, so I was at both sides of the Kincardine move.

Mary Smith, who was the then County Librarian, was retiring in Angus and the job was advertised. I applied and got it. Each job has been exciting and I've got a buzz out of each job as I've gone along. Maybe one prepares you for the next one.

Angus was maybe a bad move at that time because Angus was a very tight, miserable authority. Compared to Aberdeenshire it was like stepping back 100 years. It was just not in the 20th century at all. Nice people. I'd met some of the Angus councillors. They came for a visit to see some of our developments in Aberdeenshire when I was there. They were very sweet and charming people and I thought they were quite impressive. Some of them actually interviewed me when I applied for the job here and I was aware of the tight financial position.

When I came, we did manage to see a few developments taking place. Then, of course, reorganisation came within a year, and that changed the situation altogether. Angus before reorganisation had a County Library and independent libraries in Arbroath, Brechin, Carnoustie, Forfar and Montrose. So you had six services serving a population of about 100,000 people which is utter nonsense, a terrible waste of resources and money. The bringing of them together made a huge difference and we were able to see things developing quite dramatically.

Not so much the staff, more locals, didn't appreciate the reorganisation at all because they saw their burgh being downgraded. But very quickly the benefit was evident to the users. Arbroath, for example, might have had a stock of about 40,000 items, whereas it came into Angus District, and they had access to just about a couple of hundred thousand items. So the scale was quite different.

The only new library building in Angus has been in Carnoustie and that was opened in 1975. The old Carnoustie Town Council started it and we finished it off. But all the buildings have been either extended or renovated over the period. Oh, there is one new building in Forfar. Forfar was in the Meffan Institute.[19] The Meffan Institute was given to the town by Miss Jane Meffan, whose father and uncle had been provosts of the town, and she gave money for a building which would improve the intellectual quality, or something like that, of the people of Forfar.

It was originally a library, a museum and a reading room, and when I came here it was run down. It was really an old-fashioned, dusty place. There was a Willie Low[20] supermarket up the road, which became vacant when they moved into a new superstore, and we took that over. That's been the library for maybe 15 years and it's been a huge improvement. The Meffan Institute we converted into a museum and gallery, and that's been another good development and that continues to improve the intellectual qualities of the people of Forfar.

The service was ripe for development, and when libraries and museums came together it was good because the two services have got so much in common – providing information about your community, about your heritage and they've been able to feed off one another.

There was no archive at that stage. About ten to 15 years ago we appointed an archivist and there's now an archive centred in Montrose Library, which has gathered a very impressive collection together. The sad thing is, I think the Scottish Record Office still doesn't consider it an approved centre because it hasn't got somebody with archival qualifications. Fiona Sharlaw, the archivist, is excellent and has done a superb job in collecting archive material from all round Angus, and collecting the Council material, because that was all over the place and has now been collected together in Montrose.

And she's been able to pull in lots of material from organisations, societies around Angus. The Brechin Guildry, for example, had material going back to about the 13th-15th century that was lying in a cupboard in a damp building. Fiona had been able to get that and it includes some absolutely superb material.

I came here as County Librarian in 1974. In 1975 I became Director of Libraries and Museums for Angus District, and then in 1996 I became Director of Cultural Services. So the whole thing developed somewhat from libraries to libraries and museums to cultural services, which took in the arts, entertainment profile.

I'm only sorry it's now disappeared because it's been absorbed into recreation services. I think if I'd still been there, I would probably have had a heart attack.

Angus has got a fairly wide director structure and the Scottish Executive have been leaning on the Council to cut the structure down, for no good reason, because when surveys have been done, Angus has come out pretty much top of local authority services. I think that's because the directors who are running the services are professionals who know something about their services and the community they're serving. Whereas when you've got the narrower structure, you've got executive directors who've no idea, don't know anything about the services they're providing, who are managers in general terms and haven't got the kind of focus. Whereas the Angus structure had, and I'm quite sad that the Cultural Services Department has disappeared now.

When I came here first of all it was an Independent council, a Tory council, who didn't want to spend much money. They were disasters because they kept falling out with one another. They'd make a decision at a committee meeting and then when it came to council there had been a fall-out in the ranks and somebody would oppose it, and there was no consistency at all. They'd no discipline in the group, so from the officials' point of view it was a difficult time to operate. SNP[21] came in in the second election and they have been extremely disciplined and good to work with, and they've been very keen to see developments. Angus is not the kind of place where you'll see massive great, dramatic developments. It's been called a douce[22] area and things happened on a gradualist basis and that's been very much the case for most of the services in Angus. They've happened gradually. The SNP councillors have been good to work with.

The conveners I've worked with have all been good and supportive and very interested in what's going on. In terms of the service I had – cultural services – if they're not going to support the development of Scottish culture, who is?

I would've liked more support obviously. I would've liked to have seen more happening over the period. But you've got to put all these things in context with the resources available to the authorities and what the priorities are. Over the period the service has developed quite significantly and it's been because there's been a team effort between the councillors and the officials. Angus has been very good from that point of view. We tend to work together as a team rather than a master-servant relationship which happens in a lot of councils, where the official is a sort of bag-carrier for the councillor. It's not been that way in Angus.

Arbroath's a very sad place now. The fishing industry has been badly hit, and of course the recent business about smokies,[23] where they're talking about smokies maybe not fitting into the European regulations, could kill that industry as well. It's not just the fishing; there was a major engineering works – Giddings, Lewis-Fraser,[24] which has closed. Most of the big employers in Arbroath have now gone. Arbroath and Brechin have been the two which have been hit most by unemployment. In Arbroath it's about one in three unemployed, which is terrible.

Forfar's the main centre for textiles – Don,[25] that's the major employer. When we came to Angus in 1974, Don's employed, oh, maybe 1,500 folk. I think it's down to about 700 now. A lot of the women were employed on the machines. Now there are two or three people in white coats with helmets on who press buttons, and it's just a huge change in the kind of employment pattern – it's polypropylene.

I really enjoyed my time in Angus and got a buzz out of everything that happened. I think I got more of a buzz in the last few years because of the cultural services element. We were able to develop a few things with that unit that we hadn't been able to do before. But I felt that I'd come to the stage where I'd done 40 years in local government; pension-wise it wasn't helping me to carry on working; the pressures were becoming huge.

In the Council the demands on chief officers I think are unreasonable. Apart from running your own department, you're heavily involved in corporate affairs and I was also involved in a lot of other professional affairs outwith Angus. I was running around like a mad thing. It seemed to be escalating rather than running down. I think as you get older it takes longer to do things, and while I really enjoyed it, I decided there's more to life than doing that for the next five years. I think I was probably meant to just sit around and do nothing, so I've quite enjoyed that. I haven't had any withdrawal symptoms. I still keep in touch with my colleagues. I'm interested in what they do but I've no interest in interfering or telling them anything.

I do more reading than I used to and also I've just started to help with the Citizens Advice Bureau.[26] I do a day a week there. I've started to play more golf than I played for ages. I've been a member of Forfar Golf Club ever since I've been in Forfar, but some years I might've played once a year and when you're paying £260 for a membership it's an expensive round of golf! So I'm getting more value for money. I'm involved in the church quite a lot as well. I've always been pretty active in the kirk.

I'm a person who accepts things pretty much. I've been very lucky, not just in the authorities I've worked with but in the fact that because of them I've been able to be involved in a lot of external activities throughout Scotland. That has really given me a much broader view of the service that the department has tried to provide over the years. I've benefited from working within a number of different authorities and also having the opportunity to be involved in professional affairs and associations and other groups – the Scottish Library Association,[27] Scottish Library & Information Council.[28] I was an adviser to COSLA[29] for many years. All these things have given me an opportunity, just broadened my viewpoint. Otherwise there's a terrible danger you sit in your own little patch and you don't see beyond the four walls of your own authority.

Libraries are in the midst of a huge change because the government has put in something like £50 million to develop a national network, a computer network, which will allow libraries to become learning centres.[30] Now I think a library has always been a learning centre. Maybe in my younger days we went into the market of trying to push the pap, the popular material, so that we could claim to have big issues. But a library has always been a place where people, everybody in the community, has the opportunity to use it as a learning centre. Using the technology, the development of learning centres in libraries where you've got computers and access to the Internet, access to learning packages, together with printed material, creates a unique facility, a unique resource for communities. I think more and more people are going to spend their time working on learning packages, and on things like genealogy researches and accessing records on the Internet. The library's going to be a resource which will allow members of the community access to all these facilities. It's going to be a struggle because money's becoming tighter and tighter in public services and the library service is going to have to fight to keep these resources up to date. All this money's been ploughed in but nothing has been ploughed in to maintain it – to replace it in five years' time on a reducing budget is going to be a huge problem.

Mr Blair's[31] quoted as saying libraries are the centre of his agenda. Now that could be a double-edged sword, but from the profession's point of view to hear that being said is something that my colleagues have got to hang on to and promote. If the government are saying libraries are at the centre of their agenda and are to be at the heart of their learning strategy, that puts them really in a central position in local authority services. I hope they can hang on to that and get the resources to deliver properly, because it's fine to talk but you've got to have the resources to be able to deliver.

I could be biased, of course, but I always remember there was a lady who used our mobile library service in Aberdeenshire, lived in a remote part of the county. She taught herself all sorts of rural skills like curing her own meat, making her own butter and suchlike, just by using some of the stock that she got from us and that said something about how her quality of life improved. That's what it's about, it seems to me. There are resources available that you can use to improve your quality of life, your understanding, your knowledge. I think it's a hugely important service to provide.

Interviewed 23 February 2002

John Preston

My name is John Preston, and I was born in the east end of Glasgow, in Dennistoun, 13th November 1946.

My father was a shopkeeper. Him and my Mum ran a wee fruit and vegetable shop. We stayed in Tollcross, the fruit shop was in Shettleston and they had it since 1938 up until the early '70s. Even up until the mid '50s we used to get a lot of deliveries; particularly the ones I remember is fae Barr's Irn-Bru[1] – still the horse-drawn drays. When the horses came they used to try and get into the vegetables that were on display at the front o' the shop.

My earliest memories date from the time we stayed at 82 Maukinfauld Road. That's Tollcross. Not a lot of money, stayed in this wee room and kitchen, not particularly salubrious but very happy family life. I have one brother. He's eight and a half year older than me. He was born in 1938. My brother and I slept in the room – it was almost like a box-room, so my brother had that and I was in a cot or a bed later on.

It was a typical Glasgow close, kept very clean. It wasnae a wally close,[2] it wasn't a posh one, it was just a plaster one, but you did wee fancy whorls on the steps – the pipeclay[3] on it. We were on the ground floor and there was one shared toilet in the back close. There was three families per landing. It was four storeys. There was no bath, no bathroom. We'd a big tin bath. We used to have to bath in front of the fire.

It was gas lighting. It was the gas in the street and the gas up the close. I can remember quite clearly the old lady lamplighter comin' in, lightin' up, but the big forward leap in technology is when they got electric lighting in after the War. We didnae have a fridge. We'd a range[4] to start wi' – I can still remember my Mum black-leadin' the old grate. But we became modern about 1954 when we put a tile fireplace in, did away with the old range and got a gas cooker. Tae us this was high-tech. There was a shared washhouse oot the back green. There was a big boiler that you could put the wood in and boil it up.

My father had a pretty poor background. He stayed off what's now the Edinburgh Road in Glasgow. At that time it was country. He come off a poor family. Quite a lot o' the family emigrated abroad because there was nothing here for them. Before he opened up the greengrocer my father emigrated to the States and did various jobs, nothing particularly exciting. He was over there for four or five year, but due to family circumstances he come back and him and my Mum met up in the mid '30s. Of course my father was away during the War. He was in the Army. He was a driver, RASC.[5] He was in Normandy. I think he was born in 1909, so he wasnae called up in the first lot, but I think he was called up in 1941. He got through the War OK. I never knew my grandparents on that side at all. They were dead long before. I just don't know what they did.

I'm no' quite sure what my mother did but she worked in some kind of factory in Glasgow. My Mum was fae West Muir Street, Parkhead. Once they got married, they wanted to try and do something on their own, hence they went into the fruit shop. My maternal grandfather was a lorry driver. I still can remember getting runs in his lorry. That was quite an adventure, you know. In fact, there was two or three lorry drivers in the family. Of course Granny didnae work as women didnae really work at that time.

Of my great-grandparents I know absolutely nothing whatsoever. I think I've an Irish connection somewhere but that's all I know.

My brother was called up to the RAF. He was one o' the last to do National Service,[6] somewhere about 1960–61. He was doin' a joiner apprenticeship at that time, but once he went down south he never really come back. So he's been away now frae Scotland for 40 plus years.

I quite enjoyed working with my hands. When I was a wee kid I used to make things like swords and tomahawks. I tried making a chair at one point because in the shop you got stuff delivered in wooden boxes, and the grapes used to come in barrels with the cork in them. I used to get a lot of comics: *The Hotspur*, *The Rover*, *The Wizard*, *The Adventure*, *The Dandy*, *The Beano*, *The Beezer*. I enjoyed reading.

My Mum and Dad didnae have a lot of money but they gave me a wonderful upbringing. Anything I got, I treasured. Things like clothes you took care of. Clothes were expensive, and when it came to Easter time I'd rather have a Dinky[7] than an Easter egg. I've still got my Dinky toys. I like cars. I played with them but I took care o' them. When my son was wee he would say, 'Dad, can we play wi' your toys?' But he knew fine he hadnae tae bash them aboot or waste them.

Of course, with them having the shop, they were tied. The shop's a seven-day thing, and it was open tae about seven o'clock at night from nine in the morning. My Dad had to go to the market in Glasgow a couple of times a week, maybe in there for half past six, seven o'clock, and they didnae have a car so it was getting the tram in and back out. They worked very hard but they never really got very much for it. To be honest, they wore themselves out – that's why they didnae last very long. Mum died in her early 60s, my Dad when he was about 68. They only got one week's holiday a year. I went every year tae friends o' theirs in Kirkcaldy in Fife, and that was really the only place we went. I would go a week myself and then they would come, because they could only get a week away.

I went to Shettleston Primary. I started when I was five. Nice school, almost open-plan in a way, quite modern for its time. There was two buildings – the old two-storey affair with the balcony round the inside, and another bit had been built sometime later. I got my first taste of power when I became a milk monitor.[8] I enjoyed the school. I've always been able to count and that stood me in good stead; I've always been quite meticulous in my English and grammar and that has stood me in good stead as well.

I must've went up tae secondary school about 1959, Eastbank Academy. It's now the John Wheatley Further College of Education. In fact, it was the 100th anniversary of the school in 1995, and I went to see it again and it's changed so much I could barely recognise it. I didnae particularly enjoy Eastbank Academy. All the folk who went there were local and I wasn't because of where I lived. Most of my friends were still frae Tollcross end.

I always enjoyed History. I always enjoyed English. Science and Technology didnae particularly interest me. I preferred subjects that were people-orientated. I think you had to do French. I got on fine with that. My written French was excellent. I've still got a prize for it for fourth year. My spoken French was dreadful, as you can imagine, coming from Glasgow. My German was the opposite. My German grammar was a' tae pot but my German spoken was great. I think it started about third year when I dropped the science subjects. You could either do Chemistry and Physics or you did a language. I enjoyed my languages, and I won't say I keep them up much but I still know enough. A few years ago the wife and I were on holiday in Bulgaria and the *lingua franca* there is German. I'm not suggesting I was fluent in it, but within a week I was speaking enough to be understood. I suppose that shows I've got a good memory which is a great help in the library world, particularly in reference studies.

I got four Highers[9] – English, History, Maths, and French. I didnae get my German Higher. As I said, my spoken German was fine but my written German wasnae particularly good. That was 1963 and I was only 16, so I didnae want to stay on another year at school. I didnae see any point, I had the Highers. My Mum and Dad didn't have a lot of cash. I really wanted a job where I could start to put some money into the house because I felt I'd been kept long enough, which is maybe silly at 16.

I didn't have any specific ambitions as a laddie. I couldn't go on to higher education because I was too young. So I went to the careers adviser and they did a kind of checklist and I said I hadnae a clue what I wanted to do but I enjoyed working with people. I'd helped my Mum and Dad in the shop so I'd been used to working with the public all my life. He said to me, 'Have you thought about being a librarian?' It had never even crossed my simple wee mind. So he made a phone call and said, 'You've got an interview with Charles Wilfred Black',[10] old C W Black of Glasgow. I remember the ultimate goal was – if you did everything properly and qualified, you could earn £1,000 a year. I thought, 'Oh, what would I do with a' this money?' I won't suggest that it was purely pecuniary, but that was a carrot. So I started in the Mitchell[11] the next week and that's been me in the library world until I'd to pack it in.

I can only speak frae my very inexperienced eyes then but Mr Black was very aloof frae the rest of the staff. He used to come back frae his holidays full of great ideas and the minute his holiday dates was due everybody tried to get the next fortnight off.

The Mitchell was very hierarchical. The front desk had somebody in charge with his number one and number two and the staff at the front desk were all numbered right down to about 12 tae 14 – the folk actually getting the books for the people because it was a closed access place. You'd tae fill in a slip and the locations were all fixed. The person in charge was sitting at the front desk and he had a' these minions sitting in the front and the place where you were on duty was numbered and used tae have a wee buzzer and he'd say, 'Go for that one', and you'd to go and serve the next person. They'd a lift where you sent the chitties up tae fifth floor, fourth floor, and somebody was on duty there and they would get the item, put the chitty into the shelf, put the book in the lift and send it back down.

Other times you'd be doing backroom work. You could be processing books. Now if I can still remember this, you'd tae stamp 'Glasgow Public Libraries' on a' the books. It was page 21 top right, page 101 bottom left. It went on fae that. So you'd tae remember a' this and the right bit of the page as well, and they were all checked.

Once you did the initial front desk thing, there was the various departments of the Mitchell. The Glasgow Room,[12] for example, because it was seen as providing a kind of specialist service was quite prestigious tae work in, but you didnae really get near that until you had some experience. The level of enquiry in the Glasgow Room tended to be quite detailed in some cases. The two special ones were the Glasgow Room and the Music Room. Music to me is tadpoles and telegraph wires so thank goodness they never put me in that. Very few folk could work in that because the level of enquiries needed specialist knowledge.

The satisfaction came when somebody you'd served walked away happy. You felt you'd achieved something. And of course there's stories. They used to get a lot of telephone enquiries maybe half past eight at night, obviously coming frae a pub, drink flowing, glasses clinking: 'Who won?' One of the favourite ones was, 'What day of the week was,' you know, 'the 14th April 1927?' We had a great big chart up for every year up tae 2000, and if they told us a date we could tell them the day of the week and they thought it was absolutely wonderful.

The other favourite one, particularly towards Christmas and New Year, was somebody would phone and say, 'The boxing match between Fred Bloggs and Jimmy Wilson – who won it?' And you would say, 'Fred Bloggs.' He'd say, 'Are you sure? My mate will no' believe you so I'll put him on.' So he'd put him on and he'd say, 'Who won?' and you'd say, 'Jimmy Wilson.'

You had two shifts. One shift was nine tae half past one and six tae nine. And one was nine tae twelve, one thirty tae six. That was Monday to Saturday, and latterly you were open the Sunday as well, in the winter. It's never really worried me what hours I worked, but a lot of the blokes liked the split shift because you got to the football in the afternoon and come back in the evening.

When I was working a split shift, I couldnae really afford to go back home during the break. That was a long afternoon, so I got quite good at snooker because there was an old snooker table down in the basement. It wasnae particularly nice but a kind of rest room. Certainly no' like a modern staff facility. The other thing was you were in the centre of town and you could wander aboot the town and go up Kelvingrove Park. It was quite pleasant in the summer. You just accepted the shift as normal. It did mean a long day because if you were starting at nine, relying on public transport you were away fae the house maybe at eight o'clock and you werenae gettin' back at quarter tae ten, ten o'clock. It was normally a rotating shift, because you got a different day off each week. You took the job, you took the hours. End of story. The Mitchell was unique. There was a certain cachet in working there. We were the largest public reference library in Europe. So we just took the shifts for granted.

When I started in libraries the pay was £315 a year, plus £75 a year because you had more than two Highers. That was 1963. We come back out frae qualifying in '66 and I think I was on £750 a year at that time.

I was in the Mitchell for a few months and then I was moved to branches. It was quite strange at that time because in '65 you had the Equal Pay Act coming in, and up until then there had been no females employed in the Mitchell. It was seen very much as a male preserve but at that point they started a conscious policy of trying to get the service to be looked on as one, rather than the Mitchell and something else. So there was a conscious policy of moving folk out and in, obviously if they wanted or didn't want, but I got the chance to go to the branches. I felt it would be nearer to people, because the Mitchell was so big and a lot of it was admin, plus the sheer scale of it meant your users were anonymous, you just didn't know them and they didn't know you. I felt if I went to the branches I would get closer tae folk, plus you'd be doing different things: you've got the lending, the reference, the children's.

Glasgow was quite a big city and they did their best to get you one in your area, not necessarily close to you but at least on a bus route or something. I spent most of the next three years in Shettleston – typical '30s branch: entrance hall, fan-shaped book stacks[13] in the middle, children's department on one side, reference department on the other. You see that layout in a lot of the '30s branches. Happy memories there.

Shettleston was one of, I think, four branches at the time tae first stock Ulverscroft[14] large print. The old Ulverscroft used to be a kind of A4; well, it wasnae an A4 size, it was a size like that, but they're now ordinary sizes. I'd a wee personal happiness tae be in at the ground floor o' that because the large print publishing market now is getting bigger and bigger and bigger.

There were 50–60 in the Mitchell, all men. There were only six members of staff in Shettleston when I was there – I think four females and two males who varied in age. Traditionally, the males had always gone to the Mitchell and the females, non-professional staff, had always gone to the branches; you had male professional staff in some branches. I was in Shettleston five or six years. I enjoyed it, and of course it wasn't exactly far frae where I stayed. You worked three Saturdays out of four and you worked two nights one week and three nights the next. Ten tae half past eight, and that was your late shift. Then you started at one o'clock. And you also had one split shift a week. It meant you were off when other people weren't.

It was at that stage that I began professional training and went to Pitt Street College of Commerce and Distribution, the Scottish School of Librarianship,[15] which merged with Strathclyde Central. It was taken over by Strathclyde University in 1965, when I was halfway through my course.

Some of the course I enjoyed. Being wi' other folk of your own age was enjoyable. I found the classification, cataloguing, indexing interesting because that was useful in information retrieval. Some of it wasnae of real relevance. There was a noticeable distinction between those of us who had worked in public services to those who hadn't, because it gave you a backcloth into which tae put the theory. There was so much emphasis on the technical aspects – what's a frontispiece, what's this? That's all very nice but most folk are no' really worried about it.

Then there was a wee bit of the philosophic basis of service delivery: what are we there for, what are we trying to do, how do we know when we get there? The biggest thing it taught me wasn't so much the technical aspects, but interrelating with other people. The teachers were very good. It was a full-time course but I found that if I worked a nine-tae-five day, Monday tae Friday, I didnae have tae do any other work. Other folk

223

wouldnae go in if they'd only one lecture a day, or they'd maybe only go in for that. I never did that. I went in and worked the five-day week – the rest of the time was my own. You'd very little revision to do.

There was an exam at the end of the first year and an exam at the end of the second year – Part 2, which was a Library Association approved exam.[16] Once you passed your Part 2 then you'd to do another year's practical before you became chartered. I got through the course and went on to become an Associate of the Library Association (ALA) in '67.

By then I met Esther, who's now my wife. She was a library assistant in Shettleston. That's where we met, really got together in '67 and I thought, 'Well, I've got to think seriously about the future.' I knew I was getting married. I started about '68 to try and escape Glasgow. No' that I didn't like Glasgow, but I felt if I stayed in the one system, particularly with the size of Glasgow, I could've ended up as a branch librarian, which is a good enough job, but I felt I could do a wee bit better. For a couple of years I applied for a few other jobs, never got anywhere, but I just kept plugging away at it.

I got a couple of interviews, but I didn't get the job. That was all good experience and in 1971 I ended up in the burgh of Motherwell and Wishaw, quite a small authority. Motherwell Library was an old, well-established place. So was Wishaw, but was probably less well off for its library service. There was a small branch at Craigneuk, kind of Apache country, a part of Motherwell and Wishaw that was not salubrious, shall we say. That was a political branch. As authorities tend to do with these things, the Council kept throwing money at it in various shapes and guises. So they ended up wi' a branch library. It was OK. In Glasgow I worked in Gorbals for a time, I worked in Dennistoun, I worked in Bridgeton and I worked in Shettleston, and they weren't the quietest of places.

Motherwell was very good because not only did it get me in at a more senior level but it got me in a different working environment. Harry Hunt,[17] who was the Burgh Librarian there, ran the staff with very few professional librarians. For a burgh – some of the small burghs paid dreadfully for professional staff – Motherwell paid well. I went for the same money as Glasgow tae Motherwell but Glasgow paid more than a lot of the smaller places. When I left Glasgow I was a depute branch librarian. I went to Motherwell and you were just called a librarian there, but you were expected to contribute to a whole cross-section of things – the audio-visual service, the reference service . . .

The big thing then was cassette tapes. This was just beginning to take over from records. The music lending library and the children's department was part of it as well, and you'd the reference library and the cataloguing, accessioning and you were involved in them all. I suppose I'd a slight reputation for cataloguing. If something got delivered before 12 o'clock and wasnae on the shelf by 12 o'clock the next day, I was not happy. We used to get the stock processed by the bookseller, so it was essentially classifying, invoice checking and checking the materials.

Harry Hunt was one of the best guys I've ever come across. He led fae the front. He would back his staff to the hilt provided you'd done your bit. He was totally trustworthy and I learned a lot from him. My favourite story about Harry is when they were building the extension in Motherwell. As happens in these type of projects, the joiner blames the plumber, the plumber blames . . . and so it goes on and on. So he got in touch with them all: 'I want to see you all in my office at three o'clock on Friday.' Harry takes the key, puts it in the door, locks it and puts it in his pocket. Then he says, 'Nobody's leaving here till we fix this.' And he got it fixed! His other favourite trick was if somebody said, 'Somebody's in to see you', and if he didn't know who it was, he'd put his coat on and say, 'Oh, just send them in.' If he wanted to talk to the person, he would say, 'Great, just timed it right, I've just got back in.' If he didnae want to talk to you, he'd say, 'Oh, well, as you can see, I'm just on my way out, I'm sorry.' One I used myself when being serious with a member of staff was to put a jacket on. I've heard him saying, 'Mr Preston wants to see you and watch it, he's got his jacket on.'

Motherwell used the photo-charging issue system,[18] which was slightly unusual in Scotland. In Glasgow it was the old Browne issue system[19] – little tickets, book card; book card in ticket; book card filed in number order or in some order in an issue tray. With photo-charging, instead o' a label you'd a pocket and you'd a number transaction card which stayed with the book all the time. So you took a photograph of it, the card was all set up, and when the book came back in you took the number transaction card out. So obviously any transaction cards that were not there, the book wasn't back. So then you'd tae look up the film and do the overdue. Photo-charging could cope wi' high volume issues but it took you a helluva long time tae chase up any overdues. It was a way to try and cope with the Browne system's inability to do high-volume transactions in a short space of time.

Motherwell later put in one of the first automated systems. It was very primitive, an early DS^{20} system, just a number cruncher, but for the time it was advanced, a vast improvement fae photo-charging. That stood me in good stead when we automated Dumfries and Galloway.

The other thing that I learned a lot from, although an unhappy experience at the time, was when Wishaw Library burned down. There was an extension being built and I think it was probably vandalism, although nobody will really know. Harry Hunt got the phone call at about two in the morning to say, 'I'm sorry to tell you, Mr Hunt, your new library is on fire.' And he says, 'Is it completely destroyed?' The reply was 'Yes.' He said, 'Good!' I couldnae understand it at the time but what he meant was, we can scrap it and start again. So they've now got a cracker o' a library in Wishaw.

Motherwell only had three branches but when the public comes intae a branch library, tae them that branch library is the service. They're not interested in how many others there are. It's a bit like when you go into a shop. You're no' interested in where the head office is or how many branches they've got. You tend to judge the service and use it by the welcome that you get there. What I liked about branch work was that you did get to know the people and they got to know you, and there was a personal feel to the service.

High-falutin' readers tended to read biographies, some of them just wanted to read Westerns and romances, some were intae crime. It's very difficult tae generalise, but certainly any branch I've been in has had its distinct range of interests. Handicraft books, you can't get enough of them. Other branches, they're hardly touched. That is what the branch librarian's there for, to suss out things like this.

Motherwell and Wishaw had a fair mix of interests. Some were quite literary, others weren't. Traditionally the public library was the abode of older folk. In my early days in Glasgow, older members of staff particularly used tae look at the kids' hands tae see if they were clean before they got in. This is the traditional image, but after the War, certainly by the mid '60s with the expansion in higher education, there was a big effort in a lot of authorities tae build up links with the youngsters. I suppose on balance they tended tae be older children rather than younger, but there was a fair spread o' ages.

When I got married in 1970 we got a house in Tannochside, and that was handy for Motherwell and Wishaw, plus by 1971 we'd a car. In

1973, I think, we moved up tae a detached house in Wishaw. I was with Motherwell and Wishaw frae 1971 tae May '75, just after reorganisation when it became Motherwell District.

There was various jobs coming up at that time including the chief's job in Kilmarnock and Loudoun.[21] I got it. Kilmarnock and Loudoun was a bit like Motherwell and Wishaw but a bit bigger: 13 branches, part of the old Ayr County, part of the old Kilmarnock Burgh. Jock Thomson,[22] who was the Burgh Librarian there, became Director of Cultural Services, and very much an influence, straight as a die, Army man – he'd been in Burma during the Second World War – a Burns fanatic. I think I learned mair about Burns in the years there than I've ever wanted tae forget since.

I moved tae Stewarton in Ayrshire, about five mile frae Kilmarnock. I felt slightly nervous. I mentioned earlier about how you werenae really taught the things you really need for later on, and for the first time ever I'd tae do things like monitor and control budgets and allocate monies and had much more to do with employing the staff. I just picked it up on the hoof. That's where a lot of your networking comes in, with your friends that you built up. Jock Thomson was there if I was stuck, but he never interfered.

There was a bit of contact with councillors in Motherwell, but I didnae have tae do the politicking. Once I went intae Kilmarnock and Loudoun, I had tae do the politicking. I quite enjoyed it. I found the councillors in Kilmarnock and Loudoun much more of a mixed bag than in Lanarkshire – different political parties, different political views. Although there was a Labour majority there was a fair mix of Tories because you had the old county areas frae Ayr. The old Kilmarnock was definitely Labour almost through and through.

But I would tell all the councillors exactly the same and didn't really worry if they didn't want tae hear what I'd tae say. If they asked me something, I'd give them an honest answer and if they didnae like it, well, that was tough luck. I always treated every councillor, whatever party they were in, in exactly the same manner, with exactly the same courtesy. I think that stood me in good stead over the years, because you do get a reputation for being honest and straightforward. They might not go wi' it and that's fair enough, that's politics, but they'll accept that you're doing your best.

What opened my eyes was it was the first time I'd dealt with a dispersed area, very different frae being able to concentrate on one or two urban service points. Ayr County did have a good reputation in the '40s, '50s and '60s, but what I found was that the further away you got fae Ayr the worse became the provision.

When I was appointed I went to introduce myself tae all the staff. I wanted tae go and see them *in situ* and talk to them there so as they felt comfortable in their bit. I always tried no' tae lose that personal management touch. I like tae think the staff knew me as a person, as an individual, not just as a name on the top o' a bit o' paper. If I wanted tae talk tae you about something, I would either lift the phone or come and see you and talk tae you face to face because I felt that was much more productive.

My base in Kilmarnock was the Dick Institute[23] – not conducive to what we think of as a modern service now. The great big wonderful hallway, which is useless for doing anything in and the two wings. It's traditional – early 20th or late 19th century barn. The museum was upstairs; the Museums Service had the museum and Dean Castle.[24]

There were 13 branches in Kilmarnock and Loudoun, including two small ones in Kilmarnock, one in Hurlford[25] – political branches – not particularly nice places. They weren't purpose-built premises – converted shops in deprived areas; you've got to give them something so put a library in, make it look good. That sounds awfully cynical. That's the reality of it. They were struggling in terms of use. Logic says there's nobody there, they're all going away, there are few folk left, it's a waste o' time. The other aspect says if anybody needed a service, they do, their place is suffering, so I don't think there's a right answer. I never had a problem with those branches, but looking at the money tae run them, I used tae kind o' grue[26] sometimes.

By the time I went tae Kilmarnock and Loudoun, I was getting further away fae the public. That's one of the paradoxes about the library world: the further on you get, the higher you get, the further you get away frae the things that brought you there in the first place. But there was a great Burns interest and although I'd been in the Glasgow Room in the Mitchell Library this was my first experience of managing a local studies collection.

I finished in Kilmarnock and Loudoun December '78. I was cutting my teeth in management, and then this job came up, Regional Librarian, Dumfries and Galloway.[27] I went for it and got it and that was definitely a culture shock. One reason was the sheer physical spread o' the authority. Dumfries and Galloway covered just under two and a half thousand square miles. The physical distances and time involved, you don't realise it. It's no' just physical journeys. Other than the A74, we've got no motorways down here, we've got very little dual carriageway. It's improved in the last 20 years, but when I came down there was no bypass round Dumfries. Most of the towns are all bypassed now.

There were 20, 22 branches, now 24 and of course mobile libraries as well. The other thing was that here there was a support service for schools. This was the first time I'd tae manage that type of service. I'd had a lot tae do with liaison with schools but no' tae actually provide a service. The background tae that is that the old burgh libraries were established under the 1853 Act and it wasn't until the 1918 Education Act that county library systems, including mobile libraries, and schools library services were established as part of education authorities.[28]

One of the things I learned quite quickly was that it may well be a local authority area but it's not a natural area. Annan's different frae Lockerbie; Lockerbie's different frae Dumfries; Dumfries is different frae Dalbeattie; Dalbeattie's different frae Castle Douglas. So the folk o' Lockerbie havenae really got a lot in common wi' the folk o' Dumfries. The folk o' Gretna havenae got a lot in common wi' Annan. Newton Stewart's different, Stranraer's different. You'd this challenge tae try on a system that was being fair tae everybody.

There was an in-built fear from Stranraer because it was 75 miles away or, say, Newton Stewart that somehow everything was coming to Dumfries. There was an unease wi' the folks who had worked in the Stewartry Headquarters because everything got taken away: the reordering, the cataloguing, the accessioning and a' the admin. One of the advantages of me getting the job was I was a foreigner to everybody, so I used that opportunity to say, 'I've got no loyalty to any particular town or area. I happen to live in Dumfries, I could happen to live anywhere. Tell me what your worries are.' So, in the first few years a lot of it was tae try and allay folk's fears, to make sure that they're no' saying, 'Oh, naebody's interested in what goes on', or, 'That lot don't know', to build up a relationship wi' staff and amongst each other. We're all part of a whole. Don't think you're forgotten about. And I think honestly I did succeed in that.

One of the first things I did was go and talk to the staff, talk to everybody. It took me a long time because a lot of the small branches were part-time with different staff working at different times. I really did make a point of physically talking to everybody. I regularly used to go oot in evenings tae visit branches – a lot were only open in the evenings and Saturdays. I just went tae say hello, and they thought it was great.

In fact, the first time I did it, I wondered why they all looked so apprehensive. Nobody had ever come out unless there was a problem. Nobody ever came out just to say, 'How are you doing? Any ideas? What's going on?' The staff responded because quite often they would hear of what was going on locally. That's how, for example, we managed to get better premises for a lot of the branches, because we knew this thing's going tae happen or this thing's coming up. When a new councillor was elected, I'd go to the branch and say, 'Tell me about him.' I made it my business to know, to find out what's going on in the locality and encourage the staff to become part of it and feed the information back.

'And,' I said, 'the other thing I want tae know is, if you've got a problem. I'm no' necessarily saying I can do anything about it but if somebody comes in and complains, tell me. I want to be prepared.' They were a wee bit wary for a while but as the years went on it worked very well. They could always come to me. There's a cliché about an open door. The only time the door in my office was shut was when I was interviewing folk or if I was talking on a private phone call. Other than that, the staff could wander in and out. I didnae like my door shut, and a couple of times a day I used to just wander round a' the departments just flying the flag, and folk noticed that.

We had a full-time equivalent staff of about 80, but in numbers 140–150 roughly. I discovered that something like 15 staff were over 65 and should have been retired. In fact, one was 80-something – they werenae sure o' her age. So in one of the first committee reports I was saying, 'I've got 15 folk going.'

The premises themselves varied from fine tae absolutely abysmal. Some of them were wee huts. That's not a criticism, that's just a fact, bearing in mind that in country villages, smaller towns, there was very little in the way of community facilities. So the library in a lot of the small places was a natural gossip-shop, meeting ground. To be fair on my predecessor, Desmond Donaldson,[29] frae '75 tae '78 he did a lot to try and break this down. There was still a tradition here of voluntary service, and it was only a year or two before they shut down some of the wee voluntary service centres, the wee deposit collections. They could be based in a church hall, in a local hall, they could be based in a school, they could be based in a wee local shop. They could be based anywhere. Just book boxes.

The mobile libraries were much appreciated by a lot of folk in the rural areas. Schools had been disappearing because the countryside population had been disappearing. There used to be a whole host of mobile shops went about – they were disappearing because they were expensive tae run. When I actually costed it, the cost per issue on a mobile was phenomenally higher than the cost per issue in an average branch. That's one of these things you don't really talk about too much in public. It was very much appreciated but a very expensive service. But politically a good service because folk noticed them going about the country and thought, 'Well, the Council's doing something.' They might no' even use it but it's doing something, you know.

One satisfying aspect was work with the local studies area, outreaching materials and resources into local areas. Of course, modern technology you can do a lot with. One of the most simple things that we did, which had an absolutely brilliant public response, was tae commission facsimile editions of long out-of-print material. It didnae cost a lot of money but folk went bananas for it. There's almost a longing in everybody tae have a wee niche somewhere that you can say, 'That's home.'

The Council and character changed in the time I was there. When I come down in January '79, the majority were very much folk wi' money, businessmen that were on the Council – paternalistic. Most of the councillors now are waving a party flag. When I came most of them were Independents. Most o' them were Tories, I have tae say.

I said earlier I treated every councillor exactly the same and I think that paid off if you look, say, at the number o' new branches or the number o' branches revamped and improved, the automation, just simple things like the book-funding that went up. I managed, with a couple o' exceptions, to get it well above average, and that was just sheer hard graft, to be honest. You know, it didnae happen overnight. Actually, one of my staff said, 'That's your job. Get the money.' That's what it boiled down to.

One thing that you just have tae learn how to do is manage budgets, which you never really got told about. When I came tae Dumfries and Galloway, you'd your budget headings – staff, buildings, heat and light

– and they were all individual and all categorised. Let's say, for example, you had £1,000 of stationery and you spent £950. You started next year at £950. So what you had was a situation where a' the folk in charge o' budgets were spending up to the penny for the sake o' spending it.

I'm glad to say the Council evolved in a positive way over a number of years and latterly as long as the bottom line at the end of the year was less than the bottom line at the start you were fine. So you were actually allowed to be a manager. Finance didnae particularly like it so there was a long process of, let's say, heartfelt negotiations to try and evolve this. I'm no' just talking about the Library Service, I'm talking about local government where you were actually encouraging folk tae manage. The other thing that I liked was that the Council went on to a three-year budgetary cycle which meant you could plan ahead.

A lot of the country users have quite high literary tastes. Prior to the county system, you'd the likes o' the Douglas Ewart High School in Newton Stewart that had a very high reputation in the world. Dumfries Academy here. You're back intae the lad o' pairts.[30] We were part of Education. I went through three directors. I got on fine with them all. The first one was J K Purves, who came frae Lanarkshire; hard as nails, straight as a die; got on absolutely brilliantly wi' him. He was always very formal. He always called me Mr Preston all the years I worked for him and he didnae call me John till after he retired. 'You know, John,' he says – I thought, well, it's the first time he's called me that – 'do you know what I liked about you? You would dae most things but if you said no, you meant no.' I says, 'Well, the only time I drew the line was when you wanted me tae do something that would actually damage the service and I says, "I'm no' doing that."' I've learned a lot o' things frae folk, and that was one of them: be honest and straightforward wi' people.

Part of the reason I settled here is that there's no' very many jobs in Scotland, no' many bigger jobs. Obviously if Glasgow and Edinburgh had come up, I'd have had a crack at that. Probably wouldnae have got it but I'd have had a crack at it. Part of it was the family. When I came here, the family were five years and six months old, and then my son was born in 1985. So they would all be going through various parts of the school and I didnae really want tae uproot them.

Money's no' everything and I was getting well paid here. When I left Kilmarnock and Loudoun I was getting £7,400 a year and I came here for £7,800 a year. When I finished my job as Regional Librarian in

October '95, I was earning £39,563. In money terms and in prestige terms, one of the things I did was keep a job profile not just frae a selfish point of view. I was asked at least three times, did I not want tae move tae Education Headquarters, did I not want tae be called Assistant Director of Education and Libraries? I said, 'No, thank you, I'll stay where I am.' So the post was accepted as carrying responsibility.

In 1995 you'd local government reorganisation again. The Library Service was taken away from Education and put into Community Resources wi' leisure and swimming pools and museums and things like that. So there was a new structure and I got the post as Head of Libraries, Arts and Museums. That was in October '95. I spent the first year not fighting for money but going through budgets and just grabbing money and I was quite successful in that. But in March '97 they said to me, 'You've done your bit.' Part of it was just to save cash, part of it was that the new bit was working OK, but a lot of it was quite simply that the director wasnae happy with me.

Looking back I enjoyed the post of Regional Librarian of Dumfries and Galloway most. I was in a position here where I could make the greatest impact on the service just by the very nature of the job. Not so much the scale, just my position in the political pecking order was higher than in Kilmarnock and Loudoun.

I think I've been quite pragmatic. I've never assumed that if I took a job I was goin' tae get everything my way. I've had disappointments and sometimes something takes you a long time. Georgetown[31] – largest private housing estate in Europe; population is something like 7,000–8,000 people; about half a dozen shops, nae doctors, nae chemist, nae dentist. No' a lot at all but private houses – so they can look after themselves. It was a fight tae get it, but we got it eventually – purpose-built library, built tae COSLA standards.[32] Georgetown Library opened 1993; going like a fair; even today it's one of the busiest branches in the system.

There was the usual panic stations: 'Oh, we've no' got enough money.' The Directors had tae go tae meet wi' the Chief Exec so the Director of Education says, 'You better go tae this.' The Chief Exec says, 'Right, we've got tae cut this capital expenditure by, say, 32 per cent.' He says tae me, 'Can you cut it by 32 per cent?' I says, 'No. If you want tae tell me that the Council's priority's no' the Library I'd be disappointed but the worse thing you can do is cut the project by that amount and end up wi' something that doesnae work. You either build it to the standard or you don't do it. You either do it right or you don't do it at all.'

I remember somebody up the pub says to me, 'It didnae take you long tae get that.' And I says, 'Do you know when the first bit of correspondence for Georgetown Library was? 1981.' So you've got tae keep plugging away and plugging away. The other big one was Lochthorn, up between Heathhall and Locharbriggs. That wasnae so bad, because it didnae take quite as long.

Although I'd only had limited experience wi' things like architects' briefs, what practicably can be done in a building, revamping buildings, looking at premises and things like that, overseeing capital projects, either new branches or revamps and so on gave a sense o' achievement because you saw at the end of it something tangible that you'd done.

When you've got lots of capital projects, you've got a five-year programme and you put in so much a year, the revenue costs. You've got to work all that out and I was always good wi' money. Because folk would just look at things like salaries and I'd say, 'No, no, no, you've got National Insurance and superannuation, and you've got travel expenses tae think aboot. If you're goin' tae put the staff up, you're goin' tae increase your recruitment costs.'

With the political character changing, the councillors themselves changing, COSLA standards was one of the greatest things that ever happened for the public library service. Something non-political from an unbiased source. We've never really managed one for the schools library service. There are standards now but they're just aspirations, they're no' tangible.

I've now been out it for four and a half years so I can only give you an impression of how libraries are going. They're having to cope wi' a much more rapid change in technology than I ever had. I think they're in danger of throwing out the baby with the bathwater, because folk look on technology as an end in itself rather than a means tae an end. As far as I'm concerned, the Internet is a working tool and the danger is that you become technology-orientated rather than service-orientated.

When we went tae automate the service in Dumfries and Galloway we didn't start frae the end of what systems were available, we said, 'Where are we? What can we do? Do we want to be able to continue to do that? Must we be able to do that? Would we like to be able to do that?' We drew up a delivery spec, sent that to companies and some of them were wonderful. You would get things like, 'in development', 'being developed', 'will be available next year.' I said, 'No, I'm no' interested.' I always took a practicable and, I hope, a rational thing tae technology, tried tae make sure it served you, you didnae serve it. You didn't end up, for example, skewing the ordering, accessioning system to suit the machines.

I think they're under a lot more political pressure now than they were, but public libraries are still thriving. I think the lending of material will be much less than in the past and information provision, research provision, will probably be more.

Interviewed 23 October 2001

John Hunter

My full name is John Gear Hunter. I was given my middle name after my grandmother – it's more predominant in Shetland than anywhere else. I was born in Lerwick on the 18th June 1949.

My father was Principal Education Officer for the Shetland Islands Council, but before that the Zetland County Council.[1] He was born in 1916 and died in 1994. Very much like my mother, circumstances at home made him leave school quite early. He did work in the bank prior to moving to Edinburgh for a while and then after he came out of the Royal Navy he joined the Education Department and he was there until he retired. I think that he would have loved to have had the opportunity to go to university. He was very well read, exceptionally good with mathematics and arithmetic, and accountancy was a speciality of his. He could turn his hand to a bit o' woodwork and cut peats as well as do double-entry bookkeeping, and obviously report writing and dealing wi' educational issues.

His father was a seaman in the Merchant Navy and he was also in the Royal Naval Reserve in the Second World War, but he died of cancer in 1943. My paternal great-grandfather was a fisherman.

My mother's family only moved to Shetland in the 1900s. Before she got married, my mother went to the gutting. Her family were all fisherfolk and had moved from Gamrie and Crovie. Gamrie is the Scots dialect word for Gardenstown. Her grandparents moved to Shetland because of the opportunities to fish and the abundance of fish. I think my grandfather made his first trip to the Lowestoft and the Yarmouth herring fishing around about 1904. He introduced the drift-net into Shetland, so he was quite a well-known fisherman, and quite successful until he had an accident and had to give up the fishing and didn't really work after that. His two sons then took on the fishing boat and they did it up until they retired.

When my mother left school at 14, it was into the fish trade, baiting lines for her father, going to the gutting for the variety of companies that were in Shetland at the time. She was based in Lerwick during the height of the herring season and then moved south as the herring moved south – Yarmouth and Lowestoft.

Interestingly enough, she told me not that long ago that she took part in a strike. They decided that they had worked for a pittance for long enough. So the 4,000 fish-workers walked oot on strike. They achieved their aim of getting an improved wage, but the agents or whoever was responsible for their accommodation simply put the price of their accommodation up. So it was give with one, take with the other but I thought her a wee bit of a militant having taken part in a strike in the early '30s. She was born in 1914, so she'd only be 16 to 20 years old when she was on strike.

More or less as soon as she got married my mother gave up work. I think that my father prevailed upon her. He was of the thinking that the wife stayed at home and looked after the family, and right through all their married life my mother never worked again.

She actually went back during the War. There was a shortage of labour obviously during the War, and she agreed to go back providing nobody told my father, who was in the Royal Navy at the time. However, he came home on leave and by the time he had gone the length of Burgh Road, which is the street on which my mother was staying at the time, he'd already been told. So he was not terribly pleased. However, it was for the war effort, I suppose.

The first house I can remember growing up was 13 Rawlinson Crescent, Lerwick. It was a semi-detached council house: two bedrooms and living room, kitchen and bathroom. It had electric light, a bath, a garden back, front and side. There was no central heating in the house. There was a fire in the sitting room which heated the boiler to provide hot water. There was a prominence of council development in Lerwick, and a building programme after the Second World War provided houses of a higher standard. The old fishermen's houses started to be demolished.

I went to school when I was five. I went to the Lerwick Central Primary School and I was there until the 11-plus.[2] I quite enjoyed the primary school. I liked reading. I liked history. Dependent on the outcome you either continued at the Central School and did commercial, technical, or modified, as it was called, or you went on to the Anderson Educational Institute, where you did more academic-based study. It wasn't confined just to children from a specific class or area, and pupils from the outlying islands came and stayed in the hall of residence or hostel, as it was called then. Quite a lot of them came for the term. Nowadays they can go home every week-end, even to the outlying islands such as Fair Isle and Foula, but at that time they came for the 11 weeks of the term. Quite a lot of them simply couldn't hack it so they went back.

I went to the Anderson Institute; I qualified by the skin of my teeth! I didnae particularly enjoy secondary school. I wasnae particularly academic nor was I particularly interested. I hated Mathematics and Arithmetic, because my father was exceptionally good at both and assumed that I should be as well. I enjoyed English literature. I enjoyed History. I enjoyed Science subjects, particularly Biology and Chemistry. I wasnae so particular aboot Physics, because it was more related to Mathematics. I developed a liking for Arithmetic. I think I did despite my Dad because he was always, 'And how's your old Maths and Arithmetic?' He didn't ask about my English or my History, which I was quite good at. He wasn't the Director of Education but he was second or third in line. He knew all the teachers and the gossip. He didna solicit the information; they normally gave it to him. It's a small community and those things happen. We had teachers' sons in our class as well.

The only sport really available in Shetland when I was young was football, and I have a problem because I wear spectacles. At the time it was discovered that I had quite bad eyesight and I had to be exceptionally careful. I was monitored by a Polish eye-surgeon who I had to see every three months from the time I was five right through until I was about 13 or 14. So I didnae play football. I sailed a lot of boats in the local loch, Clickimin Loch. I spent a lot of time round the harbour. I was always interested in nature, did a lot of climbing, just the cliffs doon at the seashore – the parents didnae really know! And we all had bicycles, some in better shape than others. At that time a lot of the roads were single track wi' passing places, pretty rough. In the wintertime, it was sledging because there was loads of snow. You could always guarantee it was going to be a white Christmas.

We played with a thing we called a chickie-mellie. It was a little sticker which you attached to somebody's window and then you had a long length of string wi' a button on it. You pulled it back and forth, the button rattled against the window, and when the person came to the door you ducked down behind the dyke. That was one you did in the winter when it was dark and you couldnae see the dark thread or the ball of string. Another one was, we took great delight in swopping everybody's gates. We simply went up and doon the street and moved all the gates around. Confused the postman no end! We used to do a lot of things like neep-raiding and lob turnips at people's door and all that sort of stuff.

My father was quite well known for the work he did for the good of the community. And I was known as 'Jackie's boy', and I could be picked oot in a crowd, where some others would get away wi' it. My own boys suffered the same fate, because their mother was a police officer and I was a Chief Librarian. So they were known through both of us.

Oh, loads of friends, yeah. We would go and scrounge fish-boxes and then go and hunt for pram wheels to make hurlies wi', and go and bother the local blacksmith for a couple of axles. Or go doon wi' your sledge to get it repaired and that sort of thing. And we roamed all over the town.

I was in the Cubs. I was head of my Cub Pack and then I moved on to the Scouts[3] but gave them up after two or three years because I developed other interests. But I enjoyed them. I was a regular at the Sunday School. My parents weren't regular churchgoers. My father would go back and forth. I suppose a lot of the fishermen who came north were Brethren,[4] very staunch religious, but not my Mum and her side. Oh, she was a God-fearing woman, but not a regular churchgoer, no. We were Methodist. There were quite a lot of Methodists in Shetland, not only in Lerwick but throughout the islands.

So I went to Sunday School and then the Bible Class and eventually became the rebel teenager and gave it up about 14, I think. Certain members of the Sunday School worked in my father's office. A message was relayed via my father, 'Would John possibly read such-and-such at Easter and Christmas?' I came home and my father said, 'You're reading that in the church.' So I was the sort of star in the church for reading. In later life it certainly helped in public speaking.

There was no television. Television only came to Shetland in 1967. So the radio was a great thing both for family entertainment but also for listening to the trawler band, which allowed my mother to know where her brothers were when they were off at the fishing. I recall the maroons would go off to summon the lifeboat in the middle of the night and I would hear my father getting up. He tuned into the radio so he could listen and reassure my mother it wasna her family.

Probably aboot 15 or 16, I started to get careers guidance, and the careers officer only seemed to know about the entrance qualifications for teaching. I wanted to join the RAF, but unfortunately, although I attended Biggin Hill[5] twice for interview, I didna pass the selection procedure for what I wanted to do simply because of my eyesight. I couldn't fly because they told me that in my initial interview, but they had spaces available for air-traffic controllers. I got the requisite O-levels[6] but for some reason or other, they said I was unacceptable.

I then didn't really know what I wanted to do and muddled through the last two years of school wi' no clear idea what I wanted to pursue as a career. I completed the sixth year. If you went to the Anderson Institute there were only 400 pupils. I canna remember how many teachers. I would think aboot 40. So you were getting pretty good tuition. Yeah, excellent school.

One teacher in particular, a woman called Nessie Robertson, for the first four years in the Anderson High School, made your life absolute hell! She could shout the whole day. She could make you feel miniscule by a verbal lambasting. But once you had indicated that you were going on for a fifth and sixth year and going to pursue some sort of career, she became a friend. She was a teacher of English and History. Her ability to convey the meaning of English literature and interpret history was excellent.

I left school in 1968 so I would have been 18. Well, I had previously worked as a labourer with a building firm in my school holidays, and when I left school I simply started with the firm again, as a labourer, but my speciality was painting and decorating. I had an aptitude for it, and I thought, 'Right, I'll maybe just stay with the firm and become a painter and decorator.'

My mother didn't say terribly much. My father was exceptionally angry: he had not put me through six years of school to be a painter and decorator. Summer sort of moved into winter, and standing at the top of a ladder with the breeze blowing up your trouser legs . . . I thought, 'I maybe should get a job inside.' There was a job advertised in *The Shetland Times* for a library assistant and I had the requisite O-levels and Highers. I only had English and History. I failed my French Higher and I re-sat it subsequently because I needed a modern language to get into library school. I started in October '68, thinking, 'I'll go there in the winter and go back to painting in the summer.' However, that was not to be.

Up to that point, it never crossed my mind that library work would appeal to me. It was a job that was inside. I automatically assumed that it would have to do with reading books, which I enjoyed. So I thought, 'Well, quite a cushy little number.' My parents were good readers and I joined the library probably when I was about six or seven. I read quite a lot.

I loved detective stories as a boy, Agatha Christie[7] particularly, but any detective story. I was also an avid reader of the *Eagle* comic. I always recall it came on a Friday and my Dad had his newspaper delivered to the education offices. So it was straight from the school, into an empty office and that was me until it was time for us to go home at five and then we went home together. That was the regular comic. I bought shillingy war comics, you know, these little comic ones. Swopped some of the *Eagles* with pals for *The Hotspur* or *The Wizard* or *Rover*. And the other thing I used to buy quite a lot when we'd pocket money was these classic comics, where it was, you know, *Kidnapped* but it was a visual interpretation. And they were great for swopping, and there was a whole group of us that used to do that, because although my family were comfortably off, there was never an abundance of money.

When I first began, the Library Service staff were Chief Librarian, the assistant, and I think there were seven other staff plus two part-time members of staff who came in to cover evenings and when the full-time staff were getting time off – holidays and sickness and so on, emergencies – plus our driver, and the caretaker of the building. We were paid fortnightly to begin with and my fortnightly salary was a little over £6, and half of that I gave to my mother for housekeeping, but then £3 at that time was a lot of money. Not that my father was particularly enamoured with me drinking beer, because he wasnae a drinker himself. A pint of beer, I recall, was 1/8. So you could get quite a lot of pints of beer for £3!

The only main library in Shetland and library headquarters were in Lerwick. The Library was open six days a week. We opened Monday, Wednesday and Friday till eight o'clock and Saturday from nine until five. You worked three evenings a week until eight o'clock. You were compensated by having the Thursday off and the following week you worked a fairly normal shift but worked a Saturday. So it wasna strictly a five-day working week. At that time we had an hour and a half for lunch and an hour for tea. So it certainly cut down your nine o'clock till eight o'clock day.

Then every five weeks we went on the mobile library. This was before the introduction of the inter-island ferries, so you were simply going around mainland Shetland rural areas. My parents didn't own a car, so my opportunity to get to rural areas was a bit limited. However, I can honestly say I've been down every road and track-end in Shetland! There was a driver and a library assistant, so I was responsible for dealing with customers and the driver simply drove the vehicle.

There was a small part-time branch in Scalloway, and branches in the outlying areas usually housed in schools. The outer isles were served by collections of books which were sent out every term, and normally it was the unpaid duty of the school teacher in the rural school to look after the library collection.

Right up until the last reorganisation of local government, the Library was part of the Education Department and we were running the School Library Service in tandem with the Public Library Service. On the Scottish mainland libraries had moved to Leisure and Recreation at the '75 reorganisation, and public and school library services were split.

We would be talking about somewhere between 36 and 40 branches in the schools, and we sent collections to about five or six lighthouses as well. Some of them, like Muckle Flugga, had a shore station where the lighthouse-keepers and their families went. Presumably because they were no' particularly accessible, we sent a collection there. Those were either delivered by truck or by a tour of the mobile library.

We made up a profile of the community, the group of people, whatever it was, and selected books accordingly and sent the collection. I think it was really symptomatic of what went on in the lighthouse community but there was always a great interest in things like DIY. The non-fiction which we were supplying was of a practical and useful nature – anything to do wi' ships and sailing, fishing, and so on. The men read the non-fiction and the women read the fiction – not generally but fairly specifically.

A lot of people were interested in history, but Scandinavian history more than Scottish history – the Sagas and so on – and obviously local history material, Shetland stuff. Lighthouse men had a lot of time to read.

There were a lot of very well-read men in the lighthouse service – very practical men, turned their hand to anything. Well, one of our caretakers was a former lighthouse-keeper, and our Library was immaculate. Everything was polished in the Lighthouse Board way – the door handle shone!

I worked as a library assistant for two years and in that two years I acquired the Higher that I needed to go to library school. I found the two years that I worked there exceptionally varied. My boss at the time was George Longmuir.[8] He was appointed the first Chief Librarian in 1950. He was a wee bit tight with his money, so for one of my first jobs I was given a wire brush and a gallon of paraffin and told to clean the chassis of the mobile library before it went for its MOT. Now if I was to offer a library assistant a wire brush today, I know what the person would tell me to do wi' the wire brush. But I must say he encouraged me, and I made the conscious decision that librarianship would be my career. Of the two places that provided courses in librarianship in Scotland, Strathclyde was predominantly post-graduate, so you'd already done a degree, whereas Robert Gordon's was a certificated course.[9] I applied to Robert Gordon's and I got in. I moved away in 1970. It was a two-year course. I hadn't been away from home at all really before then, except for a couple of holidays.

So when I went doon to Aberdeen, it was to be a student going into the 'Big Smoke' for the first time. I felt quite excited by it. I had made up my mind that I wanted to do librarianship and sort of went down and grabbed it. Stayed in digs up aroond Queen's Cross area. There were eight of us in digs, eight guys from all over: a good mix. We were all doing different things. I could find my way round any library and they were constantly coming to me to say, 'Well, can you find me information on . . .?' Not necessarily find the information but give them directions.

The librarianship course was exceptionally well taught. I had two tutors who were outstanding: Charlie Wood,[10] who taught me library management, and Graham Ewins,[11] who taught me analytical and historical bibliography and hence an interest in bookbinding and printing, and the history of printing. It was a very broad course.

There were four subjects in the first year and six in the second year. Now I'll not be able to recall them all, but there was management, cataloguing and classification, local history studies, in which I sort of majored in second year, and the study of reference material.

I have contended ever since that many people turned out by schools of librarianship are computer literate and statisticians, but we have found that taking staff immediately from library school we then have had to institute in-house training because a lot of the material that they were dealing with or going to use, they were unfamiliar with. So, I'm probably a wee bit outspoken.

The examining body was the Library Association (LA).[12] Robert Gordon's offered the training but the examinations were set by the LA, although the course in librarianship had the highest failure rates second to medicine, because in Year 1 there were 80 students of librarianship, and when we moved into Year 2 there were only 40.

The pass rates for the examinations were set quite high. You had to get three of the four subjects in the first year. You then had to have the fourth subject successfully completed by December of the following year. So it was in your interest to pass all four because obviously you were going into second year with your second year work plus your referral from the first year. It had to be three out of four. Two out of four and you were out. I think, if I recall, there were only 21 of us that graduated.

I think probably three years would have been better and would have given one or two people who failed the opportunity to get through. I suppose I was fortunate in that my room-mate Andy and I both right from the beginning studied fairly conscientiously. We set aside Saturday and Sunday for playing but Monday to Friday we were studying. Obviously the three weeks before your final exams you were in the library until ten o'clock at night. I enjoyed and benefited from the course and that confirmed my decision to remain a librarian.

You came to Easter, you were in the middle of your run-up to your exams, the final exams were in June and also you were under the added pressure of trying to find a job and go for interviews. There were very few secondments at the time. I think there were only a half a dozen students studying librarianship who were guaranteed a job.

I went for an interview as branch librarian at Bo'ness and arrived to discover that I was the only person being interviewed. In fact they were so desperate to get a librarian that the first question they asked me was when would I be able to start, and I knew from that that the job was mine. I asked to have a look at the library and was intrigued by all this metal shuttering. They said, 'Oh, that gets strapped to the front of the bookshelves in the evening before you close, to deter burglars.' I thought, 'H'm, no,

I'll decline that job.' It was an indication of my confidence that I turned down the job offered on the strength of going for another interview, which, when I look back on it was a wee bit foolhardy! So I went for the job interview in Tranent and was successful. I was interviewed by 33 people including Tranent Burgh Council and they all had to have a say. Although I was going to work for East Lothian County Council, Tranent Burgh Council wanted to know that the Council was appointing the right man. I think there were eight of us interviewed for the post and I felt quite chuffed that I got it.

It was in East Lothian where I started a long association with my colleague Jessie MacLeod. She was the branch librarian in Haddington. I was the branch librarian in Tranent. We were young and enthusiastic. We felt that we could do with independent control of our book funds[13] and so we made an appointment to see the Chief Librarian, Bill Leslie,[14] who was an exceptionally good librarian but controlled everything himself. Within a fortnight or three weeks, however, all the branch library staff had their own book funds and were responsible for their own book selection.

The branch library in Tranent was brand new. I was its first librarian. I was there when it opened, set it up and so on. Tranent was an interesting place to stay. In the '70s there were still one or two of the old miners' cottages left. There was a lot of unemployment, the pits were closing down, some people were oot o' work because of their health, others because of unemployment, there was a lot of vandalism, there was a lot of crime, house-breaking was regular. But a lot of very fine, honest people. I seem to recall there was a wee bit of a divide because one end of Tranent was becoming yuppified, a commuter area for Edinburgh. And there was the council houses and the private houses. However, it was an education. I was going into a community where I knew nobody, and a community that didna know me either and I suppose in comparison to some of them, I had had a pretty comfortable background.

There had been a part-time library in an old HORSA[15] hut in an obscure area of the playground behind Tranent Primary School. It had been run by an elderly lady who ended up being one of my part-time library assistants, which could have been problematic in that she had been in charge, whereas I was coming in to take charge of her. However, we got on exceptionally well.

A lot of her knowledge was invaluable to me when we started stock selection, because she knew what people wanted and had established customers. So that was fine, building a stock for our new customers: anything and everything – Mills & Boon's[16] romances for ladies were in constant supply; greyhound racing and horse-racing were big; football. They were very Labour orientated, good Socialists.

I think we probably had the biggest range of newspapers, including *The Morning Star*.[17] The Library was situated in the Civic Centre, which was halfway between the Miners' Welfare Club and the Tranent Labour Club. Both had different opening hours, so the old miners would go to one, stop into the Library for a read of the papers and a wee bit of a breather, because obviously some of them were affected wi' silicosis. So we had the local papers and the national papers and so on.

My part-time library assistant, Mrs Sinclair, a Tranent woman herself, knew everybody. So we never had a problem wi' overdue books because she would be walking doon the street and she would haul oot some young boy and say, 'Tell your mother her books are overdue.' I would not wish this task on any young librarian now but there was a policy where we sent out overdue letters, then we compiled a list and went round and knocked on the doors. We did it at a certain time of year. It took us aboot a fortnight because we were covering Macmerry and Ormiston as well. And obviously if you went to somebody's door wearing a collar and tie, you were thought to be the rent man.

I was head-hunted for a job with a library supply firm at one point and I was tempted to go. I'd been working for quite some time and I was a bit disappointed in the quality of work that I was doing. This would have been about 1974. I felt that my professional qualification was not being put to good use.

Librarianship, even today, is a very small profession, and particularly in Scotland word spreads quite quickly and I was approached by a company called Junior Books Ltd, which was part of the Dunn & Wilson Group, now Riley Dunn & Wilson,[18] because my old lecturer, Charlie Wood, had moved on to be their stock manager, and he was looking for an assistant and he knew that I was a bit disillusioned with what I was doing.

The problem was that to leave the profession and go into book supply, if one ever wanted to go back then you were goin' to have to start at the bottom again. And I'd set my sights on going back to Shetland because I knew my predecessor was going to retire in 1976. So my ambition was to get myself to a position of seniority so that I would be in the position to apply for the job when it was advertised. I had passed the general professional examinations of the Library Association. Then you did a one-year's apprenticeship, so to speak, and then you were awarded your Associateship if you achieved certain conditions that the Library Association laid down. And it was in attempting to gain the experience to say, yes, I can qualify here, here and here, that I became a wee bit disillusioned.

I was in Tranent about two years and then Bill Leslie died and he had no assistant to take over. The authority decided that they would appoint a new District Librarian and an assistant. So I thought that I would apply for the assistant's post and was successful and I moved up to Haddington. Brian Gall[19] was appointed Chief Librarian.

We were approaching the first reorganisation of local government in 1975, and we had the opportunity to rewrite the library plan. Unlike other reorganisations since '75, money appeared to be no object. So we devised a library workforce that we thought we would like to see as the ultimate establishment. It simply was passed through the committee, and all of a sudden we were appointing a reference librarian, bibliographic librarian and so on, which we'd never had before. We were able to appoint all qualified staff to our branches, doubled the fleet of mobiles from one to two and appointed new drivers. It was an exciting time.

We conjured up an amount for the book fund, which was 100 per cent if not 200 per cent more than we'd had. It simply went through committee at the nod. So all of a sudden we were looking at a book fund of some £90,000-odd, where we'd had £28,000 or £30,000 before. So we were then able to really utilise the staff and improve reference material and so on. I think we had about 22 staff prior to reorganisation. Six full-time and six part-time branches. We then went to about 37 staff. There was myself; there was the Chief Librarian; there was an Assistant Chief; we then had four specialist librarians at headquarters – each of those had an assistant – and there were a secretary and a clerical assistant, which we hadn't had before. It was quite an increase, generally true throughout Scotland, with the exception of, I think, Orkney, Shetland and the Western Isles which didn't really approach it the way it should have been.

I was in East Lothian from 1972 to 1976. I pursued library interests besides that. I'd become active in the politics of librarianship. I had been the student rep to the Library Association whilst I was at college. I then became involved in the Scottish Library Association, East Branch, and also in the Association of Assistant Librarians in Scotland. So I was gaining experience from the political, decision-making side of the profession as well.

I had some guides and mentors, people like Alan White from Edinburgh City, Peter Grant, the City Librarian of Aberdeen,[20] Alex Howson, the Director of Libraries in Falkirk,[21] and Robert Craig,[22] who's now the Chief Executive of the Scottish Library Association (SLA) and a close personal friend. Somehow or other they all gave me some active encouragement and advice. Probably because I was fairly unique, coming from Shetland, I was always involved and they were quite willing to propose and second me to stand for election for the SLA and I was elected. A tribute to your peers that they elect you. I was elected over 15 years before I was awarded the presidency of the Association, which was a fantastic honour and one of the few ever who was outside the Central Belt.

I often wish that I had been home in '75 rather than coming back to Shetland late on in 1976. I was only going to have one chance. Because Mr Longmuir was 65, they were going to appoint somebody considerably younger, and I had made up my mind that I would try to be in a senior enough position to have the experience to apply. I planned the whole thing like a military exercise because I just wanted to have that one opportunity.

There were eight applicants and six were interviewed – one other Shetlander. We were interviewed at specific times through the morning but we were asked to reconvene at the Town Hall at 12.30 to hear the result. I'll never forget. The lady who was the clerk to the interviewing committee came in. I stood up and started walking across the floor before she had made any announcement – I was so confident that I had got the job – and when I was halfway across the floor she said, 'Yes, Mr Hunter, you're correct. The job is yours.' I would have been somewhat embarrassed had it not.

I'd been planning it. I had thought through all the questions that were liable to be asked. What actually filled me with confidence when I walked into the interview room was that the chairman for the day was my former primary school headmaster, who knew me quite well. I'm not saying that influenced it but he made me feel a lot more at ease.

Shetland Library was exactly the same. The opportunity of local government reorganisation was completely missed. I went home for a salary of £200 less than I was earning in East Lothian and I think the princely sum of £4,685 sticks in my mind. So in fact I went back to Shetland for the good job rather than for the money.

The staff numbers were still the same. The book fund was pitifully low. It was either £13,000 or £15,000 a year. The population of Shetland was 22,000, and you were talking about book issues being in the region of 200,000 to 300,000, because Shetland is an exceptionally well-read area. So the start was to try to raise the book fund. I was young, I was enthusiastic. I think that the authority decided to give me the benefit of the doubt, and within about 18 months the book fund was somewhere in the region of £38,000 to £40,000.

North Sea oil only came along in the late '70s, but the money that the Shetland Islands Council accrued from the North Sea could not be channelled into statutory local government services. They could build as many museums as they wanted, but libraries were a statutory local government service, so we really didnae benefit at all from North Sea oil. There were spin-off things. We acquired some money via an Arts Trust for author events and so on, but it was complementary to libraries.

The inter-island ferry service in Shetland is fantastic, so all our mobiles were able to go to Yell, Unst, Whalsay, Fetlar, Bressay. The only two islands that we couldnae reach were Foula and Fair Isle. We could actually get the mobile into Skerries but it's weather-dependent. So we were visiting pretty nearly every door of every community.

That was a big change from the position when I was in Shetland before, and working practices had changed, so there was none of those sending oot collections. My biggest ambition was to establish a good school library service. I was probably the most unpopular individual with school teachers because I radically changed the way that we spent the money and the way that the service was organised, and I had quite a difficult time in the '80s convincing them that I was right.

What happened was there was an allocation of funds made to a school and the school simply selected what they wanted and bought it. I said that this was really a waste of resources because we didn't have this material catalogued and classified. We'd no idea whether we were buying one copy of a book or 30 copies or 60 copies. So I restricted the money: they ordered through our library headquarters, we catalogued material, and the material became the school library collection, not each individual school's collection. And we were able to recall material from schools. Now the school library staff, the headteachers, they were agin' this idea because they thought they were going to lose out. They didn't have the vision I think I had and my staff had that, at the end of the day, we would have a collection of material that could be moved around to every school to meet the demand when needed. Obviously if we were buying a selection of books on one subject, it was only going to be used in that school one year and not until the circle of projects came back around so we could move it around. I convinced them that that was the way to do it. It was quite difficult.

We had a lot of difficult meetings. We then in every high school and junior high school developed a school librarian in the branch library, and the feeder primaries to those junior high and high schools were serviced by the librarian in that particular school. That was a new move. They didnae understand that move either but it did allow us to keep an eye on quantity and quality of the stock. So at the end of the day we had younger teachers coming along who could see the idea, were more interested in co-operation. There was quite a lot of older teachers, I think, looked on their school as their little empire and they did not co-operate with anybody else. And of course it allowed us to enter into economies of scale. We were using major library suppliers, therefore we were able to negotiate better rates of discount because the Net Book Agreement[23] had fallen; the standard rate of discount used to be 10 per cent – that was all you could get. We were now able to negotiate rates of discount from between 21 per cent up to 31 per cent, dependent on the book firm. And all the time we were annually increasing the book fund. So when I left last year, I think our book fund was in excess of £150,000, which was adequate for what we were trying to achieve and also allowed us to move into material other than books – CD-ROM, cassette, video, and so on.

We were offering in Shetland as good a library service, if not better than anywhere else in Scotland. As the Chief Librarian, I was very privileged in that, I suppose because I was quite outspoken and had a vision of what I wanted to do, I didn't really have any problem with committees, and my style was normally to go and do it and tell them that I'd done it. I was subject to some praise from one convener at some function and he said, 'The most intriguing thing about John is, he goes and does something and he reports to committee afterwards' – which was easiest, because you didnae have to justify what you were doing!

I was in Shetland for 25 years continuously thereafter. I went home in 1976 to give it ten years and I thought a move thereafter. But I got my teeth into other things. I started to take an active part in community life and I ended up as the chairman of this, that and the next thing. I was involved in the Shetland Field Studies Trust, which was indirectly an oil-funded organisation to put supplementary teaching in environmental studies into schools. I was involved with the Shetland Council on Disability for some time. I was its first chairman when a branch was established. I was a member of the Rossness Community Council, which is the area in which I stay and I enjoyed the political aspects of that. I was obviously involved in the Scottish Library Association, so that took me outside Shetland quite a lot.

I've had an interest in freemasonry ever since I was 18 because my father was interested in freemasonry. He was both the secretary and treasurer of his lodge in Lerwick. When I went back in '76, the secretary of the lodge was retiring and I was Jackie's boy, so bound to be up for it. So I took on the secretaryship and I did it for 14 years, and then I was asked to be Provincial Grand Secretary of Orkney and Shetland, which I did for a four-year period.

I thoroughly enjoyed it. The greatest satisfaction I got from it was the ability to raise money for charity and make the donations as anonymously as possible. However, in a small community, it was always known there were children in need or whatever . . . . Also over the years we had established a fairly large benevolent fund and I tried to initiate a system to help widows and widowers who had fallen on harder times, because really the money could only be used for benevolence. We got that established quite well too.

I was looking forward to retirement and doing a whole lot of other things. I'm a keen ornithologist. The Council decided that it required to cut its workforce. A new Chief Executive was appointed and the Council at the time was exceeding the budget available to it and decided to offer any employee full pensionable rights if they were over 50 and had more than 30 years' local government service. I was right in the middle of designing a new library headquarters. The contract had just been awarded and the work was just starting, and I had to make up my mind either to go in December '99 or work on till I was 65. There were other things I wanted to do. So I decided that if I retired it would be an ideal opportunity for somebody young, like myself – I mean, I was 27 when I became Chief Librarian, I was the youngest Chief Librarian in Britain at the time – and it would give somebody of that age the opportunity to go into a brand new building and turn it into what he or she wanted.

I suppose I'm fortunate. I've never had a day's unemployment in my life. I was looking forward to taking some time out and then Robert Craig phoned me and said, 'I've got a wee job that I'd like you to have a look at.' And Robert, having helped me substantially over the years, I couldn't turn round and say no to him. So here I am in Edinburgh. I'm started in a new job where I started my first job.

In 1994, two reports to the SLA and the Scottish Library and Information Council (SLIC)[24] indicated that there was a need for a newspaper microfilm unit in Scotland to be run to conservation standards that met with the National Preservation Office[25] guidelines and to allow library authorities access to funding. There were commercial organisations available but their standards werenae high enough for conservation purposes, so the Scottish Newspapers Microfilming Unit was established in 1994.

Nineteen ninety-four was a formative year. From '95 to '98, the Unit was funded by money from the Mellon Foundation[26] administered through the British Library, so there needed to be no sort of financial vindication of the Unit's performance. After '98 the Unit was imagined to be able to stand on its own two feet financially. Through '98, '99 and 2000, particularly '99 and 2000, it was obvious that there was something far wrong with the Unit because it was running at a dramatic loss. Robert Craig decided to have an outside, independent investigation and that's why I was asked to come in. When I started in January last year the Unit was about £60,000 in deficit, but by 31st March, which was the end of the financial year last year, we had turned that deficit from £60,000 to a profit of about £50,000.

We had some post-end-of-financial-year adjustments to make. However, I was able to prove that the Unit could run in the black. This year we have done a whole lot of retooling. We've spent an awful lot of money on digital material, new lenses for cameras, new computers, new CD-writers and so on and so forth. So we are not in such a healthy position this year but we have taken the opportunity to review all our pricing, all our staffing, and the way the Unit operates. Now it's normally administered to a certain extent by SLIC and representatives of the National Library of Scotland. I have recommended that the Unit is established as a limited liability company that stands on its own and reports to SLIC or the SLA or both. SLIC, who are my employers, have now asked me to stay on to see that through. So what we'll be doing this year is looking for new premises, we'll be introducing new working practices, new terms and conditions of employment for the staff, and obviously going to organisations like the enterprise companies to get start-up funds.

Through the '70s and '80s Scottish local authority library services realised the wealth of information contained in the local paper, and local history became sort of the in-thing. It still is to an extent. In Shetland, I got enough money together, I canna recall where I got it from, but when the Microfilming Unit opened we were its first major customer, and we did *Shetland News*[27] and *The Shetland Times*[28] and all the associated papers. Other library authorities werena as well off as we were and are doing it bit by bit.

However, the New Opportunities Fund Heritage Lottery Funding[29] has backed a plan called Newsplan[30] to microfilm all local newspapers in Britain. They are prioritised: the very rare, the endangered, and so on and so forth. It will take time but at the end of the day there should be a comprehensive coverage. We had to go to the Borders for the 1999–2000 *Southern Reporter*[31] because the National Library of Scotland still doesnae get it! However, we have filmed it.

We're doing one job at the moment where we're actually disbinding the newspapers. This is for a library authority in Scotland who have given us permission to do this. What'll happen is, they will not be rebound. Once they're microfilmed, the only access to them will be by microfilm and they will then go into acid-free boxes.

I think one of the problems now is that again library services are facing cuts, and of course microfilming is not quite peripheral to libraries, but it is one of the first things to be affected. But even so, you should be able to borrow these things and libraries should co-operate. I mean, we didn't have any problem in Shetland. In Shetland there's quite a lot of people doing research, doing degrees, and we never had any difficulty getting microfilms of theses or newspapers if required. I think there are certain library authorities who are maybe loath to ask, you know.

Certain of our newspapers, the early issues, were absolutely in tatters.

But wi' microfilm, it has a guaranteed life-span of 500 years. We have a master, a negative, a working negative, so you can always get a copy.

We're now diversifying into digitisation, where you take your reel of microfilm and you scan it into a computer. It becomes optical character recognisable, you can mount it on the Web, you can burn it to a CD-ROM. So, the second half of Newsplan is mounting all this microfilm material on to the Web. At the end of the day you should be able to sit in Edinburgh or in Perth or wherever and get *The Southern Reporter*.

I've kept my house on in Shetland. The job here with the Scottish Newspapers Microfilming Unit was only for one year but it looks as if it's going to be longer. If there is a long-term future, I may sell up and move doon to Edinburgh. But I have a notion to go back and stand for the Council. I feel that I have something that I could offer. It's something to give back to the Council because the Council kept me employed for 25 years.

As to final thoughts about how libraries have changed, at the moment the Heritage Lottery Fund has made money available to libraries for training staff to use computers, to be able to advise their customers on using computers; probably too little too late, to an extent. I think some of my colleagues don't spend sufficient time training their staff. Staff is an asset. Without appropriate training, they cannot do the job. It's been interesting since I took up this job a year ago, I've travelled around a number of authorities and I have to say that the reaction I've had from front-line staff in certain authorities appalled me. It is not down to the attitude of a front-line member of staff, it's down to their training and the problem lies higher up. I feel that the emphasis shouldn't be on the specialist members of staff being trained here and there and everywhere. The point of contact the public have when they come in the door of the library is with the young boy or the young girl on the desk. Every effort should be made to have them trained so that the member of the public goes away feeling satisfied.

A lot of the problems that libraries have we have brought on ourselves. It's getting better. It's far fae perfect. There's an excuse used, 'Oh, we don't have the money.' We had a training budget in Shetland for 27 staff of £3,000, which is nothing, per head, you know. And we were able to work wonders because we trained in groups, we brought in trainers rather than sent people away. I think some of my colleagues find it easier to say, 'Oh, we don't have the money so we cannot do it', than trying to be imaginative. Councillors are totally unaware of the quantity and quality of information that libraries provide. They still think it's issuing two or three Mills & Boon romances. I don't know how one can change that, short of dragging every councillor into the library to see what happens and they don't do that, from my experience. But we, too, as a profession, have not blown our own trumpet loud enough.

Interviewed 7 January 2002

Notes

Dorothy Milne, pp 5–17

1. The Gordon Highlanders were raised originally as the 100th Highlanders by the Duke of Gordon in 1794, being renumbered the 92nd (Gordon Highlanders) Regiment of Foot in 1798. Recruitment was principally from Aberdeen and the north-east of Scotland, and it is said that the Duke was assisted by his wife, the Duchess Jean, who would place a golden guinea between her lips and offer a kiss to any man who would take the king's shilling. In 1881, the 92nd was amalgamated with the 75th Stirlingshire Regiment to form The Gordon Highlanders. The Gordons raised 21 battalions in the First World War, serving on the Western Front and in Italy. In 1994 the regiment was amalgamated with the Queen's Own Highlanders (Seaforth and Camerons) to form the Highlanders (Seaforth, Gordons and Camerons) which was later merged with several other Scottish regiments to form the Royal Regiment of Scotland.

2. The Territorial Army was created as the Territorial Force in 1908, with the individual units that made up each division or brigade administered by County Associations. Its original purpose was home defence, and although its overall strength was more than a quarter of a million the volunteers who served with the Force were under no obligation to serve overseas. Nevertheless, in August 1914, after the outbreak of the First World War, territorial units were given the option of serving in France and by 25 August in excess of 70 battalions had volunteered to do so. In 1920 the Territorial Force was renamed the Territorial Army. It is now known as the Army Reserve and its stated role is to provide support to the regular Army at home and overseas.

3. See note 14 to the interview with Philip Hancock for information about the Royal Corps of Signals.

4. The Battle of Jutland was a First World War sea battle fought during 31 May-1 June 1916, in which Admiral Jellicoe commanding the British Grand Fleet intercepted the German High Seas Fleet under Vice-Admiral Scheer off the west coast of Jutland, Denmark. Although the Battle was inconclusive and the German fleet was able to return to port, it is generally regarded as a British victory as the Germans did not again try to engage the Royal Navy other than in minor operations.

5. Information about the town of Stonehaven is given in note 24 to the interview with Margaret Crawford.

6. Sir James Taggart (1849–1929) established his own business as a granite mason in

1879, at first in partnership but from 1883 on his own. James Taggart & Son had a large workforce and extensive premises in Great Western Road, Aberdeen. Sir James was Lord Provost of the city, 1914–19, Lord Lieutenant and Admiral of the North Sea during and after the First World War. The business which he established remained active until 1950.

7. Tullahill as given by the interviewee cannot be traced in *Scotland's Places: Place Names for Aberdeenshire*, although it may be a local pronunciation of Tulloch Hill, Kincardine O'Neil parish.

8. A 'scullery' is a room, usually a small room, for rough kitchen chores such as washing and cleaning crockery and kitchen utensils. As few modern houses have a scullery the word is now rarely used.

9. The features of a kitchen range are described in note 4 to the interview with John Preston.

10. Lochnagar is a mountain in Aberdeenshire, 9 miles south-west of Ballater. Its several summits and spectacular corries encircle a small lochan of the same name. It is the subject of a well-known poem by Lord Byron and its proximity to Balmoral has given it royal associations.

11. Congregational churches, although part of the wider Protestant tradition, adopted a form of governance in which each congregation independently and autonomously runs its own affairs. Taking inspiration from the example of John Glas (1695–1773), Robert Haldane (1764–1842) and James Haldane (1768–1851), 55 churches founded the Congregational Union of Scotland in 1812. By 1824 the Congregational Union had 72 member churches, and that figure soon rose to nearly 100. Although now fewer in number, the Congregational churches in Scotland continue as members of the Congregational Federation.

12. A reference to the Church of Scotland.

13. The United Free Church was formed in 1900 as a union of the United Presbyterian Church and the Free Church of Scotland and remained independent of the established church until union with the Church of Scotland in 1929.

14. Information about the Girl Guides and Brownies is given in note 32 to the interview with Margaret Deas.

15. The Sea Rangers were originally part of the Girl Guides but they split off and continue to operate in the south of England only as a freestanding youth organisation for girls. Activities include the development of nautical skills and knowledge as well as swimming, climbing and orienteering to develop leadership and team-building skills and help members gain boating qualifications.

16. See note 24.

17. Kenneth B Milne (1894–1980) was Chief Assistant Librarian with Perth County Library Service before taking up the post of first County Librarian for Aberdeenshire in 1926. At that time the stock of 10,000 books was distributed across 105 centres throughout the County. When he retired in 1960 the service had 116,000 books in 230 branches.

18. For information about NALGO, see note 15 to the interview with Andrew Fraser.

19. See notes 9 and 10 to the interview with Margaret Crawford for information about Highers and Lowers. Note 6 to the interview with John Hunter gives further details.

20. Professional qualifications awarded by the Library Association are described by Professor Reid in his Foreword.

21. Martha Paton (1906–42) commenced service with West Lothian County Library

Service in 1925, and on the departure of Charlotte Adams to take up a post with East Midland Regional Library Scheme she succeeded as County Librarian in 1935.

22. 'Bing' originates from the 16th century Old Norse word *bingr*, meaning a heap; it is commonly used in Scotland for spoil heaps from coal and oil shale mining.

23. The Scottish Youth Hostels Association (SYHA) was founded in 1931 to provide hostel-style accommodation for those with limited means, especially young people and working class people, and so allow them to access places of interest and natural heritage. The SYHA continues to operate as a self-funding charity, and although changing demand has resulted in the closure of some hostels it still maintains a network of over 60 hostels. The standard of accommodation nowadays is much higher than in the Spartan days when Miss Milne first became a member. The SYHA is part of Hostelling International with a high proportion of its guests coming from outwith Scotland.

24. Brown Owl is the leader of a pack of Brownies. Tawny Owl is usually the second in charge.

25. See note 11 to the interview with Andrew Fraser for information about miners' institutes.

26. Early Scottish public library legislation is described in note 18 to the interview with Andrew Fraser.

27. A reserved occupation was one considered sufficiently important to exempt the post holder from military service. Not only were such people exempt from being conscripted, they were often prohibited from enlisting on their own initiative and were required to remain in their posts. In 1938, a *Schedule of Reserved Occupations* was created to identify such occupations and positions.

28. Note 47 to the interview with Peter Grant gives a definition of the term 'book fund'.

29. The Old Parish Registers comprise the records of births and baptisms, banns and marriages and deaths and burials kept by individual parishes of the Church of Scotland before the introduction of civil registration in 1855.

30. In 1921 the Carnegie United Kingdom Trust (CUKT) established the Scottish Central Library for Students (SCLS), modelled on the scheme in London for the provision of technical and specialised literature which individual library authorities were unable to acquire. At this time the resources of the early Scottish county library authorities were still limited and the purpose of the SCLS was to supplement their collections and also to enable residents of areas without a library service to borrow directly from a central stock. The scheme was extended to burgh libraries two years later, and the personal lending service remained in place until 1946 when the last county library service was finally established in Argyll. It was recognised, however, that the role of the SCLS as a clearing house for inter-library lending required the creation of centralised catalogues of library collections. Accordingly, with initial funding provided by the CUKT, compilation of a Scottish Union Catalogue was begun during 1939 in the Mitchell Library, Glasgow. In spite of wartime difficulties, library authorities supported the project financially, the catalogue grew steadily and its usefulness was recognised. Eventually premises in Fisher's Close in the Lawnmarket, Edinburgh, were acquired and officially opened in 1953 by the Duke of Edinburgh as headquarters for the renamed Scottish Central Library (SCL). The principal function of the SCL was to be the completion and maintenance of the Scottish Union Catalogue, but to this were added responsibility

for lending services in support of library authorities, the operation of an overseas inter-library lending service and the provision of a bibliographic advisory service. Despite these developments over 30 years, it was not until the Public Library (Scotland) Act 1955 that the inter-lending of books between public libraries was legalised. In 1974 the Scottish Central Library was merged with the National Library of Scotland (NLS) which took on responsibility for the functions of the SCL within the newly-created NLS Lending Services. Elsewhere in this book Isabella McKinlay describes her work as editor with the Scottish Central Library and note 62 to the interview with Margaret Deas gives information about the Inter Library Lending Scheme.

31. The British Motor Corporation (BMC) was formed in February 1952 when the two former competitors, the Austin Motor Company and the Nuffield Organisation, merged to become the largest motor manufacturing business in Europe, and the third largest in the world. Government regional development policy of the time sought to direct investment to the depressed 'Development Areas', including Central Scotland, and it was decided that something had to be done for an area where the shale oil and other traditional industries were in serious decline. Accordingly, in 1960 it was announced that BMC was to set up its truck and tractor assembly plant at Bathgate. The new £9 million factory was sited on Mosside Farm on the outskirts of the town and major infrastructure projects were put in place to support the development. Thousands of new skilled and semi-skilled jobs were created at the factory and at its peak more than 6,000 people worked in the plant which had the capacity to make 1,000 lorries and 750 tractors per week. The plant closed in 1986.

32. The Grand Orange Lodge of Scotland, popularly known as the Orange Order, is a Masonic-style organisation that promotes Protestantism, conservatism, Britishness and the continued unity of the United Kingdom. It claims to have 50,000 members, the vast majority of whom are working class Protestants from the Scottish Lowlands. The Orange Order was formed in 1795 by Ulster Protestants, many of whom had Scottish roots. It was brought to Scotland in 1798 and, consequently, the Scottish branch has strong links with Northern Ireland and Ulster loyalism. The Order is best known for its yearly marches, the biggest of which are held on and around 12 July. Orange marches in Scotland have been associated with public disorder and sectarian violence.

33. This is a reference to the Library Association (LA), now renamed the Chartered Institute of Library and Information Professionals (CILIP). Further information about the LA, CILIP and the relationship between the UK parent body and the professional association in Scotland is in note 27 to the interview with Gavin Drummond.

34. Soroptimist International is a global volunteer movement for business and professional women with around 80,000 members in more than 130 countries and territories. It works at local, national and international levels to educate, empower and provide opportunities for women and girls. The name Soroptimist was coined from the Latin *soror* meaning sister, and *optima* meaning best. Soroptimist is perhaps best interpreted as 'the best for women'. The first Soroptimist club was founded in Oakland, California, in 1921.

Isabel McKinlay, pp 19–36

1. Glencraig is a small village in Fife, between Crosshill and Lochgelly. The village's population decreased significantly with the decline of the coal-mining industry during the 1970s and '80s.
2. Information about the territorial units of the British Army is given in note 2 to the interview with Dorothy Milne.
3. Following the Jacobite rising of 1715, 'watch' companies were created to patrol the Highlands. The force was known as 'the black watch', a description which may have come from its dark tartan uniform. In 1739 they were incorporated into the regular forces of the British Army. Although in 1751 the regiment was titled the 42nd (Highland) Regiment and later had 'Royal' added to its title, it continued to be known as the Black Watch. In 1881, when the 42nd amalgamated with the 73rd Regiment of Foot, the new regiment was named The Black Watch (Royal Highlanders). The regiment adopted the motto of Scotland's Stewart monarchs, *Nemo me impune lacessit* 'No one provokes me with impunity'. During the First World War, the Black Watch fought mainly in France and Flanders, but also in Mesopotamia, Palestine and the Balkans. Battalions of the Black Watch fought in nearly every major British action in the Second World War. In 1948 the two regular battalions were merged into one which fought in the Korean War and then served during the Mau Mau Uprising in Kenya, the Malayan Emergency, the Troubles in Northern Ireland and was the last British military unit to leave Hong Kong in 1997. During the present century the Black Watch has fought in both Iraq and Afghanistan. Since 2006 it has been merged with five other Scottish regiments to form the single Royal Regiment of Scotland. The Black Watch, however, retains its distinctive red hackle insignia and its name, with its battalion number as a subtitle. Accordingly, it is now known as The Black Watch, 3rd Battalion, The Royal Regiment of Scotland. The battalion's primary recruiting areas are in Fife, Dundee, Angus and Perth and Kinross.
4. Pencaitland is a parish and village in East Lothian. The village lies 5 miles south-west of Haddington and is divided by the River Tyne.
5. 'Dominie' is the Scots term for a schoolmaster, usually employed by the Church of Scotland. As the national church from 1560, the Church of Scotland sought to provide universal education throughout the country with a schoolmaster in every parish, although sometimes the minister himself served as the dominie.
6. The 1872 Education Act had established in Scotland a system of elementary state-funded education and compulsory school attendance up to the age of 12. Many new schools were built, run by local school boards. Thereafter, attention increasingly turned to secondary education, and vocational education up to the age of 14 was introduced in the elementary schools. Larger urban school boards established what were called higher grade (secondary) schools, mostly in inner-city areas. The Education (Scotland) Act 1918 introduced the principle of universal free secondary education, whereby most of the advanced divisions of the primary schools became junior secondaries and continued to provide a vocational education until the age of 14 while the higher grade schools became senior secondaries, giving a more academic education, presenting students for the leaving certificate. Selection between the two types of school was determined at age 12 by the Qualifying Exam, known colloquially as 'the Qually'. The significance of the Qualifying Exam is described in note 2 to the interview with John Hunter.

7. The Leaving Certificate Examination had been introduced by the Scottish Education Department to set national standards for secondary education.

8. Information about *The Pilgrim's Progress* is given as note 18 to the interview with Margaret Crawford.

9. *Annals of the Parish; or, the Chronicle of Dalmailing during the Ministry of the Rev Micah Balwhidder*, published in 1821, is the best-known novel of the Ayrshire-born John Galt (1779–1839). Micah Balwhidder is Galt's finest character and the book provides a truthful picture of the old-fashioned Scottish pastor and of life in a country parish. Galt's other novels of Scottish rural life are *The Ayrshire Legatees* (1820), *The Provost* (1822) and *The Entail* (1823). Together, they foreshadow the 'Kailyard school' of Scottish fiction of the late 19th century. In addition to being a writer, Galt was an entrepreneur and administrator. In 1804, having been commissioned by a commercial firm to establish trade agreements in the Mediterranean area, he met Byron, with whom he travelled to Malta and Athens. (In 1830 he wrote *The Life of Lord Byron*.) Other commercial ventures took him to France and the Netherlands (1814) and to Canada (1826). He opened up a road between Lakes Huron and Erie and founded the city of Guelph in Upper Canada (now Ontario). However, he did not continue to prosper and returned to Scotland almost a ruined man. Often labelled a forgotten writer, at least six of John Galt's books are in print.

10. Hall Caine – Sir Thomas Henry Hall Caine CH KBE (1853–1931) – was an Isle of Man author, a writer of romantic fiction and non-fiction, including biographies and literary criticism, as well as theatre and film scripts. His 1897 novel, *The Christian*, which was filmed in 1914 and 1924, was the first novel in Britain to sell over one million copies. As a young man Caine had trained as an architect and surveyor in Liverpool while self-educating himself through wide reading. He became a lecturer and theatre critic, which introduced him to influential people such as Sir Henry Irving and Bram Stoker, who dedicated *Dracula* to him. He became the secretary, factotum and nurse to Dante Gabriel Rossetti (1828–82) in the last years of the poet's life. Caine's biography of Rossetti (1882) sold reasonably well but he began to consider that his future might lie in writing fiction. His first novel, *Shadow of a Crime* (1885), was still in print in the 1900s (as it is today) and launched him on a career that was to span 40 years and produce 15 novels, a number of them based on 'the eternal triangle'. *The Woman Thou Gavest Me* (1913) caused the biggest furore of any of his novels. Libraries objected to its morals, dealing as it did with the divorce laws of the time and illegitimacy. It was reprinted five times before the end of the year, and made Caine's reputation as a popular novelist, so popular that crowds would gather outside his house to get a glimpse of him. In the words of his biographer, Vivien Allen, he was 'accorded the adulation reserved now for pop stars and footballers'. Caine received a knighthood in 1918, largely because of his work in connection with the creation of the League of Nations during the First World War. In 1922 he was made a Companion of Honour for services to Literature. There are some ten of Hall Caine's books still in print, mainly those with an Isle of Man or Lake District connection.

11. Information regarding miners' institutes is given in note 11 to the interview with Andrew Fraser.

12. The novelist and dramatist Sir James Matthew Barrie (1860–1937) was born in Kirriemuir, the son of a handloom weaver. Initially working as a journalist, his

published sketches of life in his native town, disguised as 'Thrums', were followed by a number of novels. From 1890 he wrote for the theatre and his plays enjoyed considerable success. Although critics have regarded Barrie's work as belonging to the 'Kailyard school' and sentimentalising life in Scotland, his supreme achievement, *Peter Pan* (1904), is a complex and perceptive work about childhood. Barrie's grave is in Kirriemuir and his birthplace is now a museum maintained by the National Trust for Scotland.

13. Grace Cecilia Gaston Bonthrone, known as Eila, was born in 1905. Her father was a prominent figure in local politics in Fife. Eila Bonthrone was appointed Fife County Librarian in 1930 and thereafter oversaw a significant expansion of the authority's library provision. In particular, she championed children's library services, advocating that children themselves be allowed to choose what to read. She retired sometime after the Second World War and during her retirement wrote a book published by Fife County Council in 1951 and entitled *Fife and its Folk: a Key to the Kingdom.*

14. Lawrence Daly (1924–2009) was born in Fife and began work as a miner at Glencraig Colliery at the age of 15. His father, also a miner, was a founder member of the Communist Party of Great Britain (CPGB). Daly became involved with the Scottish Mineworkers' Union and British Trades Union Congress (TUC), initially through youth committees and activities. Although active in the CPGB from 1940, he found himself in disagreement with party doctrine from the late 1940s and left the Party in 1956 over the Soviet invasion of Hungary. He was elected as a County Councillor for the Ballingry division in May 1958, and eventually joined the Labour Party in 1964. Rising through the ranks of the National Union of Mineworkers (NUM), Daly was elected to its Scottish Area Executive Committee in 1962 and became General Secretary of the Scottish Area NUM in 1965. He was prominent in the campaign in the mid-1960s for the abolition of piecework at the coalface, and its replacement by a national day-wage structure. In 1968 Daly was elected General Secretary of the NUM, and steered the union through two major strikes in 1972 and 1974 in response to a falling behind of miners' wages generally, and of coalface workers' wages particularly. Daly sustained a serious injury in a road accident in 1975, and had prolonged leave of absence following it. In 1984 he stepped down as NUM General Secretary.

15. Information about the publisher, Mills & Boon, is given as note 16 to the interview with John Hunter.

16. W & M Duncan Ltd, best known as 'Duncan's of Edinburgh', was originally established as a cake business by Mary Duncan and her son William in Dundee in 1861 before moving to Edinburgh in 1884 where the company began to produce chocolate confectionery. The Walnut Whip was launched in 1910, although Duncan's Hazelnut was undoubtedly the best-known Scottish-made chocolate bar. The business was acquired by Rowntree Mackintosh in 1947, and although the Edinburgh factory was closed in 1987 it was reopened immediately by new owners, trading as 'Duncans of Scotland'. Within ten years the new Duncan's business moved to Bellshill, Lanarkshire, and passed through several owners before becoming part of J E Wilson & Sons (Kendal). It is reassuring that the Walnut Whip continues to be manufactured by Nestlé which acquired Rowntree's in 1988.

17. Thomas Edward Lawrence, known as Lawrence of Arabia (1888–1935), first encountered the Bedouins when working with Sir Flinders Petrie's archaeological

team on the Euphrates, 1911–14. On the outbreak of war, he worked for Army intelligence in North Africa, and in 1916 became British liaison officer to the Arab Revolt against the Turks and entered Damascus in 1918. To escape his subsequent fame, he enlisted under assumed names in the ranks of the RAF (twice) and the Royal Tank Corps. He retired in 1935 but was killed later that year in a motorcycle accident. His account of the Arab Revolt, *Seven Pillars of Wisdom*, became one of the classics of war literature.

18. The dedication in *Seven Pillars of Wisdom* is 'To S A' and consists of a poem written by Lawrence and edited by Robert Graves. It begins: 'I loved you, so I drew these tides of men into my hands.' It is uncertain whether the work is dedicated to the Arab race, to Saudi Arabia as Miss McKinlay thinks, or to an individual. It has been suggested that 'S A' was a young Arab boy, Selim Ahmed, of whom Lawrence was especially fond and who died shortly before Damascus was taken.

19. Eric Henri Kennington (1888–1960) was an English painter and sculptor. He was an official war sculptor in both world wars and designed many memorials.

20. Agnes B Luke started work in Kirkcaldy Library in 1923 and was appointed Burgh Librarian in 1946, a post she held until she retired in 1967. She served on the Council of the Scottish Library Association for a period. She died in 1985.

21. *Seven Pillars of Wisdom* was first published in 1926 as a subscribers' edition with a print run of only about 200 copies, each with handcrafted binding and illustrations by a number of distinguished artists, including Eric Kennington. Copies command a very high price if they become available. Although a heavily abridged version was published under the title *Revolt in the Desert* in 1927, it was not until after Lawrence's death in 1935 that the 1926 edition was republished for general circulation. It is uncertain which edition Miss McKinlay refers to in her interview, although it seems unlikely that copies of the subscribers' edition would have been purchased for several libraries in Fife.

22. *The Times Literary Supplement* (the abbreviation *TLS* has been used as the masthead since 1969) is a weekly literary review first published in 1902 as a supplement to *The Times*, but a separate publication since 1914. Reviews were normally anonymous until 1974 when signed reviews were introduced. As well as book reviews the *TLS* publishes essays and poems. It boasts many famous names among its contributors over the years, including T S Eliot, Henry James, Virginia Woolf, Philip Larkin and Gore Vidal. For many years the *TLS* carried advertisements for library vacancies and was regularly checked by members of the profession.

23. Scottish secondary education awards are described in note 6 to the interview with John Hunter.

24. Information about the Library Association and the Scottish Library Association is given in note 27 to the interview with Gavin Drummond.

25. Professional qualifications awarded by the Library Association are described by Professor Reid in his Foreword.

26. The professional training of librarians at the Scottish School of Librarianship is described in note 9 to the interview with John Hunter.

27. The life and career of William B Paton are described in note 29 to the interview with M W (Bill) Paton.

28. John Robertson (1909–90) began his career in 1926, working with the County Library service in Stirling before his appointment as Librarian in Grangemouth in 1934. During the Second World War he served as a rating and thereafter as a

lieutenant in the Royal Navy Volunteer Reserve. He was appointed Burgh Librarian in Stirling in 1946 in which post he remained until his retiral in 1975. During this time he initiated a number of improvements including the introduction of school class visits and the opening of a reference room and adults' and children's reading rooms.

29. The term 'public library' here refers to a burgh library authority. Note 18 to the interview with Andrew Fraser discusses the development of burgh and county library authorities prior to 1975 when the reorganisation of local government in Scotland created unitary library authorities.

30. The work to compile a Scottish Union Catalogue and the role of the Scottish Central Library are described in note 30 to the interview with Dorothy Milne, and information about the Inter Library Lending Scheme is given as note 62 to the interview with Margaret Deas.

31. Matthew Cecil Pottinger joined the staff of the Mitchell Library in 1925 and then worked at Fulham Public Library during 1930–31. For nine years thereafter he was employed first as Deputy then as Librarian with the Newcastle Literary and Philosophical Society before war service as lieutenant-commander of a flotilla of assault landing craft, for which he won the Distinguished Service Cross and was mentioned in dispatches. After the War he travelled widely on library and UNESCO business before his appointment as Librarian of the Scottish Central Library in 1946 (see also note 30 to the interview with Dorothy Milne). Pottinger was active on various library committees and government working parties and was elected President of the Scottish Library Association in 1962.

32. Alexander Small joined Dundee Public Libraries as a message boy in 1910, and after holding various positions in the service was appointed City Librarian in 1949. He retired in 1961 after 51 years with the Library Service and died in 1967 aged 70.

33. The purpose of the library catalogue is to find a book or other type of material, to show what the holdings of the library are and to assist in the choice of an item from the collection. For each stock item the catalogue record provides author, title, subject, bibliographic details and any other information which identifies that specific item. In a card catalogue this information is presented in a standard format on an individual card of uniform material and size (traditionally 5 inches x 3 inches). Cards, typically arranged by author or subject, are filed in drawers and usually in a cabinet or other piece of furniture designed for the purpose. For long, the card catalogue was a familiar sight to library users but most libraries have now replaced it with the online public access catalogue (OPAC) which offers several advantages over a physical catalogue, including efficiency of updating and maintenance, enhanced searching, remote access and reduction in storage space. See note 54 to the interview with Joe Fisher for further information about an OPAC.

34. This refers to the City of Edinburgh Central Library on George IV Bridge. See also the interview with Alan White, especially note 43.

35. This refers to the British Museum Library. The British Library was a later creation, owing its origin largely to the 1969 report of the National Libraries Committee under the Chairmanship of Lord Dainton, followed two years later by a White Paper recommending the setting up of a national library for the UK. In 1972 The British Library Act was passed by Parliament, bringing the Library into operation with effect from 1 July 1973 and incorporating within it the library departments of the British Museum, the National Reference Library of Science and Invention, the

National Central Library (see note 32 to the interview with Philip D Hancock) and the National Lending Library for Science and Technology (the centre for inter library lending, located at Boston Spa in Yorkshire). In 1974 the British National Bibliography and the Office for Scientific and Technical Information joined the British Library, the India Office Library and Records and the British Institute of Recorded Sound were added in 1982 and 1983. The British Library's new, expanded home at St Pancras was formally opened by HM The Queen in June 1998.

36. Éire is the Irish language name for both the island and the state called Ireland. The Constitution of Ireland, adopted in 1937, states that 'the name of the State is Éire, or, in the English language, Ireland'. Éire has passed out of everyday usage, however, and the state is referred to as Ireland or its equivalent in all other languages.

37. An interview with M W (Bill) Paton is included in this volume.

38. Jimmy Shand was born in East Wemyss, Fife, on 28 January 1908, the sixth of nine children. At 14 he left school to work in the local coal mines but later left the pits to work for Fife Power Company. His skill as an accordionist was recognised from an early date and in 1935 he got his first recording contract. Shand formed his own dance band in 1940 and after the War made regular radio broadcasts and recordings which sold all over the world. TV appearances followed and his signature tune, 'Bluebell Polka', reached number 20 in the charts. His musicianship and popularity were acknowledged with several honours including an MBE, an honorary MA from Dundee University and a knighthood. In East Wemyss a street was named after him and after his death in 2000 a bronze sculpture was erected in his honour in Auchtermuchty, the town where he had made his home.

39. 'Box' is a popular name for an accordion.

40. John Houston (1930–2008) was one of the most distinguished painters of the post-war period. His work was powerful, rich in colour and characteristic of modern Scottish painting. Although he included still-life and the human figure in his work, it was the landscape which inspired him most. Houston was born at Buckhaven, attended the high school there and then went to Edinburgh College of Art, leaving in 1953 with a postgraduate travel scholarship which took him to Italy for the first time. In 1956 he married the artist Elizabeth Blackadder, and they both took up teaching appointments at Edinburgh College of Art, with Houston rising to become deputy head of painting in 1989. Houston and Blackadder became Royal Scottish academicians together in 1972, and in 1990 he was awarded an OBE.

41. In 1879 William Campbell of Lossiemouth produced a new design of fishing boat called the Zulu, a hybrid boat combining the best features of earlier styles of Scottish fishing vessels. The Zulu had two masts and edge-to-edge planking which was stronger than the earlier clinker design, with an upright stem and a raked stern. These features made for a faster speed and more deck space. The boat was named after the Zulu War of that time. The Zulu design quickly became popular and many were built in the following years.

42. The National Steel Foundry was established in 1910 at Kirklands, near Leven, and produced heavy and light castings. In 1955 it became part of a larger group and continued to operate until 1983 when, due to severe financial constraints, it ceased trading. That same year, however, the assets of the company were purchased by five former managers of National Steel and it was re-formed as Glencast Ltd. The company manufactured castings for a wide range of industries until its closure in 2002.

43. Henry Balfour & Co established its Durie Foundry in Leven in 1810. It became a public limited company in 1896. By the 1960s, the Foundry had diversified to include gas and chemical engineering and the manufacture of pressure vessels and machine-cut gearing among its activities, and employed 1,000 workers. In 1962 Balfour's was acquired by Pfaudler and renamed Pfaudler Balfour. It is now part of the Robbins & Myers UK Ltd group. It has operated on the same site for over 200 years where it now makes glass-lined steel products used in the chemical and pharmaceutical industries.

44. In 1924 West Fife Agricultural Trading Society Ltd was set up as a co-operative. It later changed its name to Central Farmers Ltd, and through sales of fertilisers, animal feed and household items became a profitable and well-run organisation respected and trusted by farmers. Thereafter it manufactured its own fertilisers and animal feedstuffs, and grain purchased from farmers was sold to millers, maltings and distilleries or exported. Central Farmers also moved into the supply of farm produce direct to shops and hotels. Turnover and profits increased and enabled expansion into a wider range of services, membership grew to 2,500, Central Farmers traded all over southern and central Scotland, and Methil docks was kept busy with the importation of goods for the business. By the end of the last century, however, the sector experienced great changes owing to competition from abroad and on-line ordering. As a result, profit margins fell and in 2000 the merchant and flour milling group, Carr's of Carlisle, bought over Central Farmers Ltd.

45. Methil Power Station was commissioned in 1965 for the then South of Scotland Electricity Board. It was designed to utilise low-grade coal slurry supplied from the washeries of local mines – waste that had accumulated in coal tips at pits no longer in production. When it became exhausted operations ceased. The power station was decommissioned in 2000 and demolished in 2011.

46. Charles Brister, *This is my Kingdom: Short Stories about Miners at Work and at Play* (David Winter & Son Ltd, Dundee, 1972).

47. Ron Thompson (1929–2004) was a journalist who reported for several newspapers including *The Courier*, *Daily Herald*, *Sunday Mail* and *Sunday Express*. He was also a reporter and presenter for several Grampian Television news programmes. He was awarded an MBE in 1991 for his services to journalism.

48. *The Courier* is published by D C Thomson in Dundee in five regional editions covering east-central Scotland. It was established in 1801 as the *Dundee Courier & Argus*, and in 1926 *The Courier* was merged with *The Advertiser*. In 2012, it changed to a compact format, having previously appeared as a broadsheet.

49. Information about the *Morning Star* and *The Daily Worker* can be found in note 17 to the interview with John Hunter.

50. Armistice Day is commemorated every year on 11th November to mark the First World War armistice signed between the Allies and Germany for the cessation of hostilities on the Western Front. It took effect at eleven o'clock in the morning – being the eleventh hour of the eleventh day of the eleventh month of 1918.

51. The Kirking of the Council is a long-held custom to inaugurate a new term of the council in which councillors and council officials attend an annual church ceremony, committing themselves to the service of the local community in a very public way. In some places, the ceremony includes a procession of council representatives, local uniformed organisations, bands, etc.

52. The Citizens Advice Bureau (CAB), now named Citizens Advice Scotland, is the

country's largest independent advice service offering free, confidential and impartial advice. It provides the service in person from dozens of locations and over the phone as well as through its website, Advice for Scotland, which operates in partnership with CABs in England and Northern Ireland. The service is delivered largely by trained volunteers supported by professional and specialist staff.

53. Age Concern Scotland was created from a number of Older People's Welfare Associations established during the Second World War. Its purpose was to improve the lives of older people, to make their lives more secure, comfortable, dignified and enjoyable. As well as supporting local groups, Age Concern Scotland itself delivered a range of locally-based services using volunteers and local expertise. For many years it worked in collaboration with Help the Aged in Scotland with which it merged in 2009 to form the new brand Age Scotland the following year, becoming Scotland's largest charity for older people.

54. It is uncertain which organisation Miss McKinlay refers to as 'the Blind Society'. The Fife Society for the Blind is a well-established and successful local organisation, founded in 1865, since when it has supported generations of Fifers with sight loss to enjoy the fullest possible independence, including access to reading materials. It may be, however, that her reference is to the Royal National Institute of Blind People which, since 1868 (with several name changes), has been providing various types of support to people across the UK living with sight loss.

55. David Proudfoot, a local miners' leader in Buckhaven and Methil, was prominent during the 1926 General Strike and lock-out. He was also the main force behind the establishment of *Spark*, the highly influential paper produced by the Methil Communist Pit Group during 1925–31. In elections to the National Union of Scottish Mineworkers (NUSM) Proudfoot was one of a number of Communist Party members to be returned. Frustrated by right-wing control of the union, however, a group of left-wingers, including Proudfoot, left in 1929 to form the rival United Mineworkers of Scotland (UMS). Although the UMS initially enjoyed some success, and had members throughout the Scottish coalfields, it really only had strong support in Fife. Proudfoot became the General Secretary of the UMS in early 1931 but held that post for only seven months, to be replaced by the legendary miners' leader, Abe Moffat. The UMS rejoined the NUSM in 1936. Proudfoot remained a member of the Communist Party for some time thereafter, but very publicly supported the Labour candidate in the Kirkcaldy by-election for Westminster in 1944, and was himself elected in 1945 as a Labour councillor in Buckhaven and Methil. In this position he played a key role in post-war planning and development matters. He died in 1958.

56. J K Rowling (1965–) launched her hugely successful career as a writer for children and young people with *Harry Potter and the Philosopher's Stone* (1997) set in Hogwarts School of Witchcraft and Wizardry. Sequels proved equally popular and their hero became an internationally-renowned character. The *Harry Potter* books have sold more than 400 million copies and encouraged an interest in reading among the young at a time when children were thought to be abandoning books for computers and television. Films of the books, with all-star casts, have attracted huge audiences and critical acclaim. J K Rowling, mainly using the pseudonym Robert Galbraith, has also published novels for adults. As well as an OBE for services to children's literature, J K Rowling has received numerous awards and honorary degrees.

Andrew Fraser, pp 37–55

1. Patrick Thomson opened a small haberdashery and drapery shop on South Bridge, Edinburgh, in 1889. In 1906 the company relocated to a larger store at 15 North Bridge, expanding to 60 departments. In 1926 the store was purchased by the newly-formed Scottish Drapery Corporation, and Patrick Thomson's, or PT's as it was affectionately known, branded itself 'The Shopping Centre of Scotland'. As well as providing the latest fashions for ladies and gents and a full range of household goods, customers could relax in the Palm Court restaurant while enjoying music by the in-house orchestra. PT's was a place for Edinburgh's middle classes to shop, socialise and be seen. Although in 1952 the Scottish Drapery Corporation was purchased by House of Fraser, Patrick Thomson continued to operate. In 1976, however, House of Fraser changed the name of the store to Arnotts, a move so deeply unpopular that it continued to be referred to as PT's until its eventual closure in 1982. In 1984 the building was reopened as the Carlton Hotel.

2. By 1833 Dalkeith-born Richard Barnett Whytock had patented his new Tapestry carpet loom which was considered superior to all other contemporary looms. As a result, his company, Whytock & Henderson, experienced such growth that new premises were taken at Lasswade by the banks of the River Esk, and in 1838 Whytock became Patent Carpet Manufacturer to the Queen. In 1846, however, he left the carpet manufacturing business and Henry Henderson gained a new partner in Henry Widnell, the company becoming Henderson & Widnell. In 1856 Widnell took complete control of the company, renamed as Henry Widnell & Company. In 1868 a second site was secured for carpet manufacture at the Old Bleach Works at Roslin. During the 1870s George Stewart of Stewart Brothers of Eskbank became a partner in Henry Widnell & Company, although the two manufacturers continued to trade as separate companies until 1895 when they were both sold to Henry Widnell & Stewart Ltd. That company continued to manufacture a variety of carpets and was one of the major employers in the area until the Second World War during which all three sites converted production to the requirements of the war effort. In 1959 the company was taken over by A F Stoddard & Co Ltd although it continued to trade under the name of Henry Widnell & Stewart Ltd until 1983 when it finally ceased business. The Bonnyrigg factory was demolished in 1994. The records of the company are held in the University of Glasgow Archives.

3. The features of a kitchen range are described in note 4 to the interview with John Preston.

4. The significance of the Qualifying Exam is described in note 2 to the interview with John Hunter.

5. Scottish secondary education awards are described in note 6 to the interview with John Hunter.

6. Skerry's College was a network of colleges which primarily prepared candidates for Civil Service examinations. It was inaugurated as a small training centre in Edinburgh in 1878 by George Skerry in response to the introduction of competitive examination for entry to the Civil Service, Post Office, Customs and Excise and other Government posts. It was the first college providing such training and was an immediate success with branches later being opened in several large cities across Britain. Correspondence courses were also offered from 1880. In the early 1890s Skerry's broadened its curricula to meet the requirements of university and other

entrance exams, and inaugurated office training in shorthand and typewriting. The introduction of free state education and comprehensive schools, and the decline in the attractiveness of work in the Civil Service resulted in the eventual closure of all Skerry's Colleges in the UK by 1970. Skerry's principal college in Hill Place, Edinburgh, although closed in the 1960s, continues in an educational role as Edinburgh University's English Language Teaching Centre.

7. Angus Grant Mackay FLA (1899–1962) began his career in the Mitchell Library at the age of 16. In 1925 he became District Librarian, first at Anderston Library and later at Shettleston and Tollcross Library. In 1931 he was appointed as Midlothian County Librarian, a post which he held until his death. During this time Midlothian was considered an example of a progressive and expanding county library system. He served as Honorary Secretary of the Scottish Library Association (SLA) during 1935–40 and again during 1942–43. He was elected SLA President in 1947 and 1948 and continued to serve on the SLA Council until 1955.

8. Information about the Library Association and the Scottish Library Association is given in note 27 to the interview with Gavin Drummond.

9. Professional qualifications awarded by the Library Association are described by Professor Reid in his Foreword.

10. Midlothian County Council Education Department offices were located at 9 Drumsheugh Gardens, Edinburgh.

11. Miners' institutes, also known as miners' welfares, were opened in mining communities when the coal mining industry was flourishing. Often, they were owned, funded and run by groups of miners themselves as meeting venues and social and educational centres. Among other facilities, the institutes would normally contain a library and reading room.

12. During the 19th century and the early part of the 20th century public library users were not permitted to browse the shelves to select the books they wished to read; books were held in 'closed access' in a staff-only area. Readers had to consult the catalogue, identify the item they wished to borrow and check the indicator, which 'indicated' whether the item was available or on loan. The indicator was usually a wooden screen displaying printed numbers, each number representing a book. There were different varieties of indicator, but it was Alfred Cotgreave who invented the best-known version which featured small reversible drawers with coloured ends: blue was 'in' and red was 'out'. At the time many believed open access to be a backward system; the indicator was mechanical, it was modern. Nevertheless, increasing acceptance of open access from the late 19th century onwards rendered the indicator obsolescent.

13. Robert McCall Strathdee FLA (1909–91) commenced work with Midlothian County Library Service in 1930 and was appointed County Librarian in 1962. He continued in this position until he retired in 1975.

14. The torch of knowledge sign bearing the words 'County Library' or 'Public Library' was a familiar sight at the roadside and on buildings, especially in rural areas.

15. The National Association of Local Government Officers (NALGO) was founded in 1905. By 1914 almost 70 per cent of all white-collar local government officers were members. With the growth in membership in sectors outside local government, such as health, gas and electricity, it changed its name in 1952 to the National and Local Government Officers' Association, while retaining the acronym NALGO. By the late 1970s it was by far the largest UK public sector union, with over 700,000 members.

NALGO merged with the National Union of Public Employees (NUPE) and the Confederation of Health Service Employees (COHSE) in 1993 to form UNISON.

16. Appalled by the poor selection of paperbacks available at the time, Sir Allen Lane founded Penguin Books in 1935 to publish quality contemporary fiction at an affordable price. It was Lane's secretary who suggested a penguin as the symbol for the new business. Titles were colour coded (orange for fiction, blue for biography, green for crime) and cost just sixpence, the same price as a packet of cigarettes. The way the public thought about books changed for ever and the paperback revolution had begun. At first Penguin Books was an imprint of The Bodley Head of which Lane was a director. In 1936, however, Penguin became a separate company and within 12 months it had sold three million paperbacks. In 1937 the Pelican imprint – original non-fiction books on contemporary issues – was launched and through titles on politics, the arts and science Penguin had a significant impact on public debate. Puffin was born in 1940 as a series of non-fiction picture books for children and they proved to be such a success that Puffin started publishing fiction the following year. In 1946 Penguin Classics were launched. Firmly established as a major force in publishing and British life, Penguin became a public company in 1961 and thereafter continued to expand through the introduction of new imprints and the acquisition of other publishing houses. Penguin Books is now an imprint of the worldwide Penguin Random House, a conglomerate formed in 2013 and one of the largest English-language publishers with offices in 15 countries and more than 5,000 titles in print at any time.

17. The 1931 Census of Scotland gives the population of the County of Midlothian, excluding the City of Edinburgh, as 87,286. The 1951 Census reports the Midlothian County population as 98,974.

18. The Public Libraries (Scotland) Act 1853 and subsequent legislation permitted burgh councils to establish and operate a free public library service. Adoption of the Acts, however, required the assent of ratepayers, and 25 years after the 1853 Act had been passed there were only six rate-supported libraries in Scotland; two others had adopted the Acts but did not commence a library service until later and four towns had rejected the Acts. Despite the disappointing uptake, further public library legislation was enacted. Indeed, the Public Libraries Consolidation (Scotland) Act 1887 remains the principal Act for Scotland to this day, while an Act of 1894 allowed the town council in a burgh to adopt the Acts by resolution at a special meeting. It was not until Andrew Carnegie made grants available, however, that there was a great increase in the number of places adopting the Acts.

Nevertheless, by 1914 only 50 per cent of the population of Scotland lived within library areas. The smaller towns and country districts remained to a great extent unprovided for. There was still no legislation allowing the establishment of libraries for areas beyond the burgh or parish, apart from the little-used power for neighbouring burghs or parishes to combine in implementing the Libraries Acts.

The critical change came with the passing of the Education (Scotland) Act 1918 which permitted the education authority of a county to provide books for general reading, not only to children and young people but also to the resident adult population. In contrast to the slow development of burgh libraries, this Act was interpreted by county education authorities as a mandate to set up library services to serve communities outwith burghs which had adopted the Libraries Acts. Within five years the majority of Scottish counties were operating public libraries. As was the case with burgh libraries, an important factor in this rapid development was undoubtedly the support and financial assistance of the Carnegie Trust.

It was increasingly realised that the county library movement, originally created to provide services to rural areas, had a responsibility for the towns and small burghs in their area that had not yet adopted the Acts. One of the first county library branches in the UK was opened by Midlothian County Library in Musselburgh in September 1925.

At the same time, one problem experienced by burgh libraries was that Carnegie grants had often been used to construct grand library buildings, the maintenance of which could exhaust library budgets and leave insufficient funds for the purchase of books and other materials. The Education (Scotland) Act 1918, however, had explicitly permitted county education authorities to 'enter into arrangements with public libraries' and it was soon appreciated that co-operation could be mutually advantageous, especially if small burgh libraries were involved. As early as 1921, for example, the education authority of Midlothian had arranged that the lending department of Bonnyrigg Public Library should be incorporated in the county scheme. Other authorities made similar arrangements, although for the large burgh libraries with their greater resources co-operation with the county library service was at this stage unnecessary.

This impetus towards the adoption of mutually beneficial arrangements between county library authorities and burgh libraries within their areas was accelerated by the Local Government (Scotland) Act of 1929 under which every burgh library authority had to apply, in addition to its own library rate, its proportion of the expenditure on the county library service. Co-operation between burgh and county library services, however, remained far from universal until the reorganisation of local government in Scotland in 1975 created unitary library authorities.

For further information about early public library legislation in Scotland see Professor Reid's Foreword.

19. Information about private circulating and subscription libraries, including Boots Book Lending service, is given in notes 10 and 11 to the interview with Alan White.
20. In 1922 the Scottish Library Association (SLA) began a series of schools in librarianship to prepare those attending for the Library Association (LA) exams. Other schools followed in 1923, 1925 and 1926 and until 1934 schools were held during the autumn every second year alternately in Edinburgh and Glasgow. In 1936 the school was arranged for the summer as a residential course, and for the three years thereafter Newbattle Abbey College was used as the venue. No summer schools were held during the war years and it was not until 1948 that the next one was presented. Although changes to the LA's exam syllabus and the opening of the Scottish School of Librarianship caused a rethink of the purpose of the summer schools, they resumed annually at Newbattle Abbey College from 1951. For many years they remained a feature of the SLA's work, delivering informal learning opportunities not directly aligned to professional qualification. Information about Newbattle Abbey is given as note 37 to the interview with Alan White, and note 44 to the interview with Margaret Deas refers to the Marquess of Lothian's bequest of the Newbattle Collection to the National Library of Scotland.
21. Information about the Scouts and Cub Scouts is found in note 9 to the interview with Gavin Drummond.
22. Some 20 years before Baden-Powell started the Boy Scouts, William Smith

founded the Boys' Brigade in Glasgow in 1883. Thereafter, the movement spread rapidly to other Scottish cities, to English cities and then internationally. Each company was to be affiliated to its local church, usually non-Roman Catholic, and a high priority was given to religious instruction, discipline and drill as well as to leisure, sporting and outdoor activities.

23. The King's Own Scottish Borderers (KOSB) were raised in Edinburgh in 1689 by the Earl of Leven for the defence of Edinburgh against the Jacobites. The regiment fought at the battles of Killiecrankie (1689), Sherrifmuir (1715) and Culloden (1746), the only Scottish regiment to have fought for the Government in all three decisive engagements of the Jacobite wars. During the Second World War, the KOSB fought in France, Burma and north-west Europe. In 2006 the Regiment became The King's Own Scottish Borderers' Battalion of The Royal Regiment of Scotland. In August of that year, the Royal Scots and KOSB Battalions merged to form the 1st (Royal Scots Borderers) Battalion of the new Regiment.

24. The Bren gun, usually called simply the Bren, was a series of light machine guns adopted by Britain in the 1930s and used in various roles until 1992. It is best known for its role as the British and Commonwealth forces' primary infantry light machine gun in the Second World War. The name was derived from Brno in the Czech Republic, where the prototype was originally designed, and Enfield, site of the British Royal Small Arms Factory.

25. It was from the port of Dunkirk in northern France that over 200,000 British troops and 120,000 French were evacuated during late May and early June 1940 following the capitulation of the Belgian Army to the north and the thrust of German tank forces to the south cut off the British Expeditionary Force and the French First Army. Over 850 vessels took part in the evacuation, half of them small craft hurriedly sent across the English Channel.

26. 'Tattie-howkin" is a Scots phrase meaning the harvesting of potatoes by digging them out of the ground and picking them up.

27. Victory in Europe Day, generally known as V-E Day, was the public holiday celebrated on 8 May 1945 to mark the formal acceptance by the Allies of Nazi Germany's unconditional surrender of its armed forces. It thus marked the end of the Second World War in Europe. Upon the defeat of Germany, celebrations erupted throughout the world, and in the United Kingdom more than one million people celebrated in the streets.

28. The Mark was the currency of Germany from the time of the country's original unification in 1871. Under variations of that name at different times and during the division of the country following the Second World War, it continued as the main unit of currency until the reunited Germany joined the Euro in 2002. The subdivision unit of the Mark was the Pfennig.

29. Professional qualifications awarded by the Library Association are described by Professor Reid in his Foreword.

30. Fisherrow School was closed as a school in 1958. It served as the Midlothian County Council Library HQ for many years with the result that at the time of local government reorganisation in 1975 the Midlothian District Council Library HQ was located within the area of East Lothian District Council. This arrangement continued until a Midlothian home for Library HQ was secured in the former school buildings in Roslin during the 1980s. It has subsequently transferred to the former Burgh Council offices in Loanhead.

31. Following reorganisation in Scotland in 1975, local authorities were organised on a two-tier basis. The higher tier comprised nine regional councils under which there were 53 district councils. In addition, three islands councils were given responsibility for the functions of both district and regional authorities. Education, including school libraries, became a function of the regional councils while public libraries were administered by the district councils (other than in Borders, Dumfries & Galloway and Highland Regions which were responsible for public and school library services). Lothian Regional Council covered the geographical area spanned by the City of Edinburgh, East Lothian, Midlothian and West Lothian district councils. At the same time, the boundaries of the former local authority areas were changed. As a result of the transfer of parts of the former Midlothian County to other districts within the new Lothian Region as well as to Scottish Borders Region, Midlothian District became the smallest of the authorities within the new Lothian Region area.

M W (Bill) Paton, pp 57–69

1. Information about the King's Own Scottish Borderers is given in note 23 to the interview with Andrew Fraser.
2. The Military Medal (MM) was a decoration for bravery in battle on land awarded to personnel of the British Army and other services below commissioned rank. It was established in 1916. It was the other ranks' equivalent of the Military Cross (MC), which was awarded to commissioned officers. The MM ranked below the Distinguished Conduct Medal which was also awarded to non-commissioned members of the Army. Over 115,000 awards were made for actions during the First World War. In 1993, the Military Medal was discontinued. Since then the Military Cross has been awarded to personnel of all ranks within the British honours system.
3. A face man works at the coal face. A fireman is responsible for supervising the ventilation of the mine workings.
4. A rake of hutches is a train of the box-like wheeled wagons or trucks in which coals are conveyed from the face.
5. An engine-keeper was in charge of the winding engine at a mine, taking his instructions from the banksman, the person at the surface in charge of the pit bank and responsible for loading and unloading the cage and signalling to the engine-keeper.
6. Patons & Baldwins Ltd was a leading British manufacturer of knitting yarn. The business began as two separate companies, founded in the late 1770s by James Baldwin of Halifax and in 1814 by John Paton of Alloa. Both companies produced mainly yarns for commercial knitting machines. The two companies merged in 1920 and diversified into producing wool for home knitters as well as publishing knitting patterns. By the mid-1930s, the company had establishments across Scotland and the North of England, as well as in Canada, New Zealand and Tasmania. Kilncraigs Mill in Alloa produced a range of hand-knitting yarns, hosiery yarns, manufacturing yarns and tweed yarns. At one time it employed over 2,000 workers. The company prided itself on staff welfare, and the Paton family were regarded as generous benefactors in Alloa, funding public buildings such as the town hall, the public library, a school, swimming pool and gymnasium. After the Second World War the

company developed new products such as nylon and Terylene. It was merged with J & P Coats Ltd in 1961, and its yarn production in Alloa ceased in 1999.

7. The features of a kitchen range are described in note 4 to the interview with John Preston.

8. A description of a 'scullery' is given in note 8 to the interview with Dorothy Milne.

9. The significance of the Qualifying Exam is described in note 2 to the interview with John Hunter.

10. In Scotland, people traditionally call their midday meal 'dinner' and their evening meal 'tea', whereas middle-class people would call the midday meal 'lunch' and the evening meal 'dinner' or 'supper' (often eaten later in the evening). Increasingly, however, 'lunch' is now the norm among all social classes.

11. 'Rector' is the title given to the head teacher in some Scottish secondary schools.

12. Richmal Crompton (1890–1969) taught for some years but was struck down by polio in 1923. She became a full-time writer thereafter and published 50 adult titles. She is best known for her *Just William* books – 38 short-story collections and a novel about the perpetual schoolboy, 11-year-old William Brown. The character has remained a favourite with generations of children for his escapades and his ability to reduce ordered adult life to chaos.

13. For information about the writing career of Percy Francis Westerman see note 7 to the interview with Joe Fisher.

14. See note 8 to the interview with Alan White for information about Biggles, and his author Captain W E Johns (1893–1968).

15. Robert Michael Ballantyne (1825–94) was born in Edinburgh, a nephew of John and James Ballantyne, Sir Walter Scott's printers and publishers. He joined the Hudson's Bay Company in 1841 and worked at the Red River Settlement in northern Canada until 1847. On his return to Edinburgh he began writing adventure stories for young people. He wrote more than 100 books, many of which were informed by personal knowledge of the scenes he described. *The Coral Island* is the most popular of Ballantyne's novels, one which influenced Robert Louis Stevenson and inspired parts of *Treasure Island*. Ballantyne was also an accomplished artist and exhibited some of his watercolours at the Royal Scottish Academy.

16. 'The shows' is a commonly-used Scots expression for a travelling funfair with rides such as roundabouts, dodgems, etc, as well as sideshows and stalls.

17. Common children's street games include hide and seek in which the player chosen to be 'it' counts to the agreed number while the rest of the group run off to hide. The seeker then sets off from the 'block' to search for his companions, calling out the name of anyone spotted. Kick the can is a similar hiding/capture game although those captured can be released by an unseen player kicking the can in the absence from the 'den' of the player who is 'it'. This game is particularly interesting because the den-keeper has to guard the den as well as go seeking. Levoy (also known as leavo, leevoi, reelyfo and relievo) is another chase-and-capture game in which, again, those held prisoner in the den can be freed by a player who is still free shouting 'levoy!', or something similar, while the chaser is absent. Margaret Crawford, in her interview, mentions street games she played as a child in Edinburgh. Further information can be found in *Golden City: Scottish Children's Games and Songs* by James T R Richie (Mercat Press, Edinburgh, 1999).

18. Information about the Scouts and Cub Scouts is found in note 9 to the interview with Gavin Drummond.

19. 'Ten bob' was the slang term for the sum of ten shillings in pre-decimalisation coinage, there being twenty shillings in a pound.
20. Scottish secondary education awards are described in note 6 to the interview with John Hunter.
21. William George Bunter (known as Billy Bunter) is a fictional schoolboy created by Charles Hamilton (1876–1961) using the pen name Frank Richards. Set at Greyfriars School, the stories in which Bunter features were originally published in the boys' weekly story paper *The Magnet* from 1908 to 1940. Bunter has since appeared in novels, on television, in stage plays and in comic strips. His defining characteristic is his greediness and dramatically overweight appearance. His eyes are ever on the lookout for 'tuck' parcels, no matter whose. Despite his many defects, he succeeds as a highly entertaining and comical character. At one time Charles Hamilton was regarded as the most prolific writer in the world.
22. Gloy is the brand name of paste and glue used mainly for sticking paper and card. It has been defined as 'a cheap brand of glue used by schools that can't afford anything better'.
23. Jack Egarr FLA was a native of Bradford and received his early training in that city's public library service. In 1932 he was appointed Chief Library Assistant with Dumfries County before moving to Clackmannanshire where he gained a reputation as an extremely successful County Librarian. He took an active part in Scottish library affairs and had been viewed as a future President of the Scottish Library Association. He was reported missing, presumed killed, in 1942 while serving in the Royal Navy.
24. It is assumed that 'an advance' here refers to an increase in pay.
25. Evanton lies a mile north of the Cromarty Firth, four miles south-west of Alness. It was named after Evan Fraser of Balconie in the early 19th century. The Cromarty Firth had become established as an important naval base and in 1922 a military airfield was built on the north shore a mile east of Evanton. Originally known as RAF Novar, it had become RAF Evanton by the 1930s (it was known as HMS Fieldfare to the Royal Navy), when its main role was to service the Fleet Air Arm aircraft based on the ships of the fleet. The airfield closed in 1947.
26. Named after Arthur Wellesley, 1st Duke of Wellington, the Vickers Wellington was a British twin-engined, long range medium bomber designed in the mid-1930s. It was widely used as a night bomber in the early years of the Second World War before being superseded by larger, four-engined heavy bombers such as the Avro Lancaster (see the interview with Tom Gray, note 27). The Wellington continued to serve throughout the War in other duties, particularly as an anti-submarine aircraft. It was the only British bomber to be produced for front-line service during the full duration of the War.
27. Cesenatico is situated on the Adriatic coast of Italy about 20 miles south of Ravenna. Founded in 1302, its port and canal were built in 1500. The canal, originally planned to reach Cesena, nine miles inland, was surveyed and plans for it drawn by Leonardo da Vinci at the request of Cesare Borgia. In 1722 James Francis Edward Stuart, the Old Pretender, stayed in Cesenatico's Capuchin monastery. Today Cesenatico is a popular tourist resort with a population of about 20,000.
28. The professional training of librarians at the Scottish School of Librarianship is described in note 9 to the interview with John Hunter.
29. One of the most influential figures of Scottish librarianship, William Bryce Paton

(1907–88) was born in Glasgow and began his career in the Mitchell Library in 1925. After a brief period at Watford, he was appointed Chief Librarian of Airdrie in 1931 when he was only 24 years old. Paton moved to Greenock in 1939 but his work there was interrupted by his service in the Royal Artillery during the Second World War. When the Scottish School of Librarianship was set up in 1946, he became its first and only full-time lecturer. Although a gruelling period of his professional life, Paton made the School a success and laid the foundations for future developments. In 1950, however, he left to take up the position of County Librarian of Lanarkshire. When he retired from this post 22 years later, the small, basic system which he had inherited had been transformed beyond recognition and the reputation of Lanark County Libraries was known around the world. At the same time, Paton was immersed in professional affairs at national and international levels, serving on the Council and committees of the Scottish Library Association (SLA) from as early as 1933, becoming SLA Secretary and then President in 1955 and 1956. In addition, he was appointed President of the Library Association and was active on library business for the International Federation of Library Associations and UNESCO. His was a distinguished and eventful life which earned him considerable affection and respect. Further information about W B Paton may be found in the interviews with Peter Grant and Tom Gray.

30. The life and career of W R Aitken are described in note 10 to the interview with Gavin Drummond.

31. A 'leet' is a list of candidates for a job, with a 'long leet' usually whittled down to a 'short leet', the latter being those applicants in serious contention.

32. The career of Neil McCorkindale is described in note 18 to the interview with Gavin Drummond.

33. See note 31 to the interview with Andrew Fraser regarding public library responsibilities following Scottish local government reorganisation in 1975.

34. Early Scottish public library legislation is described in note 18 to the interview with Andrew Fraser.

35. *The Press and Journal*, commonly *The P&J*, is a daily newspaper, primarily associated with Aberdeen but serving the wider area of northern Scotland with a number of editions. One of the oldest surviving newspapers in the world, it was first published as a weekly title, *Aberdeen's Journal*, in 1747, changing its name the following year to the *Aberdeen Journal*. It was published weekly until August 1876 when it became a daily. In November 1922 the paper was renamed *The Aberdeen Press and Journal* when its parent firm joined forces with the *Free Press*. *The Press and Journal* has been criticised for its regional perspective on global events, but perhaps because of its local focus it has retained a high circulation level. The paper is published by Aberdeen Journals Ltd and is now owned by the Dundee-based D C Thomson & Co Ltd.

36. The development of Scotland's two schools of librarianship is described in note 9 to the interview with John Hunter.

37. The Stimpson report (*Non-teaching Staff in Secondary Schools: Youth and Community Workers, Librarians, Instructors: Report of a Working Party appointed by the Secretary of State for Scotland*. Chairman D E Stimpson. HMSO, Edinburgh, 1976) recommended that a qualified librarian be appointed to high schools with more than 600 students and responsibility for the school library be placed with a member of the school's senior management team. These are features often in place

today although the principle of a qualified librarian in every high school is under threat because of local authority budget restrictions.

38. Information about the Library Association and the Scottish Library Association is given in note 27 to the interview with Gavin Drummond.
39. 'Couthy' is a Scots word which, when used to describe people, means pleasant, kind, tender, friendly, sympathetic.
40. As outlined in note 31 to the interview with Andrew Fraser, following local government reorganisation in Scotland in 1975, responsibility for school libraries became a function of the regional councils.
41. Information regarding the People's Network initiative is described in note 51 to the interview with Margaret Crawford and discussed by Gavin Drummond in his interview.

Tom Gray, pp 71–86

1. A shipyard plater cuts the metal, forms it and prepares it for welding. Platers usually work with thicker metal plate for the bulkhead, deck and side plating of ships and use heavy-duty cutters, burners and large rolling and pressing machines.
2. Lithgows Ltd is a family-owned Scottish company that had a long involvement in shipbuilding based in Kingston, Port Glasgow. It was established by Joseph Russell and his partners Anderson Rodger and William Lithgow who started trading as Russell & Co in 1874. In 1881 they acquired the Kingston Shipyard and although the partnership was dissolved in 1891, Lithgow took over the Kingston Yard. In 1908 William Lithgow's sons, James and Henry, assumed control and expanded the company, renamed Lithgows Ltd in 1918. Eventually Lithgows took over all the other large Port Glasgow shipyards and, in addition, owned several engine-building companies. Following many acquisitions, mergers and name-changes, much of the company was absorbed into the state-owned British Shipbuilders in 1977. Lithgows Ltd continued to trade separately, however, and remained in family hands, their business interests diversified into hotels, electronics and aquaculture. Lithgows continue to operate the Marine Resources Centre at Barcaldine, near Oban. Final traces of the Kingston shipyards were removed in 2005, the site being redeveloped for housing. The legacy of the company is considerable: over 1,200 ships were built by the Lithgow yards, with several hundred more by subsidiaries under their own names.
3. Mesopotamia is the area of the Tigris-Euphrates river system, roughly corresponding to modern-day Iraq, Syria and Kuwait, including regions along the Turkish-Syrian and Iranian-Iraqi borders. During the First World War the Mesopotamian campaign was fought between British Empire troops, mostly from India and Australia, and the Turkish Ottoman Empire which Germany had developed as an ally and whose army was led by German 'advisers'. Britain relied heavily on oil from the area to keep its dominant navy at sea and so, on the outbreak of the war with Germany, she determined to protect her interests by occupying the oilfields and pipeline near Basra. Thereafter victory over the Turks came to be seen as a less costly way towards defeat of Germany than the slaughter on the Western Front. Against fierce Turkish resistance Baghdad and the Berlin-Baghdad railway were captured in March 1917, but despite this achievement no decisive victory was gained before the armistice with Turkey in October 1918. Conditions in Mesopotamia were very bad, with high casualty rates and appalling levels of sickness and death through disease.

4. Under the lend-lease policy the United States supplied Free France, the United Kingdom, the Republic of China, and later the USSR and other Allied nations with food, oil, warships, warplanes and other weaponry between 1941 and August 1945. In general, the aid was free but the agreement provided that the material be used until returned or destroyed. (Although in practice very little equipment was returned, some hardware, including ships, was returned after the War.) This programme effectively ended the United States' pretence of neutrality and was a decisive step away from its non-interventionist policy which had dominated its foreign relations since 1931.

5. The Merino Mill was the name popularly used for the premises owned by Fleming, Reid & Co Ltd. Although founded in 1840 by John Fleming and James Reid, it was not until 1890 that the mill began to spin wool from the Australian merino sheep. The Greenock mill buildings occupied six storeys and there were also knitting sheds, warehouses and washhouses. Fleming, Reid's had an excellent reputation as spinners of carpet yarns and later became well known for tweed yarns. To retail their products, the company had 380 shops, known as the Scottish Wool and Hosiery Stores, throughout the UK, three of which were in Greenock itself. In 1959 there were around 1,000 women and 150 men employed by Fleming, Reid & Co but the business finally closed down in 1981.

6. For information about PT, see note 8 to the interview with Margaret Crawford.

7. Information about the Boys' Brigade is given in note 22 to the interview with Andrew Fraser.

8. A palliasse is a straw mattress, usually consisting of a jute sack filled with straw.

9. The McLean Museum and Art Gallery, Greenock, is the main museum in the Inverclyde area. It was established in 1876 out of the collections developed by the Greenock Philosophical Society. The Museum's fine art collection includes works by Scottish, English, European and American artists, and its displays feature items related to the engineer James Watt, Inverclyde's maritime and industrial traditions as well as world cultures, Egyptology and natural history.

10. Loch Fyne in Argyll extends 40 miles inland and is the longest of the west coast sea lochs. For hundreds of years and well into the 20th century, the Loch Fyne fishery was of great importance. The herring caught there had a reputation for high quality and the Loch Fyne kipper became a famous delicacy. Huge landings were made and often catches were bought while the boats were still at sea so that fish could be fast-tracked to Glasgow for sale at the fish markets almost as fresh as when it was caught. Although the herring fishery had always been subject to huge year-to-year fluctuations by the mid-1960s there was such a lack of herring that fishing was stopped and has never recovered.

11. Quakers are members of a group of religious movements known in Europe and some other parts of the world as the Religious Society of Friends. The first Quakers lived in mid-17th century England. The movement was originally, and is still predominantly, Christian in basis. Members of the movements profess the priesthood of all believers and avoid creeds and hierarchical structures. Quakers are known for their refusal to participate in war, plain dress, refusal to swear oaths, opposition to slavery and teetotalism.

12. *National Geographic*, formerly *The National Geographic Magazine*, is the official magazine of the National Geographic Society. It has been published continuously since its first issue in 1888, nine months after the Society itself was founded. It

contains articles primarily about geography, history and world culture. The magazine is known for its thick square-bound glossy format with a yellow rectangular border and its extensive use of dramatic photographs. *National Geographic* is published monthly, and additional map supplements are included with subscriptions. It is available in a traditional printed edition and through an interactive online edition. The magazine is published worldwide in nearly 40 languages and has a global circulation of almost seven million copies per month. In 2015 National Geographic Partners, controlled by 21st Century Fox, took over as publishers.

13. James T Hamilton began his career with Greenock Corporation Library Service during the 1930s. After serving in the Second World War he studied at the Scottish School of Librarianship. Following qualification as a chartered librarian in 1948 he was appointed Depute Burgh Librarian of Greenock. His involvement with the post-war development of libraries in the town culminated in his promotion to the post of Burgh Librarian in 1971 and the opening of the new Greenock Central Library the same year. Hamilton's professional and academic distinctions included the award of a Research Fellowship from the Library Association for his study, *Greenock Libraries, a Development and Social History* (Greenock Public Libraries, Greenock, 1969). He was also awarded a postgraduate degree by Strathclyde University for his research thesis on the development of central libraries in Scotland. In anticipation of local government reorganisation he was appointed as Chief Librarian and Cultural Services Officer of the newly-created Inverclyde District in 1974. He retired from that position in 1978.

14. See note 8 to the interview with Alan White for information about Biggles, and his author, Captain W E Johns (1893–1968).

15. Scottish secondary education awards are described in note 6 to the interview with John Hunter.

16. The life and career of William B Paton are described in note 29 to the interview with M W (Bill) Paton.

17. An interview with Peter Grant is included in this work.

18. James Neill was District Librarian, East Kilbride, with Lanark County Library Service before taking up the position of Deputy Borough Librarian at West Hartlepool in 1960. During the period 1958–60 he was the editor of *SLA News* (see note 41 to the interview with Alan White). He later became a lecturer in librarianship at Newcastle upon Tyne Polytechnic.

19. This currently operates as Northumbria University, Department of Mathematics and Information Sciences, Newcastle upon Tyne, offering CILIP-accredited distance learning courses in information and library management.

20. The career of Neil McCorkindale is described in note 18 to the interview with Gavin Drummond.

21. Greenock Morton Football Club was founded as Morton Football Club in 1874, making it one of the oldest senior Scottish clubs. Morton was renamed as Greenock Morton in 1994 to celebrate the links with its home town. Their ground is Cappielow Park. Morton won the Scottish Cup in 1922, and achieved their highest league finish in 1916–17, finishing as runners-up to champions Celtic.

22. *The Tablet* is a Catholic weekly journal that has been published continuously in the UK since 1840. It reports on religion, current affairs, politics, social issues, literature and the arts, with a special emphasis on Roman Catholicism while remaining ecumenical. It was launched by Frederick Lucas, a Quaker convert to Catholicism,

and is the second-oldest surviving weekly journal in Britain after *The Spectator*, which was founded in 1828. Since 1976 *The Tablet* has been owned by The Tablet Trust, a registered charity. It was described in 2009 as 'Britain's most notorious liberal Catholic magazine'.

23. The professional training of librarians at the Scottish School of Librarianship is described in note 9 to the interview with John Hunter.

24. The Air Training Corps (ATC) is a British youth organisation sponsored by the Ministry of Defence and the Royal Air Force (RAF). It was established in 1938 as the Air Defence Cadet Corps (ADCC) by Air Commodore Sir John Chamier, a former First World War pilot, to train young men in various aviation-related skills. With the outbreak of the Second World War, the ADCC was re-formed in 1941 as the Air Training Corps, to provide training to teenagers and young men and prepare them for entry to the RAF. Within the first month of its existence, the size of the ATC virtually doubled from that of the ADCC to more than 400 squadrons and continued to grow thereafter. ATC activities now include sport, outdoor activities and some flying experience to offer a taste of military life. Although many ATC cadets go on to join the RAF or other services, the ATC is no longer set up as a recruiting organisation.

25. During the Second World War, Durban was a busy waystation for convoys on their way to North Africa and the Far East. Perla Siedle Gibson, a South African soprano, became internationally celebrated as the Lady in White who serenaded troopships passing in and out of the harbour. Clad in white with a red hat, her repertoire included such patriotic songs as 'There'll always be an England' and 'Land of Hope and Glory'. Gibson died in 1971 and the following year a plaque donated by men of the Royal Navy was erected to her memory on Durban's North Pier. In 1995 Queen Elizabeth unveiled a statue of her in Durban harbour.

26. The Lysander was a two-seat, high-winged monoplane built by Westland as an army co-operation aircraft. It began service with the RAF in 1938 and was the first British aircraft stationed in France during the Second World War but was soon found to be vulnerable because of its relatively slow speed. Withdrawn from frontline service, the Lysander became famous for its nocturnal flights into occupied Europe, dropping supplies and agents behind enemy lines to help the resistance movements. It was ideal for this work being able to take off and land in the most difficult of terrain and flying at a low altitude, below radar.

27. The Avro Lancaster was a British four-engined Second World War heavy bomber, designed by Roy Chadwick and built by Avro for the Royal Air Force (RAF). It first saw active service with RAF Bomber Command in 1942 and, as the strategic bombing offensive over Europe gathered momentum, it became the central implement for the night-time bombing campaigns that followed. The Lancaster could take the largest bombs used by the RAF, and its versatility was such that it was chosen to deliver the 'bouncing bomb' designed by Barnes Wallis for the 'Dambuster' raid. It was powered by four Rolls-Royce Merlin engines and heavily armed with eight machine guns in various turrets on board. It carried a crew of seven.

28. Labuan is an island off the coast of Borneo in East Malaysia. Through a treaty with the Sultan of Brunei in 1846, Labuan was acquired by Britain as a naval base from which to suppress piracy in the South China Sea. The British also believed the island could be the next Singapore. During the Second World War, Labuan was occupied by Japan from December 1941 until June 1945, during which time the Japanese

developed it as a naval base. After the War the island came under the British Military Administration together with the rest of the Straits Settlements. Labuan Island, along with six smaller islands, is now a federal territory of Malaysia. Its capital is Victoria, and is best known as an offshore financial centre offering international financial and business services. It is also an offshore support hub for deep-water oil and gas activities in the region.

29. Siam was the name formerly used for Thailand, which means 'land of the free', the change taking effect from May 1949. The name had been changed before, in 1939, under the country's fascist military dictatorship, although the Allies refused to recognise this name after Siam allied herself with the Japanese and in 1942 declared war on the United States and the United Kingdom. After the War the United States decided that the Thai regime had acted under duress and no objection was raised to the change of name.

30. Seletar is an area of Singapore within its north-east region. RAF Seletar was established as a seaplane station in 1928. The airfield was the target of carpet bombing when the Japanese launched their invasion of Malaya and Singapore during the Second World War and was subsequently abandoned. After the War the base went back to the RAF, and in the late 1940s and '50s was heavily involved in the Malayan Emergency. The RAF station closed in 1971 and Seletar was handed over to the Singapore Air Defence Command (later the Republic of Singapore Air Force).

31. Edwina Cynthia Annette, Countess Mountbatten (1901–60), was the wife of Louis, Earl Mountbatten 1900–79), a great-grandson of Queen Victoria, who was supreme Allied Commander South East Asia in 1943–45. Countess Mountbatten rendered distinguished service during the London Blitz to the Red Cross and St John Ambulance Brigade, of which she became superintendent-in-chief in 1942. On her husband's appointment as Viceroy of India (1947), with a remit to oversee the transition to independence, her work in social welfare in that country brought her the friendship of Gandhi and Nehru.

32. See note 11 to the interview with Andrew Fraser for information about miners' institutes.

33. Photo-charging is a library circulation system which microfilms the borrower's membership card together with details of the borrowed item and a sequentially-numbered date of issue or date due slip. On return of the item, the numbered date of issue/return slip is removed. The system was introduced during the 1960s, mainly by public library authorities, its attractions being the elimination of the drudgery of filing and maintaining extensive card files as required by the Browne issue system (see note 40 to the interview with Margaret Crawford), as well as the speed of the issue and discharge functions. Photo-charging had major disadvantages, however, as identifying who had borrowed an item and when it was due back could only be done, in theory, by searching reels of microfilm and, in turn, such procedures as reserving items and managing overdues were cumbersome.

34. See note 9 to the interview with John Hunter for information about librarianship courses in Scotland and the establishment of a School of Librarianship at Robert Gordon's Institute of Technology in Aberdeen.

35. Information about the Library Association and the Scottish Library Association is given in note 27 to the interview with Gavin Drummond.

36. Note 47 to the interview with Peter Grant gives a definition of the term 'book fund'.

37. Alex Dow started his career as a librarian in the Mitchell Library in 1923. Like so

many Scottish librarians at this time, he moved south and served as branch librarian in Bolton Public Libraries for six years. In 1934, again following the example of colleagues, he returned to Scotland on his appointment as Burgh Librarian of Coatbridge, a post in which he served until retiring in 1968. Believing that a strong central service was preferable to the spread of resources among smaller branch libraries, his energies were directed to the main Carnegie Library, other parts of the authority area being provided with a mobile library service. He contributed significantly to the work of the Scottish Library Association over many years, serving at various times as Council member, Honorary Treasurer, Honorary Secretary and President. Alex Dow died in 1977.

38. From 1949 to 1960, Richard D Milne (1911–2001) was Librarian and Curator of Peterhead Public Library and Arbuthnot Museum (which formed part of the Library from 1893 to 1975). He was appointed Librarian of Inverness Burgh Library in 1960, and one of his earliest tasks was to move the Library from its old building to temporary accommodation to allow the creation of a large modern development incorporating a new library and museum which opened in 1966. Milne retired in 1975 at the time of local government reorganisation, but continued to work a few days each week for several years, using his knowledge and skills to help build a fine local history collection.

39. The writer Eric Linklater (1899–1974) was born in Wales, his father was from Orkney and his mother was the daughter of a Swedish ship's captain. Linklater spent much of his childhood on Orkney and was educated at school and university in Aberdeen. He is best remembered for the novel *Juan in America* but it was Orkney which was his abiding inspiration as revealed in such novels as *White-Maa's Saga*, *The Men of Ness* and *The Ultimate Viking*. His wife, Marjorie MacIntyre, has been described as 'one of the most beautiful and accomplished women of his time'.

40. See note 31 to the interview with Andrew Fraser regarding public library responsibilities following Scottish local government reorganisation in 1975. Highland Regional Council was responsible for provision of a public library service across a very large geographical area to a population of more than 200,000, most of whom, other than those in Inverness, were resident in small towns, villages and rural areas.

41. Note 32 to the interview with John Preston describes the introduction of *Standards for the Public Library Service in Scotland* produced by COSLA in 1986.

Joe Fisher, pp 87–109

1. William Beardmore & Co was an engineering and shipbuilding company based in Glasgow and the surrounding areas. It was active between about 1890 and 1930. It was founded and owned by William Beardmore (later Lord Invernairn), after whom the Beardmore Glacier was named. The shipbuilding activity consisted largely in the manufacture of heavy forgings for marine engine work and large quantities of armour plate (up to 3 or 4 inches in thickness) for the Royal Navy and foreign navies. On the engineering side it produced armaments, tanks, airships, aircraft, commercial vehicles, taxi cabs, motor cars and motorcycles. At its peak, the company employed about 40,000 people. By 1914, the workforce was down to 12,000 or 15,000, but the range of products continued to increase until 1930, when the diversification activities were closed. In 1951 the company was nationalised

under the Iron and Steel Act and six years later it was sold to Thomas Firth and John Brown. (The above note is a summary of the entry in *Grace's Guide to British Industrial History*.)

2. 'Fiche' is the shortened version of microfiche, transparent film used to store printed information in miniaturised form. To read the fiche, a user places it under the lens of a reader, which magnifies it greatly. The thinness and smallness of the film allows it to be stored easily and efficiently, allowing libraries, for example, to increase their resource collections without the need for additional storage space. Microfiche records are still created and used but digital storage now has precedence. The 'Mormon fiches' consulted by Joe Fisher were the microfilmed world-wide records of genealogical importance created from 1938 onwards by the Genealogical Society of Utah, an arm of The Church of Jesus Christ of Latter-day Saints. In 1998, the enormous task of digital imaging began. The website first opened to the public the following year. By that time the total number of entries was 640 million. From 2013, the FamilySearch.org website became the essential tool for researching family history.

3. A currier is someone who prepares tanned hides for use by soaking, colouring or other processes.

4. Arthur & Co was established in 1855 to handle the expanding textile manufacturing and wholesaling business of Arthur & Fraser of Glasgow. The partners were James Arthur and Hugh Fraser. The partnership was dissolved in 1865, by which time the firm had acquired impressive warehouse premises in Queen Street, Glasgow. Arthur & Co continued in business with James Arthur as senior partner. Hugh Fraser went on to set up a retailing business that continues today as House of Fraser, from whose archive this note has been compiled.

5. Between 1903 and 1950, George Warwick Deeping (1877–1950) wrote over 50 books and countless novellas, short stories and essays. He qualified as a doctor and served in the Royal Army Medical Corps in the First World War. Returning to civilian life, he became a full-time writer. His heyday was in the 1920s and '30s, when seven of his novels became best-sellers. His early books consist mainly of historical romances; the later ones deal with challenging issues of 20th century life: for example, social work and medicine in the slums, euthanasia, wife abuse, shell shock and pollution of the water supply. His best-known book, *Sorrell and Son* (1925), in which, after the War, Captain Sorrell MC finds himself having to carry out menial work in which he is bullied by people of less education, deals with euthanasia. Ironically, high-brow critics of the time dismissed Deeping as being among the writers who, in George Orwell's words, 'simply don't notice what is happening'.

6. Arthur Henry Mee (1875–1943) was a writer, journalist and educator. The publications for which he is best remembered are *The Children's Encyclopaedia, The Children's Newspaper* and *The King's England*. He began work on the first of these in 1908. *The Children's Newspaper* continued until 1965. All three works were published by Alfred Harmsworth's Amalgamated Press.

7. Percy Francis Westerman (1876–1959) was an even more prolific writer than Warwick Deeping (see note 5 above). He wrote over 170 adventure books, many of them with military and naval themes. Blackie & Son Ltd of London and Glasgow published most of his books. The total sales in his lifetime were over one and a half million copies. He was voted the most popular author of stories for boys. In the First World War, like W E Johns, the author of the Biggles books, Westerman was commissioned in the Royal Flying Corps. See note 8 to the interview with Alan

White for information about Biggles, and his author Captain W E Johns (1893–1968).

8. The significance of the Qualifying Exam is described in note 2 to the interview with John Hunter.

9. The renown of Shettleston Harriers is world-wide. It was set up in East Glasgow in 1904 as a cross-country running club. It won the National title for the first time in 1920. During the 1920s and '30s, as membership increased, there was diversification into other areas of athletics. Since the 1940s, 'Shettleston Harriers' has stood for excellence and consistency in Scottish and British athletics, with gold-medal winners in Empire Games and Commonwealth Games events.

10. Andrew B Paterson (1893–1961) began his career with Glasgow Libraries in 1908, serving at the Mitchell Library before taking over as Librarian at Kingston Library in 1923. In 1936 he was appointed Burgh Librarian of Paisley and then returned to Glasgow as City Librarian in 1945. During his 13 years in this position many developments were carried out including the opening of ten new branch libraries, the move of the Stirling's and Commercial Libraries to the Royal Exchange building in Queen Street, work on an extension to the Mitchell Library and the modernisation of several older branches. Paterson contributed to the affairs of the Scottish Library Association throughout his career, serving as a Council member for 34 years and Honorary Secretary for three years. He held office as President in 1953 and 1954. He was also a Council member of the Library Association for 14 years and Vice-President during 1958–60.

11. Stephen Mitchell (1789–1874), the great-grandson of the founder of Stephen Mitchell & Son, tobacco manufacturers in Linlithgow, was born in that town. On the death of his father in 1820 he continued to run the family business and then, in 1825, transferred it to Candleriggs in Glasgow. The business moved again in 1832, this time to St Andrew's Square in the city. Mitchell retired to Moffat in 1859 and died there 15 years later, leaving a bequest to establish and maintain a public library in Glasgow, to be known as the Mitchell Library. The Library was opened in November 1877 and is now the largest public reference library in Europe. The tobacco business merged with W D & H O Wills in 1901 and later amalgamated with other tobacco companies to become the Imperial Tobacco Company. See also note 11 to the interview with John Preston.

12. Francis Thornton Barrett, born in Liverpool in 1838, was appointed Sub-Librarian of the Reference Department of Birmingham Free Libraries in 1866. In March 1877 he took up the newly-created position of Librarian of the Mitchell Library. A visionary and ambitious library manager, Barrett established a model for the public library service in Glasgow which inspired the opening of 'district libraries and reading rooms' in various parts of the city. In recognition of the developments under his leadership, he was elected the first City Librarian in May 1901, a post he held until his retiral in 1915. Barrett contributed significantly to the profession in Scotland, playing a prominent role in the formation of the Scottish Library Association in 1908, acting as the Association's first President during the period 1908–11 and contributing papers on professional practice to conferences and journals. Information about the Mitchell Library is to be found in note 11 to the interview with John Preston and in note 11 above.

13. Information about Charles W Black is given as note 10 to the interview with John Preston.

14. Harold Laski (1893–1950) was born in Manchester and attended the Grammar School there. His father was a cotton exporter and a leading figure in the Liberal Party. Laski junior won an exhibition to read history at Oxford but later transferred to science. While still at Oxford he eloped to Scotland with Frida Kerry. This caused conflict with his parents who were opposed to marriage between Jews and Gentiles. After leaving Oxford he lectured at McGill University (1914–16), Harvard (1916–20) and Yale (1919–20) and contributed to the *New Republic* magazine. His support of left-wing causes resulted in his vilification as a 'Bolshevik' and precipitated anti-Semitic attacks. In 1920 he joined the staff of the London School of Economics (LSE) and six years later became professor of political science. Kingsley Martin, who taught under Laski at LSE, said: '[Laski] was still in his late twenties and looked like a schoolboy. His lectures on the history of political ideas were brilliant, eloquent and delivered without a note . . .' In 1936 Laski joined with Victor Gollancz to form the Left Book Club, which at one point had a membership of 50,000. *Tribune* magazine was launched in 1937. Laski was a strong critic of the leadership of the Labour Party but became Chairman in 1945. However, his left-wing views meant that he clashed with Clement Attlee, the prime minister.

15. Don Martin for a time worked in the Mitchell Library and it was during this period that he researched traditional Scottish songs and founded with other Mitchell librarians the highly influential folk group, The Clutha. At local government reorganisation in 1975 he was appointed Principal Assistant Librarian with responsibility for reference, local studies, archives and, for a period, museum services with the newly-created Strathkelvin District. During this time he researched and published a number of publications about the area. When Strathkelvin became part of East Dunbartonshire Council in the next round of local government reorganisation in 1996, he retained these responsibilities for the larger area. For long, Martin has been highly-regarded in the field of local history. Since retiring, he has been prominent in the Scottish Local History Forum and is co-ordinating editor of the Forum's magazine, *Scottish Local History*. Most recently he has played a leading role in the Thomas Muir 250 project commemorating the life of the 'Father of Scottish Democracy'.

16. Anthony G Hepburn (1904–66) died on duty at the Mitchell Library where he had worked for the previous 43 years. Appointed Chief Cataloguer in 1961, he succeeded George Jack as Librarian of the Mitchell Library in 1963. An authority on the works of Robert Burns, he was responsible for editing the catalogue of Burns material in the Mitchell, and in 1959 he edited a standard edition of the poet's poems and letters for publication by Collins. Between 1950 and 1955, as founder editor of *SLA News*, Hepburn established the 'news sheet', as it was originally subtitled, as an important means of communication among librarians in Scotland.

17. *Catholic Truth* is a bi-monthly newsletter, one of the publications of the Catholic Truth Society. The Scottish version is 'written by, and for, ordinary Catholics in Scotland and beyond'. It espouses 'Keeping the Faith', which entails 'reminding ourselves of what is and is not Catholic doctrine . . .' and 'Telling the Truth', which entails 'reporting facts about the state of the Church, when necessary, however unpalatable . . .'.

18. 'Split-day duties', usually referred to as 'split shifts', involve working a morning shift and an evening shift, with the afternoon free. The purpose is to provide adequate staff coverage across the long opening hours of libraries. Split shifts are

also described in the interview with John Preston. As will be gathered, they were and are unpopular with staff.

19. The law of the Medes and Persians: that which is unalterable (a Biblical reference to the Book of Daniel, chapter 6, verse 8).

20. The Stone of Destiny, also known as the Stone of Scone, and often referred to in England as The Coronation Stone, is a block of sandstone that for centuries was associated with the crowning of Scottish monarchs and later the monarchs of England and the Kingdom of Great Britain. According to Celtic legend, in the 9th century the stone was taken by Kenneth McAlpin to the village of Scone, near Perth, having originated in the Holy Land. At Scone, historically, the stone was encased in the seat of the royal coronation chair. John de Balliol was the last Scottish king crowned on it in 1292. Four years later, following the English invasion of Scotland, the stone and other Scottish regalia were taken to London as spoils of war. There, at Westminster Abbey in 1307, Edward I had a special throne built so that the stone fitted under it. It was to be a symbol that kings of England would be crowned as kings of Scotland also. When King James VI of Scotland who became James I of England was crowned on the Stone of Scone, patriotic Scots said that the legend had been fulfilled: a Scotsman ruled where the Stone of Scone was. The stone remained in England for another six centuries. On Christmas Day 1950 a group of four Scottish students removed the stone from Westminster Abbey. A search ordered by the British Government was unsuccessful, and not until four months later was it recovered, on the altar of Arbroath Abbey. It was returned to London, but in 1996, in response to growing dissatisfaction among Scots, it was decided by the government that it should be kept in Scotland when not in use at coronations. The stone remains alongside the crown jewels of Scotland (the Honours of Scotland) in the Crown Room at Edinburgh Castle.

21. The Periodicals Stock Book (PSB) recorded the acquisition, location and binding of periodicals taken by the Mitchell Library. It also recorded missing issues of titles and copies which had been passed for binding within the Mitchell's own bindery or to Dunn & Wilson (see note 39 to the interview with Alan White).

22. Professional qualifications awarded by the Library Association are described by Professor Reid in his Foreword.

23. An accession number is the unique number assigned to a book or other stock item in the order in which it is added to the library collection. Most libraries assign accession numbers in a continuous numerical sequence, although others may use separate sequences to indicate the type of material, the year of accession, etc.

24. A library's classification system allows the subject matter of each stock item to be identified and assigned a distinguishing number, letter or other mark, usually within a hierarchical arrangement of main subject classes and subclasses. Even where the collection is in closed access and not arranged by subject, as was the case with most of the Mitchell Library stock, classification facilitates access and retrieval via the catalogue.

25. Cosmo Nelson Innes FRSE (1798–1874) was a Scottish advocate, judge, historian and antiquary. He was educated at King's College, Aberdeen, Glasgow University and Balliol College, Oxford. He was Sheriff of Moray (1840–52), Principal Clerk of Session (1852) and Professor of Civil History at the University of Edinburgh (1846–74). He edited *Rescinded Acts* and assisted in the folio edition of *Acts of the Scottish Parliament 1124–1707*. He also edited many historical manuscripts for the

Spalding and Bannatyne Clubs and published works on Scottish history. In the 1830s he lived in Allan Ramsay's former house, Ramsay Lodge, at the top of the Royal Mile.

26. 'Stick or twist' is an expression from card games. You can keep the cards you have and say 'stick' or risk losing and say 'twist' for more.

27. A description of a 'scullery' is given in note 8 to the interview with Dorothy Milne.

28. The professional training of librarians at the Scottish School of Librarianship is described in note 9 to the interview with John Hunter.

29. Information about the Library Association and the Scottish Library Association is given in note 27 to the interview with Gavin Drummond.

30. 'Overdues' were issues of a periodical title which had not been received from the publisher or other supplier and which had to be 'chased' to ensure the file was complete.

31. In 1786 Thomas Edington and William Cadell junior, in association with Carron Iron Works, which had been set up in Falkirk in 1759, built Clyde Iron Works on the north bank of the Clyde, a few miles south-east of Glasgow, primarily to relieve the pressure on Carron for armaments. Clyde Iron began with two blast furnaces and a foundry, employing about 100 men. It was dependent on local supplies of coal and ironstone under the control of James Dunlop (1741–1816) of Garnkirk (see note 34 below) who contracted to supply 20,000 tons of coal a year. His bankruptcy in 1793 led Cadell and Edington to open up new seams with Dunlop's agreement. During the Napoleonic Wars the short-barrelled naval guns known as 'carronades' were made there. Before 1820, when the streets of Glasgow were lit by gas, the blaze from Clyde Iron's furnaces illuminated the area for miles around. The company was bought in 1810 by Colin Dunlop, who was at that time working the coal seams. The invention of the hot-blast process in 1832, in which Clyde Iron had an interest, transformed the cost of iron production and led to the meteoric rise of the Scottish iron industry. The company remained in business until 1978. (The above note is a summary of the entry in *Grace's Guide to British Industrial History*.)

32. The Brisbane Papers are those of Major-General Sir Thomas Makdougall Brisbane (1773–1860), 1st Baronet, GCH, GCB, FRS, FRSE, who was born at Brisbane House, a little north of Largs in North Ayrshire. At the University of Edinburgh he studied astronomy and mathematics. After graduating he was commissioned as an ensign in the 38th Regiment in 1789, at the same time as Arthur Wellesley, who later became the Duke of Wellington. Brisbane had a distinguished career, serving in Flanders, the West Indies, Spain and North America. On Wellington's recommendation he was made Governor of New South Wales (1821–25), where he introduced a number of reforms and authorised the establishment of a convict colony at Moreton Bay, which became today's city of Brisbane. He also established Australia's first observatory at Parramatta, west of Sydney. On returning to Scotland he developed the Brisbane estate and that of his wife at Makerstoun, near Kelso. On the latter estate he built and equipped a magnetic observatory.

33. From *Ode on a Distant Prospect of Eton College* by Thomas Gray, 1742.

34. The Dunlop Papers, covering the years c1587–1893, were transferred to the Glasgow City Archives in 2007 and housed in the Mitchell Library. (For further information about the Dunlops of Garnkirk, see note 31 above.)

35. The Glasgow Chamber of Commerce is the oldest Chamber in the English-speaking world. Glasgow prospered in the 18th century largely due to trade with tobacco plantations in Virginia. American independence ended the dominance that Glasgow

merchants had in the tobacco trade throughout Europe. The Chamber's early priorities were to raise the quality of the goods produced and to lobby the government to lower taxes, reduce tariffs and abolish smuggling. The Chamber also opposed the East India Company's trade monopoly with India and territories beyond the Cape (see note 38 below). The Chamber's records, covering the years 1782 to 1986, are in the Glasgow City Archives, housed in the Mitchell Library.

36. It is assumed that 'a lawyer, Bell' refers to George Joseph Bell (1770–1843). At the age of eight Bell entered Edinburgh High School but received no university education other than attending the lectures of A F Tytler and Dugald Stewart. Later he attended law lectures by David Hume, Professor of Scots Law at the University of Edinburgh, and nephew of the philosopher Hume. Bell became a member of the Faculty of Advocates in 1791. In 1804 he published a *Treatise on the Law of Bankruptcy in Scotland*, which he enlarged and published in 1826 as *Commentaries on the Law of Scotland and on the Principles of Mercantile Jurisprudence.* In 1821 he was elected Professor of Scots Law at the University of Edinburgh. Bell's *Principles* is still in print.

37. Sir Ilay Campbell, Lord Succoth (1734–1823), was an advocate, judge and politician. His father, Archibald Campbell of Succoth, was Principal Clerk of Session to the Scottish Courts. Sir Ilay Campbell studied law at Glasgow University and graduated in 1751 and became an advocate in 1757. He was appointed Solicitor General for Scotland in 1783 and Lord Advocate the following year. In that year he became Member of Parliament for Glasgow Burghs. He was a 'Pittite'. Later he became Lord President of the Court of Session and Lord Justice General, where he sat as Lord Succoth. On his resignation in 1808 he was created a baronet and lived at Garscube, about 4 miles from Glasgow on the River Kelvin. The family had owned the estate since 1687. Lord Succoth was succeeded by his son, Sir Archibald Campbell, 2nd baronet (1769–1846), who, like his father, became a Scottish advocate and judge.

38. The East India Company, as it became known, was founded by royal charter in 1600 as the Governor and Company of Merchants of London trading into the East Indies. The Company was the enterprise of London businessmen who banded together to make money importing spices from South Asia. Previously, the spice trade relied on land routes across Asia and the Middle East, but by the 16th century improvements in merchant ships and navigational skills made it possible to journey round the Cape to where the spices were produced and thus cut out the middlemen. At the outset, each voyage was a separate business venture with its own subscribers and stockholders. In 1612 the Company switched to temporary joint stocks and finally, in 1657, to permanent joint stocks. Some 50 years later the Company, which was virtually a monopoly, faced competition from another group of investors and merchants, and in 1708 the two merged as the United Company of Merchants of England Trading to the East Indies. The goods imported included not only spices from south India but also cotton and silk, indigo and saltpetre, and voyages were being made to the Persian Gulf and South East Asia and East Asia. The size of the operation attracted encounters with foreign competitors which made it necessary for the Company to assemble its own military and administrative departments. It was described as being an imperial power in its own right. Later in the 18th century, the British government reined back the Company's activities in the Regulating Act of 1773 (see note 35 above) and Pitt's India Act of 1784. The Company's monopoly ended in 1813 and it went out of existence in 1873.

39. In 1807 Glasgow merchants were 'trying to stem the emancipation of slaves in the West Indies'. That was also the year when 'An Act for the Abolition of the Slave Trade' was enacted. Scots had, however, played a part in the abolition movement. In 1778 the owning of personal slaves was banned in Scotland; and in 1792, the year that produced the most petitions for abolition, there were 561 from Britain, a third of which came from Scotland. The 1807 Act banned the slave trade but not the keeping of slaves, and it was not until 1833 that the Slavery Abolition Act came into force. In that year 700,000 Caribbean slaves were released, perhaps 30 per cent of them owned by Scots. The bicentenary of the 1807 Act prompted television programmes and the publication of several books and articles on the Scottish connection with the slave trade. Of the books, see *Recovering Scotland's Slavery Past: The Caribbean Connection*, edited by Professor T M Devine (Edinburgh University Press, 2015), and *Scotland and the Abolition of Black Slavery, 1756–1838* by Rev Dr Iain Whyte (Birlinn, Edinburgh, 2006). Reference should also be made to the availability online of the 46,000 records of compensation given to British slave owners.

40. The William Patrick Library in Kirkintilloch, originally the William Patrick Memorial Library, was named in memory of the minister of Free St David's Church, Kirkintilloch, from 1878 to 1892. Thereafter, William Patrick became minister of Free St Paul's Church, Dundee, and in 1900 he took up the post of Principal of Manitoba College, Winnipeg, Canada. He returned to Kirkintilloch when he became seriously ill, and he died in 1911. In 1929 his younger brother, David Patrick, Town Clerk of Kirkintilloch from 1887 until his death in 1941, purchased Camphill House in the town and donated this to Kirkintilloch Town Council as a library to be named after his brother. The William Patrick Memorial Library remained in Camphill House until 1994 when it moved to the purpose-built William Patrick Library at Kirkintilloch Cross. It is the main library for East Dunbartonshire Council, housing lending, reference, local history and archive services. Camphill House has been returned to private residential use.

41. The St Andrew's Halls were built between 1873 and 1877. They took up an entire city block. The building contained three major and many minor halls plus a ballroom. The Grand Hall could hold 4,000 people. It was an important venue for classical music. The fire on 26 October 1962 (the date is better known for marking the height of the Cuban missile crisis) gutted the building, leaving only the front façade standing. Not until 1990, with the opening of the Royal Concert Hall, did Glasgow again have a large auditorium for classical music.

42. For information about NALGO see note 15 to the interview with Andrew Fraser.

43. 'The Audubon' probably refers to *Birds of America*, or a plate from the book, by John James Audubon (1785–1851), the American ornithologist and bird artist. He was born in Haiti and sent to America in 1804 to look after his father's property near Philadelphia. He spent several years seeking out every species of bird in America in order to catalogue them. In 1826 he took his work to Europe where he affected a backwoodsman image. He visited Scotland five times between 1826 and 1839. In Edinburgh he met, among other men, William Home Lizars, an artist and engraver, who played a key role in the production of Audubon's book. He also met Sir Walter Scott, whose works he admired, and Robert Knox, the anatomist, one of whose lectures he attended. In 1827 Audubon published the first of the 87 portfolios of *Birds of America* (1827–38). Later, a seven-volume 'miniature' edition

became a best-seller. The National Audubon Society, dedicated to the conservation of birds in the USA, was founded in his honour in 1866.

44. William Andrew Greig Alison (1916–2005) had been in charge of Edinburgh's Art Library in his early days. He was appointed Superintendent of Branches in Glasgow Public Libraries in 1962. In due course he was promoted to Depute City Librarian and then in 1974 to City Librarian. In 1975 his post was redesignated as Director of Libraries. Alison inherited, among other modernising projects, the task of completing the extension to the Mitchell Library which, on its completion, he reorganised. He also established a divisional organisation for the lending libraries; he created new posts and a new career structure for staff; he introduced computerised issue and catalogue systems; libraries were extended and modernised; new libraries were built. Alison was President of the Scottish Library Association in 1975 and President of the Library Association in 1978 before retiring in 1981.

45. In 1863 George Baillie (1784–1873), a Glasgow lawyer, arranged for a capital sum, from his own savings, to be invested for 21 years and then for the accrued amount to be used to set up an educational establishment, Baillie's Institution, with its own free library. However, the final amount could only support a library, which opened to the public in 1887. During the 20th century the Library built up an impressive collection of material, mostly of Scottish interest. Although it attracted a number of bequests and collections belonging to local societies, by 1981 it was struggling with financial pressures and an agreement was made to transfer the stock to the Mitchell Library. Today, Baillie's Institution is a registered charity the aims of which are to advance education, citizenship, community development, the arts, heritage, culture and science.

46. *The Illustrated London News* was founded by Herbert Ingram (1811–60) as the world's first illustrated weekly news magazine. The first issue was published on Saturday 14 May 1842 and sales increased over the next 20 years to more than 300,000 copies in response to a huge demand for illustrated news and shocking stories. The magazine was published weekly until 1971, but circulation figures for all the illustrated magazines fell during the post-war period and the title switched to monthly publication in 1971 and then to six issues annually in the 1980s. Publication ceased in 2003.

47. *A Glasgow Collection: Essays in Honour of Joe Fisher.* Edited by Kevin McCarra and Hamish Whyte (Glasgow City Libraries, 1990).

48. Elizabeth (Biff) Carmichael began her career with Glasgow Libraries during the 1970s, working in community libraries before moving to the Mitchell Library during the 1980s. In the Mitchell she worked in the Science & Technology and History & Topography departments before moving to the Glasgow Room. It was there she worked closely with Joe Fisher and was later promoted to the post of Senior Librarian. In 2001 she took on the role of Education Officer, developing family history courses for members of the public and Burns for Bairns classes for schoolchildren as well as giving local and family history outreach talks to hundreds of groups in the West of Scotland. She retired in 2008 although for a few years thereafter she remained active in LOCSCOT, the Scottish branch of the Local Studies Group of CILIP.

49. Cliff (Clifford Leonard Clark) Hanley (1922–99), born in Shettleston, in Glasgow's East End, was a journalist, novelist, playwright, broadcaster and humourist. His best known book is probably *Dancing in the Streets*, an account of his early life in

Glasgow. He wrote thrillers under the pen-name Henry Calvin and also wrote the words of Scotland's unofficial national anthem, 'Scotland the Brave'. Among his many documentary and television scripts was an episode of *Between the Lines* that attracted the attention of Mary Whitehouse, the 'Clean-Up TV' campaigner.

50. Nennius (fl 796) was reputedly the Welsh author of the early Latin compilation known as the *Historia Britonum*, an account of British history from the time of Julius Caesar to towards the end of the 7th century. It contains material of doubtful historical significance, but it has its place in the study of Celtic literature and of the Arthurian legend in particular.

51. The political career of Margaret Thatcher is described in note 50 to the interview with Peter Grant.

52. Note 47 to the interview with Peter Grant gives a definition of the term 'book fund'.

53. An MBA is a Masters degree in Business Administration (management). It originated in the USA in the early 20th century when companies were seeking scientific approaches to management. Courses – which can be full time, part time, executive, distance-learning or specialist – cover accountancy, finance, marketing, human resources and operations in a manner most relevant to management analysis and strategy. Accreditation bodies specifically for MBA programmes ensure consistency and quality of education.

54. OPAC stands for Online Public Access Catalogue. It is an online database of materials held by a library or a group of libraries on which users can search a library catalogue to locate books and other library materials. Search technologies are improving all the time serving, for example, inter-library loans and world-wide access to library materials in digitised form.

55. Charles Dickens's *Our Mutual Friend*, his last complete novel, published in 1865, has been described as a satiric masterpiece encompassing the great themes of his earlier works: the pretensions of the *nouveaux riches*, the ingenuousness of the aspiring poor and the unfailing power of wealth to corrupt all who crave it.

Peter Grant, pp 111–128

1. For further information about the employment of agricultural workers at this period see note 1 to the interview with Gavin Drummond.

2. Although 'bothy' now usually refers to a hut providing temporary and overnight accommodation for hillwalkers and mountaineers, traditionally it was the name given to permanent living accommodation for workmen, especially unmarried farmworkers.

3. A grieve was a farm overseer or foreman.

4. The Scottish Renaissance was a mainly literary movement of the early to mid-20th century that arose from a desire to re-establish Scottish artistic values and reflect the ideas of the new century and modernism. Although driven by writers, its influence went beyond literature into music, the visual arts, politics and the revival in the nation's indigenous languages. Although there were connections with the Celtic Twilight and Celtic Revival movements of the late 19th century, which helped reawaken a spirit of cultural nationalism, the modernist-influenced Renaissance sought a rebirth of Scottish national culture that would both look back to the medieval 'makar' poets, William Dunbar and Robert Henrysoun, as well as to contemporary

influences. Early signs of a new era were there in the writing of George Douglas Brown, Violet Jacob and Marion Angus. In other spheres the work of Patrick Geddes, John Duncan and Charles Rennie Mackintosh revealed the flowering of Scottish creative activity. It was only through the literary efforts of Hugh MacDiarmid and his insistence on writing in Lallans that the Scottish Renaissance properly began, however. This had an electrifying effect on the literary landscape, and other writers – Edwin Muir, Neil Gunn, Eric Linklater, Lewis Grassic Gibbon and many others – soon followed in MacDiarmid's footsteps, writing in Scots, exploring the Scots identity, rejecting nostalgia and parochialism and engaging with social and political issues. Although the Scottish Renaissance continued well beyond the Second World War, its momentum had flagged by the 1960s and 1970s. Nevertheless, beyond its cultural impact, it has had a longer-lasting effect on Scottish society and politics, creating conditions for the formation of the Scottish National Party in 1934 and its subsequent success.

5. The Clyde had been deepened to allow larger ships to travel up-river to the docks in Glasgow but the deep channel and dock entrances were narrow, the river was extremely busy with shipping and quay space in the city was limited. Throughout the 19th century, therefore, many of the cargoes for Glasgow were carried by lighters plying between the city and the Tail of the Bank where ocean-going ships anchored. In 1856 a Greenock man, James Steel, acquired several lighters and formed James Steel & Sons. In 1877 Steel took David Bennie into partnership, forming Steel & Bennie. As well as carrying cargo themselves the company's boats towed dumb barges, thus originating what was to become the firm's sole business – towing. Further development followed with the purchase of the company's first tugs, employed to tow ships into and out of harbour. By 1900 the boom in Clyde shipbuilding was such that launches and repairs were everyday occurrences, many of which were attended by the firm's tugs, perfecting techniques in towing which are used to this day. In addition, the regular liner services operating from Glasgow to all parts of the world kept the tugs fully employed, and during the First World War they were taken into Admiralty service. Despite the downturn during the Depression, tug companies benefited from relatively prosperous times for the Clyde in the late '30s. During the Second World War, the two main towing companies, the Clyde Shipping Co and Steel & Bennie, were amalgamated for the war effort to deliver an effective tug service. In the 1960s they again combined until Steel & Bennie was sold to a Dutch company in 1971.

6. The Free Presbyterian Church devolved on doctrinal grounds from the Free Church of Scotland in 1893. Strongest in the Highlands and Gaelic regions, it emphasises Sabbatarianism and the minutiae of observance.

7. *The Oban Times* is a local weekly newspaper, published in Oban and covering the West Highlands and the islands off Scotland's west coast. It was established by James Miller in 1861 as *The Oban Monthly Pictorial Magazine*. In 1866 it became a weekly and changed its name to *The Oban Times & Argyllshire Advertiser.* Since 1929 it has been published as *The Oban Times and West Highland Times.* Following the death of James Miller in 1882, *The Oban Times* was purchased by Duncan Cameron and remained in the Cameron family's hands until 1976 when it was acquired by the Johnston Press. Control of the paper reverted to private ownership in 1983 and it is now part of the Oban Times Group which publishes a number of Scottish local newspapers and Scottish-interest magazines.

8. Eric Arthur Blair (1903–50), who used the pen name George Orwell, was an important British novelist, essayist, journalist and critic. His best known works include *Animal Farm* (1945), *The Road to Wigan Pier* (1937), which documents working class life in the north of England, and *Homage to Catalonia* (1938), an account of his experiences in the Spanish Civil War. In May 1946 Orwell moved to Barnhill, an abandoned farmhouse near the northern end of the Isle of Jura. Off and on for the next three years Orwell used this remote location to work on the novel *Nineteen Eighty-Four.* The book was almost never completed, however, for in August 1947 the writer led a disastrous boating expedition in which he, his son and two friends almost drowned while trying to cross the notorious Corryvreckan. In June 1949 *Nineteen Eighty-Four* was published to immediate critical and popular acclaim. It remains the work for which he is best remembered.

9. Secondary school education following the 1872 Education Act is described in note 6 to the interview with Isabella McKinlay.

10. The Argyll and Sutherland Highlanders (Princess Louise's) was a line infantry regiment of the British Army created in 1881 by the amalgamation of the 91st Regiment of Foot and the 93rd Regiment of Foot. It was expanded to 15 battalions during the First World War and nine during the Second World War. The 1st Battalion served in Korea, Suez, Cyprus, Borneo, Aden and Northern Ireland. As part of the restructuring of the infantry in 2006, the Argyll and Sutherland Highlanders was amalgamated into the single Royal Regiment of Scotland. The Argyll and Sutherland Highlanders traditionally recruit from the counties of Argyll and Bute, Dunbartonshire, Renfrewshire, Inverclyde and Stirlingshire.

11. The Dardanelles, part of the waterway linking the Mediterranean and the Black Sea, was the scene of an unsuccessful Allied campaign during the First World War. With stalemate on the Western Front and with the intention of overcoming Turkey and coming to the aid of Russia, it was decided to undertake a naval operation to capture Constantinople by forcing a route up the Dardanelles. Many of the Anglo-French ships were destroyed during the attempted passage, however, and from April 1915 efforts concentrated on the land attack on Gallipoli. Allied casualties were very high, the operation was abandoned as a costly failure and all remaining troops were evacuated in January 1916.

12. Rankin & Blackmore of Greenock were makers of steam engines for marine use. The company was founded in 1862 when the Eagle Foundry was bought by Daniel Rankin and Edward Blackmore. The firm was very successful, inventing various marine engine improvements and providing engines for paddle steamers and tugs and then cargo and passenger steamers. Rankin & Blackmore became known by its apprentices as 'The College' on account of the wide range of training provided. In 1923 the company was bought by Lithgows (see note 2 to the interview with Tom Gray). Its Greenock foundry ceased to operate in 1954 and the firm was finally closed in 1964.

13. In 1845 John Hastie, an engineer and millwright, opened a small works in Greenock producing sundry engineering products. During the two decades thereafter he produced marine steering gears based on his own patented designs. In 1870 the firm began making steam steering gears. Taking on limited liability status in 1898 it became John Hastie & Co Ltd. From 1903 the company devoted itself to the production of steering gear and in the years before the First World War was a pioneer in the use of electric hydraulic steering gear. The firm remained privately

owned until 1972 when it was acquired jointly by the Weir Group plc and Lithgows Ltd, although it remained an independently operated company. It was finally dissolved in 1991.

14. The name MacBrayne is synonymous with sea connections to the Western Isles and Highlands. Caledonian MacBrayne started life in 1851 as a steamer company under the name of David Hutcheson & Co. In 1878, the company passed to David MacBrayne and rapidly became the main carrier on the West Highland routes, providing passenger and freight services to most islands. MacBraynes remained in the hands of the family until 1928 when it was re-formed, with ownership divided between Coast Lines Ltd and the London, Midland and Scottish Railway. The new owners rebuilt the ageing fleet, and bus services, which had begun on the mainland in 1906, were expanded to the islands after the Second World War. In 1948 the company was partially nationalised and then five years later the state-owned Scottish Transport Group (STG) was formed to operate not only MacBrayne's services but also those of the Caledonian Steam Packet Company (CSP) on the Clyde. Soon after, the shipping companies were amalgamated and renamed Caledonian MacBrayne Ltd. In 1990 Caledonian MacBrayne became wholly owned by the Secretary of State for Scotland and, since 2006, by the Scottish Government.

15. The Clarks were members of the J & J Clark family, thread makers in Paisley. During the industrial revolution Paisley's transformation into an important industrial town was based largely on textiles. It became the world centre for thread making, the history of which is synonymous with the Coats and Clark families. Originally established as manufacturers of silk thread, when the supply of that material dried up during the Napoleonic Wars, members of the Clark family developed a fine cotton thread as an alternative and erected a factory in the town under the name of J & J Clark. From here their business continued to expand, and although most of its output was for the home market, they built a large mill at Newark, New Jersey, in the 1860s. Successive generations of the Clark family continued to develop the business and eventually formed a limited liability company in 1896 and amalgamated with their arch rivals J & P Coats the same year. The company, now owned by Guinness Peat, continues to work in the clothing industry under the name Coats Group plc.

16. The features of a kitchen range are described in note 4 to the interview with John Preston.

17. The significance of the Qualifying Exam is described in note 2 to the interview with John Hunter.

18. Scottish secondary education system awards are described in note 6 to the interview with John Hunter.

19. A 'kist o' whistles' is a Scots expression for an organ, especially a church organ. It is often used as a derogatory description since it was only in the 19th century that organs of any size became widely available in Scotland as they had been frowned upon by the Presbyterian churches.

20. In Presbyterian churches the precentor is the person who leads the singing. Especially in the absence of an organ, the congregation relied on the precentor to set them off on the right tune at the right pitch and with the right words

21. The life and career of William B Paton are described in note 29 to the interview with M W (Bill) Paton

22. Information about the Dewey Decimal Classification (DDC) may be found in note 15 to the interview with Alan White.

23. Sir Pelham Grenville Wodehouse (1881–1975), better known as P G Wodehouse, was an English author of almost 100 books and a contributor to a variety of periodicals including *Punch* and the *Globe*. He is best known as the creator of Bertie Wooster and his legendary valet, Jeeves, and for tales of Blandings Castle. As well as his novels and short stories, he wrote lyrics for musical comedies and at one time had five musicals running simultaneously on Broadway. Although he became a US citizen in 1955, he received a knighthood in the New Year's Honours List of 1975, only to die on St Valentine's Day some 45 days later.

24. See note 17 to the interview with Margaret Deas for a description of the life and writing career of John Buchan.

25. Information about Richmal Crompton and her much-loved *Just William* stories is given in note 12 to the interview with M W (Bill) Paton.

26. Information about the *Children's Encyclopaedia* is given in note 6 to the interview with Joe Fisher.

27. The land now occupied by Glasgow University has been called Gilmorehill as far back as the 17th century. It was successively owned by a series of merchants who made their money from the sugar, rum, cotton and tobacco trades that brought wealth to the city. The land was bought by the University of Glasgow in 1864, after a plan to use it as a necropolis fell through. The main building was designed by Sir George Gilbert Scott, its most recognisable feature being the soaring ventilation tower at the centre of the south front. The University kept within its Gilmorehill boundary for some time but increasing teaching, study and research demands have since been addressed by the construction of many new University buildings nearby.

28. Richard Wilson, originally Ian Colquhoun Wilson, was born in Greenock in 1936. He trained at RADA and is best known for his roles in many television comedies, especially that of Victor Meldrew in *One Foot in the Grave* (1990–2000). He has also appeared in a number of television dramas and films, and in the theatre he has worked extensively as an actor and director.

29. The Citizens Theatre is a venue and theatre company based in the Gorbals area of Glasgow. The building was designed by Campbell Douglas and first opened in 1878 as The Royal Princess's Theatre, seating 1,200. There is now a 500-seat main auditorium with two studio theatres. The Citizens Company was founded in 1943 by James Bridie, the pseudonym used by Osborne Henry Mavor, now considered to be a founding father of modern Scottish theatre. The Citizens Theatre was permanently established at its present location in 1945, since when it has been one of Scotland's major producing theatres presenting a programme of contemporary versions of classic plays and new Scottish drama.

30. Robert McLellan (1907–85) was born at Kirkfieldbank, Lanarkshire. His childhood, spent on his grandparents' farm, inspired his *Linmill* stories. It is as a playwright, however, that McLellan is best known. He was influenced by Hugh MacDiarmid and the Scottish Renaissance, and although he always wrote in Scots about Scotland and the Scots character, his plays are never parochial. His best known plays include *Jamie the Saxt* (1937) and *The Flouers o' Edinburgh* (1948).

31. The professional training of librarians at the Scottish School of Librarianship is described in note 9 to the interview with John Hunter.

32. See note 11 to the interview with Andrew Fraser for information about miners' welfares or institutes.

33. Note 21 to the interview with Gavin Drummond provides information about the Scottish National Party.

34. Tomas Garrigue Masaryk (1850–1937) was born in Moravia and entered politics in the nationalistic atmosphere of the 1880s. As a deputy in the Czech and Austrian Imperial parliaments and through his writings, he earned a reputation as a man of courage and common sense. His main political success was achieved after the onset of the First World War when he travelled to France, Britain, Russia and the United States, winning support and recognition for an independent Czechoslovakia. In 1918 he was elected the country's first President and remained in this position until he retired in 1935 in favour of Eduard Benes.

35. Information regarding NALGO is given as note 15 to the interview with Andrew Fraser.

36. Information about the Library Association and the Scottish Library Association is given in note 27 to the interview with Gavin Drummond.

37. Too often public library performance was measured solely by the number of items loaned. It is now common for a number of performance measures to be employed to obtain a clear understanding of whether the service is achieving its aims, objectives and targets.

38. The International Federation of Library Associations and Institutions (IFLA), an independent, non-governmental, not-for-profit organisation, is the leading body representing librarianship in matters of international interest. It promotes freedom of expression and the need for universal and equitable access to information, ideas and works of imagination. It recognises the role of library and information services in guaranteeing such access and so supports the continuing education of library personnel and develops guidelines for library services. IFLA works in close partnership with UNESCO, and several IFLA manifestos are recognised as UNESCO manifestos. IFLA was founded in Edinburgh in 1927 and has grown to over 1,600 members in approximately 150 countries. It maintains headquarters at the National Library of the Netherlands in The Hague.

39. For information about St Andrew's Halls see note 41 to the interview with Joe Fisher.

40. See note 11 to the interview with Dorothy Milne for information about Congregational churches in Scotland.

41. See note 32 to the interview with Dorothy Milne for information about the Orange Order.

42. Fenians, from the Gaelic *Fianna*, 'warriors', was the short title of the Irish Republican Brotherhood, a nationalist organisation founded as the Fenian Brotherhood by John O'Mahony (1816–77) in New York in 1857 and as the Irish Republican Brotherhood by James Stephens (1825–1901) in Ireland in 1858. Its military wing was known as the Irish Republican Army (IRA).

43. For information about the Scottish Library Association magazine see note 41 to the interview with Alan White.

44. Marcus Kelly Milne (1902–89) joined the staff of Aberdeen Public Library in 1920 and by 1928 was Chief Assistant. His appointment as City Librarian was made in 1938 and within a year he had opened the reference library and converted the lending library into a modern space with lowered bookcases and more attractive stock. As

Professor Reid writes in his Foreword to this work, despite the pressures on library services during the Second World War Marcus Milne saw opportunities to innovate. In 1942 he joined the RAF as an officer but returned to his role as City Librarian after the War. The period thereafter saw further development and modernisation of the library service in the city with the opening of new branch libraries, the introduction of the mobile library service, commencement of a housebound readers' service and restructuring of the central library. Milne strongly supported the argument for the establishment of a second Scottish school of librarianship in Aberdeen and was active in the campaign to overcome the opposition of the Library Association in London. In recognition of his services to the profession in Scotland, Marcus Milne was appointed President of the Scottish Library Association in 1967. He retired the following year.

45. William E G Critchley (1923–72) was educated at Robert Gordon's College, Aberdeen, and joined the staff of the City Libraries in 1940. After serving during the Second World War he returned to Aberdeen and, studying independently, became a Fellow of the Library Association in 1952. After spells as librarian of Berwick-upon-Tweed and Depute Librarian at Motherwell, he returned to Aberdeen as Depute. He was appointed City Librarian in 1968 and during the next four years he reorganised all library procedures, planned an extension to the central library, opened two branch libraries and introduced a gramophone record service. At various times he was a correspondence course tutor, a part-time lecturer at the Scottish School of Librarianship and a Library Association examiner. At the time of his death he was vice-president elect of the Scottish Library Association.

46. 'Coup' is a Scots word meaning to tip, overturn or tumble.

47. 'Book fund' is the commonly-used term for budgets available for the purchase of library materials, especially books. As public libraries now provide a wider range of materials and services in different formats, the terms 'materials budget' and 'resources budget' are now more generally used.

48. Mobile shelving is designed to maximise the storage capacity of a given space by incorporating movable shelving units on tracks. Because it is considerably heavier than normal shelving when filled, mobile shelving requires more structural support, an important design consideration in the construction and renovation of library facilities.

49. *The Sweeney* was a 1970s' British television police drama focusing on two members of the Flying Squad, a branch of the Metropolitan Police specialising in tackling armed robbery and violent crime in London. The programme's title derives from 'Sweeney Todd', cockney rhyming slang for 'Flying Squad'. It starred John Thaw as Detective Inspector Jack Regan, and Dennis Waterman as his partner Detective Sergeant George Carter. Such was its popularity in the UK that it spawned two feature film spin-offs.

50. Margaret Thatcher (1925–2013) was Prime Minister of the UK from 1979 to 1990 and Leader of the Conservative Party from 1975 to 1990. She was the longest-serving British Prime Minister of the 20th century and, until recently, the only woman to have held the office. A Soviet journalist called her the 'Iron Lady', a nickname that became associated with her uncompromising politics and leadership style. Her political philosophy and economic policies emphasised deregulation (particularly of the financial sector), flexible labour markets, the privatisation of state-owned companies, and reducing the power and influence of trade unions – policies which have come to be known as Thatcherism.

51. Robert Craig (1943–) started his career in librarianship as a library assistant with Hamilton Burgh Library in 1966 before studying librarianship at the University of Strathclyde. He later successfully applied for a position as a librarian with Lanark County Library Service under W B Paton, and following various promotions rose to become Depute County Librarian. After local government reorganisation in 1975, he was appointed Principal Educational Resources Librarian for Strathclyde Region's Glasgow Division. In 1978 he became a lecturer in the University of Strathclyde's Department of Librarianship and Information Studies. In 1981 he was elected Honorary Secretary of the Scottish Library Association (SLA) and three years later was appointed Executive Secretary (now Director) of the SLA, its first full-time, paid officer. It was under his guidance that standards for libraries in the public, college and school library sectors were produced. At the creation in 1991 of the Scottish Library & Information Council (SLIC), the advisory body to the Scottish Government on library and information matters, Robert Craig was appointed its Director. He was to hold jointly the posts of Director of the SLA and of SLIC until his retiral in 2002. In 2000 he was made an OBE for services to librarianship.

Philip D Hancock, pp 129–142

1. The Corps of Army Schoolmasters was formed in 1845 to educate and instruct personnel in skills relevant to the Army's requirements and to equip soldiers for post-Army civilian life. A Royal Warrant established the Army Educational Corps (AEC) in 1920 with the bulk of the teaching done by regimental officers. In 1946 the AEC was honoured with the title of 'Royal'. In 1992 the RAEC lost its Corps status and became the Educational and Training Services Branch of the new Adjutant General's Corps.
2. Information about the Black Watch is given as note 3 to the interview with Isabella McKinlay.
3. The Queen's Barracks were established in Perth as a home for cavalry regiments in 1793 and were subsequently converted to take infantry regiments. The Barracks served as the depot of the Black Watch from 1830 until they closed in May 1961. The buildings were then demolished and the site used for a police headquarters. In the 1960s the Regimental Headquarters and the Regimental Museum moved to Balhousie Castle where the Museum still remains. The Army Reserve Centre in Perth has since adopted the name of Queen's Barracks.
4. Bulford Camp is on Salisbury Plain in Wiltshire. It was established in 1897 as a mixture of tents and huts, with permanent barracks being built only during the inter-war years. The site continues in use as a large British Army base.
5. 'Scullery' is described in note 8 to the interview with Dorothy Milne.
6. The Abyssinian Crisis resulted from friction on the Eritrean and Somali frontiers between Italy and Ethiopia (then commonly known in Europe as 'Abyssinia'). Although in 1928 Italy and Ethiopia had signed a treaty of friendship, Mussolini pursued a policy of provocation, determined to secure a military success. Following an incident at Walwal between Italian colonial troops and Ethiopian forces, the Italians invaded in 1935 without a declaration of war, capturing Addis Ababa with the aid of air power and chemical weapons the following year. Despite branding Italy as the aggressor and imposing sanctions, the intervention of the League of

Nations was ineffective and gave encouragement to the alliance between Fascist Italy and Nazi Germany.

7. Sliema is a town in the Central Region of Malta, named after Our Lady of Good Voyage Chapel, a beacon and reference point for sailors and fishermen. In 1855 a new church dedicated to Our Lady Star of the Sea was opened and around this the small village grew into a town in the second half of the 19th century with the construction of elegant villas and town houses lining the streets. During this period the British built a number of fortifications on the Sliema peninsula and barracks (demolished in 2001) were created on the Tigné peninsula. The town is now a centre for shopping, restaurants and café life, and has witnessed significant modern development of apartment blocks and hotels.

8. A warrant officer (WO) in the British Armed Forces is a member of the highest group of non-commissioned ranks, holding the Queen's (or King's) warrant. Warrant officers are not saluted, but are addressed as 'Sir/Ma'am' by subordinates. Although often referred to along with non-commissioned officers (NCOs), they are members of a separate group. In the British Army, there are two warrant ranks, warrant officer class 2 (WO2) and warrant officer class 1 (WO1), the latter being the senior. The rank immediately below WO2 is staff sergeant (or colour sergeant).

9. Hornby Railways is a British model railway brand. Hornby was at first a trade name for the railway toys of Meccano (see note 10 below). Its first clockwork train was launched in 1920, and although the first successful electric train was introduced in 1925 clockwork remained the mainstay of Hornby trains until the late 1930s. In 1938 the company launched its first 00 gauge train leading to the adoption of 00 as the UK modelling standard. In 1964 Hornby and Meccano were bought by their competitor, Tri-ang, and sold on when Tri-ang went into receivership. Hornby Railways became independent in the 1980s and continued to produce a range of detailed British steam and diesel locomotives. Since then the company has acquired a number of well-known brand names including Airfix, Humbrol and Corgi.

10. Meccano is a model construction system consisting of reusable metal strips, plates, angle girders, wheels, axles and gears, with nuts and bolts to connect the pieces. It enables the building of working models and mechanical devices, the only tools required to assemble models being a screwdriver and spanners. The ideas for Meccano were first conceived by Frank Hornby who developed and patented the construction kit as 'Mechanics Made Easy' in 1901. The name was later changed to 'Meccano'. It was more than just a toy: it was educational, teaching basic mechanical principles, and the name is thought to have been derived from the phrase 'Make and Know'. It was manufactured by the British company, Meccano Ltd, between 1908 and 1980 and, following various changes of ownership, is now made in France and China.

11. The English novelist, short-story writer, historian and political commentator Herbert George Wells (1866–1946) started as a draper's assistant and through study became a lecturer until the success of his short stories allowed him to concentrate full-time on writing. He achieved fame as a novelist, pioneering science fiction with such titles as *The Time Machine*, *The War of the Worlds* and *The First Men in the Moon* and also wrote some well-known comic novels including *Love and Mr Lewisham, Kipps* and *The History of Mr Polly*.

12. (Joseph) Rudyard Kipling (1865–1936), after education in England, returned to India where he had been born. He worked as a journalist there until the success of his early verses and short stories encouraged him to move to London to pursue his

literary career. During the late 19th century and early years of the 20th century he produced many of the titles by which he is best known, including the collection of verse entitled *Barrack Room Ballads*, the two *Jungle Books*, which are counted among the most-loved animal stories, *Stalky and Co*, *Kim* and the children's classic *Just So Stories*. He was awarded the Nobel Prize for Literature in 1907.

13. The Intelligence Corps is responsible for gathering, analysing and disseminating military intelligence and also for counter-intelligence and security. The first Intelligence Corps of the British Army was formed in August 1914 but was disbanded in 1929 as a consequence of failures during the Irish War of Independence. In 1940 a new Intelligence Corps was created and has existed since that time.

14. The Royal Corps of Signals is one of the combat support arms of the British Army, providing battlefield communications and information systems. It was founded in 1870 as a Telegraph Troop of the Royal Engineers and first saw action in 1879 during the Anglo-Zulu War. In 1908 responsibility for signalling was taken over by the Royal Engineers Signal Service and as such provided communications during the First World War. In 1920 it was recognised as a distinctive part of the British Army and established as the Royal Corps of Signals. It served in every theatre of war during the Second World War and in every war and area of conflict involving the UK since then.

15. Information about George Watson's College is given as note 4 to the interview with Alan White.

16. George Heriot's School is an independent Edinburgh primary and secondary school. It was established in 1628 as George Heriot's Hospital, by bequest of the royal goldsmith George Heriot who, on his death in 1624, left around 25,000 pounds Scots – equivalent to several tens of millions today – to found a 'hospital', then the name for this kind of charitable school, to care for poor orphans. The main building of the School, notable for its renaissance architecture, opened in 1659. A statue of the founder is located in a niche within the quadrangle. As its finances grew the School began to take in other pupils and in the 1880s introduced fees. Nevertheless, to this day it serves its charitable object, providing full-fee remission for children of widows and widowers who need financial assistance. Such pupils are referred to as 'foundationers'. In 1979 it became co-educational and now has around 1,600 pupils.

17. Information about the Merchant Company of Edinburgh is given as note 5 to the interview with Alan White.

18. Scottish secondary education system awards are described in note 6 to the interview with John Hunter and in notes 9 and 10 to the interview with Margaret Crawford.

19. Information about the system of National Service may be found in note 6 to the interview with John Preston.

20. Professor William Croft Dickinson (1897–1963) was appointed Sir William Fraser Professor of Scottish History and Palaeography at the University of Edinburgh in 1940, becoming the first English-born occupant of this Chair, the oldest and most distinguished Scottish History professorship in the world. Following his appointment, Dickinson's work focused on the Scottish Reformation and general works for students, but he continued to pursue major editorial projects, including the writings of John Knox and the records of the medieval burgh of Aberdeen. He also raised the profile of *The Scottish Historical Review* which came to be regarded as the world's leading periodical for research on Scottish history. In addition to his academic work Dickinson was an accomplished author of children's fantasy stories

and traditional ghost stories for readers of all ages. He was made a CBE in the 1963 New Year honours list, just months before his death.

21. Sir Arthur Mitchell and C G Cash, *A Contribution to the Bibliography of Scottish Topography*. 2 vols (The University Press, Edinburgh, 1917).

22. Edinburgh University was founded by Royal Charter from King James VI in 1582 and opened in 1583. The Library predated this, however, as its initial collection was a bequest of 276 theological books by the advocate Clement Litill made to the town in 1580 (see note 40 below). By the time of Robert Lumsden's catalogue of 1637 the collection had grown to almost 2,500 volumes. In 1827 the Library moved to William Playfair's Upper Library in the Old College building. The collections in Edinburgh University Old College were moved in 1967 to the purpose-built eight-storey Main Library building in George Square (see note 31 below).

23. Dr Lauriston William Sharp (1897–1959), after distinguished study at Edinburgh and Cambridge universities, was appointed Assistant Librarian in the Department of Manuscripts in Edinburgh University Library in 1925. He rose to become University Librarian in 1939 and retained that position until his death. For a number of years he served on the Council of the Scottish Library Association and was President of the Association during 1949–50. He also contributed to the work of the profession through his chairmanship of the Standing Conference of National and University Libraries and of the Scottish Group of the University and Research Section of the Library Association.

24. *A Bibliography of Works Relating to Scotland, 1916–1950*. 2 vols (The University Press, Edinburgh, 1959–60).

25. Information about the Inter Library Lending scheme is available in note 62 to the interview with Margaret Deas.

26. The British Museum cataloguing rules, originally published in 1841, were devised by Sir Anthony Panizzi and his colleagues. Thereafter they appeared in revised versions until 1936. In 1893 the *Cataloguing Rules* of the Library Association (LA) were published and later revised on the basis of the British Museum rules. In light of the similar work being done on both sides of the Atlantic, Melvil Dewey (see note 15 to the interview with Alan White) suggested that there should be co-operation to produce Anglo-American rules. The first international cataloguing code was published in 1908 in separate American and British editions. Following further US/UK joint working during the 1950s and '60s the Anglo-American Cataloguing Rules (AACR) were published in 1967 to provide international rules and standards. In 1978 the current, second edition (referred to as AACR2) was published jointly by the American Library Association, the Canadian Library Association and the Library Association in the UK. AACR2 is designed for use in the construction of catalogues and other lists in general libraries of all sizes, and the rules cover the description of all types of library materials. Over the years AACR2 has been updated by occasional amendments and revisions.

27. Dr James Clarkson Corson (1905–88) graduated from Edinburgh University with honours in History in 1928 and with a PhD in 1934. He joined the University Library staff as an Assistant Librarian in 1930, rising to the position of Deputy Librarian in 1939, from which post he retired in 1965, having been Acting Librarian in the interim between the sudden death in 1959 of Dr L W Sharp (see note 23 above) and the arrival of his successor, E R S Fifoot (see note 36 below) late the following year. Corson was a leading authority on the bibliography of Sir Walter Scott and had

begun collecting printed editions of Scott in the secondhand bookshops of Edinburgh while still at school. Eventually his collection expanded to fill the old church at Lilliesleaf, near Melrose, in the old manse of which he lived and died. His zeal was recognised by his appointment as Honorary Librarian of Abbotsford in the 1950s. The collection was purchased by the University in 1975 and his widow bequeathed funds to ensure its upkeep and development. Consequently, Edinburgh University Library has one of the leading collections of books by and about Sir Walter Scott.

28. The King's Buildings is a campus of the University of Edinburgh, and contains most of the schools within the College of Science and Engineering. In 2014 the University renamed a number of the streets on King's Buildings campus in honour of scientists who had worked there, including Sir James Dewar, Thomas Bayes, David Brewster, James Hutton and Charlotte Auerbach.

29. New College opened in 1846 as a college of the Free Church of Scotland. Candidates for the Church of Scotland studied in the Divinity Faculty of Edinburgh University. From the 1930s, when the two churches came together, the New College site on the Mound has been the home of the School of Divinity of the University of Edinburgh and continues to offer a programme of academic preparation for ministry in the Church of Scotland, a programme also made use of by ministerial candidates from other churches. In the 1970s it began offering undergraduate degrees in Theology and Religious Studies, and students in these programmes now make up the majority of the School's undergraduates. It also offers several postgraduate programmes. New College Library was founded in 1843 as the Library of the Free Church College. It is one of the largest theological libraries in the United Kingdom, holding a large collection of manuscripts.

30. The guard book catalogue has been in use since medieval times and is a variation of a printed, book catalogue. It consists of printed or typed entries on slips, often cut from accessions lists, mounted and arranged on the leaves of large books into which additional sheets can be inserted to allow for the expansion of the catalogue. Space has to be left between each entry for additional entries, and when a leaf is completely full it must be cut and the slips redistributed. Although a guard book catalogue, unlike a printed catalogue, can be updated, it is far from ideal for libraries with large numbers of additions and withdrawals as the work and process of updating is time-consuming and complicated. In a large library more than one copy of a guard book catalogue has to be maintained to ensure that it is not out of use while repasting is carried out.

31. The Main Library of Edinburgh University is situated on the south-west corner of George Square, chosen as it was the quietest part of the Square. Opened in 1967, the eight-storey building was designed by Sir Basil Spence with the horizontal exterior designed to look like a bookcase. At the time of its opening, it was the largest university library in the UK, with each floor an acre in size.

32. The National Central Library was founded in 1916 as the Central Library for Students. It was financed out of grants from the Carnegie United Kingdom Trust, and its primary purpose was to lend books to adult class students who had no other sources for borrowing. It became the National Central Library in 1931 with an expanded remit to operate as the official clearing-house for inter-library lending, to provide a bibliographic service and to continue the original role in servicing adult classes. In 1973 the National Central Library was one of the national organisations

which were brought together within the newly-created British Library (see note 35 to the interview with Isabella McKinlay for more information about the formation of the British Library).

33. Information about the Scottish Central Library is to be found in note 30 to the interview with Dorothy Milne. Isabella McKinlay, in her interview, describes her work as editor with the Scottish Central Library.

34. Note 27 to the interview with Gavin Drummond gives information about the Library Association (LA), and professional qualifications awarded by the LA are described by Professor Reid in his Foreword.

35. The Association of University Teachers (AUT) was a trade union and professional association that represented academic teaching and research staff as well as academic-related staff, including librarians, at universities in the United Kingdom. It was formed in England in 1919; the equivalent Scottish body – the Association of University Teachers (Scotland) – was set up in 1922 and joined the AUT in 1949. The post-war expansion in education saw considerable growth in the Association's membership, due to the union's success in recruiting academic-related staff and amalgamation with smaller associations. In 2006 the AUT merged with the National Association of Teachers in Further and Higher Education (NATFHE) to form the University and College Union (UCU).

36. Erik Richard Sidney Fifoot (1925–92) had previously worked at the libraries of Leeds University and Nottingham University before his appointment as Librarian of Edinburgh University in 1960, in which post he remained until 1979. During 1979–81 he was Librarian of the Bodleian Library, the main research library of the University of Oxford and one of the oldest libraries in Europe.

37. Dr Brenda Moon (1931–2011) held various positions as a librarian at the University of Sheffield and the University of Hull between 1955 and 1979 before her appointment as Librarian at Edinburgh University in 1980, the first woman to head a Scottish university library. She remained in this post until retiring in 1996, and under her leadership Edinburgh University became the first university library in the UK to deliver an automated, computer-based service. She also upgraded and broadened the Special Collections which resulted in the University attracting important archive collections. Dr Moon was an energetic advocate for collaborative library activities and co-founded the Consortium of University Research Libraries which she chaired from 1991 to 1995.

38. Peter Freshwater graduated in History and English from Edinburgh University in 1964. He was employed as Superintendent of Reader Services at Birmingham University Library from 1971 until his appointment as Deputy Librarian at Edinburgh University Library in 1977, a position he held until 1999. He retains his association with the University as editor of the *University of Edinburgh Journal* for the Graduates' Association and as Secretary of the Friends of Edinburgh University Library.

39. The noble, with the value of one third of a pound sterling, was introduced during the reign of Edward III (1327–77) and was the first English gold coin produced in quantity. It was minted for the last time during the first reign of Edward IV (1461–70). The unicorn was a gold coin that formed part of Scottish coinage between 1484 and 1525. It was initially issued in the reign of James III (1460–88) with a value of 18 shillings Scots, but rising gold prices during the reign of James V (1513–42) caused its value to increase. The obverse of the coin shows a crowned unicorn, a heraldic symbol which occurs in the royal coat of arms of Scotland. The unicorn was replaced

during the reign of James V with the gold crown, or abbey crown, which had a value of 20 shillings.

40. Clement Litill (1527–80) was admitted to the Faculty of Advocates in 1553. By the Reformation he had converted to Protestantism and begun his collection of Reformist theological works. By 1561 he was serving as an elder on Edinburgh Kirk Session, and was regularly sent by the Town Council as a commissioner to the General Assembly of the Church of Scotland. The highest point in his career as a lawyer came in 1577 when he was appointed advocate depute, licensed to stand in for the king's advocate in the civil courts. In association with his brother William, a prominent Councillor, and Rev James Lawson, first minister of Edinburgh, Litill was a proponent of the scheme to establish a university in the city. In 1579, he was appointed to a Council committee to take the matter forward although discussions as to a suitable site for the University and the nature of the curriculum were still ongoing when Litill died. In his will, he bequeathed his library of 276 volumes to the Town and Kirk of Edinburgh for the use of the town's clergy, divinity students and other scholars. The collection was handed over to the newly-founded University in 1584, forming the basis of Edinburgh University Library.

41. Charles Sarolea (1870–1953) was born in Belgium and educated at the University of Liège. In 1894 he was appointed lecturer in French at Edinburgh University and in 1918 became the University's first Professor of French. He held the Chair of French and Romance Philology until his resignation in 1931. Sarolea was a linguist (claiming a knowledge of at least 18 languages), a bookman and author. His book collection of some 200,000 works was said to be the largest private library in Europe. He wrote books on a wide range of topics, especially international affairs, and edited the literary magazine *Everyman* from 1912 to 1917. Sarolea became a naturalised citizen of the UK in 1912, but for over 50 years represented Belgium as its Consul, latterly Consul-General, in Edinburgh. He held honorary degrees from the Universities of Brussels, Montreal, and Cleveland, and was awarded the Chevalier of the Belgian Order of Leopold. The Sarolea Collection covers the years 1897–1952 and relates to all of the Professor's various activities and interests. It was acquired by the University of Edinburgh Archives by purchase in 1954.

42. 'Red brick university' is the term originally used to refer to six 'civic science' universities founded in the 19th century in major industrial cities in England as a reflection of the increasing need for university-level study of technical, science, design and engineering subjects. The universities usually identified as red brick are Birmingham, Bristol, Leeds, Liverpool, Manchester and Sheffield. However, the term is often extended to include the group of a further 12 universities granted a charter between 1900 and 1963. Since books from the Sarolea collection 'went to form the start of one of the red brick universities' it is likely that the latter group is referred to.

43. Information about the microfiche format is included in note 2 to the interview with Joe Fisher.

44. *The Scotsman* was first published in Edinburgh in 1817 as a liberal weekly newspaper by lawyer William Ritchie and customs official Charles Maclaren. After the abolition of newspaper stamp tax in Scotland in 1850, *The Scotsman* was relaunched as a daily newspaper. Its premises were originally in Edinburgh's High Street and it then moved into purpose-built offices on Cockburn Street in 1860 before building extensive new premises facing on to North Bridge. These were occupied for the first time in 1902. In 1953 the newspaper was bought by the

Canadian millionaire Roy Thomson who was in the process of building a large media group. The paper was purchased in 1995 by David and Frederick Barclay and they moved the newspaper from its office on North Bridge (now an upmarket hotel) to modern offices in Holyrood Road. In 2005, *The Scotsman* was acquired by its present owners Johnston Press, a company founded in Scotland and now one of the largest local newspaper publishers in the UK. They have since downsized to premises in Queensferry Road.

45. *The Times* is a British daily national newspaper based in London. It began in 1785 under the title *The Daily Universal Register* and became *The Times* in 1788. *The Times* and its sister paper *The Sunday Times* (founded in 1821) are published by Times Newspapers, since 1981 a subsidiary of News UK, itself wholly owned by the News Corp group headed by Rupert Murdoch. Traditionally, the whole emphasis of its editorial comment and news reporting has been on important public affairs treated with an eye to the best interests of Britain. It has been heavily used by scholars and researchers because of its widespread availability in libraries and its detailed index.

46. Charles Pringle Finlayson (1911–85) graduated from Edinburgh University in 1933 and joined the staff of the University Library as a junior assistant two years later. Apart from military service during 1939–45, he remained on the Library staff, holding the position of Keeper of Manuscripts from 1946 until retiring in 1978. His knowledge of the collections under his care was invaluable to researchers and authors. Finlayson was himself a scholar, his published work including translations from the Greek and Latin and many articles in various magazines and journals.

47. Bing hand-cranked projectors could be used to show short Pathéscope films. These were popular with enthusiasts who wanted to make home movies and show commercially-made films at home, including Disney, Popeye, Betty Boop and other cartoons, comedies by such stars as Laurel and Hardy and Chaplin, as well as general-interest films of the period. In addition to selling films, Pathéscope distributed in Britain its own range of projectors and cameras during the years before the Second World War and for some years afterwards. After the War, however, the earlier home movie format suffered strong competition from Kodak's 8mm film especially the Super 8mm film, a motion picture film format released in 1965 by Eastman Kodak.

48. The widely known Grundig company, established in Nuremberg by Max Grundig in 1945, is a manufacturer of high-end household appliances and electronic goods including a full range of audio-visual products. Reel-to-reel audio recording uses magnetic tape held on a reel rather than being securely contained within a cassette. Reel-to-reel tape recorders were widely used for voice recording in the home and in educational establishments before the compact cassette, introduced in 1963, eventually replaced reel-to-reel recording.

49. *Railway Modeller* has been published monthly since 1949 and remains Britain's most popular model railway title.

Margaret Deas, pp 143–158

1. The Royal Lyceum Theatre, Grindlay Street, Edinburgh, was built in 1883 for J B Howard and F W P Wyndham who, two years later, founded the Howard & Wyndham theatrical company. The building is largely in its original state and is located adjacent

to the Usher Hall (see note 14 below). It was purchased by Edinburgh Corporation in 1965 to provide a home for the Royal Lyceum Theatre Company. Its present capacity is 658.

2. Boys: male members of the cast requiring accommodation during a play's run.

3. The Regal Cinema, Lothian Road, now the Odeon, formerly the ABC Regal, opened in 1938.

4. The King's Theatre, Leven Street, opened in 1906 as a rival to the Royal Lyceum Theatre (see note 1 above). It was commissioned by an Edinburgh business group but the project was transferred to the King's Theatre Company when the group experienced financial problems. Its principal role at the outset was as a venue for touring companies. In 1928 it became part of the Howard & Wyndham company under whose management summer shows, pantomime and variety were introduced in addition to theatrical performances. In 1969 the theatre was sold to the City of Edinburgh Council which carried out major renovations in 1985 and 2012. The original capacity was 2,500; it is now 1,336.

5. The Empire Palace Theatre, Nicolson Street, was opened in 1892, the first in the Moss Empire chain. It seated 3,000 people on four levels. In 1911 there was a disastrous fire on stage. The large audience escaped swiftly, but 11 people backstage lost their lives, as did a lion. The theatre reopened within three months. There was a refurbishment in 1928 and the programme of top-level, light entertainment continued. In the years from 1947 to 1963 it was also used as a venue for the Edinburgh International Festival. For about 30 years thereafter it was a bingo hall. It was rebuilt in 1994 as the Edinburgh Festival Theatre, with a capacity of 1,915. There has been a theatre on the site for 185 years.

6. The Theatre Royal, Broughton Street, was also known over the years as the Adelphi, the Caledonian and the Queen's, etc. From 1788 onwards various theatres and places of entertainment stood on the site. The Theatre Royal closed in 1946 after a fire and was demolished in the late 1950s.

7. Wrens: Women's Royal Naval Services (WRNS). Founded in 1917, by 1919 there were 7,000 Wrens: 'Women for the Navy – a new shore service.' In 1939, 3,000 women were recruited and given jobs as radio operators, meteorologists and bomb range markers, together with boat's crew Wrens. By 1944 the complement was 74,000. The service was integrated into the Royal Navy in 1993.

8. For information about Moray House School of Education see note 32 to the interview with Margaret Crawford.

9. James Gillespie's High School is in the Marchmont area of Edinburgh, a short distance from the city centre. It was founded in 1803 as a result of the legacy of James Gillespie, a tobacco merchant. Until 1908 it was administered by the Merchant Company of Edinburgh (the Royal Charter of which, awarded in 1681, protected the trading rights of the city's merchants; see also note 5 to the interview with Alan White). Thereafter, the Edinburgh School Board and its successors took over. The School was attended by the novelist Muriel Spark whose 'Miss Jean Brodie' was based on one of her teachers.

10. The Qualifying year, in which the Qualifying Exam (aka the 'Qually') was taken. See note 2 to the interview with John Hunter.

11. The Allied invasion of Normandy (Operation Neptune), 6 June 1944 (D-Day).

12. Parents and professionals came together in the 1940s to establish an organisation to support children with cerebral palsy to go to school, get a job and enjoy an independent

lifestyle. In 1946 the Scottish Council for the Care of Spastics, as it was then known, opened Westerlea School in Ellersly Road, Ravelston. The opening ceremony was performed by Mary, Princess Royal (1897–1965). Today the School is run by Capability Scotland.

13. 'Bless This House' was published in 1927, with music by May Brahe and lyrics by her friend Helen Taylor. One of the first singers to perform it was John McCormack (1884–1945).

14. The Usher Hall, situated in Lothian Road, was built in 1914, funded by Andrew Usher, a whisky distiller and blender, who donated £100,000 for a new concert hall. The final cost was £134,000. Andrew Usher died before the building work got underway. The capacity of the Hall is 2,200 and the auditorium is renowned for the quality of the acoustics. The Usher Hall is the Edinburgh home of the Royal Scottish National Orchestra. It is constantly in use for performances of all kinds of music and it is the key venue for the Edinburgh International Festival. Major, phased refurbishment carried out this century by the City of Edinburgh Council has greatly improved the building's accessibility and facilities. Adjacent to the Usher Hall is the Royal Lyceum Theatre (see note 1 above).

15. Information about *The Sunday Post* will be found in note 14 to the interview with Margaret Crawford.

16. George Bernard Shaw (1856–1950) was an Irish playwright, a socialist and a co-founder of the London School of Economics. He won the Nobel Prize for Literature in 1925, by which time he had written *Arms and the Man* (1894), *Mrs Warren's Profession* (1898), *Man and Superman* (1903), *Major Barbara* (1905), *Pygmalion* (1913), *Heartbreak House* (1919) and *Saint Joan* (1923). Over the course of his life he wrote more than 60 plays. Nearly all of them address prevailing social problems, but include a vein of comedy. Shaw examined education, marriage, religion, government, health care and class privilege. His adaptation of *Pygmalion* for film in 1938 won a Best Screenplay Oscar. The musical adaptation by Alan Jay Lerner and Frederick Loewe, *My Fair Lady*, came in 1956. Most of Shaw's books remain in print – *Pygmalion*, for example, having gone through over 320 editions.

17. John Buchan, 1st Baron Tweedsmuir of Elsfield (1875–1940), was made Governor General of Canada in 1935 and served until his death. He was a diplomat, politician, historian and novelist. After graduating from Oxford in 1900 he worked for two years as private secretary to Lord Milner, 'the seer of Empire', in South Africa. Returning to London, he went into partnership with the Edinburgh publisher, Thomas Nelson (see note 18 to the interview with Alan White). During the First World War, after brief military service, he worked for the British War Propaganda Bureau and also as a correspondent for *The Times*. His best-known book, the spy thriller *The Thirty-Nine Steps,* was published in 1915. The hero, Richard Hannay, based on a friend from South Africa, appeared in five other novels. In 1927 Buchan, by this time a full-time writer, was elected Member of Parliament for the Combined Scottish Universities and served until 1934. His writing career had begun while he was at Oxford, producing five books between 1895 and 1899, including three novels, one of which, *John Burnet of Barns* (1898), was set in the Scottish Borders. Of the novels from this period, *Prester John* (1910), set in Africa, is perhaps the best remembered, having been published in many languages and adopted as a school reader. In office as Governor General of Canada he was well received, travelling extensively, promoting unity and Canadian identity and encouraging the arts. On

his death, the Prime Minister, Mackenzie King, said that Canada had 'lost one of the greatest and most revered of their Governors General, and a friend who, from the day of his arrival in this country, dedicated his life to their service'.

18. Frances Parkinson Keyes (1885–1970) was born in Virginia. Between 1919 and 1968 she was a prolific journalist, editor, memoirist and biographer but is remembered as a best-selling novelist. She wrote about politics, murder, religion, and life in the southern states. *Came a Cavalier* (1947) and *Dinner at Antoine's* (1948) each sold a million copies. At the age of 18 she married Henry Wilder Keyes (which rhymes with 'prize') and the couple lived on his family's estate in New Hampshire. He became the State Senator and later Governor. After his death in 1938 she spent time travelling in Europe and the United States before settling in the French Quarter of New Orleans.

19. Dennis Wheatley (1897–1970) was born in London, the son and grandson of Mayfair wine merchants. From 1908 to 1912 he was a Royal Navy cadet, then spent a year in Germany learning about wine making. At the age of 17 in 1914 he received his commission and later fought at Cambrai, St Quentin and Passchendale. He was invalided out of the Army and entered the family wine business, becoming its owner. In the early 1930s, however, because of the slump, he was forced to sell up. Encouraged by his wife, he wrote a murder mystery which introduced the characters of the Duke de Richleau and his friends who became Wheatley's most popular inventions, but the book was not published. His next book, *The Forbidden Territory* (1933), was reprinted seven times in as many weeks and translated into many languages. There followed at regular intervals a string of thrillers, non-fiction titles, short-story collections, crime dossiers and articles on the occult. During the Second World War he was recruited on to the Joint Planning Staff and worked on top-secret operations. After the War, with the increasing popularity of paperbacks, sales of his books rocketed. In the UK alone, during the 1960s, he sold over one million copies a year.

20. *The Scarlet Pimpernel*, published in 1905, was the first book in a series of historical romances by Baroness Orczy (Emmuska Magdalena Rosalia Maria Josepha Barbara Orczy) (1865–1947). Inspired by Paris and the memories of the French Revolution it brought to her romantic mind, and a clear vision of her hero, Sir Percy Blakeney, she wrote the book in five weeks. At first, it was rejected by the London publishers, but it succeeded in play form. Dismissed as 'old fashioned' by the critics, it became a popular success, playing more than 2,000 performances. In book form, a year later, it too was an immediate success throughout the world, encouraging the author to write many sequels over the next 35 years.

21. Robert the Bruce (1274–1329) was King of Scots from 1306 until his death. He led Scotland during the first of the Wars of Independence against England. During his reign he fought to regain Scotland's place as an independent country. William Wallace (1270–1305) was one of the leaders during the Wars of Scottish Independence. He was appointed Guardian of Scotland and served until his defeat at the Battle of Falkirk in 1298. Seven years later he was captured and handed over to Edward I of England. He was hanged, drawn and quartered for high treason and crimes against English civilians. Statues of Robert the Bruce and William Wallace, sculpted by Alexander Carrick (1882–1966), were built into either side of the Edinburgh Castle Gate in 1929.

22. Field Marshal Douglas Haig, 1st Earl Haig (1861–1928), commanded the British Expeditionary Force (BEF) from 1915 to the end of the War. An equestrian statue of him stood on the northern edge of the Castle Esplanade from 1923 until 2011

when, after being cleaned and repaired, it was relocated inside the Castle walls to the Hospital Square, next to the Scottish National War Museum. It was moved because each year for some weeks it was hidden below temporary scaffolding erected for the Edinburgh Tattoo. The sculptor of the statue was George Edward Wade (1853–1933). It was cast in bronze and weighs 10½ tons. It was gifted to the city by a wealthy Indian merchant, Sir Dhunjibhoy Bomanji.

23. Ensign Charles Ewart's grave was moved to the Edinburgh Castle Esplanade in 1938. Charles Ewart (1769–1846) enlisted in the Royal North Dragoon Guards (the Scots Greys) at the age of 20 and fought in the French Revolutionary Wars, emerging as a sergeant. At the Battle of Waterloo he seized the regimental eagle of the 45th Regiment of the Line in a close fight with a number of Frenchmen. He was hailed a hero and given his commission as an ensign (second lieutenant) in 1816. The Eagle captured by Ewart is on display in the Royal Scots Dragoon Guards Museum in Edinburgh Castle. His name lives also in that of a pub, down from the Castle on the left side.

24. William Burke (1792–1829) and William Hare (1792 or 1804-date of death unknown), 'the Edinburgh bodysnatchers' and murderers, 'scratched' an unknown number of corpses and killed 16 people in 1828, the bodies being supplied to Dr Robert Knox, an anatomist at Edinburgh Medical School, who was cleared of complicity in the murders. Tanner's Close, in the West Port, just south of Edinburgh Castle, was the scene of most of the crimes. Burke was hanged in the Lawnmarket on 28 January 1829 and the following day his body was publicly dissected in the Old College of the University. Hare, who testified against Burke, was granted immunity.

25. The Braid Hills and adjacent Braidburn Valley Park are on the south-west edge of Edinburgh. The Valley Park has been a public park since 1933. The Hermitage of Braids, the grounds of the old Hermitage House, were gifted to the city as a public park in 1937, and are now a local nature reserve. The evidence of glacial activity in the Braids, Braidburn and the nearby Blackford Quarry excited Victorian geologists.

26. Joppa, an eastern suburb of Edinburgh, fronts on to the Firth of Forth. The main attraction is Portobello beach. The Joppa rocks yield fossil shells and plant remains. The rocks and the Joppa quarries were studied by, among other geologists of the period, Hugh Miller (1803–56), who died at Portobello, having committed suicide.

27. Standard Life was founded in Edinburgh in 1825 as The Life Insurance Company of Scotland. This was changed in 1832 to The Standard Life Assurance Company. In 2006 the company demutualised as Standard Life plc, with a London Stock Exchange listing. The head office is in Lothian Road, Edinburgh, and there are offices in many parts of the world.

28. Tynecastle Stadium is situated in the Gorgie area of Edinburgh, on the west side of the city. It is the home ground of the Scottish Premiership football club Heart of Midlothian. The team first played there in 1886. There were changes to the stadium in 1903 and 1906 when the extent of the terracing was increased, giving a capacity of over 60,000. This has now been reduced to 17,500.

29. Piershill lies to the north-east of the city. To the east is Portobello (see note 26 above). Piershill Barracks were built in 1794 and housed various regiments, including the Inniskilling Dragoon Guards and the 17th Lancers. The Barracks were demolished in 1938. The Piershill Danse Hall (*sic*) is listed in the Edinburgh & Leith Post Office Directory of 1961 as being at 18 Piershill from 1934 to 1949.

30. Murrayfield Stadium is 'the home of Scottish Rugby' and of 'Edinburgh Rugby'. It has a seating capacity of 67,141, making it the largest stadium in Scotland and the sixth largest in the UK. It is located in the west end of the city. The first Murrayfield was built in 1925 and could accommodate over 100,000 people. It was completely rebuilt in 1994 at a cost of £50 million. Currently the official name is BT Murrayfield.

31. House: a division in some schools that groups together children of all ages, especially for competitive sports.

32. The Girl Guide movement evolved because girls wished to join the Boy Scout movement, founded by Lord Robert Baden-Powell in 1908. He decided that girls should have their own organisation, and the Girl Guides came into being in the UK in 1910. In the early years his sister, Agnes Baden-Powell, was in charge of Guiding. There are now member organisations in 145 countries and millions of Guides taking part. Two principal themes have been followed from the beginning of the movement: domestic skills and 'a kind of practical feminism which embodies physical fitness, survival skills, camping, citizenship training, and career preparation'. The Brownies, for girls aged from seven to nine years, were organised by Lady Baden-Powell in 1914. In 1918 Lord Baden-Powell's wife, Lady Olave, took over the responsibility for the Guides and the Brownies. The name comes from *The Brownies*, an 'improving' story by Juliana Horatia Ewing, written in 1870. The original name, Rosebuds, was not popular.

33. Thomas Chalmers (1780–1847) was a Presbyterian minister, theologian, author and political economist. On 18 May 1843 he was one of the 121 ministers and 73 elders who withdrew from the General Assembly of the Church of Scotland to walk down the hill from St Andrew's Church in George Street, Edinburgh, to Tanfield Hall in Canonmills, where the first meeting of the Disruption Assembly was held. Chalmers was the first moderator of the Free Church of Scotland. He has been described as 'Scotland's greatest nineteenth-century churchman'.

34. Scottish secondary education awards are described in note 6 to the interview with John Hunter.

35. Dr Henry William Meikle (1880–1958) was Keeper of Manuscripts in the National Library of Scotland from 1927 to 1931 and Librarian from 1931 to 1946. He became Historiographer Royal in 1940. The post was founded in 1681 and now has no formal responsibility or salary. It is held under the Great Seal of Scotland.

36. Professor William Beattie (1903–86) was Keeper of Printed Books at the National Library of Scotland from 1931 to 1953 and Librarian from 1953 to 1970. He was elected President of the Scottish Library Association in 1960. Besides being awarded honorary doctorates from St Andrews University and Trinity College, Dublin, he was created a CBE in 1963. After he retired from the National Library in 1970 he became the first Director of the Institute of Advanced Studies in the Humanities at Edinburgh University.

37. Dr Alan Marchbank joined the National Library of Scotland in 1971 and was Director of Public Services when he retired in 2003/4. He was Margaret Deas's line manager for many years.

38. The Laigh Hall lies beneath Parliament Hall where the single-chambered Scottish Parliament met between 1639 and 1707. The Laigh Hall housed Scotland's records until 1789 when they were moved to Register House.

39. The Advocates Library is the law library of the Faculty of Advocates and contains

a comprehensive range of materials built up over 300 years. It was inaugurated in 1689 and was the national deposit library of Scotland until 1925, when the National Library of Scotland was established. The Faculty gifted to the nation its whole collection of some 750,000 law books and other materials. The Advocates Library retains the copyright privilege for law publications (see note 49 below).

40. The Royal Infirmary of Edinburgh was, from 1879 to 2003, located in Lauriston Place (perhaps a five-minute walk from the National Library on George IV Bridge). It now occupies a greenfield site at Little France, on the south-east fringe of the city.

41. Marryat Ross Dobie CBE (1888–1973) took up a position as an assistant in the National Library of Scotland in 1929 before his appointment as Keeper of Manuscripts in 1931. During both world wars he served as an officer in the Intelligence Corps (see note 13 to the interview with Philip Hancock) but resumed his post as Keeper of Manuscripts in 1944 until becoming Librarian of the National Library in 1946. He continued as such until he retired in 1953.

42. James Spence Ritchie (1916–94) began his career in the Department of Manuscripts in 1947, becoming Keeper from 1972 until he retired in 1981. He built up a special knowledge of the 19th century manuscript collections, one of the Library's great strengths. There were Scott and Carlyle materials of great importance, but it was the archives of the Edinburgh publishing house of Blackwood in which he was particularly interested. The National Library's fine collections of the papers of modern Scottish authors, especially those of Lewis Grassic Gibbon, also owe much to his encouragement.

43. James (Hamish) Robert Seaton OBE (1918–2012) began his career with the National Library of Scotland in 1947 as Assistant Keeper in the Department of Printed Books. He became Deputy Keeper in 1964 and Keeper in 1966, with special responsibility for the catalogue and the introduction of automation. In 1974 he was appointed Principal Keeper of Printed Books, a post he held until he retired in 1983. Promoting greater accessibility to library collections, he supported such initiatives as micro-filming the Library catalogue as the basis for automation, the introduction of the *Bibliography of Scotland* and greater co-operation among research libraries in Scotland.

44. The Newbattle Collection consists of a major portion of the library formed by the Lothian family over three centuries. It was formerly housed at Newbattle Abbey in Midlothian. A number of important items from the library were sold in New York in 1932, but the remainder was bequeathed to the National Library of Scotland by the 11th Marquess of Lothian and acquired in 1950. The collection comprises 5,158 printed volumes and 112 manuscripts and is rich in foreign books of the 15th to the 18th century. The collection includes illustrated books of antiquities, architecture, natural history, geography and topography, as well as maps and atlases. The printed books were retained at the Lothian family home at Monteviot House in the Scottish Borders. The books are periodically inspected by the Library staff to ensure that none are missing and that the environmental and security arrangements are adequate. Further information about Newbattle Abbey is given as note 37 to the interview with Alan White. Information about the Newbattle summer schools is given in note 20 to the interview with Andrew Fraser.

45. Dr Ann Matheson was Keeper of Printed Books at the Library from 1983 until retiring in 2000. In the latter year she became Chairman of the Consortium of European Research Libraries. From 1997 to 2003 she was Chair of the Literature Committee of the Scottish Arts Council.

46. The Pentland Hills extend some 20 miles from south-west of the Edinburgh boundary towards upper Clydesdale. The five highest peaks are between 1,800 and 1,900 feet. At the northern end of the range, accessible by public transport from the centre of the city, there is now a regional park covering 35 square miles and providing 60 miles of marked routes.

47. A political crisis focused on the Suez Canal in 1956 when Egypt's President Nasser nationalised the Canal. Given the strategic interests of Britain and France in the Canal, they sought to overturn Nasser's decision, but they lost their appeal to the International Court. Thereafter, they worked to overthrow Nasser himself. They colluded with Israel to provoke a conflict. Israel invaded Sinai in October 1956, followed by British and French forces in the cities of the Canal Zone. Diplomatic action by the USA and the USSR forced Britain and France to withdraw and Israel to relinquish Sinai.

48. David Alexander Robert Lindsay, 28th Earl of Crawford (11th Earl of Balcarres) (1900–75), became Chairman of the Trustees of the National Library of Scotland in 1944. In 1951 he was made a Knight Grand Cross of the Order of the British Empire for his services to the arts. He was further awarded the Thistle in 1955 for his time as Rector of the University of St Andrews from 1952 to 1955. The title Earl of Crawford is one of the most ancient titles in Britain, having been created for David Lindsay in 1398. The family seat is Balcarres House, Colinsburgh, Fife.

49. It is a legal requirement that a person or group (a publisher or publishing company) must submit copies of their publications to a repository, usually a library. Legal deposit, which has existed in English law since 1662, helps to ensure that the nation's published output is collected systematically, to preserve the material for the use of future generations, and to make it available for readers in the designated legal deposit libraries. The National Library of Scotland is one of six legal deposit libraries in the UK and Ireland. The others are the British Library, the Bodleian at the University of Oxford, Cambridge University Library, the library of Trinity College, Dublin, and the National Library of Wales. For the purposes of the legislation, 'book' includes pamphlets, magazines, newspapers, sheet music and maps. There is now provision for the deposit of non-print works.

50. See note 6 to the interview with Margaret Crawford for information about the Civil Service.

51. The Civil Service Clerical Association was formed in 1921 as a trade union representing civil servants. Although the Association had been required to disaffiliate from the Labour Party and the Trades Union Congress following the 1926 general strike, it rejoined the TUC in 1946. In 1969, the union was renamed as the Civil and Public Services Association (CPSA). As a result of various mergers and departures, since 1998 the CPSA has become the Public and Commercial Services Union.

52. The London agent was the Agency for the Legal Deposit Libraries: the agency that, before 2009, distributed books on behalf of publishers to the legal deposit libraries. The agency outgrew its premises in central London and the National Library of Scotland took over the ownership and management. It operates from premises in Causewayside, Edinburgh.

53. William George Pottinger (c1906–98) was a former civil servant in the Scottish Office. He was imprisoned for corruption in 1974, the sentence being reduced to four years on appeal. On release he became a full-time author. Among his books are *Whisky Sour* (1979), *The Secretaries of State for Scotland, 1926–76: Fifty Years of*

the Scottish Office (1979), *The Afghan Connection* (1983) and *Muirfield and the Honourable Company* (1979).

54. Ian Rankin (1960–), who also writes as Jack Harvey, is best known for his Inspector Rebus novels, set mainly in Edinburgh, ten of which have been adapted for television. The first Rebus novel was published in 1987, the twentieth in 2015.

55. Gordon Brown (1951–) was elected as Rector of the University of Edinburgh in 1972 while still a student. The Lord Rector is elected every three years by students and staff and chairs the University Court and, in the absence of the Chancellor, the General Council. In recent years the role has been described as being akin to that of an ombudsman for the university community, dealing with student and staff issues. The office of rector exists in five Scottish universities: St Andrews, Glasgow, Aberdeen, Edinburgh and Dundee. Gordon Brown was the UK Prime Minister from 2007 to 2010.

56. Robin Cook (1946–2005), an Edinburgh University graduate, was elected to the House of Commons as Member of Parliament for Edinburgh Central in 1974. When the constituency boundaries were revised, he transferred to the new Livingston constituency, which he served from 1983 until his death. He was Foreign Secretary from 1997 to 2001. From the latter year until 2003, when he resigned in protest against the invasion of Iraq, he was Leader of the House of Commons.

57. Sir Jonathan Miller (1934–) is a theatre and opera director, actor, author, TV presenter, humourist and doctor of medicine. In the early 1960s he performed in the comedy review *Beyond the Fringe*, with others who had been members of the Cambridge University Footlights Drama Club (founded in 1833). Miller left the show in 1962 when it moved to Broadway and took over as editor and presenter of the BBC arts programme, *Monitor.*

58. John P Mackintosh (1929–78) was a Labour politician, an advocate of Scottish devolution and a pro-European. He was elected Member of Parliament for Berwick and East Lothian in 1966. He lost his seat in the February 1974 general election but regained it in the October election that year. Later he became Chair and Professor of Politics at the University of Edinburgh. His books include *The Devolution of Power* (1966) and *The British Cabinet* (1968).

59. Lord Cooper, 1st Baron Cooper of Culross (1892–1955), was a politician, judge and historian. From 1935 to 1941 he was Conservative Member of Parliament for Edinburgh West. He was appointed Solicitor General for Scotland in 1935. He later became Lord Justice General and, in 1947, Lord President of the Court of Session. He resigned in 1954 and was created a peer. He died after his peerage was created and the barony became extinct.

60. Professor Denis Roberts (1927–90) taught in the Department of Modern History at Queen's University Belfast prior to being engaged in 1955 as an Assistant Keeper in the Department of Manuscripts in the National Library of Scotland. The post was created, along with others, in anticipation of the opening in 1956 of the Library's new building on George IV Bridge. For the next 11 years he was involved with important acquisitions, such as that of the Iona Psalter, and with exhibitions, one of which was the Dead Sea Scrolls in 1966. In that year he was promoted to be Secretary of the Library. In the following year he took up the post of Librarian of Trinity College Dublin. He returned to the National Library of Scotland in 1970 when he succeeded Professor William Beattie (see note 36 above) as Librarian. Professor Roberts was in the post until his death 20 years later. In those two decades he oversaw

the continued expansion of the Library's services and the delivery of them. Significant developments included the absorption of the Scottish Central Library in 1974, the building up of the Scottish Union Catalogue and the organisation of inter-library lending (see note 62 below). Lack of space was inhibiting planned developments – for example, the public online catalogue, the creation of the Scottish Science Library and the Business Information Service – and it was not until 1989 that Phase 1 of the Causewayside building was opened, making it possible to provide these and other services. It was fitting that shortly before Professor Roberts died he heard that the government had agreed to fund Phase 2 of the Causewayside development.

61. The Library of Trinity College, Dublin, was established in 1592, at the same time as the College. Like the National Library of Scotland it is a legal deposit library (see note 49 above).

62. The Inter Library Lending (ILL) scheme allows a library, on behalf of its members, to borrow books from other libraries, or be supplied with a copy of articles and other print materials which it is unable to supply from its own holdings. The scheme operates both nationally and internationally, but does not extend to works of fiction. The ILL scheme originated in Scotland with the establishment in 1921 of the Central Library for Students, later renamed the Scottish Central Library. In 1974 the services provided by the Scottish Central Library were taken over by the National Library of Scotland and financed from government funds. This opened up new areas of co-operation among all types of libraries in Scotland. For further information about the Scottish Central Library, see note 30 to the interview with Dorothy Milne, and Isabella McKinlay's description of her work as editor with the Scottish Central Library.

Margaret Crawford, pp 159–173

1. Carrick Knowe is a suburb on the west side of Edinburgh, some 3 miles from the centre of the city. It was mainly built in 1936 by Mactaggart & Mickel (see note 2 below) as a private for-rent housing estate. The properties are four-in-a-block flatted villas most of which are now privately owned.

2. Mactaggart & Mickel Ltd, housebuilders, was founded in 1925 as a Scottish company. During the past 90 years it has built houses in several parts of the UK. Celebrating its longevity in 2015, it claimed that the firm had 'maintained quality in design, construction and "crafting" homes'.

3. A surge in the number of pupils entering primary education, increasing the normal intake, will necessitate the setting up of two reception classes.

4. The significance of the Qualifying Exam is described in note 2 to the interview with John Hunter.

5. Information about James Gillespie's High School can be found in note 9 to the interview with Margaret Deas. Information about George Heriot's School is given in note 16 to the interview with Philip D Hancock. Information about George Watson's College is given as note 4 to the interview with Alan White.

6. Her Majesty's Civil Service is the permanent bureaucracy or secretariat of Crown employees supporting the Government, which is composed of a cabinet of ministers chosen by the Prime Minister of the United Kingdom of Great Britain and Northern Ireland, as well as two of the three devolved administrations: the Scottish Government and the Welsh Assembly, but not the Northern Ireland Executive.

7. The Regent Road Institute was handily situated near one of the main places of Civil Service employment, St Andrew's House (building completed in 1939), which initially housed the Scottish Office. Since 1999 St Andrew's House has accommodated part of the Scottish Government. Some 1,400 civil servants work there.

8. PE, physical education, is also known as PT, physical training. Currently, in Scotland, there is a government-supported weekly entitlement of a minimum of two hours of quality PE in primary schools and two periods (50 minutes) in secondary school years S1 to S4. In fifth and sixth years, PE is voluntary.

9. In the Scottish education system, 'Highers' (Higher Grade) are the national school-leaving exams and the university entrance qualifications of the Scottish Qualifications Authority. See note 6 to the interview with John Hunter for further information.

10. Under the Scottish Leaving Certificate, the lower level of assessment was originally intended to suit the General Medical Council entrance requirements, but only as an accompaniment to Highers. This was later revised to suit the requirements of banking, insurance and business.

11. The *Daily Express*, a national middle-market newspaper, was founded in 1900 by Sir Arthur Pearson, who sold it to Lord Beaverbrook in 1916. It was in broadsheet format until 1977, when it became a tabloid. The present owner is the publisher Richard Desmond.

12. The *Edinburgh Evening News,* first published in 1873, is printed daily, except on Sundays. It covers matters that are relevant to readers in Edinburgh and the Lothians. The present owners, Johnston Press, also own *The Scotsman* about which further information may be found as note 44 to the interview with Philip D Hancock.

13. The *Sunday Express* is the sister paper of the *Daily Express* (see note 11 above).

14. *The Sunday Post* is a weekly newspaper published in Dundee by D C Thomson & Co Ltd. It was founded in 1814 and circulates widely in Scotland, Northern Ireland, parts of Northern England and copies can be found much further afield. It is claimed that at one time it had three to five million readers. The paper has described itself as 'A thoroughly decent read'. (See also notes 15 and 16 below.)

15. *Oor Wullie* is a cartoon strip published in *The Sunday Post* since 1936. Wullie (Willie) seems to be about eight to 11 years old, has spiky hair, wears dungarees and uses an upturned bucket as a seat. With his pals he roams the streets of the town where he lives (Auchenshoogle, so it has been learned; also see below), getting up to mischief. The cartoon strip was drawn by Dudley D Watkins from the outset until his death in 1969. Since then it has been the work of several artists.

16. *The Broons* (Browns), like *Oor Wullie,* appear in *The Sunday Post* and again the cartoon strip was first drawn by Dudley D Watkins, beginning in 1936, with R D Low as the writer/editor. The strip features the couthy goings-on in the Broon family, who live in a tenement flat in Glebe Street in Auchenshoogle, a Scottish industrial town, perhaps modelled on a district of Glasgow or Dundee. There is a biennial *Broons* Christmas annual, alternating with the *Oor Wullie* annual.

17. The Band of Hope was founded in 1847 by a Baptist minister, the Reverend Jabez Tunnicliff, who was moved to do so following the death of a young man whose life was cut short by alcohol. Its objective was to teach children the principles of sobriety and teetotalism. Within eight years the Band of Hope was a national organisation, holding meetings in churches throughout the country. Millions of people signed the pledge to abstain from alcohol. The movement was at its height in the 1930s, with

three million members. Twenty years later, submitting to changing society, the support had dwindled. It functions today as Hope UK, remaining concerned about children's welfare and promoting alcohol and drug awareness.

18. *The Pilgrim's Progress* by John Bunyan (1628–88) was published in 1678. He began the work while in the Bedfordshire county prison for holding religious services outside the auspices of the Church of England. The book centres on the tortuous journey of Christian from his home in the City of Destruction ('this world') to the Celestial City ('that which is to come' – Heaven). *The Pilgrim's Progress* is regarded as one of the most significant works of religious literature. It has been translated into more than 200 languages and has never been out of print.

19. Information about the Girl Guides and the Brownies is given in note 32 to the interview with Margaret Deas.

20. Note 17 to the interview with M W (Bill) Paton describes children's street games, and further information can be found in *Golden City: Scottish Children's Games and Songs* by the late James T R Richie (Mercat Press, Edinburgh, 1999).

21. The Royal Burgh of Burntisland (population about 4,000) is in Fife and situated on the north shore of the Firth of Forth. It has a history of herring fishing, shipbuilding, oil shale processing, alumina refining and offshore oil and gas fabrication. The town is well known to generations of day trippers, among the attractions being the summer fairground and the Highland Games – the second oldest in the world, starting in 1652.

22. Kirn is a village in Argyll on the west shore of the Firth of Clyde. It lies between Dunoon and Hunters Quay, facing Gourock on the opposite shore.

23. Leven (population about 9,000) is in Fife and situated on the north shore of the Firth of Forth. For visitors the main attractions in the area are the extensive sandy beaches, the woodland parks and the many golf courses.

24. Stonehaven (population about 12,000) is in Aberdeenshire, 15 miles south of Aberdeen, built round a sheltered bay. It has grown rapidly with the oil boom. In the 19th century it was an important centre in the herring trade. At one time there was a peak catch of about 15 million fish per annum and more than 1,200 people were employed in the fishing industry. For visitors there is the Olympic-size swimming pool. When Margaret Crawford visited the town, probably in the 1950s, there was an open-air swimming pool, on the edge of the North Sea and, in the evenings, dances in the town hall. Today, the visitor numbers have increased as a result of the town's proximity to Dunnottar Castle (see note 25 below).

25. Dunnottar Castle, which is a scheduled monument, can be approached from Stonehaven harbour using the coastal path, or the A92 road. The castle stands on a precipitous, rocky headland – an area of 1.4 hectares – joined to the mainland by a narrow strip of land. The site was fortified in the Early Middle Ages and the remaining buildings, all of which are listed, are largely of the 15th and 16th centuries. Dunnottar is best known as the place where the Honours of Scotland, the crown jewels, were hidden from Cromwell in the 17th century. The castle is in private ownership and was restored in the 20th century.

26. The National Hospital Service Reserve (NHSR) was a civil defence organisation set up under the 1948 Civil Defence Act. It was staffed by uniformed volunteers who received training in first aid and auxiliary nursing. Local authorities were responsible for their administration. The NHSR was stood down in 1968 and disbanded along with other civil defence organisations.

27. The International Red Cross and Red Crescent Movement started in 1863, inspired by a Swiss businessman, Henry Dunant. The British Red Cross began three years later. During the First World War there were 90,000 Red Cross volunteers. In 1919 the League of Red Cross Societies was formed and extended the role of national societies to work in times of peace. When war was declared in September 1939, the British Red Cross and the Order of St John formed the Joint War Organisation. Since 1945 the role of the British Red Cross has been to help people in crisis, whoever and wherever they are. It helps vulnerable people in the UK and abroad to prepare for, withstand and recover from emergencies in their own communities. It is part of a global voluntary network, responding to conflicts, natural disasters and individual emergencies.

28. The nursing home next to Edinburgh Zoo in Corstorphine Road is now a privately run hospital.

29. Leith Links is the principal open space in Leith, the docks area of Edinburgh. The park extends to 18.5 hectares and is used for many forms of recreation, including bowls, cricket, petanque and tennis. It appears in the annals of golf: both Charles I and the future James IV were said to have played on the Links and records show that for many years up to 1824 there was a five-hole course. The rules of golf developed in Leith were adopted by the Royal and Ancient Company of Golfers in 1777. The Links were formalised as a public park in 1888 and golf was discouraged. In 1905 it was banned.

30. The firm of Crawfords was founded in 1899 and went on to become a Scottish institution with its chain of bakers' shops and tearooms the length and breadth of the country. It closed down in 1996. Currently, a firm of bakers operates in Edinburgh under the name of D S Crawford Ltd, the original designation of the company.

31. Labour Exchanges were introduced in 1909 to address the chaos of the labour market and the problems of casual employment. From 1917 they came under the new Ministry of Labour and were renamed Employment Exchanges (presumably the old name had long currency as far as the public was concerned). 'Jobcentre' was the branding from the mid-1970s to 1994, followed by 'Employment Service Jobcentre' until 2002, when the 'Jobcentre Plus' arrived.

32. Moray House School of Education is a school within the College of Humanities and Social Science at the University of Edinburgh. It operates from the Holyrood Campus. It has existed in one form or another since the mid-19th century. Currently it offers programmes of teacher training, Community Education, Digital Education, Physical Education and Sports Science.

33. The Scottish Union & National Insurance Company began business in Leith as the Scottish Union Insurance Company in 1825, offering 'insurances on property against loss by fire, with power to embrace insurance in lives and survivorship if it shall be so determined'. In 1877 it merged with the Scottish National Insurance Company and combined the two names in the title. Its offices were at 35 St Andrew Square, formerly known as the Douglas Hotel. In 1959 the company was acquired by the Norwich Union Fire Insurance Company. In 2002 it changed its name to the Union Insurance Company and went into liquidation in 2008.

34. The Assembly Rooms, George Street, Edinburgh, opened on 11 January 1787 for the Caledonian Hunt Ball. It is now used for public events, including the Edinburgh Festival Fringe and the Hogmanay celebrations. Four rooms are available for private functions. On the ground floor at the rear of the building there is a restaurant.

35. Brown Owl is the leader of a pack of Brownies. (Information about the Girl Guides and the Brownies is given in note 32 to the interview with Margaret Deas.)

36. A Ranger is a senior Girl Guide, usually between the ages 14 and 25. The role was introduced into Guiding by Olave Baden-Powell, then the Chief Guide, in 1920.

37. The Women's League of Health & Beauty was founded in 1930 by Mary Bagot Stack (1883–1935). Its 'health training' classes included elements from dance, callisthenics and exercise to music. Combining hard work and fun, the League attracted large numbers of women. Its activities were necessarily restricted during the Second World War, however, and with the return of peace its earlier success was not repeated. In 1999 it changed its name to the Fitness League and became a joint founder of the Exercise, Movement and Dance Partnership in 2006.

38. In the 1950s many of the firms with offices in central Edinburgh allowed their staff an extended 'lunch hour', sometimes an hour and a half. A contemporary of Margaret Crawford who worked in George Street was told that it was for the benefit of those who lived at the extremities of the tram system (old style). It gave them time to travel home, enjoy an unhurried lunch and return to work.

39. Hurlford is a village in East Ayrshire, on the A71 road, a short distance east of Kilmarnock. In the 19th century, coal, fireclay and ironstone were worked extensively until production ceased in the 1970s. Today, the activities are brake pad manufacturing and whisky production.

40. This refers to the daily issue: ie, the number of books and other items issued for loan that day. Using the Browne issue system, when an item is borrowed the member of library staff stamps the return date on the date label (in a book this is usually on the first right-hand page facing the board of the book) and inserts the ticket from the item into one of the reader's cards – this constitutes a 'charge'. Charges are filed together and are usually arranged in trays by return date and within date by a system allowing easy retrieval: by author's surname for fiction items or classification number for non-fiction, or by a unique number, eg, accession number, these details being shown on the ticket from the item. When the item is returned, the reader's card is removed from the file of the day indicated by the stamp and given back, and the book card is replaced in the item. The total number of items on loan at any time is referred to as the library issue.

41. Information about Mills & Boon novels is to be found in note 16 to the interview with John Hunter.

42. See note 31 to the interview with Andrew Fraser regarding Scottish local government reorganisation in 1975.

43. Kilmarnock and Loudoun was one of 19 local government districts in the Strathclyde Region from 1975 to 1996. The district was formed by the Local Government (Scotland) Act 1973 from part of the county of Ayrshire and abolished by the Local Government etc (Scotland) Act 1994. The name Kilmarnock and Loudoun continues to be used for constituencies of the House of Commons and of the Scottish Parliament. (See also the interview with John Preston.)

44. Note 23 to the interview with John Preston gives information about the Dick Institute.

45. Book rotation involves moving stock from one library location to another within the authority. Often this is done according to an agreed timetable as well as to the size of each branch library, local interests and other relevant factors. This allows stock in individual libraries to be refreshed from time to time and is especially important in smaller branches. It also allows the physical condition of stock to be monitored and cleaning and repairs to be carried out. Stock rotation procedures are greatly facilitated

by the ability of automated library systems to identify stock to be relocated and to update catalogue information.

46. Prior to the introduction of automated library systems, a request for an item had to be formally submitted by completing a form, often a postcard, with as many bibliographic details as possible – author, title, ISBN, publisher, etc. When the item became available, library staff might either phone the reader or post the card advising that it should be collected by a certain date.

47. In the event of failure of the on-line automated library system, an off-line backup procedure would allow the library to continue to issue and discharge stock items.

48. It is common practice for overdue reminders to be issued to borrowers when items on loan are retained beyond their return date. Traditionally much staff time was spent in manually preparing these reminders although automated library management systems and electronic communications have replaced or at least simplified these procedures. Usually the wording of reminders becomes sterner the longer items remain overdue and borrowing entitlements may be suspended. Ultimately, recourse to legal action might be threatened but is seldom implemented.

49. The *Ghostbusters* franchise began in the United States in 1988, publishing comics and comic books. Since then there has been a plethora of films, DVDs, electronic games and toys, etc.

50. Reader development schemes and initiatives in public libraries aim to promote reading, learning, literacy skills and library use among both adults and children. These take various forms including book groups, author visits, summer reading schemes for children and reading activities for pre-school children. The library authority may work in partnership with other local and national agencies, including, for example, The Reading Agency, in delivering reading-oriented activities. Staff training is recognised as a key factor in the success of such initiatives.

51. As more books, information resources and government services are delivered online, public libraries have developed their traditional purpose and services and have taken on the role of helping to bridge the digital divide, providing access to the Internet and public computers for those who otherwise would not be able to use these facilities. This development was realised by the launch in 2000 of what was entitled the People's Network, using monies from the UK National Lottery. Administered through the New Opportunities Fund, this significant investment across all public library authorities in the UK delivered a programme which integrated broadband connectivity with the provision of computer equipment and software, staff training and the digitisation of learning materials. The introduction of the People's Network transformed the public library service in this country. See also the interview with Gavin Drummond.

52. IT is the standard abbreviation for information technology, the study or use of systems (especially computers and telecommunications) for storing, retrieving, manipulating and sending information.

Alan White, pp 175–198

1. The Elsie Inglis Memorial Maternity Hospital opened in 1925 and had 20 beds. It was built on a site at Abbeyhill, backing on to Holyrood Park. It was founded as a memorial to Dr Elsie Maud Inglis (1864–1917) who, in 1894, working with Jessie MacLaren, a fellow student at the Edinburgh School of Medicine for Women, had

opened a maternity hospital for poor women. 'The Hospice', as it was called, occupied a building on the Royal Mile and also housed a midwifery resource centre. Dr Inglis's deep concern about the standard of medical care available to women led to her becoming politically active. From 1906 to 1914 she was honorary secretary of the Scottish Federation of Women's Suffrage Societies. At the beginning of the First World War she was instrumental in setting up the Scottish Women's Hospitals for Foreign Service Committee which was funded by the women's suffrage movement to provide female-staffed relief hospitals for the Allied war effort. The organisation sent teams to France, Serbia and Russia. Elsie Inglis herself went with the teams sent to Serbia by the French government. She worked on improving hygiene in order to reduce typhus and other raging epidemics. In 1915 she was captured and repatriated. Back in Scotland, she raised funds to set up a Scottish Women's Hospital team in Russia. She headed the team when it set off, but after a year was forced to return, suffering from cancer. She died in November 1917. The maternity hospital in Edinburgh that bore her name was closed in 1988.

2. The LMS (London, Midland and Scottish Railway) Coronation Scot express passenger service, running from London to Glasgow, began in 1937. Five Coronation Class locomotives were designed by Sir William Stanier (1876–1965), and built at Crewe. The locomotives were, at the time, the most powerful ever built in Britain, beautifully streamlined and painted Prussian blue with white stripes, and capable of speeds of over 100mph. The purpose-built coaches were soundproofed and air-conditioned. Up to the outbreak of the Second World War there were further refinements of the locomotives and the passenger accommodation. The building of Coronation Class locomotives continued until 1948, but by that time it had been found that the iconic streamlining was of little value at speeds below 90mph. The London, Midland and Scottish Railway company was created in 1923. In 1948, together with the other three railway companies set up at the same time – London and North Eastern Railway, Great Western Railway and Southern Railway – it was nationalised to form British Railways.

3. G & J Maclachlan started their brewing business in Glasgow. Towards the end of the 1890s, when it became too small to cope with demand, the company decided to move to a new site on the east side of Edinburgh. The construction of a building on Duddingston Road was commissioned in 1900 and the brewery – the Castle Brewery – was completed the following year. It closed in 1966 following the takeover of Maclachlan's Ltd in 1960 by J & R Tennent Ltd. The building was demolished and there is now residential property on the site. It is clear that Alan White is mistaken in saying that he travelled as far as Maclachlan's brewery on his tricycle, since Duddingston Road is on the other side of Edinburgh from Slateford. It is more likely that the brewery he arrived at was either Lorimer & Clark's Caledonian Brewery (which still stands), or T & J Bernard's Edinburgh Brewery (which is all but demolished), or McEwan's maltings in Slateford (now converted to housing). (Acknowledgement is made to the Scottish Brewing Archive Association for their assistance in the preparation of the above note.)

4. George Watson's College is a co-educational independent school in the Merchiston area of Edinburgh. It began as a hospital school in 1741 and became a day school in 1871. It is a Merchant Company of Edinburgh school (see note 5 below). The school was established on the instructions of George Watson (1654–1723) who bequeathed the bulk of his estate to found a school for the provision of post-primary

boarding education and commissioned the Merchant Company to implement the terms of his will. The initial roll consisted of 11 boys, aged 9–10 years; by 1870 the pupils numbered 86. In 1868 the Merchant Company applied to Parliament for powers to reorganise their schools so as to make education more widely available. When Watson's reopened in September 1870 the roll was 800 boys. Between 1741 and 1932 the school occupied various sites in the Lauriston Place area where the Royal Infirmary of Edinburgh was, like the school, expanding. It became necessary to build anew and a site adjacent to its playing fields was selected. The new building was opened in September 1932. George Watson's College School for Young Ladies – later, George Watson's Ladies College – came into being in 1871. The two Watson Colleges amalgamated in 1974 with a roll of over 2,400 pupils.

5. The Company of Merchants of the City of Edinburgh, also known as the Merchant Company of Edinburgh, was founded by Royal Charter in 1681 to protect the trading rights of the merchants of Edinburgh. Consistent with its Guild of Merchants origins, it took an interest in the running of the city regarding such matters as taxation, postal services and the water supply. The Company was also involved in educational and charitable work. The receipt of charitable trusts left to the Company to be administered made it possible to operate several 'hospital schools': at that time, charitable schools for the 'puir, faitherless bairns' of Edinburgh. The schools included The Merchant Maiden Hospital (now the Mary Erskine School), George Watson's Hospital (now George Watson's College), Daniel Stewart's Hospital (now part of Stewart's Melville College) and James Gillespie's Hospital and Free School (now James Gillespie's High School the management of which was handed over to the Edinburgh School Board in 1908: see note 9 to the interview with Margaret Deas). By the middle of the 19th century the hospital school system was falling into disrepute. The report of a Royal Commission concluded that the provision of education should be widened and, to make this possible, the rules governing educational trusts were changed. The Company took advantage of this and the hospital schools became mainly day schools (see note 4 above). Today, the Company's schools are operated by the Merchant Company Education Board, a registered Scottish charity.

6. Sir Banister Flight Fletcher (1866–1953) was an English architect and architectural historian, as was his father, also named Banister Fletcher. Together they produced *A History of Architecture* the 6th edition of which, revised in 1921 by the former and his first wife, became the standard text. A centenary 20th edition, edited by Dan Cruickshank, was published in 1996.

7. The Nicolson Institute, in Stornoway, is the largest school in the Western Isles and the only six-year secondary school on the Isle of Lewis. It was founded in 1873 as a result of a bequest by Alexander Morrison Nicolson (1832–65), the fifth child of a family of seven sons whose father was a fish curer. Alexander Nicolson received his early education in the Stornoway Parish School and proceeded to the High School in Glasgow for his secondary education. Thereafter, he served an apprenticeship with J & G Thomson, shipbuilders, Glasgow. He then made his way to the Far East, where he flourished. In due course he acquired a partnership in a foundry and shipbuilding business in Shanghai. In 1865, at the age of 33 he was killed in a boiler explosion in one of his own vessels. He left an estate of £5,672, one third of which was to be donated to 'the most approved charitable institution in my native town for the education and rearing of destitute children in the hope that I may be the indirect means of rendering some assistance to the children of

some of my oldest acquaintances'. The sum of £1,898 was used to build a new school for a boys' institution run by a noted and much respected figure in the town. Thus the Nicolson Institute came into being. The school now occupies extensive, modern premises, built in 2012. The school roll is around 1,000. (The above note is largely compiled from a paper, 'The Nicolson Institute: The First 50 Years', prepared by the Stornoway Historical Society.)

8. The first of the Biggles books, of which there are nearly 100, was published in 1932, the work of William Earl Johns (1893–1968), 'Captain W E Johns'. Biggles, 'James Bigglesworth', born in India in 1899, ace pilot and adventurer, was one of several inventions by Johns, but he is the most enduring. He was a survivor and his ability to fly to the rescue was never dimmed. The reader is told about the young Biggles, his adventures in the First World War, his career as a charter pilot, his Second World War heroics and his post-war work in the Special Air Service. Some of the stories match Johns's own experiences. In the 1960s Biggles went through a sticky patch when the books in which he featured were removed from libraries and children's lists owing to the perception of racial prejudice. Biggles has survived; many of the books are being reprinted, with footnotes explaining slang and military terms. The output of W E Johns was huge; between 1922 and 1968 he penned over 160 books and scores of magazine articles and short stories.

9. Presumably, Alan White read the Blyton books before he read the Biggles books. Many of the former consisted of early readers for boys and girls, while the latter immediately appealed to readers – boys mainly – aged perhaps 10 plus. Enid Blyton (aka Mary Pollock) (1897–1968) was the most successful children's writer of her generation. She completed over 400 books in her lifetime – often at the rate of 50 a year – and the total sales were over 600 million copies. Some 300 of her titles are still in print. She is best remembered for her Noddy, Famous Five and Secret Seven series, from all of which, in the 1940s onwards, there were spin-offs in the form of card games, board games and jigsaw puzzles. Her books were not, however, universally popular. From the 1930s to the 1960s the BBC operated a ban on dramatising them for radio, considering the author to be a 'second-rater' whose work was without merit. There was also criticism of the snobbery in her books and an assumed level of privilege. Some librarians felt that her restricted use of language was prejudicial to an appreciation of more literary qualities. Noddy was once described as an 'unnaturally priggish . . . sanctimonious . . . witless, spiritless, sneaking doll', bursting into tears at any sign of trouble in Toytown. Worst of all, from the mid-1960s to the early 21st century, there were accusations of racism, xenophobia and sexism. Since 2012, world rights in the Enid Blyton estate have been owned by the publisher Hachette UK. The franchise includes the Famous Five series, but not the rights to Noddy, which have been sold to DreamWorks, a film production company. Mindful of the criticisms levelled, some of the titles have been altered to reflect more liberal attitudes towards issues such as race, gender and the treatment of children. In the modern reprints of the Noddy series, for example, teddy bears or goblins have been substituted for golliwogs. At the risk of seeming to be patronising, the language used in the books has been 'subtly' updated, especially in the dialogue rather than the narrative. For example, 'school tunic' becomes 'uniform', 'mother and father' becomes 'Mum and Dad' and 'bathing' is replaced by 'swimming'. The biggest change, however, will be seen in the expansion of the formats in which Enid Blyton's work will appear.

10. Boots Book Lending service was established in 1898 at the instigation of Florence Boot, the wife of Jesse Boot, 1st Baron Trent, the son of John Boot, the founder of The Boots Company. The libraries were set up originally in the small number of shops that had stationery departments, and were stocked with second-hand books. By 1903, when there were 300 Boots shops across the country, 143 had a Booklovers Library. Members could take out a book at any one of the library branches and return it to any other. Membership cost from 10/6 a year for one volume, up to 42/- for six and 7/- for each additional volume. Library catalogues were issued and these stressed the library's reputation for the circulation of clean books and the beautifully fitted libraries. These libraries were placed on the first floor or at the back of the branch, which drew customers through many of the departments of the shop as they made their way. The libraries in Edinburgh and Glasgow were on the first floor. The librarian's job was to know the book stock and advise readers and to make sure that they never left empty handed. In addition to the normal service, there were 'On Demand' subscriptions, holiday and juvenile subscriptions, a postal service, and special arrangements for country members. By 1920 there were 500,000 subscribers and by 1938 books were being exchanged at the rate of 35 million a year. Light romance and whodunits were the most popular. During the Second World War the number of subscribers increased to a million. Boots were buying books at the rate of 1,250,000 a year, giving the company considerable influence in the publishing world – an influence on print runs and also an influence (seen as malign by some critics) on the types of book that publishers of fiction in particular saw as the most marketable. By the 1960s such libraries became less popular owing to the expansion of paperback publishing, the increase in the numbers of television viewers and growing investment in public libraries. In 1965, with only 121 Boots Booklovers Library branches remaining and 140,000 subscribers, the decision was taken to close down the service.

11. Douglas & Foulis, booksellers and librarians, were in business at 9 Castle Street, Edinburgh, having been founded probably in the early to mid-19th century. The National Library of Scotland website refers to a catalogue of Douglas & Foulis's circulating library in which the books added from 1913 to 1917 are listed and gives the subscription prices. The lowest price was 5/- ; for one guinea (21/-) a year, a person could borrow one book a month; ten guineas a year entitled the subscriber to 30 books a year. The business closed in the late 1960s.

12. See note 6 to the interview with John Hunter for information about Highers.

13. Information about the Scottish School of Librarianship is given as note 9 to the interview with John Hunter.

14. The Library of Congress Classification (LCC) is a library classification scheme developed for the Library of Congress. It is used by most research and academic libraries in the United States and in several other countries. Edinburgh Library Service is unusual in having adopted it; in the UK most public libraries and small academic libraries use the Dewey Decimal Classification (DDC) scheme. LCC was invented by Herbert Putnam in 1897 just before he was appointed Librarian of the Library of Congress. It has been criticised for lacking a sound theoretical basis as it was designed specifically for the collection there and is not a classification of knowledge as such.

15. The Dewey Decimal Classification (DDC) is a library classification system created in 1876 by Melvil Dewey, a librarian and founding member of the American Library

Association. Since then it has been revised and expanded through 23 major editions, and has grown from a four-page pamphlet with fewer than 1,000 classes to a four-volume set. It is also available in an abridged version suitable for smaller libraries and in an online version. It is currently maintained by the Online Computer Library Center (OCLC), a non-profit co-operative. DDC introduced the concepts of relative location and relative index which allow new books to be added to a library in their appropriate location based on subject. Libraries previously had given books permanent shelf locations in the order of acquisition rather than topic. The classification's notation makes use of three-digit numbers for main classes, with decimals allowing expansion for further detail. The number makes it possible to find any book and to return it to its proper place on the library shelves. DDC is used in 200,000 libraries in at least 135 countries.

16. Sandy Barker (1931–85) worked in Grangemouth and Edinburgh Public Libraries before being appointed Burgh Librarian of Grangemouth in 1960. He held that post until 1974 when, after a brief spell as Depute District Librarian of Falkirk District Libraries, he became Branch Librarian at Grangemouth.

17. The Stockbridge Colonies, which lie to the west of Edinburgh city centre, were built between 1861 and 1911 by the Edinburgh Co-operative Building Company. The purpose was to provide owner-occupied, low-cost housing for, and organised by, working people. Over a third of the shareholders were stonemasons and other tradesmen. The Stockbridge Colonies consist of cottage-style, two-storey houses (some with basements), each with a front garden, arranged in 11 parallel terraces. Today, because of their unique architectural features and proximity to the city centre, the Royal Botanic Garden and parkland, they are regarded as desirable residences. Elsewhere in Edinburgh there are other colonies, built for similar purposes.

18. Thomas Neilson (1780–1861) began business as a second-hand bookseller in the West Bow, just off the Grassmarket in Edinburgh, in 1798. Twenty years later, by which time he was also publishing inexpensive books and reprints, he changed his name to 'Nelson' because customers were frequently misspelling his original name. His two sons joined the firm in the 1830s and it expanded rapidly. By the time of the founder's death, Thomas Nelson and Sons had become the largest printing and publishing house in Scotland, with offices in Edinburgh, London and New York. The passing of the English and Scottish Education Acts in 1870 and 1872 respectively provided impetus to the publishing of textbooks and readers, which became a major part of the firm's business. The second element, 15 years later, was the publication of its first Bible. By 1900, Thomas's two sons having died, the company was being run by his two grandsons, assisted by a cousin. Three new series of non-copyright pocket books were launched: the New Century Library, Nelson's Sixpenny Classics and Nelson's Classics. John Buchan became a director and literary adviser in 1907 (see note 17 to the interview with Margaret Deas), and in the 22 years that he served, he developed the history – especially war history – and contemporary fiction lists, important adjuncts to the cheap reprints, and the traditional educational and general lists for children and adults, which were to serve the company well until the Second World War. Further offices were opened in Paris, Leipzig and Toronto. There were agents in Australia and South Africa, and the Toronto and New York offices became independent companies. Offices were opened in Lagos and Nairobi. In 1958, the head of the firm, Ian Nelson, one of the founder's grandsons died. (His brother, Thomas III, had been killed in combat in

1917.) By that time, the education list had become all important, and overseas markets for textbooks were being nurtured. But perhaps largely as a result of the expansion of paperback publishing by other companies, the cheap reprints had gone, as had much of the general list. In 1962 Thomas Nelson and Sons Ltd was taken over by the Thomson Organisation. The office was moved to London and the bound stock to Surrey. In 1968, the pride of the company, the magnificent 'baronial-style' Parkside printing and binding works, built in 1907 in the shadow of Arthur's seat, was sold and the site cleared for redevelopment. It is now occupied by an investment company. The American parent company of Thomas Nelson is now HarperCollins, the publishing arm of News Corp, with headquarters in Nashville, Tennessee. The 'publication types' are 'Bibles, books, curriculum and digital content'. There is also a Canadian company, Nelson Education Ltd, describing itself as 'Canada's Learning Advantage'. (The above note has been prepared from a timeline published on the Sapphire.ac.uk website. The site carries much information about Thomas Nelson, including the recollections of people who worked for the company.)

19. For information about the *Edinburgh Evening News*, see note 12 of the interview with Margaret Crawford.

20. The building of prefabs (prefabricated houses) in the United Kingdom was outlined in the Housing (Temporary Accommodation) Act 1944, the purpose being to address the post-Second World War housing shortage. The wartime coalition government decided that 500,000 prefabricated houses, with a lifespan of up to ten years, should be built within five years of the end of the War. A year later, the post-war Labour government agreed to deliver 300,000 units within ten years at a cost of £150 million. The Ministry of Works developed common standards for the construction and wartime production facilities were used. The approved prefab units had to have a minimum floor space of 635 sq ft and a maximum width of 7.5 ft to allow for transportation. The specification allowed for some differences in design and materials, but all designs had to include a 'service unit'. This was a back-to-back kitchen and bathroom, constructed in a factory to an agreed size. The layout meant that water pipes, waste pipes and electrical services were all in the same place and easy to install. There was a coal fire with a back boiler to provide central heating and hot water. The kitchen facilities included a water heater, built-in oven and refrigerator. The prefabs came pre-decorated. The erection time was as low as four hours. Many were constructed on the edges of public parks or green spaces. However, only 156,623 prefabs were completed between 1945 and 1951. Some are still in existence, their habitability improved with insulation and extensions. A few of those that are in their original state have Listed Building status.

21. Charles Sinclair Minto (1905–96) was born in Brighton but spent his youth in Edinburgh where his father, John Minto, was Librarian of the Signet Library. Charles Minto was appointed to Edinburgh Public Library as a junior assistant in 1923 and, like many others recruited at that time, spent his entire career in the city. He became a Fellow of the Library Association in 1931 and held a number of key posts during the rapid development of the service, notably in cataloguing and classification, the Reference Library and in the newly-created Fine Art Library. He was appointed Depute Librarian in 1942, Principal Librarian in 1953 and City Librarian and Curator in 1954. Post-war austerity and financial constraints meant that it was only during the late 1950s that further service developments could be introduced. These included the creation of the Central Fiction Library, the

rehousing of the Local Collection and the Scottish Library and the introduction of a housebound service. During many years of service on the Council of the Scottish Library Association he organised a number of the early post-war summer schools and served as President in 1957 and 1958.

22. Tulliallan Castle, near Kincardine, in Fife, built in 1818–20 for George Elphinstone, 1st Viscount Keith, has been the home of the Police Scotland College since 1954. It is the only central police college in the United Kingdom. On the creation of the unified Police Scotland in 2013 it also became the force's corporate headquarters, apparently on a temporary basis.

23. Ernest Albert Savage (1877–1966) was Principal Librarian of Edinburgh Public Libraries from 1922 to 1942 during which time he transformed the service in almost every aspect, introducing direct public access to books, adopting the Library of Congress Classification (see note 14 above) and establishing special subject departments. Savage was President of the Scottish Library Association from 1929 to 1931, President of the Library Association in 1936 and President of the Edinburgh Bibliographical Society. He wrote extensively on libraries and library science and had a career-long concern with the training and professional status of librarians. He received an honorary LLD from Edinburgh University in 1944.

24. Marie A Balfour joined the staff of Edinburgh Public Libraries in 1924. When the new Department of Economics and Commerce was established in 1932 she became its first Librarian and then in 1942, after a period as Librarian at Morningside, she took charge of the Edinburgh Room. During her long tenure there Miss Balfour developed a service which proved of great value to historians of her native city. She died in 1955.

25. Irvine Welsh was born in Leith in 1958 (and for a time lived in a prefab in West Pilton, Edinburgh: see note 20 above). He left school at the age of 16 and completed a City and Guilds course in electrical engineering and had a series of jobs before moving to London where, in 1978, he joined the punk scene and fell foul of the law. In the late 1980s he worked for Hackney Borough Council and studied computing. Returning to Edinburgh, he worked in the housing department of the city council. (There is no mention of his working as a library assistant, but apparently it was of short duration. On his website he says 'the jobs are a bit too boring to recount'.) He then studied for an MBA at Heriot-Watt University. Energised by the rave scene in Edinburgh, and drawing on experiences of a life of addiction, boredom and brutality lived in the seamier parts of the city by a group of characters, he began to write, producing a draft of the novel that became *Trainspotting*. Parts of the manuscript were published as pamphlets and in magazines including *Rebel Inc.*, the Scots counter-culture magazine. It was read by the editorial director of Secker & Warburg, who decided to publish *Trainspotting*, despite thinking it was unlikely to sell. It came out in 1993, dividing the critical establishment, receiving as many good reviews as ones 'swathed in disgust and outrage – establishing a tradition that continues to this day'. The book became a best-seller and Irvine Welsh shot to fame and gave up his day job. In 1994 there was a stage adaptation of the book and two years later a film version, which was a world-wide success. He has remained a controversial figure whose novels, novellas, short story collections and stage and screen plays have proved difficult to assimilate but have nevertheless been a commercial success. *Trainspotting* has sold nearly one million copies, and other titles, notably *Ecstasy* and *Filth*, have gone to the top of the best-seller list on publication. Currently (2016), there are 11 Irvine Welsh novels and four short story collections in print.

26. Information about NALGO is given in note 15 to the interview with Andrew Fraser. The National Union of Public Employees (NUPE) was a British trade union founded in 1908 as the National Union of Corporation Workers. It became NUPE in 1925 and grew rapidly in membership especially among 'blue collar' public sector workers. In 1993 NUPE merged with NALGO (the National and Local Government Officers Association) and COHSE (the Confederation of Health Service Employees) to form UNISON.

27. Professional qualifications awarded by the Library Association are described by Professor Reid in his Foreword.

28. For information about the Advocates Library, see note 39 to the interview with Margaret Deas.

29. The Signet Library is located in Parliament Square, adjacent to Scotland's Supreme Courts. It is the library of the Society of Writers to Her Majesty's Signet, founded in 1594. The full title is abbreviated to WS Society, whose members are entitled to put the letters 'WS' after their names. The shell of the Library, regarded as one of the finest buildings in Georgian Edinburgh, was built in 1809–12 but is overshadowed by the splendour of the colonnaded interior which has become, in recent years, a venue for weddings, corporate events and conferences. Away from the public rooms, the Signet Library offers members an outstanding collection of legal books, journals, legislation, case reports and databases.

30. See note 23.

31. James Gordon Herbert Ollé, *Ernest A Savage, Librarian Extraordinary* (The Library Association, London, 1977).

32. Robert Butchart (1888–1964) held senior library posts in Arbroath, Lanark and England. He was a district librarian in Glasgow and was appointed County Librarian of Midlothian in 1927. In 1930 he moved to Edinburgh Public Libraries and became City Librarian in 1942, a position he held until his retiral in 1953. He served on the Council of the Scottish Library Association for 30 years, becoming President during 1942–43. He was awarded an honorary degree of MA by Edinburgh University in 1955.

33. James Watson Cockburn (1908–80), joined the staff of Edinburgh Public Libraries in 1926. After work in several departments of the Central Library he was appointed Librarian-in-Charge of a branch library. Following war service he was promoted to the newly-created post of Superintendent of Branch Libraries. In 1953 he was appointed Deputy City Librarian, a post which he held for 17 years before his elevation to the position of City Librarian and Curator. For many years Cockburn served on the Council and committees of the Scottish Library Association and became President in 1968.

34. J Alan Howe became City of Edinburgh Librarian in 1973 after service as Borough Librarian of Luton. His term of office in the capital saw further expansion of the Library Service with the opening of Gilmerton and Craigmillar libraries in 1974 and Newington (with Edinburgh's first audio library) in 1975. In that latter year the Plessey automated library issue system was introduced. Following local government reorganisation in 1975, Howe moved from Libraries to become Head of Cultural Services in the city.

35. Herbert Coutts held senior local government cultural posts for more than 40 years. As Edinburgh's City Curator he oversaw, among many other things, the establishment and subsequent extension of the City Art Centre, the extension of the

Museum of Childhood and the restoration of the Scott Monument. In the final period of his career, he directed the city's Culture and Leisure Department. His achievements in the arts field included the establishment of Edinburgh's Cultural Partnership, the renovation of the Usher Hall (see note 14 of the interview with Margaret Deas) and the development of Makars' Court (Scotland's Poets' Corner), in the courtyard next to the Scottish Writers' Museum, at the top of the Mound.

36. Jack Kane (1911–99) became Edinburgh's first Labour Lord Provost in 1972 having been elected as a councillor in 1938. He represented Liberton first and then, after six years of service in the Royal Artillery, Craigmillar, one of the poorest areas in the city. It was said that 'he was not a man to give up easily . . . . A steadfast fighter, he would put his group's case with determination and conviction'. In 1974, when his time as Lord Provost was coming to an end, he refused the offer of a knighthood, although the award was regarded as automatic for the Lord Provosts of Edinburgh and Glasgow. He said that he thought the honour would separate him from the kind of people he tried to represent, adding: 'I did not come into local government looking for anything like this.' From 1936 to 1955, Jack Kane was the librarian of the P M Dott Memorial Socialist Library, which was opened by Harold Laski (see note 14 of the interview with Joe Fisher) at 8 Grosvenor Crescent. It was set up as a private limited company with Dr Eric Dott, the younger son of the late Peter McOmish Dott (1856–1934), art dealer and critic, proprietor of Aitken Dott, art dealers in Edinburgh (now the Scottish Gallery), as director. Jack Kane was supported by a group of volunteers and an advisory committee for advice on book selection. After nine months it had 1,000 members and had made 8,000 issues. It moved to premises at 9 George IV Bridge, next to the Edinburgh Central Library (see note 43 below). It advertised a stock of 3,000 books on socialism, fascism, peace, war, Spain, China, Czechoslovakia, the Soviet Union, and 'hundreds of left novels and plays', which could be borrowed for 2d a book. The opening hours were 3pm to 10pm daily. There was space in the building for lectures. The Library and its programme of events attracted activists from all sections of the movement, and remained in business throughout the War, although Jack Kane had been called up for military service. In 1947, after he had returned to his post and the building having been acquired by the Central Library, the Dott Memorial Library moved to 138 Dalry Road. It was opened this time by John Wheatley MP, the Lord Advocate. Within a few years, however, it closed and the stock was disposed of. From 1955 to 1978 Jack Kane was the South East Scotland district secretary of the Workers' Educational Association.

37. Information about the Newbattle summer schools is given in note 20 to the interview with Andrew Fraser. Newbattle Abbey in Midlothian was a Cistercian monastery founded in 1140 by monks from Melrose Abbey. The patron was King David I of Scotland. The Abbey soon became prosperous and at one time the community numbered 80 monks and 70 lay brothers. It suffered, however, from English incursions in the 14th century and by the time of the Reformation few of the monks remained. It became a secular lordship for the last commendator, Mark Kerr (Ker), who converted to Protestantism and retained the land around the Abbey. His son, also Mark, became Lord Newbattle in 1596 and Earl of Lothian in 1606. Part of the Abbey was converted into a house and further work was carried out over the next 250 years. Newbattle Abbey remained the home of the Marquesses of Lothian until it was gifted to the nation in 1937 by the 11th Marquess, to be used

as a college of education. Newbattle Abbey College, founded in 1937 – 'Scotland's Life-Changing College' – provides adults, most of whom have few or no qualifications, with the opportunity to experience high-quality, transformative learning. There is also a Higher National programme and courses have been developed for young people at points of transition. (See also note 44 of the interview with Margaret Deas which refers to the Marquess of Lothian's bequest of the Newbattle Collection to the National Library of Scotland.)

38. The life and career of William B Paton are described in note 29 to the interview with M W (Bill) Paton.

39. Dunn & Wilson, one of the UK's leading bookbinding companies, was established in Edinburgh in 1909. For most of the 20th century, from factories in Falkirk and Huddersfield, it provided services to the country's library suppliers and libraries. For the former, the company's principal function was to strengthen publishers' bindings to increase the books' shelf life; for the latter, it was to repair or rebind well-worn or damaged books and to bind journals, etc. For some years, however, very little rebinding has been commissioned by public libraries. The vast increase in the availability of paperbacks, which are discarded once worn out, is one reason; another is the discarding of titles, especially works of fiction, once their popularity has passed. In response to this, Dunn & Wilson – renamed Riley Dunn & Wilson in 1966 – has perforce moved its focus towards book and paper conservation, periodical binding, heritage digitisation, and the production of craft-bound editions and leather bindings.

40. The Association of Assistant Librarians (AAL), formerly a group of the Library Association, catered for members of a particular status rather than for those engaged in a specialist aspect of librarianship, as in the case of other groups. It was organised in divisions which operated at local level. Originally known as the Library Assistants Association, it was formed in 1895; the name was changed to the AAL in 1922. It was an independent association until 1930 when it became a section of the Library Association. It published its own members' journal, *Assistant Librarian*. Since 1998 it has ceased to operate as a separate group of CILIP.

41. Strangely enough for an organisation dealing so closely with the written word, it was not until 1950 that the Scottish Library Association (SLA) produced an A5-size members' magazine entitled *SLA News: the Official News Sheet of the Scottish Library Association*. Later, and perhaps in recognition of its importance as a forum for professional opinion, the subtitle was changed to *The Official Journal of the Scottish Library Association*. Between 1987 and 2002 an A4 format was adopted and the title changed to *Scottish Libraries: the Journal of the Scottish Library Association*. Since its inception the title flourished under a series of honorary editors, prominent figures in the profession, and it was only from 1992 that a professional editor was appointed. With the renaming of the SLA as CILIPS, the old title was deemed inappropriate and *Information Scotland* was launched as a full-colour publication. With the CILIPS website seen increasingly as the main means of communication with members, *Information Scotland* ceased publication in 2009, to be replaced by a four-page newsletter *IS News: Information Scotland News*. This final print version of a members' newsletter lasted only three years, replaced in turn by electronic newsletters composed and circulated from CILIPS office.

42. George Cunningham was born in Fife in 1931. He was elected to serve as a Labour MP for Islington South West from 1970 to 1974 and after boundary changes that year

he was elected for Islington South and Finsbury. He opposed Scottish devolution and it was at his prompting that the House accepted an amendment to the 1978 Scotland Act that a majority voting 'Yes' in the devolution referendum would have to constitute at least 40 per cent of the Scottish electorate. As expected, the threshold was not achieved. He resigned from the Labour Party in 1981 and defected to the Social Democratic Party in 1982. He lost his seat narrowly at the general election the following year and again in 1987 when he contested the seat.

43. The architect of the Edinburgh Central Library, built in the French Renaissance style, was in fact Sir George Washington Browne (1853–1939). (It is possible that Alan White 'misspoke' the third element of the man's name in the interview or that it was misheard.) Browne established his own independent practice in 1885 and two years later won the competition for the Central Library. He went on to design the Royal Hospital for Sick Children, the Caledonian Hotel, the Edinburgh College of Art and several British Linen Bank branches throughout Scotland. The building of Edinburgh Central Library was funded with £50,000 from Andrew Carnegie who, on 9 July 1887, laid the foundation stone (see Professor Peter Reid's Foreword). In 1890, its first full year of operation, over 400,000 book loans were issued. Today, the Library issues over 500,000 book loans annually. The Central Library, as with all public libraries in Edinburgh, organises its adult collections using the Library of Congress Classification system (see note 14 above).

Gavin Drummond, MBE, pp 199–216

1. At this period farm workers were rarely employed on a permanent basis and often lived quite a nomadic life. They were usually hired on a temporary basis at a feeing market, typically held every six months, in May and November. On accepting the fee, the farm servant would be bound to the farmer for the next six months or a year. He probably wouldn't see much of his fee in hard cash but would be provided with a roof over his head and some basic food and fuel. If he was a married man, he might be lucky enough to be taken on by one of the larger farms that provided accommodation for his family. Otherwise he would have to stay in the bothy with the single men while his family stayed elsewhere, perhaps with the wife's parents.

2. Arthur Kinmond Bell (1868–1942) was born in Perth and followed his father and grandfather into the family business of Arthur Bell & Sons Ltd, whisky distillers. On his father's death he became managing director and continued to expand the business despite the obstacles of the Great Depression and US prohibition. In 1921 Bell's became a limited company and grew further through the takeover of three other distilleries during the 1930s. Later in life, A K Bell saved the Perth linen industry by financially backing the town's one remaining company and re-equipping it for artificial fibre production. Bell is also remembered as a philanthropist, determined to use his wealth for the benefit of his native city. His first major philanthropic project was the building of the Gannochy Housing Estate between 1924 and 1932 to benefit a generation which had experienced the rigours of war and were now looking to better themselves. Many of the original tenancies were granted to Bell's employees. In 1937 he set up the Gannochy Trust, partly to maintain the Gannochy Estate and partly to ensure the continuing improvement of his native city. To the latter end he was active in securing a supply of clean water for Perth and surrounding villages

by establishing sewage treatment works. In March 1938 A K Bell was granted the Freedom of Perth which he described as his greatest honour. In death he was as generous as in life, awarding significant sums to senior employees of the company, to all staff with ten years' experience in the firm and to his gardeners, chauffeurs and servants in his employ for ten years or more. In 1995 Perth's new multi-million-pound library was officially opened as the A K Bell Library in honour of the man who had played such a large part in the city's history and whose legacy has had such a large impact on the city.

3. Soldiers and officers of the Royal Electrical and Mechanical Engineers (REME) are the technicians, mechanics and fabricators who inspect, repair, modify and maintain the equipment that the British Army employs. It was formed in 1942. Today, it is made up of seven Regular, two Training and six Army Reserve battalions.

4. A K Bell's philanthropic works included the provision of inexpensive, well-designed rented accommodation for the artisans of Perth and other deserving people in the area. See note 2 above for further details of Bell and his philanthropic projects.

5. See note 8 to the interview with Alan White for information about Biggles, and his author, Captain W E Johns (1893–1968).

6. See note 9 to the interview with Alan White for information about the children's author, Enid Blyton.

7. The significance of the Qualifying Exam is described in note 2 to the interview with John Hunter.

8. Scottish secondary education system awards are described in note 6 to the interview with John Hunter and in notes 9 and 10 to the interview with Margaret Crawford.

9. The Boy Scouts was founded as a uniformed organisation by Robert Baden-Powell in 1908. He got the idea from his experiences with the British Army in South Africa. In his book *Scouting for Boys* he describes the Scout method of outdoor activities aimed at developing character, citizenship and personal fitness. These include camping, woodcraft, first aid, aquatics, hiking, backpacking and sports. Personal progression is recognised by the award of badges. Scouts are organised into troops under the guidance of one or more Scout Leaders; troops subdivide into patrols of about six Scouts. The movement grew rapidly to become the world's largest youth organisation. Originally, the Scout programme was aimed at 11 to 16 year old boys. In response to demand from younger boys, the Wolf Cub section was started in 1916. This was renamed as the Cub Scouts or Cubs and serves those aged 8 to 10½. This section follows on from the Beaver Scouts for 6 to 8 year olds. Some troops, especially in Europe, have been co-educational since the 1970s, allowing boys and girls to work together. Older Scouts can continue their personal progression through Exploring, Venture or Rover Scouts.

10. William Russell Aitken (1913–98) was born in Calderbank, Lanarkshire, a son of the manse. His first job after University in Edinburgh was in the Scottish Central Library for Students. He was later County Librarian of Clackmannanshire (1946–49), Perth & Kinross (1949–58) and Ayrshire (1958–62). During his time in Perth & Kinross he was involved with the establishment of the Scottish Fiction Reserve and completed his PhD thesis on *The History of the Public Library Movement in Scotland* which was later published by the Scottish Library Association (SLA). In 1962 he joined the staff of the Scottish School of Librarianship which later became part of the University of Strathclyde and where he achieved the title of Reader in Librarianship before retiring in 1978. Aitken was always professionally active and

was President of the SLA in 1965 and became Honorary Vice-President in 1995. He was passionate about the Scots language and Scottish literature. His literary work was considerable: he edited the poems of William Soutar (1961) and, with Michael Grieve, the complete poems of Hugh MacDiarmid (1978). In 1982 he published *Scottish Literature in English and Scots.*

11. The professional training of librarians at the Scottish School of Librarianship is described in note 9 to the interview with John Hunter.

12. Information about the system of National Service may be found in note 6 to the interview with John Preston.

13. The 'Primary Memorandum' (1965) required a primary school curriculum that integrated different subjects – History, Geography, Science, Technology, Health and Expressive Arts. It was pioneered at Jordanhill College of Education in Glasgow, now the University of Strathclyde, and a methodology emerged that was originally called Topic Work, and is now known more widely, and internationally, as Storyline. Its main feature is that it recognises the value of the existing knowledge of the learner, tested with evidence and research and often employing art and craft techniques.

14. The Public Libraries & Museums Act 1964 remains the principal piece of legislation governing public libraries in England and Wales. It makes public library services a statutory duty for local authorities and requires that they provide a comprehensive and efficient library service for all persons in the area that want to make use of it, promote the service and lend books and other printed material free of charge for those who live, work or study in the area.

15. The word 'bing' is defined in note 22 to the interview with Dorothy Milne.

16. An interview with M W (Bill) Paton is included in this volume.

17. Following the passage of the Public Libraries and Museums Act of 1964 (see note 14 above), which applies in England and Wales only, the Scottish Education Department set up a working party to examine the public library service in Scotland and to make recommendations (Scottish Education Department. *Standards for the Public Library Service in Scotland: Report of a Working Party,* 1969). Named after the working party Chairman, the Robertson Report's recommendations followed very closely those contained in the Roberts Report (Ministry of Education. *The Structure of the Public Library Service in England and Wales,* 1959) which formed the basis of the Public Libraries and Museums Act 1964. In Scotland, however, the Robertson Report, while identifying opportunities for service development, did not result in any legal obligation upon authorities to provide an adequate library service. This remained the case until the Local Government (Scotland) Act 1973 required local authorities to secure adequate library facilities for all residents. In more recent times, guidance in interpreting the word 'adequate' was provided by the Confederation of Scottish Local Authorities' *Standards for the Public Library Service in Scotland* and subsequent public library improvement models created by the Scottish Library & Information Council. Such guidance has undoubtedly driven service development. (See also note 32 to the interview with John Preston.)

18. Neil Russell McCorkindale started his career in Greenock Public Library in 1939. After the War, in which he was decorated with the Distinguished Flying Medal, he studied at the Scottish School of Librarianship. After a period as a branch librarian in Greenock he spent three years in Stoke Newington, 17 years as Burgh Librarian of Galashiels, six years as County Librarian in Aberdeenshire and two and a half

years as Chief Librarian of the North East of Scotland Library Service. He was very active in the Scottish Library Association of which he was Secretary during 1961–66 and then President in 1971. He died in 1977.

19. The Meffan Institute, now Meffan Museum & Art Gallery, is in the centre of Forfar and houses a variety of exhibits of local interest in Angus, including a collection of Pictish stones, particularly the Dunnichen Stone and the Kirriemuir Sculptured Stones, as well as Roman and medieval artefacts found in the area. A reconstruction of Forfar street scenes includes representations of daily life as it would have been around the beginning of the 19th century, as well as a depiction of the execution of one of the women accused of witchcraft in the Forfar witch hunts of 1661–66. In addition, a diverse programme of art exhibitions throughout the year brings the work of local, national and internationally renowned artists to Forfar.

20. William Low (popularly referred to as Willie Low's; latterly marketed as Wm Low) was a chain of supermarkets based in Dundee. The company was founded by William Rettie and James Low in 1868 and remained independent until it was bought out by Tesco in 1994. As a group it was smaller than most of its competitors and often served small towns, although it still had several large supermarkets, including two in Dundee and two in Perth. Most towns in the Tayside region had at least one large William Low store and it had branches throughout Scotland, North East England, Cumbria and Yorkshire.

21. The Scottish National Party (SNP) supports and campaigns for Scottish independence. It was founded in 1934 with the merger of the National Party of Scotland and the Scottish Party. Although it had enjoyed electoral success in Angus during the final quarter of the 20th century onwards, for long it trailed the other main political parties in support and representation at a national level. Since then its fortunes have much improved. The SNP came to power in the 2007 elections to the Scottish Parliament as a minority government, before going on to win the 2011 election and forming Scotland's first majority government.

22. 'Douce' is a Scots word mostly applied to places and meaning quiet and sedate.

23. A smokie is a type of smoked haddock. Although a speciality of Arbroath, it is said to have originated in the small fishing village of Auchmithie, 3 miles north-east of the town. In 2004 the European Commission registered the designation 'Arbroath smokies' as a Protected Geographical Indication under the EU's Protected Food Name Scheme, acknowledging its unique status.

24. Giddings & Lewis-Fraser Ltd was one of the main Arbroath engineering firms. Douglas Fraser started the business in Friockheim in 1832 and initially specialised in making equipment for the burgeoning weaving industry. The company soon moved to new premises in nearby Arbroath. Fraser's was a highly successful firm with many engineering innovations to its credit. The firm expanded over the years and became one of the biggest employers in the Arbroath area. It was bought by an American company in the 1950s and given the name Giddings & Lewis-Fraser. Like so much of the town's heavy industry, the Giddings & Lewis-Fraser factory closed during the recession of the 1980s, the entire plant eventually being demolished to make way for a supermarket.

25. Like other parts of Angus, Forfar was home to a very successful textile industry during and after the Industrial Revolution. In the late 18th century the firm of William Don & Co (later William and John Don & Co) was founded in the town. The firm originally bought and sold webs of linen woven in local cottages, and also

operated a small weaving shed. In 1865 the firm merged with a Dundee-based firm to form Don Brothers, Buist & Co Ltd and constructed several works in Forfar which contained 1,000 power looms. Workers' housing was also built by the firm in Forfar. In the 1920s high US tariff duties led to a slump in linen production and the company concentrated its weaving business on jute. After the Second World War the company expanded and diversified partly because in 1948 jute was rationed owing to an acute shortage in Pakistan. In 1960 it merged with another Dundee firm, Low Brothers & Co (Dundee) Ltd, eventually becoming Don & Low (Holdings) Ltd. The firm retains premises in Forfar, mainly producing woven and non-woven polypropylene industrial textile products and plastic food packaging.

26. Information about the Citizens Advice Bureau will be found in note 52 to the interview with Isabella McKinlay.

27. The Library Association (LA) was founded in 1877 as a result of the first International Conference of Librarians and was awarded a Royal Charter in 1898. In 2002 the LA merged with the Institute of Information Scientists, founded in 1958, to form the Chartered Institute of Library and Information Professionals (CILIP), the leading professional body for librarians, information specialists and knowledge managers in the UK, although membership is not compulsory for practice. CILIP's vision is a fair and economically prosperous society underpinned by literacy, access to information and the transfer of knowledge. CILIP accredits degree programmes in library and information science at universities in the UK, including Robert Gordon University and Strathclyde University. The Scottish Library Association was established in 1908 and affiliated with the LA in 1931, retaining its own constitution and separate governance arrangements. As the professional body within the devolved nation, CILIP in Scotland funds its own office in Glasgow, is registered as a Scottish charity and is responsible for all policy, financial and operational matters relating to its internal affairs and for those professional matters solely affecting the operation, development and promotion of library and information services in Scotland.

28. Information about the Scottish Library & Information Council is given in note 24 to the interview with John Hunter.

29. COSLA (the Convention of Scottish Local Authorities) is the national association of Scottish councils and acts as an employers' association for its member authorities. Formed in 1975, COSLA exists to promote and protect the interests of the country's councils by providing a forum for discussion of matters of common concern. COSLA represents and communicates the views of member councils to central government, other bodies and the public. It is the successor to the Convention of Royal Burghs which dated back to the 12th century but was dissolved after local government reorganisation in 1975.

30. Information regarding the People's Network initiative is described in note 51 to the interview with Margaret Crawford.

31. Tony Blair (1953–) was born in Edinburgh and educated at Fettes College there and at St John's College, Oxford. He was elected to parliament as Labour MP for Sedgefield in 1983. In 1994 he succeeded John Smith as Leader of the Labour Party and, following Labour's landslide victory in the general election of 1997, became Prime Minister. The Labour Party under his leadership was returned to government at the general elections of 2001 and 2005 and Blair remained Prime Minister until he resigned in 2007. As part of Blair's modernising agenda, in 2000 monies were made available to introduce the People's Network.

John Preston, pp 217–235

1. Irn-Bru is a carbonated soft drink, produced by A G Barr of Glasgow. It was first produced in 1901, in Falkirk, under the name 'Iron Brew'. In 1946 a change in the law required that the word 'brew' be removed from the name as the drink is not brewed. The chairman of the company came up with the idea of changing the spelling of both halves of the name, thereby inventing the Irn-Bru brand. Innovative and sometimes controversial marketing campaigns have included the slogans, 'Scotland's other national drink' (ie, comparable to whisky), and 'Made in Scotland from girders', a reference to its rusty colour. Such promotion has probably helped keep Irn-Bru as the most popular soft drink in Scotland and it is sold throughout the UK and the rest of the world.

2. Tenement flats were accessed from an entrance passage, or close, and common stair. In grander tenements, especially in Glasgow, these would be lined with decorative, often ornate and colourful tiling on the walls. Such 'wally' closes were considered to indicate higher social standing and their residents were proud of them and cleaned them communally.

3. The *Oxford English Dictionary* defines pipeclay as a 'fine white kind of clay which forms a ductile paste with water'. As well as being used for making tobacco pipes and pottery, it is traditionally used for all sorts of polishing and whitening purposes. Once the common stair and close of a tenement had been washed it was the recognised material for adding the finishing touch.

4. Ranges were to be found in the kitchens of many homes until well into the 20th century. Usually they were in three sections. The main coal fire (the grate) was in the middle with a water boiler on the left and an oven on the right. The water boiler had a tap on the bottom to let the hot water out. People also used to boil water by putting a kettle on top of the fire. The grate was black in colour and made of cast iron. It would be completely cleaned regularly and coated with 'black lead', a form of liquid graphite which came in a small tin, one popular brand being Zebrite or Zebo.

5. The Royal Army Service Corps (RASC) was responsible for land, coastal and lake transport, air despatch, barracks administration, the Army Fire Service, staffing headquarters' units, supply of food, water, fuel and domestic materials such as clothing, furniture and stationery and the supply of technical and military equipment. In 1965 the RASC was merged with the Transportation and Movement Control Service of the Royal Engineers (which was responsible for railway transport, inland water transport, port operations and movements) to form the Royal Corps of Transport (RCT). All its supply functions were transferred to the Royal Army Ordnance Corps (RAOC), leaving the new RCT solely responsible for transport and movements. In 1993 the RCT and RAOC were merged to form the Royal Logistic Corps.

6. National Service was a system of military conscription in the UK from 1939 to 1960. After the Second World War peacetime conscription was formulated by the National Service Act 1948. From 1 January 1949 healthy males between 17 and 21 years old were to serve in the armed forces for 18 months, and remain on the reserve list for four years. Exemption applied to men employed in the 'essential services' of coal mining, farming and the merchant navy for a period of eight years. In 1950, in response to British involvement in the Korean War, the service period was extended to two years. National Service personnel were used in combat operations, including the Malayan Emergency, the Cyprus Emergency, the Mau Mau Uprising

in Kenya, the Korean War and during the Suez Crisis. National Service ended gradually from 1957. In November 1960 the last men entered service, call-ups formally ended on 31 December 1960 and the last National Servicemen left the armed forces in May 1963.

7. Dinky Toys are die-cast miniature vehicles produced by Meccano Ltd – makers of Hornby Trains, which were named after founder Frank Hornby (see notes 9 and 10 to the interview with Philip D Hancock). Dinky Toys were made in England from 1935 to 1979. By the time of the Second World War there were around 200 different products in the Dinky Toys range including die-cast ships, aeroplanes, small trains, cars, trucks, buses and military vehicles. The golden age of Dinky Toys was in the post-war period when they were produced with greater accuracy and detail. Due to the lack of competition, however, development of new models was slow until the appearance of a rival under the Corgi brand name. The most obvious difference was the addition of clear plastic window glazing. Meccano responded by updating the Dinky Toys range and the models from both companies became more sophisticated, featuring such things as suspension, 'fingertip steering', detailed interiors and jewelled headlights. Changing fashions in the toy industry, international competition and cheap labour overseas meant that the days of British-made toy vehicles like Dinky Toys were numbered. The factory in Liverpool where they had been manufactured closed in 1979, although Corgi Toys struggled on until 1983. The Dinky trade name has since changed hands many times and continues to be used.

8. For many years schoolchildren were given a one-third of a pint bottle of milk free of charge each day. This was consumed through a waxed paper straw issued with the milk. In many schools the distribution of the milk and collection of the empties in crates was a task allotted to pupils who gloried in the title of milk monitor. On her appointment as Secretary of State for Education & Science, Margaret Thatcher abolished free milk for schoolchildren aged seven to eleven, provoking a storm of protest and left her dubbed 'Thatcher, Thatcher, Milk Snatcher'. Note 50 to the Interview with Peter Grant further describes the political career of Margaret Thatcher.

9. Scottish secondary education system awards are described in note 6 to the interview with John Hunter.

10. Charles Wilfred Black (1909–78) held posts in Manchester and Fulham before joining the City of Glasgow Library Service in 1938 as Superintendent of District Libraries. He was appointed Depute City Librarian in 1952 and succeeded A B Paterson as City Librarian in 1958. Black has been described as 'an energetic perfectionist with a relentless interest in detail', and it was he who was largely responsible for the post-war development of Glasgow's Library Service following a decade of expenditure restrictions. He opened seven new libraries and completed the modernisation of other pre-war libraries. He retired in 1974 and is best remembered for his work in developing the extension to the Mitchell Library, a project which he did not live to see completed. He was active within professional circles and served as Vice-President of the Scottish Library Association from 1961 to '63, although he declined the nomination of the Presidency. A short time prior to his death Black was ordained as a non-stipendiary priest in the Scottish Episcopal Church. In his interview in this volume Joe Fisher describes Black's management style.

11. The Mitchell Library is one of Europe's largest public libraries and the centre of the public library system of Glasgow. It was established with a bequest from Stephen Mitchell, a wealthy tobacco manufacturer, whose company, Stephen Mitchell & Son,

would become one of the constituent members of the Imperial Tobacco Company. The Library opened originally in temporary premises in Ingram Street before moving to more suitable accommodation in Miller Street. Thereafter, it moved to North Street where the original building with its distinctive copper dome surmounted by a bronze statue by Thomas Clapperton, entitled *Literature* (often referred to as Minerva, the Roman goddess of wisdom), opened in 1911. The Extension Building, built between 1972 and 1980, is located to the west of the original building. It incorporates what were the St Andrew's Halls, designed by James Sellars and opened in 1877. This was Glasgow's pre-eminent venue for concerts and meetings but was gutted by fire in 1962. Its facade survived, however, and was later incorporated into the Extension Building which also houses the Mitchell Theatre. The Mitchell contains a large public reference library with over one million volumes as well as a substantial lending facility. More recently the Library underwent a major internal refurbishment to create a stylish new café bar, a large learning centre offering IT facilities and a business lounge. The building also houses Glasgow City Archives, the official records of the city dating back to the 15th century. See also note 11 to the interview with Joe Fisher.

12. The Glasgow Room was opened in 1959 but its origins go back to the opening of the Mitchell Library when a decision was taken to preserve there all material relating to the history of Glasgow. This unique collection was developed over the years to become a valuable record of the history, life and people of the city. It contains a huge variety of material – books, maps, plans, directories, newspapers, pamphlets, valuation and voters' rolls, photographs and engravings – and is of immense importance to researchers and the local community. See the interview with Joe Fisher for further information about the Glasgow Room.

13. For the maximum surveillance of public areas traditional library design often featured a fan-shaped arrangement of book stacks, radiating from a central point, usually the issue desk or some other staff control point.

14. Ulverscroft Large Print Books Ltd was founded in 1964 by Dr Frederick Thorpe, the first publisher in the world to provide large print books for the visually impaired. The company came into being following concerns expressed by the Women's Institute that its elderly members were not able to read books due to the small font. The main market for Ulverscroft and its sister companies, Magna Large Print and Isis Publishing, is the public library sector world-wide to which it supplies a wide variety of large print titles in hard and soft cover formats as well as abridged and unabridged audio books. Many of its titles are by the world's favourite authors. It has now launched its own digital products, including audio and e-books.

15. The professional training of librarians at the Scottish School of Librarianship is described in note 9 to the interview with John Hunter.

16. Professional qualifications awarded by the Library Association are described by Professor Reid in his Foreword and information about the Library Association and the Scottish Library Association is given in note 27 to the interview with Gavin Drummond.

17. Harold I Hunt was born in Middleton, Manchester, around 1915. He began his library career with posts in Middleton and Norwich before seeing active service with the Royal Artillery during the Second World War. On returning from military duty he became Chief Librarian in Rawtenstall, Lancashire, and qualified as a Fellow of the Library Association in 1948. He was appointed Burgh Librarian of

Motherwell and Wishaw in 1956 and thereafter oversaw developments which included an internal refurbishment of Motherwell Library and the extension of lending services to include audio cassettes, charts, slides and prints. By the time of his retiral in 1980 four new branch libraries had been opened under his management and a computerised library management system had been introduced.

18. Note 33 to the interview with Tom Gray describes the photo-charging issue system.

19. Note 40 to the interview with Margaret Crawford describes the Browne issue system.

20. Many of the computerised library management systems were developed during the 1980s, and by the 1990s they comprised a number of modules to deliver library housekeeping functions including acquisitions, cataloguing, membership records, circulation, on-line public access catalogue facilities, etc. Most library management systems are now integrated; data is only held once by the system and then used across all the modules and functions. DS, a British library management system supplier, became a market leader during the 1990s.

21. See note 43 to the interview with Margaret Crawford for information about Kilmarnock and Loudoun District.

22. John F T Thomson began his career as Depute Librarian at Morningside Library in Edinburgh before taking a post with Dearne Urban District in Yorkshire. He was appointed Director of Libraries and Museums with Kilmarnock Town Council in 1958. At local government reorganisation in 1975 he became Manager of Cultural Services with Kilmarnock and Loudoun District Council. He was active within the library profession as a tutor to the Association of Assistant Librarians and a member of the Panel of Assistant Examiners of the Library Association. For many years he was Secretary and Treasurer of the Robert Burns World Federation. He was also an active member of the Burma Star Association and was involved in several local community organisations. He was awarded the MBE in 1976, and died in 1981.

23. The Dick Institute in Kilmarnock was opened in 1901 with funding from James Dick, a native of the town who had emigrated to Australia. It is an important cultural venue, containing the central library of what is now East Ayrshire Council and featuring the largest museum and art gallery space in Ayrshire. Permanent displays of the museum's own collections illustrate the local and social history of the area as well as natural history, the sciences and archaeology. Its gallery programme includes nationally-important exhibitions and work by contemporary artists.

24. Dean Castle is situated in the Dean Castle Country Park in Kilmarnock. It was the stronghold of the Boyd Family, who were lords of Kilmarnock for over 400 years, and has strong connections with many people and events famous in Scottish history: Robert the Bruce who gave the Boyds these lands; King James III whose sister married a Boyd; the Covenanters, some of whom were imprisoned here; Bonnie Prince Charlie, whose rising was joined by the 4th Earl of Kilmarnock and Robert Burns who was encouraged to publish his poetry by the Earl of Glencairn who owned the Castle at that time. Gifted to the people of Kilmarnock by the 9th Lord Howard de Walden in 1975, the Castle and Country Park are open all year round to visitors. The Keep, dating to around 1350, and the Palace or Place, built about 100 years later, house outstanding displays of historic weaponry, armour, musical instruments, medieval tapestries as well as changing exhibitions and events.

25. In the interview with Margaret Crawford she describes her work as a library assistant in Hurlford Library. Note 39 to that interview gives information about Hurlford village.

26. 'Grue' is a Scots word meaning to shudder with fear, horror or revulsion.

27. See note 31 to the interview with Andrew Fraser regarding public library responsibilities following Scottish local government reorganisation in 1975.

28. Early Scottish public library legislation is described in note 18 to the interview with Andrew Fraser.

29. Desmond Donaldson (1918–2011) was born in Perthshire and served as County Librarian there before becoming County Librarian with Moray and Nairn. He held that position for eight years before his appointment in 1968 as Dumfriesshire County Librarian. He became the first Regional Librarian of Dumfries and Galloway in 1974 in anticipation of local government reorganisation the following year. His major professional achievement was successfully bringing together the three county library services of Dumfriesshire, Kirkcudbrightshire and Wigtownshire to form a single library service. He was also responsible for the substantial remodelling of the Ewart Library in Dumfries. His main enthusiasm was local studies and he published four volumes of old photographs of Dumfries and Galloway. He also wrote the introduction and notes to *The Glenriddell Manuscripts of Robert Burns* (E P Publishing Ltd, Wakefield, 1973). He retired in 1978.

30. 'Lad o' pairts' is a term describing a boy from humble origins who demonstrates academic talent and is able to achieve success in spite of his background. The expression is associated with the deeply-rooted conviction which developed during the 19th century that Scottish education is among the best and that the Scots have a love of learning quite out of the usual. This conceit is not always based upon hard evidence.

31. Originally a hamlet 2 miles south-east of Dumfries, Georgetown is now one of the town's numerous suburbs as a result of extensive housing development from the 1960s onwards.

32. *Standards for the Public Library Service in Scotland: Report by a Working Group Appointed by the Arts and Recreation Committee of COSLA* were produced in 1986 to guide public library authorities in identifying appropriate standards of service. The *Standards* were adopted widely by local authorities and achieved their purpose in fostering service development. Although revised in 1995, the *Standards* focused more on inputs than on outcomes and were subsequently replaced by the Public Library Quality Improvement Matrix (PLQIM) developed by the Scottish Library and Information Council and intended to form part of authorities' corporate performance measurement. PLQIM has since been revised as *How Good is our Public Library Service? A Public Library Improvement Model for Scotland*.

John Hunter, pp 237–256

1. The Norse *Hjaltland* (High Land) has been variously rendered as Hetland, Yetland, Zetland and Shetland. The last is now the most usual form although Zetland survived until 1975 in the title of Zetland County Council.

2. Prior to the introduction of a system of comprehensive schools, the traditional pattern of education in Scotland had long been one of selection according to ability. At the end of primary school, each pupil would sit the Qualifying Exam – the dreaded 'Qually' – also known as the 11-plus, and would be assigned to either senior secondary or junior secondary school on the basis of their performance.

3. Information about the Scouts and Cub Scouts is found in note 9 to the interview with Gavin Drummond.

4. Although there are several types of Brethren, the Brethren movement in general emerged as part of the Protestant evangelicalism of the 19th century. Its features are the zealous spirituality of its members and its conservatism in theology. The name 'Brethren' was applied to those within the movement because of their habit of referring to each other as 'brother' or 'sister'. There remain Brethren congregations in various parts of Scotland.

5. The Royal Air Force station, RAF Biggin Hill, is best known for its role during the Battle of Britain in the Second World War when it served as one of the principal fighter bases protecting London and south-east England from attack by Luftwaffe bombers.

6. For many years the Scottish secondary education system awarded the Scottish Certificate of Education at two levels. The now-discontinued Ordinary Grade (commonly known as the O-Grade or O-level) was the predecessor of the Standard Grade qualification. Courses were available in a wide range of subjects and were studied over two years, during the third and fourth years (age 14–15) of a pupil's time at secondary school. A good pass at O-Grade would normally allow a pupil to take the same subject at Higher Grade (commonly known as Highers) in fifth or sixth year. This did not always follow, however, as many pupils left school at the end of their fourth year. Highers are recognised as university entrance qualifications in Scotland.

7. Dame Agatha Mary Clarissa Christie (1890–1976) wrote more than 70 classic crime novels including those featuring such well-known characters as Hercule Poirot, the Belgian private detective, and Miss Jane Marple, an elderly English spinster and amateur sleuth. Her best-known titles include *The Mysterious Affair at Styles*, *The Murder of Roger Ackroyd*, *Murder at the Vicarage*, *Murder on the Orient Express*, *Death on the Nile* and *And Then There Were None*. She is reputed to be the best-selling novelist of all time, and many of her books and short stories have been adapted for television, radio, comics and even video games. More than 30 feature films have been based on her work, and her play, *The Mousetrap*, which opened in London's West End in 1952, is still running after more than 25,000 performances. She also wrote under the pen name of Mary Westmacott.

8. George Watson Longmuir (1911–79), Zetland County Librarian, 1948–76. Longmuir was the first professionally qualified librarian to hold this post. In the pre-oil era, he developed the Zetland Library into a modern service including lending framed art prints and recorded music on vinyl (LPs). In 1966 he supervised the move of the Library into the purpose-built Shetland Library & Museum building and during the 1970s, in response to the establishment of inter-island vehicle ferries, he introduced the first mobile library service. He was also active in gathering manuscripts and collections which led to the creation of Shetland Archives with an archivist appointed in 1976. (See note 1 above for the derivation of 'Zetland'.)

9. The Scottish School of Librarianship was established in 1946 as part of the Glasgow and West of Scotland Commercial College which became the Scottish College of Commerce in 1956. It prepared students for the examinations of the Library Association (LA). The courses consisted of one year's study leading to the Registration Examination and one further year of study for the final examination. These qualified students for, respectively, the Associateship and the Fellowship of the LA after appropriate practical experience had been completed. In 1964 the

Scottish School of Librarianship was established as the Department of Librarianship in the University of Strathclyde which was created by the merger of the Royal College of Science and Technology and the Scottish College of Commerce. As part of this change the courses related to the LA syllabus and examinations were replaced with new degree and postgraduate courses delivered by the Department of Librarianship. The first Head of the Scottish School was William B Paton who left in 1950 to become the County Librarian of Lanarkshire. On his retiral from that post in 1972, he returned to the Department as Visiting Professor. (The life and career of William B Paton are described in note 29 to the interview with M W (Bill) Paton and in the interview with Peter Grant.) At the same time as the establishment of the Department of Librarianship in Strathclyde University, there arose concerns about the direction of professional education in Scotland and about the number of places available for those wishing to study librarianship. As a result, in September 1967 the second School of Librarianship in Scotland was opened at the Schoolhill Campus of Robert Gordon's Institute of Technology in Aberdeen, now Robert Gordon University.

10. Charles B Wood began his career in Lanark County Library Service under W B Paton (see note 29 to the interview with M W (Bill) Paton). Like so many of his Scottish contemporaries, however, Wood could achieve career advancement only by heading to England and so took up the position of Deputy Librarian of Grantham. Returning home at an early opportunity he was appointed Depute County Librarian of Aberdeenshire and then in 1967 secured a post as lecturer when Scotland's second school of librarianship opened at Robert Gordon's Institute of Technology in Aberdeen, now Robert Gordon University (see note 9). Wood later became a Director of Junior Books, a specialist supplier within the Dunn & Wilson Group (see note 39 to the interview with Alan White). He developed services for school libraries and this led to the creation of a separate specialist supplier – Audio Visual Library Services – of which he became managing director. Latterly he became proprietor of his own video business and also formed Schiltron Books to produce 'talking books' on tape of mainly Scottish material, much of which was otherwise unavailable. Before retiring he joined one of Scotland's leading library suppliers, T C Farries, as Bibliographic Services Manager. He died in 2000.

11. Graham W Ewins was one of a number of teaching staff appointed on the opening in September 1967 of Scotland's second school of librarianship at the Schoolhill Campus of Robert Gordon's Institute of Technology in Aberdeen, now Robert Gordon University (see note 9). Prior to his appointment Ewins had been Central Lending Librarian at Gillingham Public Library.

12. Information about the Library Association and the Scottish Library Association is given in note 27 to the interview with Gavin Drummond.

13. Note 47 to the interview with Peter Grant gives a definition of the term 'book fund'.

14. William Leslie (1920–73) was appointed County Librarian of East Lothian in 1960 and has been credited with the 're-birth' of the Library Service there through the introduction of a catalogue of stock, a request service, co-operation with the Scottish Central Library (see note 30 to the interview with Dorothy Milne) and the introduction of a mobile library service to replace library centres in the smaller, rural communities.

15. With the raising of the school leaving age following the Second World War, Britain faced an urgent need for bigger school premises. The short-term response was the

construction of huts with concrete walls, asbestos roofs and metal-framed windows – the Hutting Operation for the Raising of the School-leaving Age, or HORSA for short.

16. Founded in 1908 by Gerald Rusgrove Mills and Charles Boon as a general publisher, Mills & Boon began to concentrate on romances for women during the 1930s. Mills & Boon novels continue to be hugely popular, as shown by the fact that over 100 titles are released each month. While the modern titles cover a wide range of romantic situations, styles and explicitness, their comforting familiarity and inevitability of a happy ending ensures that they meet reader expectations.

17. Originally called *The Daily Worker*, the *Morning Star* was founded by the Communist Party of Great Britain and first published on 1 January 1930. Since 1945 the paper has been owned by a readers' co-operative, the People's Press Printing Society, and offers a broad left perspective on political, industrial and international issues. The newspaper was renamed the *Morning Star* in 1966 and continues to be published daily.

18. Information about Dunn & Wilson and Riley Dunn & Wilson is given in note 39 to the interview with Alan White.

19. Brian Gall held the post of Senior Assistant Librarian with Motherwell & Wishaw Public Libraries before his appointment as East Lothian County Librarian in 1974. In anticipation of local government reorganisation he was appointed Librarian of East Lothian District Council the same year. He was later promoted to become the Council's Director of Leisure and Tourism

20. Interviews with Alan White and Peter Grant are included in this volume.

21. After study at the Scottish School of Librarianship, Alex Howson (1938–) held various posts with Lanark County Library Service during 1956–66 before appointment as Students' and Reference Librarian with Stafford County Library. Between 1967 and 1969 he was Deputy County Librarian of Aberdeenshire and then was appointed Burgh Librarian of Falkirk, a position he held until local government reorganisation in 1975 when he became Director of Libraries and Museums of Falkirk District Council and then Director of Leisure Services in 1990. He retired from that post in 1995. Howson was active within the Scottish Library Association over a long period and became the Association's President in 1981.

22. The career of Robert Craig is described in note 51 to the interview with Peter Grant.

23. The Net Book Agreement (NBA) was an agreement between publishers and booksellers in the UK which set the prices at which books were to be sold to the public. Under the NBA public library authorities were entitled to receive a discount of 10 per cent on the set retail price. It was argued that the NBA allowed income from the sales of best-sellers to subsidise the publication of important works with lower sales potential. It operated from 1900 until the 1990s when it was abandoned by some large bookshop chains and then ruled against the public interest and therefore illegal in March 1997 by the Restrictive Practices Court.

24. The Scottish Library and Information Council (SLIC) is the independent advisory body to the Scottish Government on library and information services. Its members include public libraries, further and higher education establishments, NHS Trust library services and other specialist and information services. Its purpose is to support and promote the role of library services in the social and economic development of Scotland's communities through funding, training and quality assurance frameworks and evaluation tools.

25. The National Preservation Office was formed by the British Library in 1984 and

was jointly funded by the Library and other major national institutions. Its aim was to develop and promote preservation management of library and archive materials in the UK and Ireland. It was renamed the Preservation Advisory Centre in 2009. The Centre has now closed although the British Library continues to provide information and advice on preservation of materials.

26. The Andrew W Mellon Foundation of New York City was established in 1969 as a private, not-for-profit corporation endowed with wealth accumulated by Andrew W Mellon of the Mellon family of Pittsburgh, Pennsylvania. Through the award of grants, the Foundation supports the work of educational and cultural institutions in the humanities, the arts and heritage.

27. *Shetland News* was a weekly newspaper published between 1885 and 1963. It is now a website providing 'daily news, views and other items'.

28. *The Shetland Times*, established in 1872, is a weekly newspaper. It is owned by The Shetland Times Ltd which also operates a bookshop and a printing company. The company publishes a range of Shetland-related books.

29. Using money raised through the National Lottery, the Heritage Lottery Fund (HLF) gives grants to support and develop the UK's heritage. Museums, parks, historic places, archaeology, the natural environment and cultural traditions have all received investment since the Fund opened for applications in 1994. The HLF is a non-departmental public body, and although it operates under the direction of the UK Department for Culture, Media & Sport there is a decision-making committee in Scotland.

30. Newsplan Scotland, based at the National Library of Scotland, is one of ten regional groups which took part in the Newsplan 2000 Project, the aims of which were to preserve fragile newspapers from further deterioration by microfilming them on 35mm archival-standard microfilm; increase access to the content of these newspaper titles in local libraries; raise awareness of the availability of titles and the richness of this resource. In 2001 the Heritage Lottery Fund (see note 29 above) awarded a grant of £5 million in support of the Newsplan programme with match funding from the newspaper industry and 'in-kind' support from libraries across the United Kingdom.

31. *The Southern Reporter*, established in 1855 and now owned by Johnston Press plc, is based in Selkirk and provides news coverage across the Scottish Borders.

Index

Entries such as '258n21' refer to the Notes at the end of the book. In this case it would be note 21 on page 258.

The Scottish Working People's History Trust

Founded in 1991, the Scottish Working People's History Trust finds and encourages the depositing in libraries and archives of all surviving documentary sources of working people's history north of the border. A key element of its activities is recording and making accessible the oral testimony of the lives of working men and women throughout Scotland. The Trust has been responsible for a number of publications based on the collected oral testimony.

Over the last twenty years the Trust's research worker, Dr Ian MacDougall, has interviewed in depth hundreds of working men and women in many occupational groups – including miners, journalists, Leith dockers, railway workers, Borders farm workers, textile millworkers, librarians, co-operative society workers, blacksmiths, shipyard workers.

As a result of the work of the Trust many important historical records, banners, artefacts and photographs have been deposited in Scottish libraries and archives.

The Trustees come from a wide cross section of occupations and institutions. They are people of experience in a variety of areas who feel it is vital that these priceless written and oral records of the past be preserved and, at the same time, that the scholarship behind their presentation is of the highest quality.

The experiences of so-called 'ordinary working people' in Scotland deserve to be a much better known part of history than has hitherto been the case. The hope is to arouse greater awareness of the important contribution that oral recollections about work, housing, education and recreation can make to the understanding of our heritage. It will encourage people to identify working men and women in their own areas whose spoken recollections can be recorded and preserved for posterity before it is too late. For veteran working men and women to recollect and record their experiences can contribute distinctly both to their recognition that their own lives have been meaningful and to a greater knowledge and better understanding of history by other people.

The Trust is glad to receive names and addresses of veteran working men and women in Scotland who might have their recollections recorded. It is also always keen to learn of any documentary sources of working people's history in Scotland, such as minutes of organisations, photographs, reports, financial records, membership lists. The Trust can give advice on how these might best be preserved in such a way as to make them accessible to as wide an interested audience as possible. If you know of such people or of records please contact the Trust Secretary:

Janet McBain, 86 Marlborough Avenue, Glasgow G11 7BJ
e-mail secretary@swpht.org.uk

Why not become a Friend of the Scottish Working People's History Trust?

The Trust is wholly dependent on voluntary donations to finance its activities. Joining the Friends is an easy way to support the Trust's activities. For just £10 per annum you will be kept informed of the Trust's activities and receive mailings of new publications.

www.swpht.org.uk